Palladium Books® Presents . . .

ROAD HOGS

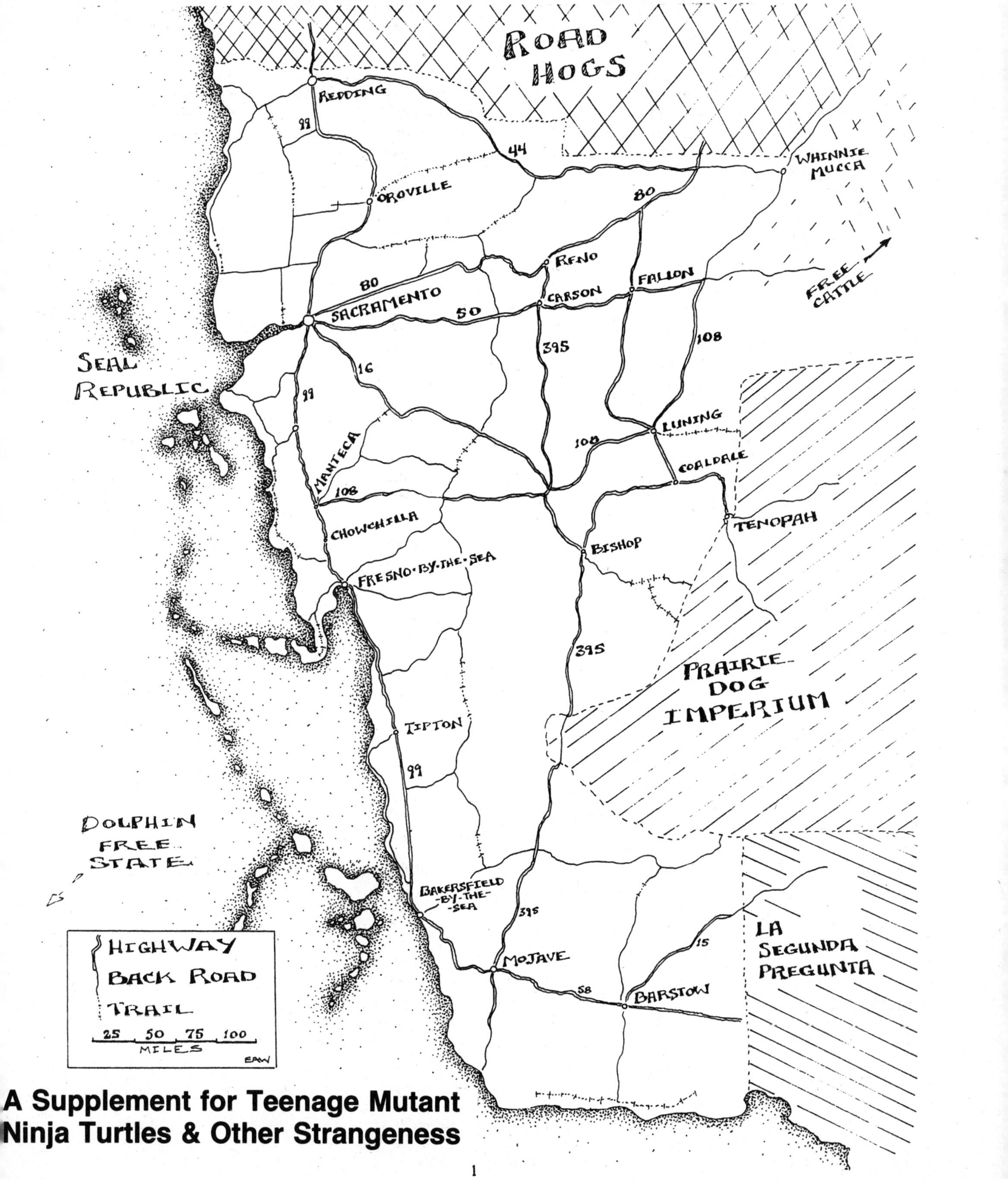

A Supplement for Teenage Mutant Ninja Turtles & Other Strangeness

Road Hogs Dedication:

A role-playing game is never better than its best players. I'm grateful for eight years of brilliant and incisive play. This dedication is for loyal role-players everywhere, but most especially for *Trow*, stalwart from the onset, and *Alaric*, scribe without peer, the ever-defiant *Bolton, Thorn,* whose convolutions baffle even the gods, *Jason*, juvenile deliquent extrordinaire, *Damien*, master/slave of grim reality, and the late-comers; *Chartock* and *K'Chagga, Arknel'D* and *Djia*.

Third Printing — March 1989

The Teenage Mutant Ninja Turtles comic book is available from:

Mirage Studios
P.O. Box 417
Haydenville, Mass. 01039

ROAD HOGS **is published by Palladium Books, 5926 Lonyo, Detroit, Michigan 48210**

Palladium Books® Presents . . .

ROAD HOGS™

Written By: **Erick Wujcik**

Compatible with Heroes Unlimited®

Editors: **Alex Marciniszyn**
Kevin Siembieda
Florence Siembieda

Cover Painting: **Kevin Eastman**

Interior Art: **Walter Storozuk**

Comic Strip: **Wujcik & Siembieda (script)**
Brent Carpenter (pencils & Ink assists)
Kevin Siembieda (inks & tones)

Typography: **Maryann Siembieda**

TABLE OF CONTENTS

INTRODUCTION

Yup! We're back again.

Some of you may recall an invitation we made in the Introduction to *After the Bomb*. Since *After the Bomb* only covered the Northeastern Seaboard of the U.S. we said, ". . . if you want more then, by all means, let us know!"

Well, you sure let us know. We're grateful for your cards and letters, your comments and criticisms. Even more impressive was the way you bought out the entire first printing of *After the Bomb*! Like nothing else, that told us you want more.

This time we're presenting the West Coast of the *After the Bomb* world. What remains of California, the southwestern U.S., and the northwestern tip of Mexico, is our new playground. Of course, you can bring your *After the Bomb* characters out on a journey of exploration. On the other hand, we've presented everything you need, including 24 NEW! animal descriptions, to create a whole new campaign.

And, if you like this one as much as the last one . . . well, let us know what you'd like to see next!

CREATING A CHARACTER: ROAD HOG STYLE!

You start *Road Hog* characters the same way as any other TMNT or After the Bomb characters. **Step 1: The Eight Attributes**. The next step is a little different because the possible animals are slightly different:

Step 2: Animal Type

The following table can be used for any adventure set in the United States' West Coast. It works for both contemporary TMNT and for After the Bomb/Road Hogs character generation.

ANIMAL HERO CHARACTERS

First roll to determine animal category:

ANIMAL CATEGORY

1-15	Urban
16-25	Rural
26-45	Forest
46-70	Desert/Plains
71-75	Aquatic Animals
76-95	Wild Birds
96-00	Zoo

Second, roll on the corresponding table for the specific animal type.

URBAN ANIMALS (01-15)

1-25	Dog
26-45	Cat
46-50	Mouse
51-55	Rat
56-58	Hamster
59-60	Guinea Pig
61-65	Squirrel
66-75	Sparrow
76-83	Pigeon
84-85	Parrot
86-88	Bat
89-92	Turtle
93-95	Frog
96-97	Lizard
98-00	Chameleon

RURAL ANIMALS (16-25)

1-10	Dog
11-15	Cat
16-20	Cow
21-35	Pig
36-45	Chicken
46-50	Duck
51-58	Horse
59-62	Donkey
63-65	Rabbit
66-75	Mouse
76-80	Jumping Mouse
81-85	Sheep
86-90	Goat
91-94	Turkey
95-00	Bat

FOREST ANIMALS (26-45)

1-3	Wolf
4-6	Fox
7-13	Coyote
14-16	Badger
17-20	Black Bear
21-24	Grizzly Bear
25-30	Mountain Lion
31-32	Bobcat
33-34	Lynx
35-36	Wolverine
37-40	Weasel
41-45	Raccoon
46-54	Ringtail
55-60	Opossum
61-65	Skunk
66-70	Porcupine
71-76	Mole
77-78	Squirrel
79-84	Marten
85-94	Deer
95-00	Elk

DESERT/PLAINS ANIMALS (46-70)

1-15	Coyote
16-20	Mountain Lion
21-30	Armadillo
31-35	Peccary (treat as a Boar)
36-40	Coati
41-45	Gila Monster
46-55	Lizard
56-65	Pack Rat
66-75	Prairie Dog
76-80	Pronghorn
81-90	Road Runner
91-95	Kangaroo Rat
96-00	Jumping Mouse

AQUATIC ANIMALS (71-75)

1-20	Otter
21-30	Beaver
31-50	Muskrat
51-55	Dolphin
56-60	Whale
61-65	Octopus
66-70	Sea Turtle
71-80	Sea Lion
81-90	Seal
91-00	Walrus

WILD BIRDS (76-95)

1-10	Sparrow
11-15	Robin
16-18	Blue Jay
19-21	Cardinal
22-23	Wild Turkey
24-25	Pheasant
26-27	Grouse
28-29	Quail
30-34	Crow
35-39	Duck
40-45	Owl
46-50	Condor
51-55	Buzzard
56-65	Vulture
66-70	Hawk
71-75	Falcon
76-85	Goose
86-90	Eagle
91-00	Hummingbird

ZOO ANIMALS (96-100)

1-10	Lion
11-15	Tiger
16-20	Leopard
21-25	Cheetah
26-30	Polar Bear
31-35	Crocodile (or Alligator
36-40	Aardvark
41-45	Rhinoceros
46-50	Hippopotamus
51-60	Elephant
61-65	Chimpanzee
66-70	Orangutan
71-75	Gorilla
76-85	Monkey
86-90	Baboon
91-95	Camel
96-00	Buffalo

Step 3: Mutation Background

The average citizen of the Road Hogs world is pretty much like the average citizen anywhere, content to sit at home and watch the world go by. Player characters in a *Road Hogs* game are a different breed. They're the mutant animals that have been touched with wanderlust, the ones who love traveling on the open road.

Note: "Vehicle Expenses" are to be used for constructing cars, trucks and motorcycles ONLY! This money *cannot be used for any other purpose*. For details see the Vehicle Construction Rules.

01-15 Mechanics. In the world of Road Hogs, mechanics are highly valued as the magicians who keep the machines going. Raised as an apprentice in one of the many garages and mechanic shops along Highway 99. Training focuses on *Auto Mechanics*, so the character automatically gets the secondary skill of *automotive mechanics* equal to 5th level, with a 65% diagnosis and a 50% repair skill. Each additional level of experience gives them a +10% (this also applies to group characters). These characters also have a good general education. No Scholastic Bonus, but with 6 High School Skills, 2 College Skills and 8 Secondary Skills. The character can put together a $12,000 car (vehicle expense) and has $300 to $1,800 (3D6 times $100) to spend on personal possessions. Most mechanics are easy-going and self-confident, since they know their skills are always in demand.

16-35 Bikers. Before the Road Hog Rebellion there were hundreds of small motorcycle gangs along the highways of New America. These were mostly family affairs, and their mutant offspring were initiated early into their customs. Driving skills and combat are the main interests, so Biker characters start with first level Piloting Skills of Automobile – Automatic Transmission (S), Manual (S), Race Car (S), and ½ Ton Truck (C). Also *Pilot Motorcycle*, which is equal to 4th level. Four (4) Military Weapon Skills and four (4) Secondary Skills are also available. No Scholastic Bonus. The character has $200 to $1,200 (2D6 times $100) to spend on personal possessions and $6,000 for vehicle expenses. The character's family biker gang was destroyed by the Road Hogs, so the character will be very interested in revenge.

36-45 Troopers. The *California Road Patrol* is a multigeneration organization. This character was brought up in a military tradition and trained to be a future trooper. The character can take any **One**, Pilot Automobile, Truck or Motorcycle Skill at 5th level proficiency. +10% Scholastic Bonus with 6 High School Skills, 6 Secondary Skills and 4 Military Skills. Starting money includes $300 to $1,800 (3D6 times $100) for personal possessions and $10,000 for vehicle expenses. Trooper characters are often lone vigilantes; helping innocents, villages, and tracking down and fighting Road Hogs wherever they're found.

46-55 Feral Mutant Animals. There are still quite a few mutant animals who grow up lost and alone in the wilderness. Survivors like this character have a hard time trying to fit into "civilized" life and prefer to keep moving on the open road. Feral Mutants tend to be tougher, but not as well educated as the average mutant animal. No Scholastic Bonus. 2 Secondary Skills, 2 Military Skills, plus Basic Survival, Climbing, Escape Artist, Prowl, Tracking, and Hunting. There is a S.D.C. bonus of +15, a P.E. bonus of +6, a P.S. bonus of +3 and a P.P. bonus of +2. Starting money is just $10 to $60 (1D6 times $10) with NO vehicle expenses. Feral Mutants are usually loners who like to help others, but who feel uncomfortable in large crowds.

56-75 Ninja. The character was adopted into a Ninja school. Knows 5 High School Skills, 3 Military Skills, 2 College Skills, 6 Secondary Skills and Hand to Hand Ninjitsu. In addition, the character can choose 3 ancient or ninja weapon proficiencies. Outfitting includes $250 of weapons, equipment and supplies. In addition, the ninja's teacher provides one, high quality, traditional weapon (or pair of weapons) to match the character's main weapon skill. NO vehicle expenses are given.

76-85 Truckers. The truckers who operate the armed convoys along the highways are highly trained specialists. They have Pilot Freight Truck (Semi) starting at 4th level proficiency and Automotive Mechanics (Secondary Skill) at 2nd level proficiency. No Scholastic Bonus; 6 Secondary Skills, 3 Military Skills and 3 High School Skills. Character has $200 to $1,200 (2D6 times $100) worth of personal possessions and has $15,000 for vehicle expenses. Truckers are usually more interested in making money than in fighting Road Hogs, but they are fierce enemies of anyone who threatens the highways.

86-95 Highway Engineers. Building and maintaining the road is an honorable profession respected by almost everybody. Highway Engineers are well educated with a +10% Scholastic Bonus. Two Skills: Highway Design & Engineering (40%+5% per level; ability to construct or repair roads, bridges and tunnels) and Surface Materials Technology (30%+5% per level; knowledge of concrete, tar and gravel construction) are available ONLY to Highway Engineers. They also have 1st level skill in Explosives and Demolitions, Mechanical Engineering, Mathematics, Pilot Heavy Machinery, Pilot Automobile (both), and Pilot Freight Hauler (Semi) Truck. 4 College Skills, 4 Secondary Skills and 2 Military Skills can be selected as well. $400 to $2,400 (4D6 times $100) is for personal possessions and $8,000 is the character's vehicle expense.

96-00 Natural Mechanical Geniuses. This rare character has a natural affinity for machines. Instead of *studying* Automotive Mechanics the character just *senses* what's wrong with machines. This is a sort of psionic skill where the character seems to communicate directly with the machine and can diagnose and fix it with 100% reliability!

There is, however, one tiny problem with the Mechanical Genius' talent. The "fixed" machines only work as long as the character stays within 250′ of the device. As soon as the character leaves there's only a 5% chance that the thing will keep working. It's because of this that Mechanical Geniuses have gotten a bad reputation along the highways. Not that the Genius characters are dishonest, they really *believe* that they've done serious, permanent repairs and they tend to blame others for "mistreating" the machine while they were gone. Although Mechanical Geniuses know they have a "special talent" they find it hard to believe that it only works while they're around.

So long as the character stays with a vehicle it will continue working. After a number of "repairs" the vehicle becomes completely dependent on the character, dismantling into a pile of parts when he/she leaves. No Scholastic Bonus with 4 Secondary Skills, 2 High School Skills, and 2 Military Skills. Mechanical Genius Characters have a M.E. bonus of +5. Character starts with $20 to $120 (2D6 times $10) of personal possessions (many of which wouldn't work for anyone else). There's also a $2,000 vehicle expense allowed. Mechanical Geniuses tend to be friendly, good-natured and talkative; in fact, they even talk to their machines.

Steps 4 & 5

Same as TMNT and Other Strangeness. See Economics and More Equipment for prices.

Note: Although characters *must* spend their vehicle expenses on a vehicle, they can *pool* their money, thus a group of any two or more characters can make a shared vehicle.

NEW ANIMAL DESCRIPTIONS

BIRDS

BUZZARD

Original Animal Characteristics

Description: There's a common misconception (the result of a certain Hollywood cartoon character) that Buzzards are similar to vultures. Wrong! Buzzards are actually predatory birds (vultures are scavengers) who look pretty much like hawks.

Size Level: 3

Length: 18 to 22 inches

Weight: to 18 pounds

Build: Medium

Mutant Changes & Costs

Total BIO-E: 70

Attribute Bonuses:

P.P.: +3

Spd.: +2

Human Features

Hands: 5 BIO-E for Partial
10 BIO-E for Full
20 BIO-E for Extra Limbs with Human Hands

Biped: Full Automatic

Speech: 5 BIO-E for Partial
10 BIO-E for Full

Looks: None; sharp, hooked beak; eyes on the side of the head, feathers, talons on feet.

5 BIO-E for Partial. Face with beak and large eyes, feathered body, bird-like legs and feet.

10 BIO-E for Full. Sharp features, hair that is actually very thin feathers, powerful upper body, skinny legs.

Natural Weapons: 5 BIO-E for 1D8 Talons on Feet.
10 BIO-E for 1D10 Beak

Powers: 10 BIO-E for Glide
20 BIO-E for Flight
5 BIO-E for Enhanced Vision

CONDOR

Original Animal Characteristics

Description: The largest flying animal in the Americas is a carrion eater like its vulture relatives. The huge Condor never attacks a living creature. Thick feathers, especially in a ruff around the neck, to protect it from the cold of its high altitude homeland.

Size Level: 5

Length: to 50 inches

Weight: to 30 pounds

Build: Medium

Mutant Changes & Costs

Total BIO-E: 50

Attribute Bonuses:

P.S.: +4

P.E.: +1

Human Features

Hands: 5 BIO-E for Partial
10 BIO-E for Full
20 BIO-E for Extra Limbs with Human Hands

Biped: Full Automatic

Speech: 5 BIO-E for Partial
10 BIO-E for Full

Looks: None; large body with large wings, scaly head with hooked beak and eyes on the side of the head, long crooked neck, taloned feet.

5 BIO-E for Partial. Prominent hunchback, face with beak, crooked neck, feathers, bird-like legs and feet.

10 BIO-E for Full. Head with sharp features and no hair, long neck, slight hump in back, and huge shoulders; short, skinny legs.

Natural Weapons: 5 BIO-E for 1D6 Talons on Feet
10 BIO-E for 1D8 Beak

Powers: 10 BIO-E for Glide
20 BIO-E for Flight
5 BIO-E for Enhanced Vision
5 BIO-E "Terrain Awareness" is a hard power to describe. Condors commonly fly in rough mountain terrain in the middle of dense fog without running into anything. There are numerous reports of hikers hearing the rattling of the Condor's wings (they are very noisy flyers) as they pass overhead by less than three feet. Thus, this power is a sort of psionic, intuitive sense of jutting objects while flying, and the ability to avoid bumping into that object even when visually impaired. Adds +1 to dodge while in flight.

HUMMINGBIRD

Original Animal Characteristics

Description: These tiny birds feed mainly on flower nectar and pollen. Their incredible flying speed makes them invulnerable to most predators. Their feathers are multicolored and seem to change constantly in the light. Black-Chinned and Calliope Hummingbirds are common on the West Coast.

Size Level: 1

Length: to 4 inches without tail.

Weight: ranging to less than 1 ounce.

Build: Short

Mutant Changes & Costs

Total BIO-E: 70

Attribute Bonuses:

P.P.: +3

Spd.: +10 for flight, +5 on land

Human Features

Hands: 5 BIO-E for Partial
10 BIO-E for Full
Note: Hummingbirds cannot hold things in their wings and fly at the same time!
20 BIO-E for Extra Limbs with Human Hands.

Biped: Full Automatic

Speech: 5 BIO-E for Partial
10 BIO-E for Full

Looks: None; long pointy beak; eyes on the side of head; thick, brightly feathered body; taloned feet.

5 BIO-E for Partial, face with beak and large eyes, feathered body, bird-like legs and feet.

10 BIO-E for Full, sharp features, hair that is actually very thin feathers, powerful upper body, skinny legs.

Natural Weapons: None

Powers: 30 BIO-E for Advanced Flight. Hummingbirds fly like nothing else. They can hover in mid-air, fly backwards or upside down, and stop or turn instantly. Most birds have long, rigid wings that can also be used for gliding, Hummingbirds cannot glide because they have short, stubby wings that can rotate or flex completely around. Hummingbirds are NOT quiet in flight, with wing flaps of 50 to 75 beats per second; at Size Level one they put off a steady hum. The noise doubles with each increase in size, at Size Level 10 they're as loud as airplane engines (in other words, forget about Prowling in Flight).
+3 to Strike while in flight
+4 to Dodge while in flight
+1 Attack per Melee Round
No plus to Parry or Damage while in flight.

Note: Like the Weasel's Increased Metabolic Rate (*see TMNT, pg. 51*), a Hummingbird with Advanced Flight is also hyperactive. They eat constantly, sleep in short naps and are easily bored.

ROAD RUNNER

Original Animal Characteristics

Description: As the name and cartoon character suggests, these birds are great runners. They eat mostly insects and fruit, but will also attack fairly large reptiles.

Size Level: 2

Length: to 18 inches without tail

Weight: to 5 pounds

Build: Medium

Mutant Changes & Costs

Total BIO-E: 65

Attribute Bonuses:

P.P.: +2

Spd.: +3

Human Features

Hands: 5 BIO-E for Partial
10 BIO-E for Full
20 BIO-E for Extra Limbs with Human Hands

Biped: Full Automatic

Speech: 5 BIO-E for Partial
10 BIO-E for Full

Looks: None; sharp beak; eyes on the side of the head, feathers, talons on feet.

5 BIO-E for Partial. Face with beak and large eyes, feathered body, bird-like legs and feet.

10 BIO-E for Full. Sharp features, hair that is actually very thin feathers, powerful upper body, skinny legs.

Natural Weapons: 5 BIO-E for 1D8 Talons on Feet
10 BIO-E for 1D10 Beak

Powers: 20 BIO-E for Flight. **Note:** Road Runners are lousy flyers; maximum air speed is only 40mph. Maximum +2 to Dodge while flying. No plus to damage.
15 BIO-E for Heightened Speed. This is an increase in running speed that allows the mutant Roadrunner to run up to 45mph for extended periods, and in bursts of speed up to 60mph (can maintain maximum speed for up to 6 minutes).
+3 to Strike
+3 to Dodge
+2 to Damage for each 20mph.

VULTURE

Original Animal Characteristics

Description: Carrion eaters who feed exclusively on dead bodies and the remains left by other predators. Both Turkey Vultures and King Vultures are found in the western U.S. They will fly in circles over a dying creature while waiting for their next meal.

Size Level: 4

Length: to 50 inches

Weight: to 20 pounds

Build: Medium

Mutant Changes & Costs

Total BIO-E: 55

Attribute Bonuses:

M.E.: +2

P.E.: +3

Human Features

Hands: 5 BIO-E for Partial
10 BIO-E for Full
20 BIO-E for Extra Limbs with Human Hands

Biped: Full Automatic

Speech: 5 BIO-E for Partial
10 BIO-E for Full

Looks: None; large body with large wings; leathery, red head with beak, and eyes on the side of the head, long crooked neck, taloned feet.

5 BIO-E for Partial. Prominent hunchback face with beak, crooked neck, feathers, bird-like legs and feet.

10 BIO-E for Full. Head with sharp features and no hair; flushed, red skin; long neck, slight hump in back, and huge shoulders; short, skinny legs.

Natural Weapons: 5 BIO-E for 1D6 Talons on Feet
10 BIO-E for 1D8 Beak

Powers: 10 BIO-E for Glide
20 BIO-E for Flight
5 BIO-E for Enhanced Vision

COATI

Original Animal Characteristics

Description: If anything looks like a cross between a raccoon and an oppossum it's the Coati. Their furry tails are as long as the rest of their bodies and are always kept fully upright, as if they were carrying flagpoles around.

Size Level: 5

Length: to 21 inches of actual body (42 inches from nose to tail tip).

Weight: to 25 pounds

Build: Long

Mutant Changes & Costs

Total BIO-E: 60

Attribute Bonuses:

I.Q.: +2

M.E.: +1

M.A.: +3

Human Features

Hands: 5 BIO-E for Partial
10 BIO-E for Full

Biped: 5 BIO-E for Partial
10 BIO-E for Full

Speech: 5 BIO-E for Partial
10 BIO-E for Full

Looks: None; pointed, triangular head with upturned nose. Lean bodied with long tail.

5 BIO-E for Partial. Short tail, brown fur, and pointed features.

10 BIO-E for Full. Very sharp features, brown hair with white highlights, lean body.

Natural Weapons: None

Powers: 5 BIO-E for Advanced Hearing
10 BIO-E for Prehensile Tail. Use as Partial Hand.

DOLPHIN

Original Animal Characteristics

Description: Dolphins come in quite a variety, ranging from creatures almost whale-sized down to much smaller species. The description here is for the common Bottlenosed Dolphin (like 'Flipper'). Note that the vast majority of mutated dolphins are aquatic. Dolphin player characters will be lonely outcasts who must live on land because of their mutation.

Size Level: 14

Length: to 16 feet

Weight: to 400 pounds

Build: Medium

Mutant Changes & Costs

Total BIO-E: 40

Attribute Bonuses:

I.Q.: +5

M.E.: +5

M.A.: +4

Human Features

Hands: 5 BIO-E for Partial
10 BIO-E for Full

Biped: None. Flukes and tail have developed into four legs.
5 BIO-E for Partial
10 BIO-E for Full

Speech: 5 BIO-E for Partial
10 BIO-E for Full

Looks: None; rounded head and body with thick, grayish skin; awkward, flat legs and arms.

5 BIO-E for Partial. Rounded head with bottlenose snout, eyes on side of head; thick, grey skin; short arms and legs.

10 BIO-E for Full. Rounded features; hairless, pale skin; fat-looking.

Natural Weapons: 5 BIO-E for 1D8 Bite

Powers: 5 BIO-E for Sonar
5 BIO-E for Thick Blubber; Protection against cold (½ normal damage) and adds 20 S.D.C.

DONKEY

Original Animal Characteristics

Description: Also called an "Ass" or "Burro", they are distant relatives of horses. Although Horses and Donkeys can interbreed the result is a *sterile* Mule.

Size Level: 12

Length: to 54 inches at the shoulder

Weight: 200 to 400 pounds

Build: Medium

Mutant Changes & Costs

Total BIO-E: 15

Attribute Bonuses:

M.E.: +2

P.E.: +5

Human Features

Hands: 5 BIO-E for Partial
10 BIO-E for Full

Biped: 5 BIO-E for Partial
10 BIO-E for Full

Speech: 5 BIO-E for partial
10 BIO-E for Full

Looks: None; large, long head with large, tubular ears on top; short hair; large rounded body; tail with tuft on end; short, bristly mane; long, thin legs.

5 BIO-E for Partial. Large, muzzled face, large ears on top of head, mohawk-style hair going all the way down the back, short tail, thin arms and legs.

10 BIO-E for Full. Short, bristly, mohawk-style hair; large, pointed ears; stocky, powerful build.

Natural Weapons: 5 BIO-E for Hoofed Feet, Kick does 1D8 damage.

Powers: 5 BIO-E for Advanced Hearing

LIZARDS

LIZARD (typical)

Original Animal Characteristics

Description: There are an enormous variety of lizard species in just about any color imaginable. They are generally insect eaters.

Size Level: 1

Length: to 12 inches

Weight: to 1 pound

Build: Long

Mutant Changes & Costs

Total BIO-E: 90

Attribute Bonuses:

P.P.: +2

Spd.: +3

Human Features

Hands: 5 BIO-E for Partial
10 BIO-E for Full

Biped: 5 BIO-E for Partial
10 BIO-E for Full

Speech: 5 BIO-E for Partial
10 BIO-E for Full

Looks: None; long, skinny body with tail of equal length; wedge-shaped head with protruding eyes, luminescent scales of bright colors.

5 BIO-E for Partial. Long, thin body with skinny arms and legs; short tail, large head and eyes, bright scales.

10 BIO-E for Full. Bald, wrinkled skin that shines with highlights of lizard color, slender build, long fingers.

Natural Weapons: 5 BIO-E for 1D6 Claws (climbing)

Powers: 15 BIO-E for Light Natural Body Armor; A.R.: 9 and S.D.C.: +20
30 BIO-E for Medium Natural Body Armor; A.R.: 13 and S.D.C.: +35
25 BIO-E for Accelerated Dodge, the ability to dart back and forth with blinding quickness. +4 to Dodge, +6 to speed
10 BIO-E for jump/leap; can spring 10ft high and 10ft long.

Lizard Species and Color Table

ROLL	TYPE	COLORATION
1-20	Fence Lizard	shiny brown
21-50	Anole	bright green
51-60	Collared	bright blue with yellow spots
61-80	Horned	pointy scales in shiny red and yellow
81-00	Desert Night	bright yellow with mottled brown spots

CHAMELEON

Original Animal Characteristics

Description: These lizards are not native to North America, but frequently have been imported as pets.

Size Level: 2

Length: to 12 inches without tail

Weight: to 2 pounds

Build: Medium

Mutant Changes & Costs

Total BIO-E: 80

Attribute Bonuses:
None

Human Features

Hands: 5 BIO-E for Partial; an unusual hand with three fingers on one side and two thumbs on the other.
10 BIO-E for Full; three fingers and two thumbs; one thumb on each side of the palm.

Biped: 5 BIO-E for Partial
10 BIO-E for Full

Speech: 5 BIO-E for Partial
10 BIO-E for Full

Looks: None; a fat body with loose, leathery skin covered with bumps. Legs and arms are bony and covered with loose skin; long tail equal to the length of the body. Huge, straight mouth; loose skin under chin, leathery bumps all over face.

5 BIO-E for Partial. Bloated body with skinny arms, legs and tail, ugly lizard face.

10 BIO-E for Full. Large facial features, wart-like bumps covering the skin, thick body, thin arms and legs.

Natural Weapons: 5 BIO-E for 1D6 Claws (climbing)

Powers: 5 BIO-E for Advanced Vision. Note that taking this power also means that the eye looks like a chameleon's eye, i.e., more like a rotating camera lens than a regular eyeball.
5 BIO-E for Prehensile Tail; use as partial hand.
20 BIO-E for Chameleon Camouflage Power. This is the power to change the pattern and color of the skin to blend in with the surroundings. Character can change at will with simple color changes taking under a minute, stripes or mottled patterns requiring as much as five minutes. So long as the character remains *motionless* there is only a 5% chance of being detected. Although this power is no substitute for the Prowl Skill, it does give the character a 20% bonus to Prowl.

GILA MONSTER

Original Animal Characteristics

Description: Gila Monsters are carnivorous desert dwellers. They are the only venomous lizards. A related species, the Mexican Beaded Lizard is similar.

Size Level: 2

Length: to 24 inches

Weight: to 3 pounds

Build: Medium

Mutant Changes & Costs

Total BIO-E: 80

Attribute Bonuses:
None

Human Features

Hands: 5 BIO-E for Partial
10 BIO-E for Full

Biped: 5 BIO-E for Partial
10 BIO-E for Full

Speech: 5 BIO-E for Partial
10 BIO-E for Full

Looks: None; round, tubular body; scales with bright, mottled, yellow and brown pattern; blunt, triangular head; short, stubby arms and legs; long, fat tail.

5 BIO-E for Partial. Thick, round body; short arms and legs, brightly colored scales in place of hair.

10 BIO-E for Full. Thick features; short, powerful arms and legs; bald with slightly mottled skin.

Natural Weapons: 5 BIO-E for 1D6 Claws

Powers: 10 BIO-E for Digging
20 BIO-E for Paralytic Poison Bite. The poison comes from the poison sacks in the lower jaw, along grooves in the teeth and into the victim. Victims must save vs. poison (on P.E.) to avoid being paralyzed. The bite/poison does 1D10 damage directly to hit points, even if the person saves against poison paralysis.

OCTOPUS

Original Animal Characteristics

Description: The eight legged octopus is possibly the most intelligent non-mammalian animal. There are many species, some much larger than described here.

Size Level: 2, but varies among species.

Length: varies

Weight: varies

Build: Medium

Mutant Changes & Costs

Total BIO-E: 70

Attribute Bonuses:
I.Q.: +2
P.S.: +3

Human Features

Hands: Partial hands are automatic because the tentacles are the equivalent of partial hands.
5 BIO-E for Full. One pair of tentacles has three branches at the end of each that serve as two fingers and a thumb. Note: must be bought for EACH Extra Pair of Tentacles for *full* use.

Biped: None: Crawls along with arms
10 BIO-E for Partial (two stubby legs and torso)
15 BIO-E for Full

Speech: 5 BIO-E for Partial
10 BIO-E for Full

Looks: None; huge head with loose, bulbous back (see picture); large eyes; gray, leathery skin.
5 BIO-E for Partial. Huge head and thick neck; long, flexible body; multiple tentacles protrude from upper torso, humanoid legs and body form; clearly not human!
Full Human looks are NOT available.

Natural Weapons: None

Powers: 10 BIO-E for Black Ink Spray. This is an oily chemical that forms a blinding cloud in the air or water. Reduces visibility (and smell) to zero for up to 5 minutes for about 20 square feet. Can be used 4 times per day.
15 BIO-E for Multi-limb Coordination: The ability to use more than one pair of limbs per melee. Provides one additional attack or complete action per melee. Note: Maximum is FOUR pairs (eight arms); +1 to strike.
5 BIO-E for Powerful Suction cups per pair of tentacles. Enables to climb or attach to rough and smooth as glass surfaces (climb skill 60% with one pair of suction arms, add 10% for each additional pair).
20 BIO-E for Chameleon Camouflage Power. This is the power to change the pattern and color of the skin to blend in with the surroundings. Character can change at will with simple color changes taking under a minute, stripes or mottled patterns requiring as much as five minutes. So long as the character remains *motionless* there is only a 5% chance of being detected. Although this power is no substitute for the Prowl Skill, it does give the character a 20% bonus to Prowl.

PRONGHORN

Original Animal Characteristics

Description: These grazing animals of the western plains are reputed to be the fastest animals in the Americas. Not only are they fast, but agile as well; able to take corners and come to sudden stops with surprising skill.

Size Level: 8
Length: to 5ft long
Weight: up to 140lbs
Build: Medium

Mutant Changes & Costs

Total BIO-E: 40

Attribute Bonuses:
P.P.: +1
P.E.: +3
Spd.: +7

Human Features

Hands: 5 BIO-E for Partial
10 BIO-E for Full

Biped: 5 BIO-E for Partial
10 BIO-E for Full

Speech: 5 BIO-E for Partial
10 BIO-E for Full

Looks: None; long, snouted head with large ears at the upper corners; large, widely spaced eyes; thick neck and body with long, thin arms and legs. Straight horns that branch in two near the top.
5 BIO-E for Partial. Muzzled head, large ears, thick body with thin arms and legs. Massive eyebrow ridge.
10 BIO-E for Full. Long nose, massive eyebrow ridge, large ears, powerful build.

Natural Weapons: 5 BIO-E for Small Antlers — 1D6

Powers: 15 BIO-E for Heightened Speed. This is an increase in running speed that allows the mutant Pronghorn to run up to 45mph for extended periods, and in bursts of speed up to 60mph (only a couple of minutes).
+1 to Strike
+4 to Dodge
+2 to Damage for each 20mph

RINGTAIL

Original Animal Characteristics

Description: Related to raccoons and has the characteristic ring-striped, bushy tail. They are nocturnal predators who live on mice, insects and berries. Other names include "cacomistle," "ring-tailed cat," or "civet cat."

Size Level: 2

Length: to 16 inches without tail

Weight: to 3 pounds

Build: Long

Mutant Changes & Costs

Total BIO-E: 80

Attribute Bonuses:

I.Q.: +1
M.E.: +1
M.A.: +1
P.P.: +2

Human Features

Hands: 5 BIO-E for Partial
10 BIO-E for Full

Biped: 5 BIO-E for Partial
10 BIO-E for Full

Speech: 5 BIO-E for Partial
10 BIO-E for Full

Looks: None; lean, cat-like body; elongated cat face with oversized ears and long nose. Furry, ringed, floor-length tail. Black and white facial markings.

5 BIO-E for Partial. Long-nosed with large ears on top of the head, stubby tail, distinct, black and white markings.

10 BIO-E for Full. Long nose and features, lean build, distinct white streaks in head hair and beard.

Natural Weapons: 5 BIO-E for 1D6 Claws (Climbing)

Powers: 5 BIO-E for Advanced Hearing

RODENTS OF THE WEST

KANGAROO RAT/JUMPING MOUSE

Original Animal Characteristics

Description: These small rodents are like kangaroos in appearance, with oversized back legs, and designed for hopping rather than running. Although the Kangaroo Rat (to 4 ounces) is much larger than the Jumping Mouse (less than 1 ounce) they are identical for the purposes of the game.

Size Level: 1

Length: to 2 inches

Weight: to 4 ounces

Build: Short

Mutant Changes & Costs

Total BIO-E: 80

Attribute Bonuses:

Spd.: +5

Human Features

Hands: 5 BIO-E for Partial
10 BIO-E for Full

Biped: 5 BIO-E for Partial
10 BIO-E for Full

Speech: 5 BIO-E for Partial
10 BIO-E for Full

Looks: None; oversized, muzzled head with thick neck, small arms, huge legs and feet, brown and white fur; and long, skinny tail that's longer than the rest of the body.

5 BIO-E for Partial. Large, muzzled head; thick body, huge legs and feet, tail.

10 BIO-E for Full. Thick neck; large thighs, legs and feet.

Natural Weapons: None

Powers: 5 BIO-E for Leaping Ability that doubles the maximum Jump or Leap of the character.
10 BIO-E for Digging
5 BIO-E for Advanced Hearing

PACK RAT

Original Animal Characteristics

Description: Known as the White-Throated Wood rat, this creature is a natural thief. It will often sneak into populated areas to steal any bright shiny object that catches its fancy. They are also natural builders and will construct fortresses up to 5 feet tall to keep out predators.

Size Level: 1

Length: to 12 inches without tail

Weight: to 8 ounces

Build: Medium

Mutant Changes & Costs

Total BIO-E: 65

Attribute Bonuses:

I.Q.: +1
M.E.: +2
P.P.: +4

Human Features

Hands: 5 BIO-E for Partial
10 BIO-E for Full

Biped: 5 BIO-E for Partial

10 BIO-E for Full
Speech: 5 BIO-E for Partial
10 BIO-E for Full
Looks: None; muzzled head with pointed nose, widely spaced eyes, round ears on top of head, thick fur; long, furry tail; thick body with short arms and legs.

5 BIO-E for Partial. Slightly muzzled head, ears on top of head, thick neck and body, short tail.

10 BIO-E for Full. Sharp nose and protruding ears, thick hair, rounded body.

Natural Weapons: 5 BIO-E for 1D6 Claws (Climbing)
Powers: 10 BIO-E for Natural Thieving Bonuses. Note: The character must study the skills to get these one time only bonuses:
+25% to Prowl
+30% to Pick Pockets
+10% to Pick Locks
+25% to Sleight of Hand

PRAIRIE DOG

Original Animal Characteristics
Description: Prairie dogs are communal animals, building underground cities with up to 1,000 inhabitants. They communicate using a complex code of chattering, barking, signs and odors. White-tailed Prairie Dogs are identical except that they live at higher altitudes.
Size Level: 2
Length: to 15 inches
Weight: to 3 pounds
Build: Short
Mutant Changes & Costs
Total BIO-E: 65
Attribute Bonuses:
I.Q.: +2
M.E.: +6
M.A.: +4
Human Features
Hands: 5 BIO-E for Partial
10 BIO-E for Full
Biped: 5 BIO-E for Partial
10 BIO-E for Full
Speech: 5 BIO-E for Partial
10 BIO-E for Full
Looks: None; rounded, furry body with squirrel-like head; small ears, short tail.

5 BIO-E for Partial. Rounded snout, light brown fur, rather stout body.

10 BIO-E for Full. Very small ears, thick hair, round body.

Natural Weapons: None
Powers: 10 BIO-E for Digging
20 BIO-E for Tunneling
30 BIO-E for Excavating

SEA TURTLE

Original Animal Characteristics
Description: The two main varieties are the Leatherback and the Green Turtle. Both are deep water animals who range all over the world. Their armor is more leathery, and thicker than a land turtle's.
Size Level: 17
Length: to 5ft
Weight: to 800 pounds
Build: Short
Mutant Changes & Costs
Total BIO-E: 0
Attribute Bonuses: P.E.: +4
Human Features
Hands: 5 BIO-E for Partial
10 BIO-E for Full
Biped: 5 BIO-E for Partial
10 BIO-E for Full
Speech: 5 BIO-E for Partial
10 BIO-E for Full
Looks: None; small head on a round body; large, flat arms and legs; mottled, green, brown and white pattern on leathery skin.

5 BIO-E for Partial. Bald head with large nose, leathery neck, round body and soft shell.

10 BIO-E for Full. Thick, leathery skin; green eyes, bald, and powerfully built.

Natural Weapons: None
Powers: 5 BIO-E for Hold Breath
5 BIO-E for Swimming equal to basic swim skill at 85%
15 BIO-E for Light Natural Body Armor; A.R.: 9, S.D.C.: +30
30 BIO-E for Medium Natural Body Armor; A.R.: 11, S.D.C.: +50
45 BIO-E for Heavy Natural Body Armor; A.R.: 13, S.D.C.: +75
60 BIO-E for Extra-Heavy Natural Body Armour; A.R.: 15, S.D.C.: +100

SEA LION FAMILY

Original Animal Characteristics
Description: This family of aquatic mammals includes Sea Lions and several Fur Seals. They are distinguished from other seals in that their hind flippers can be used as legs on land, and in the water, they use their *front* flippers for propulsion. There is a huge difference between male and female sizes; the data below represents a rough average.

Size Level: 13
Length: to 7 feet
Weight: to 350lbs
Build: Medium

Mutant Changes & Costs

Total BIO-E: 20
Attribute Bonuses:
M.E. +1
M.A.: +3
P.P.: +1

Human Features

Hands: 5 BIO-E for Partial
10 BIO-E for Full
Biped: 5 BIO-E for Partial
10 BIO-E for Full
Speech: 5 BIO-E for Partial
10 BIO-E for Full
Looks: None; round, furry body; long, thick neck with small, dog-like head; tiny ears, large eyes; long thin arms and legs; no tail.
5 BIO-E for Partial. Rounded body, thick neck, snouted head with whiskers, small ears.
10 BIO-E for Full. Powerful chest and neck, smallish head, short legs, large eyes.
Natural Weapons: None
Powers: 5 BIO-E for Advanced Vision
5 BIO-E for Thick Blubber; protection against cold (½ damage) and +20 S.D.C.

TRUE SEALS

Original Animal Characteristics

Description: True seals have no external ears and cannot use their rear flippers on land. In the water they use the back flippers and pull themselves around on land with the front flippers.
Size Level: 11
Length: to 6ft
Weight: to 250 pounds
Build: Medium

Mutant Changes & Costs

Total BIO-E: 30
Attribute Bonuses:
M.E.: +2
M.A.: +3

Human Features

Hands: 5 BIO-E for Partial
10 BIO-E for Full
Biped: 5 BIO-E for Partial
10 BIO-E for Full
Speech: 5 BIO-E for Partial
10 BIO-E for Full
Looks: None; round, furry body; long, thick neck with small, dog-like head; large eyes; stubby, narrow arms and legs; no tail.
5 BIO-E for Partial. rounded body, thick neck, smallish head, short legs, large eyes.
10 BIO-E for Full, powerful chest and neck, smallish head, short legs, large eyes.
Natural Weapons: None
Powers: 5 BIO-E for Advanced Vision
5 BIO-E for Thick Blubber; protection against cold (½ damage) and +20 S.D.C.

WALRUS

Original Animal Characteristics

Description: Like Sea Lions, Walruses can use their back flippers for walking on land and, like True Seals, they have no exterior ears. Their heavy whiskers are used to feel for food in the dark. Tusks are used both for fighting and for dredging the bottom of the ocean for food.
Size Level: 18
Length: to 10 feet
Weight: to 1200 pounds
Build: Short

Mutant Changes & Costs

Total BIO-E: 0
Attribute Bonuses:
None

Human Features

Hands: 5 BIO-E for Partial
10 BIO-E for Full
Biped: 5 BIO-E for Partial
10 BIO-E for Full
Speech: 5 BIO-E for Partial
10 BIO-E for Full
Looks: None; round, wrinkled body; thick neck with small, dog-like head; and huge, whiskered upper lip.
5 BIO-E for Partial. Rounded body, thick neck, snouted head with whiskers; thick, wrinkled skin.
10 BIO-E for Full. Powerful chest and neck, smallish head, short legs; heavy, handlebar mustache.
Natural Weapons: 10 BIO-E for 2D6 Tusks
Powers: 5 BIO-E for Advanced Touch
5 BIO-E for Thick Blubber; protection against cold (½ damage) and +30 S.D.C.

WHALES

Original Animal Characteristics

Description: These huge ocean mammals are only very rarely mutated into a land form.
Size Level: 20
Length: to 80 feet
Weight: to 150 tons
Build: Medium

Mutant Changes & Costs

Total BIO-E: 0 (remember you can trade size levels for BIO-E points)
Attribute Bonuses:
I.Q. +4
M.E.: +4
M.A.: +4

Human Features

Hands: 5 BIO-E for Partial
10 BIO-E for Full
Biped: None. Flukes and tail have developed into four legs.
5 BIO-E for Partial
10 BIO-E for Full
Speech: 5 BIO-E for Partial
10 BIO-E for Full
Looks: None; rounded head and body, tiny eyes, thick grayish skin, awkward, flat legs and arms.
5 BIO-E for Partial. Thick rounded head; small eyes on side of head; thick, grey skin; short, fat arms and legs.
10 BIO-E for Full. Rounded features, hairless, pale skin; short, stubby arms and legs.
Natural Weapons: 5 BIO-E for 1D10 Bite
Powers: 5 BIO-E for Sonar
5 BIO-E for Thick Blubber; protection against cold (½ damage) and +40 S.D.C.
10 BIO-E for Extra Thick Skin; protection against cold (¼ damage) and +60 S.D.C.

VEHICLE RULES FOR ROAD HOGS

Attitude: In TMNT the use of vehicles like cars, trucks and motorcycles makes combat a bit different. Yet the rules are not overtly complicated . . . the basic idea is that vehicles are treated exactly like powered armor . . . just as robots are handled in *Heroes Unlimited*, so vehicles are dealt with in TMNT . . .

When you get into a car you essentially don a suit of superpowered armor . . . this armor augments three basic things:

1. S.D.C.
2. A.R.
3. Speed

Vehicle Expense

Putting a vehicle together is a five-step process, an *expensive* five-step process. Just take 'em one at a time.

Step 1 — The Basic Vehicle

The basic vehicles in Road Hogs are free. During the Big Death, cars, motorcycles and trucks were left scattered across the landscape. Some sections of road are unused simply because they're completely jammed with cars that attempted to escape the holocaust.

Getting cars is easy. Making them *work* is another problem. The costs below represent the necessary replacement parts and specialized labor needed to get a vehicle working. NOTE: A Mechanical Genius character can use any of these vehicles without having to spend money on parts. The usual restrictions apply.

TABLE NOTES

Vehicle Type: The brand and model of the vehicle can be chosen by the player. For example, a sports car can be (player's option) a Corvette, Delorean, Jaguar, or Porsche. A luxury car can be a Cadillac, Mercedes Benz, Rolls Royce or Bently.

Price: Represents the amount of money needed to replace missing parts, repair the frame, replace the tires, and generally get the vehicle moving again.

S.D.C.: The amount of damage the vehicle can take before it ceases to operate/ride.

Max. Seats: The number of comfortable seats available. This can be modified in many ways. For example, a street bike can seat two, a passenger holding onto the driver, or three if a sidecar is added.

Max. Load: This is the absolute maximum weight, in pounds, that a vehicle can carry, including passengers. Bad roads or vehicle damage will reduce the maximum load possible. NOTE: *A vehicle cannot exceed cruising speed while carrying the maximum load.*

Turrets: The maximum number of rotating weapon turrets that can be added to the vehicle. For cars and truck cabs the turrets are built into the roof. Vans and commercial vehicles can have turrets on the sides, front or rear walls. Truck beds can have freestanding turrets.

Vehicle Type	Price	S.D.C.	Max. Seats	Max. Load	Turrets
Motorcycles (Gasoline/6 volt)					
Dirt Bikes	$200	75	1	250	0
Street Bikes	$350	100	2	450	1
Small Automobiles					
Compact	$100	250	4	1,250	1
Sports Car	$500	300	2	1,300	1
Jeep	$600	450	4	2,400	1
Large Automobiles					
2-Door Sedan	$200	350	5	1,400	1
4-Door Sedan	$200	400	5	1,500	1
Luxury Car	$300	450	6	1,700	1
Station Wagon	$250	450	8	2,000	2
Vans					
Mini-Vans	$400	400	8	1,800	1
Full-Sized	$450	450	10	2,500	2
Utility	$500	500	6	3,000	2
Small Truck					
Small	$400	350	2	1,500	1
Pick-Up	$500	450	2	3,000	2
4-Wheel Drive	$600	500	2	2,500	2
Commercial Vehicles (Diesel/24 volt battery)					
Passenger Bus	$750	500	45	9,000	8
½ Ton	$700	600	3*	15,000	6
10-Wheeler	$800	800	3*	60,000	10
16-Wheeler	$1,000	1,000	4*	160,000	16

*Seats indicated are in the cab of the truck, an additional 30, 60 or 90 can be seated or placed in the trailer of the truck, depending on the size.

Step 2 — Adding Speed to Vehicles

At this stage the vehicle isn't much more than basic transportation. Before it was fixed it had a negative Class Engine, it couldn't move at all. Now it has a Class 0 Engine and Alignment, which means the vehicle can go about 5mph. Which is fine for plowing fields, but hardly suitable for highway travel.

Important Note: When you're buying speed you're buying more than a hot engine. Without good alignment the vehicle will shake itself to pieces before it ever reaches cruising speed. Transmission, drive train, carburetor and exhaust also have to be modified in order to achieve higher speeds.

The next thing to buy is Speed. Use the following table.

Adding Speed to Vehicles

Speed Class	Spd.	Maximum	Cruise	Engine and Alignment Cost Bike	Sport	Car/Truck	Semi
1	22	15 mph	10 mph	$100	$100	$50	$500
2	44	30 mph	20 mph	$150	$200	$100	$1,000
3	66	45 mph	30 mph	$200	$300	$150	$1,200
4	88	60 mph	45 mph	$250	$400	$200	$1,400
5	110	75 mph	55 mph	$300	$500	$250	$1,600
6	132	90 mph	60 mph	$350	$600	$300	$1,800
7	154	105 mph	65 mph	$400	$700	$400	$2,000
8	176	120 mph	70 mph	$425	$800	$500	$2,250
9	198	135 mph	75 mph	$450	$900	$600	$2,500
10	220	150 mph	80 mph	$475	$1,000	$700	$3,000
11	242	165 mph	85 mph	$500	$1,200	$800	$4,000
12	264	180 mph	90 mph	$550	$1,400	$1,000	$5,000
13	286	195 mph	95 mph	$600	$1,600	$1,500	$6,000
14	308	210 mph	100 mph	$700	$1,800	$2,000	$7,000
15	330	225 mph	105 mph	$1,000	$2,000	$2,500	$8,000
16	352	240 mph	110 mph	$1,500	$2,250	$3,000	$10,000
17	396	270 mph	115 mph	$2,000	$2,500	$4,000	$15,000
18	440	300 mph	120 mph	$3,000	$2,750	$5,000	$20,000
19	484	330 mph	125 mph	$4,000	$3,000	$6,000	N/A
20	528	360 mph	130 mph	$5,000	$3,500	$7,000	N/A
21	572	390 mph	135 mph	$6,000	$4,000	$8,000	N/A
22	616	420 mph	140 mph	$7,000	$5,000	$10,000	N/A
23	660	450 mph	145 mph	$8,000	$6,000	$15,000	N/A
24	704	480 mph	150 mph	$9,000	$8,000	$20,000	N/A
25	792	540 mph	155 mph	N/A	$10,000	$25,000	N/A
26	880	600 mph	160 mph	N/A	$20,000	$50,000	N/A
27	968	660 mph	165 mph	N/A	$50,000	N/A	N/A
28	1,056	720 mph	170 mph	N/A	$75,000	N/A	N/A

TABLE NOTES

Spd: If the car were a person this would be its equivalent to Speed Attribute. A character with a Speed of 22 can run 15mph. It's the same for vehicles except they can go much faster. The land vehicle maximum is 1,056, which is 720mph or the speed of sound.

Maximum: The vehicle's absolute maximum speed. Because this is pushing the machine to it's limits there must be a roll on the breakdown table for every 12 miles driven. Note that these speeds are impossible without excellent roads.

Cruise: Safe speed for extended travel (given good roads). The vehicle should be able to drive indefinitely at Cruising Speed.

Bike: Cost of equipping any Motorcycle with matching speed.

Sport: The price of engines for sports cars and specialized racing cars. Only specially equipped sport and racing cars can be modified for the very top speeds.

Car/Truck: Engine costs are the same for luxury cars, station wagons, full-sized and mini vans, small trucks, pick-up trucks and all other medium sized vehicles.

Semi: Includes all commercial vehicles, as well as tanks, construction machinery and moving equipment.

Step 3 — Adding Vehicle Weapons

Gun Ports

Characters can easily fire out of open windows or doors. The problem is that this exposes them to enemy fire. Armored gun ports have a hole for the weapon barrel and can swivel 180 degrees.

Swivel Gun Port $100 each

Fixed Mount

This kind of weapon fires in only one direction, aiming requires turning the entire vehicle. Usually set up to shoot straight ahead, but can be mounted in any direction. Usually used by the vehicle pilot.

Weapons	Damage	Effective Range	Price
5.56mm Light Machinegun	5D6	1,200ft	$2,000
7.62mm Medium Machinegun	6D6	2,200ft	$3,000
Empty Swivel Mount			$800
Can be used with any weapon.			
2.75″ Rocket Launching Tube	8D6	5,000ft	1500ea

Rockets are disposable weapons, once used the entire thing must be replaced. Explosion does 8D6 on everything within a 20 square foot area.

Swivel Mount

The weapon extends out from the passenger compartment across the front or rear hood. The weapon can swivel up to *45 degrees to the left or right* of the mount position. In other words, a forward mounted machinegun can hit a target anywhere in front of the vehicle but **NOT** a target that's next to it. Can be used by pilot if forward mounted, otherwise by a passenger.

Weapons	Damage	Effective Range	Price
5.56mm Light Machinegun	5D6	1,200ft	$2,000
7.62mm Medium Machinegun	6D6	2,200ft	$3,000
Empty Swivel Mount			$800
Can be used with any weapon.			

Turret Mount

Weapon is mounted on a swivel that can be rotated 360 degrees. Operator must enter the turret to fire the weapon.

Weapons	Damage	Effective Range	Price
5.56mm Light Machinegun	5D6	1,200ft	$3,000
7.62mm Medium Machinegun	6D6	2,200ft	$4,000
.50 Calibre Heavy Machinegun	7D6	3,000ft	$8,000
Empty Turret			$1,000
Can be used with any weapon.			
Flame Thrower	4D6	60ft	$6,000

Does damage to everything in an 8 square foot area. All combustible items will ignite. If used on unarmored vehicles the gas tank may detonate (30% chance).

Step 4 — Adding Vehicle Armor

Having weapons is nice. Unfortunately there are plenty of other people on the road with similar ideas. To keep them from putting holes in characters and vehicles, you'll need armor.

Passenger Armor

Armor for the passenger compartment for most vehicles. Note: Passenger Armor is not available for motorcycles. *Only one set of armor per compartment.*

Light Armor with Glass Windows	A.R.: 10	S.D.C.: 200	$800
Light Armor with Plexiglass Windows	A.R.: 12	S.D.C.: 250	$1,000
Light Armor with Window Slits	A.R.: 14	S.D.C.: 300	$1,200
Medium Armor with Glass Windows	A.R.: 11	S.D.C.: 300	$2,000
Medium Armor with Plexiglass Windows	A.R.: 13	S.D.C.: 350	$2,500
Medium Armor with Window Slits	A.R.: 15	S.D.C.: 400	$3,000
Heavy Armor with Glass Windows	A.R.: 12	S.D.C.: 400	$4,000
Heavy Armor with Plexiglass Windows	A.R.: 14	S.D.C.: 450	$4,500
Heavy Armor with Window Slits	A.R.: 16	S.D.C.: 500	$5,000

Turret Armor protects both the weapon and the operator. Separate armor must be bought for *each* turret. *Only one set of armor per turret.*

Light Armor	*A.R.: 10*	*S.D.C.: 350*	*$800*
Medium Armor	*A.R.: 12*	*S.D.C.: 300*	*$1,800*
Heavy Armor	*A.R.: 14*	*S.D.C.: 400*	*$3,500*

Vehicle Armor

This armor protects the vehicle only, passengers are not covered. *Only one set of vehicle armor allowed.*

Light Armor	A.R.: 14	S.D.C.: 350	$2,500
Medium Armor	A.R.: 16	S.D.C.: 700	$10,000
Heavy Armor	A.R.: 18	S.D.C.: 1,400	$50,000

Step 5 — Optional Equipment

Some equipment is standard with any basic vehicle, including headlights and brake lights, speedometer, odometer, and trouble indicator lights for brakes, oil and temperature. Also seats, seat belts, standard pedals, steering wheel and gear-shift. AM Radio is free. Everything else must be bought from the following list.

Comfort Features

Fold-Down Bucket Seats: These seats are more comfortable than the standard bench seats. They can also be folded down and turned into temporary sleeping space. *Cost:* $200 Each.

Camper Option: Can be used with any van or larger vehicle. Includes beds (from 1 to 4), small kitchen with sink and stove, bathroom with shower, conference/dining table, and interior decorating with paneling and carpeting. *Cost:* $5,000. Of course this severely limits cargo space.

Stereo System: Picks up AM/FM/Shortwave signals and delivers the signal in stereo. Also plays tape cassettes. *Cost:* $400

Pressurized Cabin: The passenger compartment can be supplied with an on board oxygen supply. Poison gas and smoke will be kept out. Air supply will last for up to 40 minutes. Not effective in water or vacuum. *Cost:* $150,000.

Refreshment Dispenser: A built-in unit that delivers coffee, tea, hot chocolate or hot soup (pick one) from one spout, and soft drink, milk, ice water or fruit juice (pick one) from another. Must be recharged every few days. *Cost:* $450.

Sensory Equipment

Engine Readout Package: The instrument panel is modified to include a tachometer, temperature and oil pressure gauges, fuel mix indicator, and readout on the battery charge. Adds +5% to Auto Mechanics diagnosis. *Cost:* $250.

Night-sight Camera/Monitor: A forward mounted camera sees into the darkness and relays an amplified image to a monitor in front of the driver. Range is 300ft, and the camera clearly shows obstacles, vehicles and animals. Any bright lights, including the vehicles's own headlights, blind the night-sight camera. *Cost:* $20,000.

Radar Display: A monitor is mounted on the dash that displays the radar picture for an area 500ft around the vehicle. This shows solid obstacles (trees, rocks, buildings, airplanes), other moving vehicles, and moving bodies. It does *not* show pits, potholes, broken pavement or bodies smaller than Size Level 6. *Cost:* $20,000.

Radio Locator: Directional locator that lets the vehicle operators find the exact position of a radio transmission. Useful for finding planted "bugs". *Cost:* $1,000

Vehicle Modifications

Second Engine: This is a backup engine for the vehicle. Especially valuable for those characters who continually run at maximum speeds. Payment for second engine depends on Speed — see Speed Table for Cost; varies with the maximum speed.

Trailer Hitch: Allows a trailer to be attached to the vehicle. *Cost:* $150.

Winch and Cable: Mounted on the front bumper is an electric winch; basically, a motor connected to a cable. The woven steel cable is 100ft long and has a hook on one end. The winch can pull up to 300lbs, larger loads can be handled by locking the winch and backing up the vehicle. *Cost:* $500.

Fuel Efficiency Modification: Modifying the car's engine so that fuel consumption is cut by half. *Cost:* $2,000.

Super Fuel Efficiency: By careful tinkering, the vehicle consumes only 10% of the normal miles per gallon rate. *Cost:* $15,000.

Security Measures

Theft Alarm System: A tamper-proof burglar alarm. When someone attempts to open the vehicle without the alarm key, a piercing siren will sound out. *Cost:* $700.

Thief Proof Locks: The vehicle locks have been modified so that standard pry bars and skeleton keys will not work. *Cost:* $200 each.

Flashing Lights: Police car-style lights with flashing red and blue bulbs. *Cost:* $150

Searchlight: High-powered spotlight. Mounted on a swivel next to the pilot's seat. *Cost:* $200

Siren: High pitched emergency siren. Can be heard up to 2,500ft away. *Cost:* $50

Loudspeaker: Simply a large speaker/amplifier mounted outside the vehicle. Can be heard clearly, over vehicle noise, up to 400ft away. *Cost:* $300.

Oil Slick: The pilot can release oil from a tank mounted on the underside of the vehicle. Contains enough oil for three oil slicks. *Cost:* $1,200

Vehicle Caltrops: A container of broken glass, nails and metal shards can be released by the pilot. *Cost:* $300 for each container and release mechanism. $100 per each, non-reusable, container; although homemade containers can be made for about $30.

Ram-Prow: The ram-prow is a special metal reinforced ram at the front of the vehicle. The ram may be a simple foundation of metal bars, train-like cow-catcher or any variety of metal protrusion with the purpose of ramming.

The ram-prow protects the attacking vehicle from any damage that it would normally receive in a ram attack. (see "Ramming" under Combat Tactics). Also adds 75 S.D.C. to the vehicle. **Cost:** $800.

ECONOMICS AND MORE EQUIPMENT

New Americorp dollar bills ($5's, $10's, and $20's) are accepted everywhere throughout the West Coast. The only problem is that the further away you get from Sacramento, the less they are worth. $50, Americorp, Gold Coins are accepted virtually everywhere, and are a sure way of getting, at least, a 50% discount off the stated price in those remote villages.

The prices listed in TMNT are accurate for stores inside Sacramento city limits. For about 100 miles further out, expect to pay at least 25% more. By the time you get to Bakersfield-by-the-Sea prices have shot up by 4 times. And, out in the prairies, a single cotton T-Shirt, $8 in Sacramento, could go for $80 or more.

Initial Character Possessions

Since it's assumed that the characters had plenty of time to shop around for bargains, the players can buy all their *original* equipment at the prices listed in TMNT. Of course, later in the game it won't be quite so cheap . . .

Here's a few other items available for sale in New Americorp. Prices listed are Sacramento standard.

Driving Suits or Armor

Motorcycle drivers wear helmets and leathers for a reason; it helps to protect them in an accident. Characters with full leathers, including heavy boots, helmet, leather jacket, leather pants and leather gloves, will reduce the amount of damage taken in a crash. *The suit absorbs half the damage taken, up to a maximum of 24 points.*

For example, if Fran's character crashed and took 80 points of damage, she'd only have to take 56 points off her S.D.C. and Hit Points. On the other hand, if Mike crashed with 8 points of damage, he'd take 4 points off his S.D.C. (½ damage) and 4 off his Hit Points (the other ½).

Driving suits are *no protection against bullets, explosions, weapons, or hand-to-hand attacks*. They are useful for crash damage only. On the other hand, regular armor, either modern or ancient, gives *no protection against crash damage*.

Driving armor is just a safety measure. Or, according to some bikers. "You may break every bone in your body, but, at least, the leather will keep your body from coming apart. At the very least, leathers insure that your corpse will look good at your funeral."

Cost: $200 for characters of Size Level 7 or lower, $250 for up to Size Level 11, $300 for Size Level 12 and 13, add $100 for each additional Size Level.

Tool Kits

Portable Tool Kit: A portable tool kit in a leather case, about the size of a briefcase. Weighs 20 pounds and has everything needed for most Auto Mechanic diagnostics. **Cost:** $150.

Trunk Tool Kit: A metal toolbox weighing 60 pounds and with everything needed for road repairs. **Cost:** $500

Shop Kit: Actually several metal boxes and drawers worth of tools, usually installed in a garage or in a utility van (although most large vehicles could be modified to suit). This 1400 pound set has everything needed for major vehicle repairs (rebuilding engines, adjusting the frame) and modifications. Includes welding torch, hoist, and machine for mounting tires on wheels. **Cost:** $2,800

Vehicle Necessities

Gas: In the major towns along Route 99, the price of gas has been set by Americorp at *$5.00 per gallon* for both gas and diesel fuel. At remote gas stations, the price can range up to $50.00 per gallon and diesel may not be available at all.

Oil: A quart of oil goes for $4 in Sacramento. All high-performance vehicles need oil changes monthly. Under "OIL" on the table below it shows how many quarts are needed for a change.

Batteries, Tires, and **Spare Parts**: Cost varies according to the vehicle. See Table.

Vehicle Consumption Table

	Fuel	Tank	Oil	Batteries	Tires
Motorcycle	30 mpg	10	2	$50	$75
Compact Cars	20 mpg	15	4	$100	$50
Sports/Luxury Cars	10 mpg	20	6	$200	$90
Cars/Trucks/Vans	15 mpg	25	4	$300	$60
Large Trucks	10 mpg	30	8	$500	$100
Semi Trucks	10 mpg	65	12	$750	$150

Notes: Fuel is consumption in mpg = miles per gallon, Tank Size is how many gallons fit in the standard tank, Oil is the number of Quarts needed for an oil change, Batteries and Tires are unit prices.

Garage Fees

Storage: Storing a vehicle safely means paying a space rental charge which varies according to the size. Motorcycles are $15 a month. Standard Cars are $50 a month. Semi-Trucks are $500 a month.

Repairs: Mechanic's rates vary according to labor and part costs. Simple S.D.C. damage can be fixed at $2 per point.

Carburetors, radiators, fuel lines and the like, will cost about $50 for labor and from $30 to $200 for parts.

Repairing Speed Classes lost costs $25 per each level up to level 5, then $100 per level to level 10, then an additional $50 for each additional level ($150 for 11, $200 for 12, $250 for 13, etc.).

Major Engine Damage can run from $200 to $1,600 (roll 2D8 times $100); anything over $500 and it's cheaper to just replace the engine.

Note: Auto Mechanics "borrowing" the use of a garage's tools and equipment are expected to pay for their time, usually around $5 per hour.

Modifications and Additions

Characters aren't stuck with their vehicles staying the same after the initial Vehicle Expense. NPC Mechanics, player character auto mechanics, and mechanical geniuses, can keep making all kinds of modifications. Modification costs will depend on parts and labor as determined by the GM.

Here's a couple of examples. To add on a Siren would take the normal cost ($50) for parts, plus another $10 for labor.

Adding an Infrared Monitor is also possible, but nobody sells Infrared Monitors. However, if you can *find* one, a mechanic will install it for $250.

Increased Speed Class: A mechanic will charge 20% to upgrade a vehicle one Speed Class. For a player, it takes 10% in parts and three days work. Mechanical geniuses can upgrade a vehicle one Speed Class every day (limit one vehicle and one Speed Class per day).

Speed Class Example: Let's say you want to upgrade your Jaguar sports car from Speed Class 13 to Speed Class 14. It costs $1,800 to get level 14; so a mechanic will charge 20%, or $360 to "soup it up" to go 210mph. A player mechanic can do the same work for 10%, or $180. The mechanical genius doesn't need parts, but there's a 95% chance that the engine will disintegrate when he leaves.

Getting Paid

Escort Service: Armed escorts and guards receive from $30 to $180 per week, depending on the danger involved in the job. Room, board, gas and ammunition, is usually provided as well.

Government Employees: New Americorp pays very well; $200 to $1200 per week, plus perks. However, these jobs are in very high demand and usually go to "insiders", unless extremely dangerous.

Farm Workers, Store Attendants and Trade Apprentices: From $2 to $12 a week plus room and board.

Mechanic's Wages: Employee mechanics make from $5 to $20 an hour depending on experience and ability.

Instructor Services: One easy way to make money in the world of Road Hogs is as an instructor. Knowledge is highly regarded and mutant animals are willing to pay well to get it. Teaching someone how to fix carburetors might take a week's steady work and would be worth $20 to $120 a day.

For example, let's say that Mike (a mutant rabbit who's also a mechanic) posts a notice saying that his services are available and describing his specialties. As it happens, the local tailor wants to learn something about fixing carburetors. They meet, negotiate and strike a deal. For 5 days, Mike will spend his evenings with the tailor, tearing apart carburetors and teaching him as much as he can. In return, Mike will receive a new pair of pants, a new shirt, two pairs of socks, and $50 a day.

Road Hog Bounty: The government will pay for captured or destroyed, Road Hog, gang vehicles. $250 for a motorcycle, $500 for a car, and $1,000 for a large truck or commercial vehicle. The first few times that characters cash in, they must provide some kind fo definite proof that the vehicles really belonged to the Road Hogs. Special bounties for specific criminals or vehicles can be 10 times the normal rate, but this is *not* the norm.

Antiques and Artifacts: Old, pre-death items can also be scavenged, and sold in Sacramento or Fresno-by-the-Sea for about 50% of their original value.

VEHICLE CONTROL & SKILLS

Driving any vehicle in Road Hogs requires Pilot skill. Here are all the vehicle related skills. Those marked (NEW!) are additions to the game system not found in **Heroes Unlimited or TMNT & Other Strangeness.**

Skills

Pilot Automobile; Automatic Transmission: The ability to operate a car, station wagon, or van, so long as it's equipped with an automatic transmission. 90% + 3% per level. **Note:** Character's vehicle with Speed Class of 10 or less can be either automatic or manual transmission (player's choice).

Pilot Automobile; Manual Transmission: Can operate any car, station wagon, or van with either automatic or manual transmission. 82% + 4% per level. **Note:** All vehicles with Speed Class of 11 or higher must have manual transmission.

Pilot Automobile; Professional Race Car: Specialized knowledge of operating high performance vehicles at high speed. Using these vehicles, at any speed, requires this skill. All Control Rolls in high powered vehicles are done with the rating from this skill. 60% + 5% per level. **Important Note:** *Any vehicle with Speed Class 15 or greater is considered to be a Professional Race Car.*

Pilot Motorcycle: In addition to being able to pilot dirt bikes (cross-country motorcycles) and street bikes (heavier highway motorcycles), the character also has a DODGE bonus of +2. 60% + 8% per level.

Pilot Commercial Vehicles: (New!) 60% + 5% per level.

Pilot Truck; Half-Ton Pick-up: 80% + 5% per level.

Pilot Truck; Freight Hauler: 50% + 5% per level.

Pilot Military Vehicle: 50% + 5% per level.

Pilot Heavy Machinery: (New!) 40% + 3% per level.

Vehicle-to-Vehicle Combat: (New!) Practice and theory of wheeled combat. The big advantage of this skill is that there is no limit on how high a character can advance. In every other skill there is a 98% maximum proficiency. With V-to-V Combat there is no limit, and characters may have percentiles over 100%. *Use for Control Rolls only.* Can be used with one or more other Pilot skills. 30% + 5% per level.

Map Reading Skill: (New!) Reading a road map in the world of Road Hogs isn't an easy matter. Road maps are either pre-death versions, in which case the earthquakes, bombs, and road renewal projects have made them obsolete and just about impossible to follow. More recent maps are always coded in some way and, if that weren't enough of a problem, they are almost always flawed. Interpreting these difficult documents is a job for a professional. 35% + 6% per level.

Automobile Armor and Weaponry: (New!) Assembling, installing and repairing vehicle weapons and armor is a job for a specialist. An improperly installed or adjusted item of this type can offset the vehicle's alignment and cause a *decrease in Speed Class of 1D6.* 40% + 4% per level.

Automotive Mechanics: Although this skill works for all engines and systems in all the vehicles of Road Hogs, it is *not* the equivalent of a Palladium RPG "Heal Spell". Without proper tools and spare parts the character can't do much of anything. 40% + 5% per level diagnosis and 25% + 5% per level for repairs.

Control Rolls

In Road Hogs, drivers are in constant danger of losing control of their vehicle. To avoid losing control the characters must roll against their Pilot skill. *Control Rolls must be made for each of the following situations:*

Exceeding Cruising Speed: Anytime a driver exceeds the Cruising Speed for the vehicle there's the danger of losing control. Every melee round of excessive speed requires a Control Roll. See Road/Speed Table for penalties.

Exceeding Road Speeds: Going too fast on back roads or trails is dangerous no matter how well built the vehicle is. Any travel over 75mph on a back road, or over 45mph on a trail, requires a Control Roll. This is not the case with Highways; a vehicle can travel all the way up to Cruising Speed on a Highway without rolling for Control. See Road/Speed Table for penalties.

Exceeding Maneuver Speed: Every *turn, swerve* or *land change* while exceeding Cruise Speed *or* Road Speed *requires another Control Roll with a* −12 penalty.

Driving in Reverse: Attempting to drive in reverse at any speed over 25mph. Roll a Control Roll with a −30% penalty.

Poor Road Conditions: Requires a Control Roll. This can include anything from rain to steep inclines. −30% or optional. See Road Quality and Obstacle Table for specific penalties.

Avoiding Obstacle: Swerving around any object requires a Control Roll, no penalty. If the swerve or dodge involves leaving the road surface then the penalty is −40%.

Loss of Control Table

The game master or player should roll on the following table every time a character fails a Control Roll. Roll percentile dice.

01-10 **Pothole!** Vehicle slams into something and rebounds. Or, just as likely, the vehicle bottoms out, smashes the underside into broken pavement or a pothole. Vehicle takes 4D6 points of damage to S.D.C. and Speed Class is reduced 1D6.

11-25 **Out of Control!** The vehicle skids out of control. Ends up off the road, in a ditch or in some other embarrassing situation. Stuck 3D6 Melee Rounds.

26-44 Stall! Forced to make a sudden stop; the car stalls out. Getting it going again takes 2D6 Melee Rounds.

45-76 **Skid!** Skid out of control and into an object. The vehicle takes half normal damage from this minor crash. Speed Class is reduced 1D6 levels. See Crash and Damage rules.

77-90 **Crash!** Skid out of control into an object. The vehicle takes full damage and occupants take half damage. Speed Class is reduced 2D6 levels. See Crash and Damage rules.

91-97 **Totaled!** Vehicle crashes and is totally destroyed. Occupants take full damage.

98-00 **Roll and Burn!** The vehicle goes completely out of control and rolls over 1D6 times. Vehicle takes double damage, occupants take normal damage. In 1D10 melee rounds the vehicle fuel tank will explode, anyone remaining inside will be torched. See Crash and Damage rules.

Road & Speed Table

Use the following table to determine how much ground is being eaten up in V-to-V combat.

Travel Speed	Distance/Melee	Control Roll Modifiers for: Highway	Back Road	Trail/Broken Road
1 to 15mph	1/32 mile	SAFE	SAFE	SAFE
Over 15mph	1/16 mile	SAFE	SAFE	SAFE
Over 30mph	1/8 mile	SAFE	SAFE	SAFE
Over 45mph	1/6 mile	SAFE	ROLL	−5
Over 60mph	1/4 mile	ROLL	ROLL	−10
Over 75mph	1/3 mile	ROLL	−5	−20
Over 90mph	1/2 mile	ROLL	−10	−30
Over 120mph	1 mile	−5	−10	−45
Over 240mph	2 miles	−10	−15	−60
Over 360mph	3 miles	−15	−20	−70
Over 480mph	4 miles	−30	−40	−75
Over 600mph	5 miles	−45	−70	−85
At 720mph	6 miles	−60	−80	−95

Example: A motorcycle is going 240 miles per hour down a back road in a hot pursuit. Every melee the character must make a Control Roll with a −10 modifier because the character is going *over 120*. If the speed were even 241mph then the modifier would be −15. Every melee, the character covers 2 miles of ground.

CRASH AND DAMAGE RULES

Driver & Passenger Damage

Anyone *not* wearing a Seat Belt must roll to see if they are thrown clear in an accident. With percentile dice, a roll of 25% or higher indicates the character bounces around inside the vehicle and takes *double* damage. If the roll is under that, then the character is thrown clear and bounces around outside, taking *2D6 damage for every 10mph of vehicle speed.*

Characters wearing Seat Belts or other restraining straps take 1D6 damage for every 20mph. The addition of crash helmet and specially padded, asbestos suit reduces the damage by half.

Motorcycle crashes are even more deadly. With helmet and leather body covering, or some kind of protective garments, the character(s) takes 1D6 for every 10mph. Without helmet or protective garments: 2D6 per 10mph.

Lucky Fall: With all vehicles, motorcycle, car, van, truck, etc., there is a slim chance that each passenger and driver will be thrown clear, or luck-out with only minor damage even in a terrible crash. *Roll Percentile Dice:* 1-20 Lucky Fall, 2D6 total damage; 21-00, full normal damage.

Vehicle Damage

Motorcycle	1D6 per 10mph
Automobile, Small Truck, Mini Van	1D8 per 10mph
Full-Sized Trucks and Vans	1D8+1 per 10mph
½ Ton Trucks and Buses	1D10 per 10mph
10 or 16 Wheeler Semi-Trucks	2D6 per 10mph

Damage is based on relative speed. When something hits a stationary object then the only thing to worry about is the speed of the moving object. When two moving objects meet, whichever does the most damage will determine the actual damage. Round up in all cases.

If Mike is driving a *car* north at 38mph and runs into something standing *still*, like a telephone pole, then both his car and the pole take 4D8 damage. Note the 38mph is rounded up to 40; 1D8 per 10mph = 4D8 damage.

Now let's look at Mike running *head-on*. Mike is travelling at 40mph, a motorcycle approached from the opposite direction at 60mph. Their added speeds are 100mph so the damage to both vehicles is 10D8. Since Mike's car is larger/heavier and does more damage, we use the automobile damage formula rather than the motorcycle.

Pedestrian Impact Damage

Vehicle-to-Pedestrian Combat: In order to hit a moving object (mutant animal, insect or machine) requires a Strike roll from the vehicle driver. To avoid a vehicle hit/ram attack, the target must make a Dodge roll greater than the Strike roll. Unconscious characters and stationary objects do not Dodge.

Vehicle-to-Pedestrian Damage: Anything hit by a vehicle takes the full damage from the **Vehicle Damage** table according to vehicle type and speed. However, vehicles themselves also take impact damage. Creatures or items of Size Level 1 and 2 do 2D6 points of damage regardless of vehicle type and speed. With Size Levels 3 through 8 the vehicle takes one third of damage received by the target. Size Levels 9 through 12 the vehicle takes half damage. The vehicle takes three quarters of the target's damage when the Size Level is from 13 to 16. Hitting anything with a Size Level of 17 or better is the equivalent of a crash — both the vehicle and the target take full damage. Vehicles with ram-prows take no damage from any targets with Size Level 18 or less. Hitting a Size Level 19 or 20 object is still a crash even with the ram-prow.

VEHICLE COMBAT RULES

Vehicle to vehicle combat in Road Hogs shouldn't be all that different from other kinds of TMNT combat. That is, the game master should work at keeping things clean, quick and simple. The only two differences are in rolls to Dodge and rolls to Strike.

Dodge: Vehicle-to-Vehicle

In spite of their advanced Speed, vehicles have absolutely *no bonus to dodge against firearms*. Why? Well, first off, a vehicle just isn't as maneuverable as a person, it generally goes in a straight line, and, even on curves, the faster the thing is going the smoother the curve. The other thing to bear in mind is the car's size.

However, drivers *can dodge attacks from other vehicles*. When someone is attempting to cut-off, ram or sideswipe the vehicle then a Dodge roll is possible. A vehicle making a Dodge can't do anything else in that Melee Round.

Strike: Vehicle-to-Vehicle

Rolls to Strike in Vehicle-to-Vehicle combat are exactly like ordinary rolls to strike. The only difference is that a vehicle is several targets in one package. *Every strike on a vehicle must be "called"*. The attacker has to specify which target is being attacked; *the crew compartment (driver), a turret, or the vehicle itself.*

"Ramming", or striking one vehicle with another, always attacks the vehicle itself. *Area effect weapons*, like explosives and fire, can attack the vehicle, the turret and the occupant(s). *See vehicle combat tactics*.

Melee Rounds: Vehicle-to-Vehicle

The melee round system hasn't really changed for Road Hogs. The idea is still to get the combatants in close quarters and let 'em slug it out 'til somebody goes down.

Don't get carried away with the possible complexities of the systems. For example, avoid the trap of over-calculating the exact number of seconds required for a car going 187 miles per hour to catch up with a car going 193 miles per hour.

Remember that in, the real world, things are never that simple! Cars have to swerve and weave, acceleration is never constant and, at high speeds, drivers make mistakes constantly. Just read a newspaper account about a police car chase. Usually the police car is much faster than the criminal's. Even so, the chase can go on for dozens of miles at very high speeds.

Keep it simple; if the pursuer is faster, then it'll catch up. If the leader is going faster than the pursuer, then it leaves the other car in the dust. *There should only be three possible conditions*: 1) either the cars are neck-and-neck, or 2) one is behind the other in firing range, or 3) the two cars are too far away for combat.

Another important thing to remember about Melee Rounds is that the use of a vehicle as a weapon to ram or sideswipe, etc., is limited to *one attack/action per Melee Round*. So, if the driver has other Melee Actions left, he can use them to shoot out the window, grab a fire extinguisher, or get a cup of coffee.

Vehicle Combat Tactics, Maneuvers & Techniques

The Ram

Ramming is a vehicle-to-vehicle attack where one vehicle attempts to bash into the rear of another. The speed of the ramming/attacking vehicle must exceed 10mph of the vehicle it is attacking. Speeds greater than 10mph above the defending vehicle's constitutes a crash; use the Crash and Damage rules to determine the damage of both vehicles. Likewise, head-on collisions/rams and ramming stationary objects at speeds over 10mph constitutes a normal crash, damaging all parties.

Ramming damage varies with the size of the attacking/ramming vehicle.

Damage to Target Vehicle	Inflicts
Motorcycle	4D6
Automobile, small truck, mini van	6D6
Full-Sized truck or van	6D8
½ ton truck or bus	6D10
10 or 16 wheeler/semi-truck	10D10

Note: The attacking vehicle also suffers damage, but only ⅓ of that which it inflicts on its target. Only if the attacking vehicle has a ram-prow built onto it will the vehicle take no damage.

Control Rolls: Immediately after a successful ram both vehicles must make control rolls. The attacker is −25 and the defender is −40.

The Sideswipe

When cars are neck-and-neck they can attempt to shove each other off the road. Works exactly like the Ram except that damage is half those listed. **Control rolls** are the same as for Ramming.

The Cut-Off

The attacker pulls in front of the defender, cutting off the lane and forcing the defender to either hit/crash or swerve to avoid hitting. The attacker rolls to strike and must make a control roll. A failed strike means the maneuver is unsuccessful/incomplete and can be tried again. A failed control roll means a crash. If the attacker succeeds and the defender fails to dodge (either by missing the roll or by not rolling), then there is a collision. *Use the standard Crash and Damage Rules.* **Control Rolls**: the attacker at −30, and the defender at −25.

The Block

Basically this happens when the attacker wants to keep the defender in some position. A good example is where the cars are neck-and-neck, the right hand car sees an oncoming truck in the left lane and decides to force his opponent to stay in that lane. This same technique can be used to keep one's opponent from passing as well. If the attacker rolls a successful strike, and if the defender does not try to dodge or fails to dodge, then the defender is stuck in that lane until the next melee. Neither a *Sudden Brake* or a *Drag Race* is good against a Block. To execute a block may require high speeds and/or quick maneuvering, like switching lanes, swerving, etc. Control rolls should be made for each block/strike maneuver and dodge/evasive action. **Standard Control Rolls apply**.

The Sudden Brake

When two cars are side-by-side, preferably in different lanes, one of them can attempt to get behind the other by hitting the brakes. Whether or not the braking car actually pulls behind depends on a straight, twenty-sided die, initiative roll. Both cars roll; high roll wins. However, the braking car reduces speed by half for one melee. An unsuccessful Sudden Brake means the opposing car is still side-by-side. **Control Rolls** must be made with a −15 penalty. **Warning:** Don't attempt to brake with anyone immediately behind you unless you want a collision.

The Bootleg Turn

This is a special maneuver that lets the vehicle completely change direction. Basically the driver turns, slams on the brakes and "fishtails" the car into the opposite direction. While in the Bootleg the vehicle has *no chance to Dodge*. **A Control Roll** must be made with a −50 penalty.

Drag Racing — Road Hogs Style!

When two cars are neck-and-neck and trying to pull ahead of each other, that's a Drag Race. The same thing happens when one car is behind another and both decide to speed up. A lot depends on the Speed Class of the vehicle, the higher the better. However, there's a lot more to drag racing than engine performance. The driver's skill and reflexes, as well as raw luck, are just as important.

Rolls for Drag Racing are made on twenty-sided dice. There are two modifiers. First, each driver can add in the Speed Class of his/her vehicle. Second, the driver's P.P. bonus can be added.

If both cars were neck-and-neck, then the winner will be way out in front. When one car is trying to overtake another, then winning means catching up and losing means falling way behind. In case of a tie the cars maintain their current position. A Natural Twenty is perfect luck, either leaving a pursuer in the dust or coming up neck-and-neck with a fleeing prey.

Note: There is a −5 penalty when driving any vehicle for the first time. In other words, if a character just stole a car and is trying to escape in it, he'll have a −5 penalty on the initiative rolls.

Vehicle Combat Example

In this example, two characters are driving a '68 Cadillac (Speed Class 8) equipped with compartment armor, vehicle armor; fixed, forward-mounted, .50 calibre machinegun and gun ports on all four sides. Both Mike's and Fran's characters are wearing Motorcycle Leathers and packing .45 Automatic Pistols as sidearms.

GM: Well, you've been traveling at full cruising speed for the last 20 miles. So at 120 miles per hour, that takes you 10 minutes. Now I'll check road conditions (rolling dice). Uh, Oh! You see a stretch of broken pavement ahead.

Mike: Whoa! I better slow down. What are my options?

GM: Well, you can take it at 15mph and there'll be no chance of an accident.

Mike: Oh, come on! We can do better than that.

GM: Sure, you can use your Pilot skill. Let's see . . . (looking at table) . . . at 30mph it's a straight roll. 45mph and you have a −5 on your skill, −10 if you take it at 60, and −30 if you take it at 90.

Fran: Mike, don't get too crazy; we just rebuilt this clunker.

Mike: Hmmm . . . I've got a skill of 98%, so −30 seems a little risky . . . we'll take it at 60mph.

GM: Okay, you're dodging chunks of paving stones at 60mph. Roll on your Pilot skill.

Mike: No problem! I roll . . . a 38. My skill is only reduced to 88%. We're safe as houses.

GM: It looks like you're going to make it by the rocks. Ahead you see clear pavement with dense forest on the right-hand side. Oops! There must be a road in the woods.

Mike: Why? Can I see it?

GM: No, but you can see a ¾ ton truck pulling out right in front of you.

Fran: A what?!?

Mike: Am I gonna' hit it?

GM: Not unless you want to. Are you going to stop? Or are you going to try to pull around it?

Mike: Ah . . .

Fran: Don't stop; it could be a Road Hog trap!

Mike: Right. I'll hit the gas and try to drive around it.

GM: Since you're being *cut off*, I'll roll for the truck driver's Strike and you roll a Dodge.

Mike: (rolls) I've got a 7. Can I add in my attribute Dodge bonus?

GM: Nope. Since you're driving a vehicle you can only get the straight Dodge roll. Let's see if you made it . . . (rolls) . . . the trucker only rolls a 4 to Strike, so you manage to get around.

Fran: Whew!

GM: Now roll percentile.

Mike: Why?

GM: You dodged the truck, but you may have lost control of your vehicle. You've got to roll under your skill with a −30 modifier.

Mike: Ooff . . . (rolls) . . . a 9! I made it!

Fran: Do I see anyone else in the woods?

GM: You sure do. There's 5 motorcycles, a station wagon and a sleek looking sports car pulling out into the road off to your right.

Fran: Let's get outa' here!

Mike: Yeah, I punch this baby up.

GM: You were going 60 when you went around the truck. How fast do you want to go now?

Mike: Does the road look clear?

GM: The pavement's solid, but you don't know road conditions ahead.

Mike: I'll play it safe, push it up to 120.

GM: You leave the motorcycles and the station wagon in your dust.

Mike: What about the . . .

Fran: (to Mike) Keep your eyes on the road dummy! I'll check the rear. (to GM) What about the sports car?

GM: It's approaching fast. It must be going at least 60mph faster than you.

Fran: 180?!

Mike: What's the road look like in front of me?

GM: It looks fine as far as you can see; smooth, flat and straight for the next 3 miles.

Mike: And after that?

GM: Why are you asking me? I'm only the game master.

Fran: (to Mike) Mike, the GM *never* tells you about things like that. You drive and I'll check our map. (to GM) Okay, I've got out the map. What do I think we're heading into?

GM: Give me a percentile roll. Mike, through the rear view mirror you see the other car gaining on you. What are you doing?

Mike: They're goin' 180, so I'll go 180. I punch it up!

GM: Now you're going over Cruising Speed . . . this is a Highway, so you need to make a Control Roll with a −5 modifier.

Mike: Okay . . . (rolls) . . . a 78, safely below the 93 mark.

Fran: You want a roll under my map reading skill? (GM nods) . . . I rolled a 13, well under my skill. What does the map say?

GM: You figure you've got about 8 miles of straight road. Then it'll head up into the mountains. The road will twist and turn like crazy there.

Fran: Ich!

GM: Your friends just accelerated again. Now they're in *firing range*. Incidently, you can now see a machinegun turret mounted on the roof.

Fran: I'm aiming my pistol out of a rear gun port.

Mike: I gotta' outrun him. I'll punch it up to maximum, 240mph.

GM: He's in range and he's going to try to keep up. That means you're now in a *Drag Race. Roll a twenty-sided.*

Mike: I get to add in the Speed Class of the car, right?

Fran: And your P.P. bonus, don't forget that! Your P.P. is 19, so that's another +2.

GM: Right on both counts; now roll.

Mike: (rolls) . . . only a 4. With Speed Class of 8, plus 2, plus 4, that's 14.

GM: (rolls) . . . Natural Twenty! They pull up next to you on the right side. Mike, you do your Control Roll and I'll roll for them.

Fran: I'm pulling my gun out of the rear port and putting it in the right gun port.

Mike: (rolls) . . . 80, still no problem.

GM: (rolls) . . . they made their Control Roll. They're aiming for the crew . . . (rolls again) . . . a 12, they hit, but the armor absorbs all . . . (rolls) . . . 16 points of damage. Record the damage.

Mike: They're next to me?

GM: Yup.

Mike: I hit the brakes! If I'm behind them I can use my machinegun.

GM: I figure this guy was going to try *sideswiping* this round, so let's see who gets the initiative. Mike, roll twenty-sided.

Mike: Any modifiers?

GM: Nope, just straight initiative.

Mike: (rolls) . . . a 14, is that good enough?

GM: And the Road Hog rolls . . . a 9. He slams into your lane just as you hit the brakes and drop back. You're right behind him, but I still need a Control Roll, this time with a −15 because of the excessive braking.

Fran: They're in front now? (GM nods) One more time; I take my gun out of the right gun port and stick it in the front. Maybe this time I'll actually get a chance to shoot.

Mike: Don't worry. All I need is to roll under 88 for my Control Roll and you can nail 'em with our big gun . . .

OPTIONAL ROAD HOG TABLES

Vehicle Damage Table

Any time a shot on a car penetrates the armor, either by a roll over the car's A.R., or when the A.R. has been depleted, or on a called shot followed by a "natural" twenty to strike, there's a chance that the vehicle may be crippled by the damage. Roll Percentile dice.

01-05 Engine on Fire: Speed Class goes down 1D6 level. GM rolls 4D10; that's how many melees the characters have before the fire spreads to the fuel tank. If they can pull over and extinguish the fire before that, then no further damage will be taken.

06-08 Tire Shot Out: Speed reduced by a third, driver must make a Control Roll at −5 per *each* 10mph that the vehicle was traveling.

09-14 Frame is Seriously Dented: Alignment problems; drop Speed Class by 1D6.

15-20 Hole in Radiator: Over the next 6 melees, engine will get hotter and hotter. After that there's a 20% chance, every melee, that the engine will suddenly stop. Steam pours out from under the hood.

21-25 Hole in Brake Line: Brakes don't work anymore. No other problems until the character tries to stop.

26-30 Electrical System Damaged: Control panel inside the crew compartment catches on fire. Until the smoke is cleared and the fire is put out, Control Rolls are an additional −30 each melee, and/or manuever. All attacks are impossible until the smoke is stopped.

31-35 Steering Damaged: Take −50 on all Control Rolls.

36-50 Cosmetic Damage: Vehicle loses chrome, paint and trim. Looks bad, but no real damage.

51-60 Light Knocked Out: Depending on where the shot came from, either the headlights or the brake lights are knocked out. Could be serious at night.

61-65 Exterior Electronics Disabled: Any electronic devices on the outside of the vehicle are destroyed.

66-70 Battery Destroyed: Not a problem right away, but the vehicle can't be started again without a jump or a replacement.

71-75 Alternator/Generator Wrecked: The car stops recharging itself and is running off battery power alone. Will work for 8D4 minutes before draining the battery, then it'll quit.

76-85 Transmission Fluid Leak or Damage: Shifting becomes impossible and the transmission will start making hideous grinding noises. Vehicle will continue operating for another 4-24 melee rounds.

86-90 Leak in Gas Tank: Vehicle will loose one gallon a minute until the fuel runs out.

91-95 Fragments in Driver's Compartment: Roll 2D6 damage for each occupant. Driver make Control Roll at −50.

96-00 No Serious Damage: However, make Control Roll at −10.

Optional Critical Damage Table

Use whenever damage from one shot is over 30 points or whenever a *Natural Twenty* is rolled. This is also useful for when the S.D.C. of the vehicle is all gone. Roll percentile dice.

01-15 Vehicle Speed Class reduced by 2D6.

16-20 Vehicle S.D.C. takes double damage.

21-30 Steering Disconnected! Roll on Control Loss Table.

31-40 Drive Train Hit. Car starts rolling to a stop.

41-50 Carburetor Destroyed. Engine sputters out.

51-90 Roll on Vehicle Damage Table.

91-00 Gase Tank Explodes. Roll for crash. Everyone inside takes an additional 6D6 damage.

Note: This table may make the game too deadly.

Road Quality & Obstacle Table (Optional)

On tended roads, like Route 99, roll every 20 miles. For *well traveled*, but poorly maintained roads, the roll should come every 10 miles. *Back Roads* and *Trails* call for a roll every 5 miles. During Vehicle-to-Vehicle combat the GM may want to roll more often.

01-25 Excellent Conditions. No Problems.

26-30 Broken Pavement. Make Control Roll. Failure means the vehicle's alignment gets messed up; decrease Speed Class 1D6.

31-35 Car-Eating Potholes. Make Control Roll. Failure means the vehicle suffers 4D6 S.D.C. damage, and goes down 1D6 Speed Classes.

36-40 Stretch of Dirt Road. Reduce Speed or make Control Roll on "Trail" Column of table.

41-45 Construction Area. Road reduced to one lane for both directions. 30% chance of worker directing traffic. Otherwise vehicle takes its chances with oncoming traffic.

46-50 Road Hog Ambush. From 3 to 12 (3D4) Road Hog vehicles are ready to come out of hiding. Victim takes 3 machinegun shots (no bonuses to hit, no Dodge possible) at once.

51-60 Mutant Plant Obstacle. Yes, bunkie, some of the plants did mutate during the Big Death! They're not especially dangerous, just big and very fast growing. In other words, what was a clear stretch of road yesterday is now a thick forest of telephone pole-sized trunks. Control Roll with a −35 penalty.

61-70 Poor Visibility. Fog, rain, snow, or other weather problem, clouds the road for the next 30 minutes. Roll again.

71-75 Gas Station. Small, walled compounds with farmhouse, inn and combination gas station/country store.

76-80 Large mutant creature (above Size Level 16) is walking down the road. Control Roll with −10 to avoid.

81-85 Toll Gate. Usually a section of toll road. Fee ranges from $2 to $12, depending on the size of the vehicle. There is a 30% chance of from 2-12 vehicles already lined up.

86-88 Roadblock. Either Troopers or other officials waiting in ambush. They only do this when they know somebody, like a Road Hog group or escaped prisoners, might be headed that way.

89-90 Road Ends in Hole. Remember the earthquakes? Well, they're still around, and every now and then a chunk of road opens up into a gaping hole. Control Roll with −20 penalty.

91-95 Oncoming Traffic. No problem unless someone is trying to pass. Vehicles come by every 3D6 Melee Rounds for the next five miles.

96-00 Very Heavy Traffic. Up to 3D6 vehicles are clogging the road in both directions.

ROAD HOGS: THE EVIL FROM THE NORTH

The world as it now exists was born out of the death of an earlier civilization; a civilization made-up entirely of humans, with awesome powers that are now only fading dreams. The destruction was, if anything, worse here on the West Coast of the American continent than anywhere else. Bad enough the damage done by war, biological plague and nuclear winter. Nature, would not have her power overshadowed. With a mighty series of quakes, a huge chunk of the continent, including Baja California and the fabled cities of Los Angeles and San Francisco, fell into the ocean.

It might have been easier had the area simply sunk. Unfortunately, there were weeks of extreme shocks that served as a warning. The panic-stricken population attempted to flee, and ran right into a population already hysterical with the other elements of the Big Death. It is estimated that less than 10,000 humans were left alive from a population that must have numbered in the hundreds of thousands.

Inevitably, after such a disaster, there came a golden age. The next sixty years were a time of peace and prosperity for the growing mutant animal population along with the shrinking number of humans.

The government that followed wasn't much of a government at all, more like anarchy by consensus. Although the larger towns maintained Road Troopers, there was no state-wide militia. Biker gangs and townspeople alike labored to keep alive the one great remnant of the fallen civilization, the artifact known as Route 99. Nomadic Corps families, those hardworking Highway Engineers, spent years maintaining and repairing the roads. And not just Route 99. Eventually they spread to bring back other roads — "Great 58, Gateway to the South;" 395, 99's sister highway to the east; 108, 50, 6, 44 and even distant Highway 95.

Meanwhile, a foul presence festered in the north. While peace loving Biker clubs roamed our smooth highway, their hate-filled brethren went north, up towards Pork Land. We of the south knew nothing of their ways until the Road Hogs staged their underhanded attack. These creatures had no decency; they blew up roadways, ripped up bridges, destroyed decades of Highway Engineering in the first two weeks of their rampage through the south.

Our peaceful Biker gangs, armed with nothing more than chains, knives and clubs of their ritual gang wars, fought bravely. Against the Road Hog's grenades and automatic weapons, they were simply slaughtered. Had it not been for the secret military reserves of Sacramento, the entire land would have been lost.

We have thrown the barbarians back. Even now, five years later, they continue infiltrating, destroying and looting. Using our great freeways, they penetrate deep into our lands on their motorcycles and armored cars. No matter. Sacramento and New Americorp grow stronger every year. Some day soon we will take the battle to them!

—from Americorp The Free
a 5th Grade Reader.

The Road Hogs

Where the Biker gangs of the south were peace loving and family oriented, those who went into the northlands became brutal and savage. It was an environment where only the toughest survived and, in the end, one gang ended up supreme. Their motto, "Join or Die", was earned many times over.

When the gang wars were finally over, and when a strong leader (Catsblood) took over, the gang finally took a long look at the rich lands to the south. It looked like easy pickings indeed. They were encouraged in this outlook by their secret backers; an organization that had been supplying them with advanced weapons for almost a decade. Their only mistake was thinking that they could take a piece of Route 99 without everybody joining in.

Five years after the failed invasion the Road Hogs are getting ready to try again. They have stockpiled weapons and supplies. Even more importantly, they have scouted out the roadways and townships of the south. Many of their leaders are impatient, but the secret backers keep telling them to wait . . .

Population: Roughly 34,000 Road Hog Bikers and 180,000 serfs, slaves and servants. No actual estimate on animal breakdown, but it seems that about 25% of all Road Hogs are mutant pigs.

Government: The land is controlled by the Road Hogs, who are controlled by their leader, Catsblood. It is traditional among the Road Hogs that new leaders are chosen by combat, so there would probably be many months of disorganization if something happened to Catsblood.

Major Towns: Pork Land is the main capital and headquarters of the Road Hogs. It is an ocean-side town with rich fishing and lush rice paddies. Along the northern branch of Route 99 (called US 5 on pre-death maps) there are the other Road Hog controlled towns of *Eugene, Roseburg, Medford and Weed.*

Roadways: Except to the northern branch of Route 99, the Road Hog network is in miserable condition. Treat Route 99 as a Highway, all other major roads as Back Roads, and everything else as a Trail. Only Route 99 has regular patrols. There's only a 10% chance per day of meeting Road Hogs on any of the other roads. Road Hogs will immediately attack and pursue any outsiders they discover on "their" roads.

CATSBLOOD CLAW — Mutant Cheetah

Real Name: Paul Clearwater
Alignment: Aberrant
Attributes: I.Q. 20, M.E. 22, M.A. 15, P.S. 19, P.P. 23, P.E. 18, P.B. 19, Spd. 25
Age: 34 **Sex:** Male
Size Level: 9 **Weight:** 160lbs **Height:** 5ft 6inches
Hit Points: 44 **S.D.C.:** 41
Disposition: Egotistical, remote, superior
Human Features: Hands — Full
Biped — Full
Speech — Partial
Looks — None
Powers: None
Psionics: Sixth Sense
Level of Experience: 6th Level Assassin
Level of Education: High School Equivalent
Scholastic Bonus: +20%
Occupation: Leader of Road Hogs
Scholastic Skills:
None
Natural Weapons: None
Weapon Proficiencies:
W.P. Revolver, 6th level Expert
W.P. Automatic Pistol, 6th level
W.P. Assault Rifle, 4th level
W.P. Dagger, 6th level
W.P. Chain, 6th level
Physical Skills/Training:
Acrobatics
Hand-to-Hand Assassin, 6th level
Prowl 92%
Secondary Skills:
Automotive Mechanics, 83/68%
Pilot Automobile (All) 98%
Pilot Motorcycle 98%
Vehicle-to-Vehicle Combat 121%
Pick Locks 88%
Combat Skills:
Attacks Per Melee: 4
+6 to strike, +3 to parry, +7 to dodge, +8 to damage, +8 to roll with punch or fall, +3 to pull a punch.
Personal Profile: Catsblood feels a natural sense of superiority to any other creature. He's a natural, charismatic leader who the Road Hogs follow enthusiastically. He's never been bested in personal combat. Not because he's physically superior, but because he uses his mind calmly while he fights.
Special Weapons: Usually carries a sidearm and a couple of daggers. Wears a heavy chain over the left shoulder that does 2D6 damage.

The Prairie Dog Imperium

The Prairie Dog Imperium is a strict religious community, deriving their beliefs from pre-Death Quakers and Mormons. They are anti-technology, but *not* pacifistic, and they maintain a huge, if undisciplined, army of "believers." In recent years, there have been rumors of wars between the Prairie Dogs and the Free Cattle to the north and east.

Population: 5,800,000 Prairie Dogs, perhaps 1,000,000 mutant animals of other kinds.

Economy: With the exception of a few crafts, blacksmiths and potters, the whole area is entirely agricultural. The Prairie Dog Imperium and Americorp are major trading partners.

Roadways: Most Roadways are crude, but well maintained by local workers; treat as Back Roads. The only major Highway is Route 95, which is maintained by Americorp as far as Vegas. Prairie Dog roadways are not guarded or patrolled, and visitors, so long as they pay cash, are always treated well.

La Segunda Pregunta

Whether this is an independent state or simply part of a larger government is unknown. Certainly, visitors have seen officers in uniforms that are similar to, but unlike, those of the Pregunta soldiers. The Pregunta soldiers themselves are impressive, usually Size Level 11 or greater, and armed with Assault Rifles.

Population: Unknown; at least 400,000 mutant animals.

Economy: Although it seems, on the surface, to be largely farmers and small villages, Pregunta is Americorp's primary supplier of gas and oil.

Roadways: All persons and vehicles entering Pregunta must stop on the border and be issued identity papers. Being caught without papers, or in an area not authorized by the papers, will result in an immediate arrest. The idea of a speedy trial is unknown in Pregunta and a stay of several years in jail is not uncommon.

The roads themselves are of very high quality. At least one good Highway is known and other roads seem to be very well maintained.

GOVERNOR NUEVO VARGEZ — Mutant Condor

Real Name: Nuevo Lagaztin de la Marino Vargez
Alignment: Anarchist
Attributes: I.Q. 17, M.E. 15, M.A. 17, P.S. 13, P.P. 9, P.E. 15, P.B. 13, Spd. 16
Age: 58 **Sex:** Male
Size Level: 11 **Weight:** 208lbs **Height:**6ft 6inches
Hit Points: 34 **S.D.C.:** 50
Disposition: Calm, dignified, genteel
Human Features: None
Powers: None
Psionics: None
Level of Experience: 8th Level
Level of Education: College
Scholastic Bonus: +14%
Occupation: Governor of Pregunta
Scholastic Skills:
Political Science 98%
Law 75%
Foreign Language – English 95%
History 92%
Weapon Proficiencies:
None
Physical Skills/Training:
None
Espionage Skills/Special Training:
Interrogation/Torture 95%
Surveillance Systems 90%
Escape Artist 88%
Forgery 90%
Secondary Skills:
Wine Tasting 84%
Ventriloquism 90%
Combat Skills:
Attacks Per Melee: 1
No Bonuses to Strike/Parry/Dodge/Damage

Personal Profile: Vargez is the perfect diplomat; always pleasant, always charming, and never, never indiscreet. Characters can have lengthy conversations and come away impressed, even though Vargez never answers any questions directly. On the other hand, he will encourage others to speak freely.

The Stainless Steel Stallions

The northeastern town of Whinnie Mucca is under the control of one the last, remaining, free biker gangs; the Stainless Steel Stallions. This group has managed to fight off at least 6 Road Hog attacks over the last five years. Rumor has it that they are somehow affiliated with a group called *the Free Cattle* who live far to the east.

Population: Estimated at 6,000

New Americorp

The official name for the government is the United Towns of New Americorp, abbreviated UTNA. For some reason, the older humans tend to call it "New America" – not that anyone knows why.

Americorp is by far the strongest power on the West Coast. Based in the great industrial city of Sacramento it operates a loose confederation with all the major towns along Route 99 and with many of the small towns in the interior.

Part of the problem with Americorp is that very few people identify with the government. Inside Sacramento, the people feel more loyalty to their city than to the larger government. And in the other main population centers along Route 99, people refer to themselves mostly as "99ers". Nevertheless, the people rallied behind Sacramento during the first Road Hog invasion and they would do so again, instantly. Because Americorp is so diverse, each town will be described separately.

Roadways: All the main routes shown on the map are Highways in good to excellent condition. Any other roads (and there are hundreds) are Back Roads or Trails.

PRESIDENT LOUISA DATO — Mutant Mountain Lion

Real Name: Louisa Dato

Alignment: Principled

Attributes: I.Q. 17, M.E. 9, M.A. 13, P.S. 13, P.P. 15, P.E. 14, P.B. 17, Spd. 7

Age: 40 **Sex:** Female

Size Level: 9 **Weight:** 155lbs **Height:** 5ft 7inches

Hit Points: 38 **S.D.C.:** 41

Disposition: Friendly, outgoing

Human Features: Hands — Full
Biped — Full
Speech — Full
Looks — None

Powers: None

Psionics: None

Level of Experience: 8th Level

Level of Education: Master's Level

Scholastic Bonus: +35%

Occupation: Chief Executive Officer, Americorp

Scholastic Skills:
Architectural Design and Engineering 60%
Mathematics 85%
Law 55%

Natural Weapons: 2D6 Retractable Claws

Weapon Proficiencies:
W.P. Pistol, 3rd level
W.P. Sword, 6th level
Physical Skills/Training:
Acrobatics
Espionage Skills/Special Training: None
Secondary Skills:
Pilot Automobile (All) 90%
Pilot Motorcycle 98%
Speak Spanish 88%
Combat Skills:
Attacks Per Melee: 1
No Bonuses to Strike/Parry/Dodge/Damage
Personal Profile: Louisa is dedicated to improving and expanding Americorp. Her interest in architecture has lead her to propose a massive construction project, to include new highways, bridges and public buildings. Unfortunately, the Road Hog problem has put all this on the back burner.
Special Weapons: None

The Human Elite

This is a fringe group of human, supremacist fanatics. They've been around for at least 40 years, but, until recently, were regarded as harmless crackpots. Lately, they've started appearing with weapons and vehicles of a strange new design; high tech, but unlike other pre-Death artifacts. This is a secret society, and the members often wear hoods or face-plates when appearing in their traditional biker's costume. They are humans being secretly supplied by the Empire of Humanity on the East Coast.

The State Troopers

This organization is still called the "California Road Patrol" by insiders. It's a multi-generation organization where officers are apprenticed at a young age and grow up learning the traditions and skills of the service. "Once a trooper, always a trooper", is a common expression, so any former trooper characters will be able to speak freely with regular officers.

CAPTAIN O'HAIR — Mutant Raccoon
Real Name: Shawn Coon O'Hair
Alignment: Scrupulous
Attributes: I.Q. 14, M.E. 17, M.A. 13, P.S. 14, P.P. 9, P.E. 8, P.B. 17, Spd. 19
Age: 48 **Sex:** Male
Size Level: 8 **Weight:** 180lbs **Height:**5ft 3inches
Hit Points: 29 **S.D.C.:** 55
Disposition: Gruff, short-tempered, impassioned, impatient.
Human Features: Hands — Full
Biped — Full
Speech — Full
Looks — None
Powers: Advanced Hearing
Psionics: None
Level of Experience: 9th Level
Level of Education: College
Scholastic Bonus: +15%
Occupation: Captain of State Troopers
Scholastic Skills:
Pilot Automobile (Any) 98%
Pilot Motorcycle (Any) 96%
Pilot Truck (Any) 87%
Vehicle-to-Vehicle Combat 138%
Natural Weapons: None
Weapon Proficiencies: All 9th level
W.P. Revolver
W.P. Automatic Pistol
W.P. Rifle
W.P. Submachinegun
W.P. Machinegun
W.P. Heavy Weapons
W.P. Spear
Physical Skills/Training:
General Athletics
Body Building
Prowl, 90%
Hand-to-Hand, 9th Level
Espionage Skills/Special Training:
Pick Locks 90%
Surveillance Systems 90%
Secondary Skills:
Pilot Vehicles (All) 98%
Vehicle-to-Vehicle Combat 135%
Carpentry 66%
Speak Spanish 92%
Combat Skills:
Attacks Per Melee: 5
+3 to Strike/Parry/Dodge/Damage; +3 Roll with Punch or Fall, Knock Out/Stun on 19 or 20; Critical Strike on 18, 19 or 20; Kick Attack does 1D6 damage; +4 to Body Block.
Personal Profile: O'Hair is a perfectionist. He's hard on himself, hard on his officers and hard on the world in general. He'll be pushy, insulting, argumentative and demanding. On the other hand, he'll never, ever break his word or fail to show up when promised.
Special Weapons: Custom .38 Special Revolver.

Sacramento

As the saying goes — "All roads lead to Sacramento." This is the junction of Route 99 with Routes 80, 50 and 16. Anyone approaching the city will know instantly, from the smell and the smoke, that this is a major, industrialized city. This is the late 21st Century's biggest factory town. Technologically, Sacramento is roughly equal to the U.S. in the mid-sixties; producing heavy equipment, electronics, pharmaceuticals, and weapons. This is also the base for the State Troopers, the Americorp Mint, the University of California at Sacramento, and the State Legislature.

Population: 800,000 mutant animals of every kind. There are an estimated 2,000 humans living in the city as well.

Redding

Because of frequent Road Hog problems this entire town has been walled off. Regular patrols of the *Redding Irregulars* go "Hog Hunting" in the roads around the town. Junction of Routes 44 and 99.

Population: 7,000 mutant animals of all kinds.

Oroville

Another walled town. It has a population of only 600, but is an important repair and refueling base for highway traffic.

Manteca

The junction of Routes 99 and 108. Has a population of around 5,000 with a large percentage of felines (about 30%).

Fresno-by-the-Sea

This is a major trading port. Dolphins, seals, and other oceangoing creatures, come from many places in the Ocean to trade for manufactured goods. The southwestern edge of the town is flooded with 2 feet of saltwater for the convenience of the ocean visitors.

Population: 80,000 land dwelling, mutant animals. The offshore population of ocean animals has been estimated at anywhere from 10,000 to 2,500,000.

Bakersfield-by-the-Sea

Junction of Routes 99 and 58 and site of Americorp's major oil refinery. Crude oil comes into Bakersfield by tanker and by truck from Pregunta. There is a major chemical industry and a growing plastics industry. Just recently, the first, new microchips were fabricated.

Population: Over 100,000 mutant animals of all kinds.

Game Master Tips

In Road Hogs, the players should be confronted with a fairly visible evil, whether it be the *Road Hog Gang, the Human Supremacists or the Enslavers*. So the players should have no difficulty choosing sides.

Yet, one problem remains. How should the players be organized? That depends on you, the game master, on the preferences of the players, as well as on the kind of characters the players end up with. Let the players roll-up the characters, then talk over the choices with them. The best way to set up an organization for player characters is to let the players choose one of the following:

Choice #1: A Biker Gang. In many ways this is the most fun to play. The characters can be obvious. They can wear their 'colors' (the leather jacket with their club emblem on the back) and they can zoom around looking for Road Hogs to beat up. Let the players choose the club name, motto, standard vehicle and so forth. Not the best choice for players with subtlety and finesse, but good for lots of action.

Choice #2: Ninja Secret Society. The game master should work up a secret Ninja Master (a Sensei) who will watch over the group, send them on assignments and supply them with inside information. One or more of the player characters should be Ninjas, but the rest will be hired for their special skills. The cartoon printed in this book illustrates the kind of thing that Ninja Societies do best.

Choice #3: California Road Patrol Agents. In this case, the group will pretend to be migrant laborers, merchants or whatever. They'll infiltrate areas and try to track down Road Hog or other illicit activities. Calls for players who are more interested in intrigue and less interested in combat.

Of course, there are plenty of other choices! Players could be explorers from the East Coast of *After the Bomb*, or renegade Road Hog bikers who've switched sides, or. . . you get the idea. So long as the characters don't end up wandering around the countryside aimlessly.

ROAD HOGS: MAIL CALL!

Note: This is an introductory scenario. It's a useful device for players to "learn" the Road Hogs, Vehicle-to-Vehicle, combat systems before they generate their characters "for real." At least two playing teams are needed. Uneven numbers on the teams are okay. One neat thing about this scenario is you can play it over and over again!

PLAYER BACKGROUND:

First have the players generate mutant animal characters from this book. They need to do everything *except* create their cars. Next, have them divide into two teams. Read the following:

> "You two teams are representing two, rival Trucking companies; *The Blue Barracudas* and the *Cheetah Express*. Both teams are in contention for a major shipping contract for Americorp. Awarding the contract is simple. You meet at exactly midnight, on Route 99 at the Sacramento, southern border. There you'll each be given a letter. The first one to deliver this letter to the northern border of Bakersfield-by-the-Sea is the winner."
>
> "Here are the rules:
>
> 1. No Weapons or Ram-Prows allowed.
> 2. There are no other rules."
>
> "Each team is hereby awarded $15,000 to construct your vehicle or vehicles. This is *all the money you may use*! Now go work up your vehicles."

GAME MASTER INFORMATION

Players may use any dirty trick in the book, may buy as many vehicles as they want and can try to deceive the other players in any way they like. On the other hand, the players *cannot exceed $15,000 in vehicle expenses and they cannot buy or use weapons or ram-prows*. Any kind of Vehicle-to-Vehicle maneuver or hand-to-hand combat is okay.

THE ROAD SYSTEM:

Main Highway: Route 99 will be clear of all traffic and in good repair all the way from Sacramento to Bakersfield-by-the-Sea.

Back Roads: If you've got a real map, then by all means use it (it doesn't even have to be of California). Otherwise, explain to the players that you will roll the roads as you go along.

Trails: Although it isn't very fast, the characters can always choose to travel directly cross-country. Be sure to keep close track of compass direction while characters are using Trails. Use the following table for encounters.

01-25 Trail continues straight and clean for 1 mile.
26-30 Turn to right or left; can't go straight.
31-35 Must turn left.
36-40 Must turn right.
41-45 Absolute dead end; cliff wall.
46-70 Clear in all directions.
71-80 Fork; can go left or right.
81-90 Trail joins with Back Road.
91-95 Trail merges back onto Route 99.
96-97 Trail dead ends in forest. Vehicle is trapped for 2D6 minutes trying to get out.
98-99 Mutant Fly Swarm; roll 4D6 impact/S.D.C. damage.
100 Characters become totally lost and no longer know which way is north. GM rolls 1D6; on 1 or 2 — they're facing north, 3 or 4 — facing south, 5 — facing west, and 6 — facing east.

Note: The GM can add, modify or spice up this adventure any way he/she may desire or play it as a straight, one-on-one, combat race. The preceding road table may be used in other adventures if the GM likes.

ON THE ROAD AGAIN

Note: This is an easy mission. A good introduction to the vehicle-to-vehicle combat system. First-time, Road Hog, player characters can "shakedown" their vehicles against a fairly low-level group of Road Hogs.

PLAYER BACKGROUND:

Read:

> "You are enjoying lunch in a small diner. It's a pleasant break from driving in a pleasant little town. Suddenly, you hear the sound of gunshots outside. What are you doing?"

Anyone who looks or runs outside will see the following:

> "Right across the street, at the town gas station, you see a Mutant Vulture, wearing a Road Hogs jacket, firing a shotgun into the station. Two other Road Hogs, a Hawk and a Beaver, are revving up Street Bikes. A third motorcycle is already zooming out of town. The shotgun-wielding Vulture is backing up toward a bright red, pick-up truck. What are you doing now?"

GAME MASTER INFORMATION:

Players can start shooting from the moment they set eyes on the Road Hogs. Eliminating some of the opposition before they get out of town is a good idea. It'll take the vulture a full melee round to get in the truck. Players have three melee rounds against the two motorcycles and the truck, before they're out of range. The Road Hogs have just robbed the gas station and beatup the owner, his wife and two, young attendants.

Road Hog Vehicles

Three (3) Road Hog Motorcycles

Base S.D.C.: 100
Vehicle Armor: A.R.:14; S.D.C.: 350
Speed Class: 10 (Maximum 150mph/Cruise 80mph)
Description: Large Street Cycles with black paint and bright yellow Road Hog symbol.

Road Hog Pick-Up Truck

Base S.D.C.: 450
Vehicle Armor: A.R.: 16; S.D.C.: 465
Crew Compartment Armor: A.R.: 11; S.D.C.: 300—Light Armor with glass windows
Speed Class: 12 (Maximum 180mph/Cruise 90mph)
Forward, Swivel Mounted Light Machinegun: 5D6 Damage
Gun Ports Mounted: 1 Right, 1 Left, 2 Rear, 2 Front
Description: A 1950's Ford Pick-up Truck with crude-looking, plate metal armor. Bright red paint with bright yellow Road Hog symbol on each side.

NPC CHARACTERS:

Slymie: This mutant *Hog* is the leader of this group of Road Hogs. He's the driver of the pick-up truck. Capturing him alive would be a plus since he knows quite a bit about the Road Hog command structure. He'll try to Dodge vehicle attacks, but will attempt sideswipes, and the like, against any smaller vehicles (motorcycles, compacts and sports cars).
Size Level: 12 **A.R.:** 4 **S.D.C.:** 50 **Hit Points:** 22
Human Features: Hands — Full, Biped — Full, Speech — Partial
Driving Skills: Vehicle-to-Vehicle Combat 95%
Weapons: .45 Automatic Pistol; 4D6 Damage, Single Shot
Attacks Per Melee: 2
+3 to Strike, +2 to Parry, +3 to Dodge

Eric: A mutant *Jumping Mouse* who is already in back of the truck when the characters come on the scene. He'll stay hidden until some vehicle gets in range. Then he'll open fire. He has no armor and no protection in the back of the truck.
Size Level: 13 **A.R.:** 4 **S.D.C.:** 52 **Hit Points:** 31
Human Features: Hands — Full, Biped — Partial, Speech — Partial
Driving Skill: None
Weapons: Flame Thrower; does 8D6 Damage; range: 40 feet.
8 Fragmentation Grenades, no plus to Strike; 6D6 damage
Attacks Per Melee: 3
+2 to Strike; No plus to Parry/Dodge

Urhawl: The mutant *Vulture* who's backing toward the truck. He'll ride in the passenger seat and will fire the shotgun out of the gun ports. He'll also man the forward machinegun if a target shows up there.
Size Level: 11 **A.R.:** 4 **S.D.C.:** 42 **Hit Points:** 18
Human Features: Hands — Full, Biped — Full, Speech — Partial
Driving Skill: Vehicle-to-Vehicle Combat 60%
Weapons: Shotgun; 4D6 damage.
Attacks Per Melee: 2
+4 to Strike, +3 to Parry, +5 to Dodge

Wally: Mutant *Coyote*; wearing armor and driving one of the motorcycles. He will attempt to drive and fire over his shoulder at the same time (−20 on his Control Rolls).
Size Level: 11 **A.R.:** 4 **S.D.C.:** 48 **Hit Points:** 30
Chain Mail Armor: A.R.: 13; S.D.C.: 70
Human Features: Hands — Full, Biped — Full, Speech — Partial
Driving Skill: Vehicle-to-Vehicle Combat 105%
Weapons: Submachinegun; 4D6 damage
.32 Automatic Pistol; 2D6 damage
Attacks Per Melee: 2
+2 to Strike(weapons and H-to-H), +6 to Parry, +5 to Dodge.

Grey: Mutant *Beaver*; wearing armor and driving a motorcycle. He will avoid combat unless cornered.
Size Level: 14 **A.R.:** 4 **S.D.C.:** 65 **Hit Points:** 38
Chain Mail Armor: A.R.: 13; S.D.C.: 55
Human Features: Hands — Full, Biped — Full, Speech — Full
Driving Skill: Vehicle-to-Vehicle Combat 100%
Weapons: 9mm Automatic; 2D6 damage
Attacks Per Melee: 3
+1 to Strike, +4 to Parry/Dodge

Quince: Mutant *Hawk* wearing armor and driving a motorcycle. He will avoid any early combat, his objective will be to get *behind* any opponents and use the machinegun. If he has enough of a lead he'll hide and come at them from behind. If that's not possible then he'll do a sliding sudden brake, trying to make it look like an accident.
Size Level: 10 **A.R.:** 4 **S.D.C.:** 45 **Hit Points:** 29
Leather Armor: A.R.: 10; S.D.C.: 40
Human Features: Hands — Full, Biped — Full, Speech — Partial
Driving Skill: Vehicle-to-Vehicle Combat 78%
Weapons: Motorcycle has forward fixed light machinegun; 5D6 Damage
Attacks Per Melee: 2
+2 to Strike

LOCAL ROAD SYSTEM:

Main Highway: Route 99 is the main road through town. The Road Hogs will get on immediately and head north. They'll stay on the Highway until they realize that they're being pursued. There are side roads every two miles.

Side Roads: The roads are the equivalent of Back Roads. They twist and turn through the forest. Here's a table for randomly creating the roads:

01-15 Road continues straight and clean for 1 mile.
16-20 Gradual turn to right.
21-25 Gradual turn to left.
26-30 Sharp turn to right (Control Roll).
31-35 Sharp turn to left (Control Roll).
36-40 Four-way intersection – Clear.
41-42 Four-way intersection; truck on intersect course.
43-50 Fork; can go left or right.
51-52 Blind curve to the right with oncoming truck.
53-60 Road turns into Trail quality for 1 mile.
61-65 Road merges back onto Route 99.
66-70 Road dead ends in forest.
71-80 Broken Pavement (Control Roll).
81-85 Mutant Fly Swarm; roll 4D6 impact/S.D.C. damage.
86-90 Mutant Tree in center of Road (Control Roll).
91-95 Abandoned Truck in Road (Control Roll).
96-99 Road cuts through town.
100 Friendly mutant animal takes rifle shot at Road Hog – +4 to Strike, 4D6 damage, aimed at vehicle.

Note: Feel free to use this table in other adventures if you like.

If there are more Road Hog vehicles than the number of pursuing vehicles, then the Road Hogs will start splitting up.

SOUTH OF THE BORDER (or The Magnificent Seven, again?!)

Note: This is a moderate level adventure requiring at least five strong characters. The more characters killed in vehicle combat, the better. It is assumed that the characters have already formed some kind of group prior to the briefing.

PLAYER BACKGROUND

The GM should set the stage for the characters. This should take place in an area somewhere where the characters frequently hang out. If the characters have their own camp, garage or building, that would be best. Other possibilities include a bar, inn or restaurant. Ideally, it will be in Bakersfield-by-the-Sea. Read:

> "Your whole group is sitting around talking when you notice a rather odd-looking pair of mutant animals enter. One, a grizzled old Mule, is unusual only in that the cut of his clothes is slightly different. The other, a good-looking, mutant, Prairie Dog, would stand-out in any crowd. He's wearing a bright pink shirt embroidered with silver thread, a red ascot, red pants, a shiny black vest, matching black boots, a silver studded belt and holster, a pearl-handled revolver, and a weird, wide-brimmed hat with little round tassels. There is a shocked silence in the room, none of you have ever seen anything remotely like this before."

Give the players a chance to react. If any directly insult either of the two strangers, they will turn to leave. The Prairie Dog saying, "Let us go. There are no honorable ones here!" Otherwise, or if the characters apologize, he will say the following. Read:

> "The gaudily dressed, young Prairie Dog speaks, 'My friend Jose and I, Don Lazlo Fuego Huarez de Zapata, come to this land seeking brave drivers and powerful vehicles. The fighters we are looking for must be true of heart and of mind, willing to risk all for a noble cause and a fair lady! Could it be you that we seek?' What are you doing?"

If the characters express an interest or willingness then Lazlo will tell them his story. Read:

> "Lazlo seats himself and starts speaking, 'I come from a far-off land known as West Texas. There, I am engaged to marry the most beautiful creature on the face of the Earth. The fair, the wonderful, the incredible . . .' at this point Jose, the Mutant Donkey, kicks Lazlo under the table, '. . . ouch! Ah, the beautiful Consuela of the Realto Hacienda.
>
> "'Alas it has been hard for Consuela. After her father's death last year, her land has been threatened by banditos. Banditos

who ride cars and trucks and motorcycles. They treaten and steal from the peasants, kill and rob innocent travelers, and burn whatever they cannot drag away.'

"'Yet they are even more evil than simple bandits. They have started destroying our wells, blowing up our natural springs and pulling down our water towers. It's as if they intend to kill us with thirst and starvation, merely so they can rob our meager possessions. Surely, if this continues, it will mean death for all our people.'

"'They have not succeeded in taking our stout haciendas, but neither can we dislodge them from their fortress. We outnumber them, we are as brave as they, but we are helpless in the flat lands when they come on their machines. So now we look for a group of courageous dirvers and stout machines, so that we may drive these brutes from our lands.'"

Lazlo will then answer questions to the best of his ability. He can describe the trip from the hacienda to Bakersfield-by-the-Sea (they hitchhiked with kindly truckers), the banditos and their vehicles.

Whenever the characters ask about payment, Lazlo will reply, "This is not a job; this is a crusade against evil. And an opportunity to fight for a fair lady. What more could any brave *gunfighter* want?" He'll keep up like this until someone agrees to go. Then, when someone starts worrying about money, he'll say "no problem" and pour out a sack of seven hundred, $50 gold pieces. This, he says, is for expenses, "and for the dear friends who will come help us fight the banditos."

If a character asks why Lazlo came to Americorp, Lazlo will reply, "Why did we come here? It is because Paco, Consuela's human guardian, said that the greatest gunfighters come from Bakersfield. Although, had I known how far it was, I might never have started."

GAME MASTER INFORMATION

The entire area around the bandito's Fort, which they call Petrolia, has been assaulted during Lazlo's absence. The land is under the tight control of the bandits who are attempting to control the entire fuel and water supply. They make a regular practice of blowing up storage tanks, wells and natural springs. To make 'examples' out of rebellious villages, they will simply cut off their entire supply of water and fuel . . .

The peasant's stronghold is a walled village built around an ancient, Pueblo Indian village . . . the whole thing sits in a niche of a stone pillar . . .

GM Tip: It's suggested that Game Masters take a look at a U.S. Road Atlas before running this adventure.

CLUES AND ENCOUNTERS

This journey of almost 1,460 miles can easily provide for a long-term, Road Hog campaign all by itself. GMs should feel free to create whole new towns, countries, bandit territories or whatever they fancy. Throughout the entire trip, Lazlo and Jose will occasionally mutter something about "how could Paco say it was just a little piece down the road?"

The trip should start in Bakersfield-by-the-Sea.

Step 1: Route 58 to U.S. 40 (125 miles). About 50 miles out, they must stop at the border and get official passes and go through Pregunta. This is not a problem.

Roadways/Gas: The roads are all excellent Highways. Gasoline sells for $6 to $8 a gallon.

Step 2: U.S. 40 east until it turns north. When it turns east again, the characters will have covered another 210 miles and will exit from *Pregunta*.

Roadways/Gas: The roads in this area, formerly a U.S. superhighway, are now a little better than Back Roads. There is only one gas station in this entire stretch ("Last Chance Gas") and the asking price is $12 per gallon in gold.

Step 3: East again on U.S. 40, all the way through the Imperium of Prairie Dogs and beyond. Continue through mountainous bad lands, all the way to the Albuquerque crater (479 miles).

Roadways/Gas: Road quality varies from Trail to Back Road to Highway, and can shift at any time. There are small outposts selling gas, roughly every 150 miles. Prices are usually around $17 in gold.

Step 4: Head southeast and find U.S. 25, then continue south until meeting U.S. 10 (225 miles)

Roadways/Gas: Road quality is usually pretty good. Only one outpost selling gas (a small walled fort) about halfway. They ask $25 per gallon, but can be argued down to $15, so long as the payment is in gold.

Step 5: Take U.S. 10 south, around the *El Paso Death Zone* (posted), then southeast and east for another 380 miles. This should put the players in the ruins of Fort Stockton, Texas. Incidentally, if they go another 50 miles, they'll find out why Lazlo was told that Bakersfield was "just a little piece down the road." That's right; Bakersfield, *Texas* . . . Lazlo just turned left instead of right.

Roadways/Gas: This stretch has about half Highway and half Trail quality roads with almost nothing in between. Trading Posts carrying gas are about every 75 miles and the price is usually no more than $4 per gallon (obviously the characters should figure out that there is some gas source nearby — the traders will only say that a truck comes by every month or so).

Step 6: South along a Back Road, Federal 385, for another 40 miles and they'll finally come to the Realto hacienda. Just a mile outside of the hacienda they'll see something by the side of the road. Read the following:

> "You pull over and see the body of a human lying face down in the dirt. Lazlo and Jose both rush to him saying, 'Paco!' They turn him over and you see he's been severely beaten; he's only barely alive.
>
> "Lazlo is holding him and saying, 'Paco, what happened? Who did this to you?' The old human speaks, saying in a halting voice, 'It was (cough) Hancho! He has returned . . . (choke) . . . with a dragon . . . (gasp) . . . broke down the wall . . . (mumble) . . . leading the banditos. Lazlo! They have Consuela! You must . . .'
>
> "The man goes limp. He is obviously dead. Jose starts sobbing softly, but Lazlo gets a determined look. He fingers his gun and says, 'I will avenge you my friend, on my life's blood, I will avenge you!' The scene is interrupted by gunshots from the direction of the hacienda."

Roadways/Gas: No gas available. The road is good for a Back Road, but no Highway.

Step 7: The attack on the Realto hacienda happened the night before the characters arrive on the scene. Most of the Banditos have already left, but three remain; drinking, looting and terrorizing the few, remaining, Prairie Dog, Donkey and Vulture peasants. The three left are *Ricardo*, a mutant Road Runner who is Hancho's second in command, *Simpatico* and *Gonzi*.

Since the Banditos will be surprised by the characters, there will be minimal resistance. Ricardo will not even try to fight, instead he'll use his speed to try to get away.

Step 8: Once the Realto hacienda is taken back from the banditos, Lazlo will ask to be taken around to the other haciendas. Every single one has been taken by the Banditos. Along the way, Lazlo will find from 10-100 volunteers who still are willing to fight. Everyone else will be too afraid of the dragon.

If asked about the 'dragon', they'll respond, "You don't unerstan' senor! This is a dragon. Very, *very* large. A monster. Bullets, they bounce off! Explosives do not hurt it. What can we do against that?"

Step 9: The final step is the attack on the Bandito fort. Fortunately, there are no fortification. The Banditos will attempt to charge the attackers with their shabby vehicles (although the player character vehicles should run rings around the Bandito vehicles). As soon as it looks like the player characters are a real threat, they will deploy the Dragon.

When things are looking very bad, Hancho will take Consuela as a hostage. With Ricardo (if he escaped the player characters), he will flee in the last Bandito, ½ ton truck. The final problem for the characters will be to rescue Consuela from Hancho.

The Realto Hacienda Characters

LAZLO — Mutant Prairie Dog

Real Name: Don Lazlo Fuego Huarez de Zapata
Alignment: Principled
Attributes: I.Q. 10, M.E. 12, M.A. 13, P.S. 16, P.P. 16, P.E. 13, P.B. 17, Spd. 11
Size Level: 9 **Weight:** 145lbs **Height:**5ft 4inches
Hit Points: 28 **S.D.C.:** 40
Disposition: Courtly, honorable, good natured.
Human Features: Hands — Full
Biped — Full
Speech — Full
Looks — Full
Powers: None
Psionics: None
Level of Experience: 1st
Level of Education: High School
Scholastic Bonus: None
Occupation: Rancher
Scholastic Skills: None
Natural Weapons: None
Weapon Proficiencies:
W.P. Revolver, 9th level Expert (3/6, +5 to strike)
W.P. Quick Draw, 8th level (just means he can do fancy stuff like pull out the gun quick, spin it around, shoot over the shoulder, etc.)
Physical Skills/Training:
Prowl 88%
Running
Flamenco Dance 40%
Espionage Skills/Special Training: None
Secondary Skills:
Play Spanish Guitar 89%
Sing Spanish Songs 83%
Farming 75%
Basic Survival 80%
Combat Skills:
Attacks Per Melee: 2
No Bonuses to Strike (except weapon)/Parry, +3 to Dodge.
Personal Profile: Lazlo is a mutant *Prairie Dog* who is an incurable romantic. He is deeply and passionately in love with Consuela, and will readily sacrifice his own life for hers.
Special Weapons: Customized, .45 Revolver with pearl handles; gold inlay and a gorgeous, silver belt/holster.

JOSE — Mutant Donkey

Real Name: Jose
Alignment: Anarchist
Attributes: I.Q 14, M.E. 15, M.A. 16, P.S. 17, P.P. 15, P.E. 18, P.B. 17, Spd. 18
Age: 52 **Sex:** Male
Size Level: 9 **Weight:** 145lbs **Height:**5ft 4inches
Hit Points: 48 **S.D.C.:** 60
Disposition: Quiet, withdrawn, deep
Human Features: Hands — Full
Biped — Full
Speech — Partial
Looks — None
Powers: Advanced Hearing
Psionics: None
Level of Experience: 9th Level
Level of Education: Grade School
Scholastic Bonus: None
Occupation: Peasant Farmer
Scholastic Skills: None
Natural Weapons: 1D8 Hooves
Weapon Proficiencies:
W.P. Rifle, 9th level (Aimed 3/6, +5 to Strike)
W.P. Revolver, 4th level
W.P. Knife, 4th level
W.P. Machete, 4th level
Physical Skills/Training:
Hand-to-Hand Martial Arts, 9th level
Prowl 98%
Espionage Skills/Special Training: None
Secondary Skills:
Cook 87%
Sewing 43%
Basic Survival 98%
Combat Skills:
Attacks Per Melee: 6
+3 to Strike/Parry/Dodge/Damage, +4 Roll with Punch or Fall, Knock Out/Stun on 19 or 20. Note: Kick Attack does 2D8 damage.
Personal Profile: Jose doesn't say much; mostly "yes", "no" and "maybe, maybe not". He is also Lazlo's protector and will defend him at all costs.
Special Weapons: Always carries an old, Western-style rifle; 4D6 damage.

CONSUELA — Mutant Prairie Dog

Real Name: Consuela Delia Doraval Estevez Realto
Alignment: Scrupulous
Attributes: I.Q. 21, M.E. 15, M.A. 18, P.S. 18, P.P. 14, P.E. 13, P.B. 18, Spd. 13
Age: 19 **Sex:** Female
Size Level: 9 **Weight:** 138lbs **Height:**5ft 2inches
Hit Points: 28 **S.D.C.:** 40
Disposition: Cheerful, self-confident.
Human Features: Hands — Full
Biped — Full
Speech — Full
Looks — None
Powers: None
Psionics: None
Level of Experience: 1st Level
Level of Education: High School
Scholastic Bonus: +30%
Occupation: Mistress of the hacienda
Scholastic Skills:
Flamenco Dancing 88%
History 78%
Business Management 70%
Natural Weapons: None
Weapon Proficiencies: None
Physical Skills/Training:
Gymnastics
Dance
Espionage Skills/Special Training: None
Secondary Skills:
Audio Communications 55%
Pilot Motorcycle 40%

W.P. Rifle, 1st Level
Combat Skills:
Attacks Per Melee: 2
No Bonuses to Strike/Parry/Dodge/Damage
Personal Profile: Consuela is dedicated to Lazlo. She finds his chivalry a little silly, but is flattered by it anyway. She is fairly resourceful, and will grab any opportunity to escape that presents itself. She's also not above attacking Hancho directly, if she feels that's what will turn the situation around.
Special Weapons: None

The Survivors

Typical Hacienda Survivor: Roll percentile for type 01-20, Prairie Dog; 21-30, Cow; 31-35, Pig; 36-50, Jumping Mouse; 51-60, Pronghorn; 61-65, Coyote; 66-75, Buffalo; 76-80, Vulture; 81-85, Dog; 86-100, random animal. Typically, they have Rifles (5D6 damage, single shot), Revolvers (3D6 damage, single shot) and ancient, hand-to-hand weapons like swords, machetes and knives. Average Hit Points is 20. Average remaining S.D.C. is 30. Most have slight wounds and are still bandaged.

The Bandito Characters

HANCHO — Mutant Coyote
Real Name: Hancho
Alignment: Miscreant
Attributes: I.Q. 18, M.E. 18, M.A. 15, P.S. 17, P.P. 12, P.E. 20, P.B. 13, Spd. 12
Age: 28 **Sex:** Male
Size Level: 8 **Weight:** 140lbs **Height:** 5ft 4inches
Hit Points: 47 **S.D.C.:** 39
Disposition: mean, vindictive and cruel
Human Features: Hands — Full
Biped — Full
Speech — Full
Looks — None
Powers: Advanced Smell
Psionics: None
Level of Experience: 4th Level
Level of Education: Grade School
Scholastic Bonus: None
Occupation: Bandit Leader
Scholastic Skills: None
Natural Weapons: None
Weapon Proficiencies:
W.P. Assault Rifle, 4th level Expert
W.P. Rifle, 3rd level
W.P. Revolver, 3rd level
W.P. Automatic Pistol, 3rd level Expert
W.P. Submachinegun, 2nd level
W.P. Machete, 2nd level
W.P. Knife, 3rd level
Physical Skills/Training:
Prowl 86%
Hand-to-Hand Expert, 4th level
Espionage Skills/Special Training: None
Secondary Skills:
Pilot Automobile (All) 98%
Vehicle-to-Vehicle Combat 100%
Auto Mechanics 87/72%
Armorer — Rapid-fire Weapons 96/81%
Combat Skills:
Attacks Per Melee: 4
+3 to Strike/Parry/Dodge, +2 to Roll with Punch or Fall, +2 to Pull a Punch

Personal Profile: Hancho is a driven mutant *coyote*. He's driven to punish anyone who offends him. Years ago, when he was a worker at the hacienda of Consuela's father, he was fired for drunkenness. Now he has returned to punish all the people of the region.
Special Weapons: Prefers traveling with 7.62mm assault rifle, 9mm automatic pistol, and, at least, three daggers.

RICARDO — Mutant Road Runner
Real Name: Ricardo
Alignment: Miscreant
Attributes: I.Q. 14, M.E. 12, M.A. 13, P.S. 15, P.P. 19, P.E. 16, P.B. 16, Spd. 24
Age: 23 **Sex:** Male
Size Level: 8 **Weight:** 145lbs **Height:** 5ft 1inch
Hit Points: 32 **S.D.C.:** 43
Disposition: Irritable, impatient and fast-tongued
Human Features: Hands — Full
Biped — Full
Speech — Full
Looks — None
Powers: Speed (45mph/+3 to Strike & Dodge/+2 to Damage per each 10mph)
Psionics: None
Level of Experience: 3rd Level
Level of Education: Grade School
Scholastic Bonus: None
Occupation: Bandit
Scholastic Skills: None
Natural Weapons: None

Weapon Proficiencies:
W.P. Buffalo Rifle, 3rd level Expert
W.P. Pistol, 3rd level
W.P. Knife, 3rd level
Physical Skills/Training:
Running
Prowl 90%
Espionage Skills/Special Training: None
Secondary Skills:
Pilot Automobile — Automatic 43%
Pilot Automobile — Manual 33%
Combat Skills:
Attacks Per Melee: 2
+3 to Strike, +5 to Dodge
Personal Profile: He is a loyal follower of Hancho and the most efficient killer in the group. Out in the prairies and desert he's particularly deadly, since he'll use his speed to put some distance (4,000 feet or so) between himself and his victim. Then he'll use the Buffalo rifle to kill the victim.
Special Weapons: Carries an ancient Buffalo Rifle. This is a single shot weapon (needs a full melee round to reload) with 5D6 damage. The main advantage of this weapon is incredibly long range. He can pick something off with accuracy up to 3 miles away. Requires special shells that he carries in a small pouch.

Rondo

Mutant Gila Monster who controls "The Dragon" (he calls it 'stupid'). He will stay behind the beast, usually on a motorcycle, and control its movements. If he is captured or killed the monster becomes harmless.
Size Level: 9; **A.R.:** 4; **S.D.C.:** 35; **Hit Points:** 24
Chain Mail Armor: A.R.: 14; S.D.C.: 45
Human Features: Hands — Full, Biped — Full, Speech — Partial
Driving Skill: Pilot Motorcycle 58%
Natural Weapons: Paralytic Poison Bite
Weapons: .45 Automatic Pistol; 4D6 damage
Attacks Per Melee: 2
+1 to Strike, +2 to Parry/Dodge

THE DRAGON

This is a *mutant Gila Monster*, but a twisted creature that does **not** have human intelligence, but immense size. Rondo, is a mutant Gila Monster with Animal Speech and Animal Control and forces the simple minded creature to attack. Bullets usually do no damage but they *hurt*! Without Rondo "The Dragon" would just wander back out into the desert.
Size Level: 20+ **Weight:** 40,000lbs **Length:**45ft long
Hit Points: 210 **A.R.:** 18 **S.D.C.:** 1200
No Human Features
+2 to Strike, +30 to Damage, Claws do 4D6

EMANUAL

Mutant Armadillo who usually drives one of the two ½ ton trucks (Hancho always drives the other). He is paranoid about getting hurt and will likely surrender if things look bad. It becomes a sure thing if he's hurt or if "the Dragon" is taken out of the action.
Size Level: 10 **Hit Points:** 30
Natural Body Armor: A.R.: 10; S.D.C.: 165
Chain Mail Armor: A.R.: 14; S.D.C.: 48
Human Features: Hands — Full, Biped — Partial, Speech — Partial
Driving Skill: Pilot ½ ton truck, 85%
Weapons: 9mm Automatic, 2D6 damage
Attacks Per Melee: 2
+1 to Strike, +4 to Parry/Dodge

Typical Banditos

Average Bandito Vulture: The mutant Vultures are the gunners of the Banditos. They man all the Turret weapons and avoid driving when possible. There are 8 of them. They are fierce fighters who will only surrender when it looks absolutely hopeless. Usually second level in experience.
Size Level: 11 **A.R.:** 4 **S.D.C.:** 42 **Hit Points:** 18
Human Features: Hands — Full, Biped — Full, Speech — Partial
Driving Skill: Pilot Jeep 60%
Weapons: Either Rifle, Shotgun or Revolver
Attacks Per Melee: 2
+2 to Strike, +1 to Parry, +3 to Dodge

Average Bandito Coyote: The 18 mutant Coyote followers of Hancho are all drivers. They will drive jeeps, and when all the jeeps have been taken they'll drive motorcycles. They like the bandit life, but they won't defend it to the end. If necessary they'll try to escape rather than be captured.
Size Level: 9 **A.R.:** 4 **S.D.C.:** 43 **Hit Points:** 30
Human Features: Hands — Full, Biped — Full, Speech — Full
Driving Skill: Vehicle-to-Vehicle Combat 105%
Weapons: All use Submachinegun, 4D6 damage
Attacks Per Melee: 3
+3 to Strike (for weapon), +3 to Parry, +5 to Dodge

THE BANDITO VEHICLES

12 Motorcycles
Base S.D.C.: 100
Vehicle Armor: A.R.: 16; S.D.C.: 700
Passenger Armor: A.R.: 12; S.D.C.: 250
Speed Class: 8 (Maximum 120mph/Cruise 70mph)
Forward Swivel Mounted Light Machinegun: 5D6 Damage

4 Jeeps
Base S.D.C.: 450
Vehicle Armor: A.R.: 14; S.D.C.: 350
Crew Compartment Armor: None
Speed Class: 5 (Maximum 75mph/Cruise 55mph)

Turret Mounted Heavy Machinegun: 7D6 Damage
— No Turret Armor
Gun Ports Mounted: Open cab, none needed.
Description: A desert camouflage painted jeep.

2 Heavy Trucks (½ Ton)
Base S.D.C.: 600
Vehicle Armor: A.R.: 18; S.D.C.: 1,400
Crew Compartment Armor: A.R.: 16; S.D.C.: 500
Speed Class: 6 (Maximum 90mph/Cruise 60mph)
Forward Swivel Mounted Medium Machinegun: 6D6 Damage
Gun Ports Mounted: 1 Right, 1 Left, 2 Rear, 2 Front
Single Turret, Mounted on Cab Roof:
Armor: A.R.: 17; S.D.C.: 550
Heavy Machinegun: 7D6 Damage, 3,000ft Range
Description: An ex-army truck, still painted green. The back is an open flatbed for carrying cargo.

ROAD HOGS: GANG WAR!

Note: This is a Moderate level game that could take from two to four sessions to finish. Players should be experienced role-players, but need not know this game system. No special abilities, powers, or numbers needed. Player characters must be in the employ of either the State Troopers, a Ninja organization or some other group that can supply them with costumes and information.

PLAYER BACKGROUND:

The GM may wish to role-play the character's investigation of the Road Hog's organization. This can involve observations of an infiltration camp just before it's raided, or interrogation of a Road Hog prisoner. It's important the characters are provided with *Road Hog disguises*, and Road Hog-style weapons and vehicles.

Once the character have found out a bit about the Road Hogs they should be given a briefing. This will be presented by their contact in whatever organization they have affiliated with. Read the following:

> "Your group has been selected for a sensitive and vital mission in the Road Hog camp. We expect you to disguise yourselves as Road Hogs, to join one of their expeditions and to make your way towards Pork Land.
>
> "Once in Pork Land we have an address, 111 Washington Avenue, that requires careful investigation. It may be that one of them will yield some clues as the mysterious source of the Road Hogs' weapons and vehicles.
>
> "The reason why the mission begins today is that we have just heard about a large mobilization of Road Hogs north of Whinnie Mucca. In such a large group, at least 500, a small group of strangers should go unnoticed.
>
> "The main tricky thing will be to come toward the Road Hog camp from the north. That means you should travel to the far east, then head north, then west, then back to the south to join the Road Hogs.
>
> "We've arranged for enough captured, Road Hog weapons, vehicles and outfits, so that you should fit into their camp easily. Their loose organization makes it really unlikely that you'll be challenged.
>
> "For all our sakes, please be careful! Bringing back information on the Road Hogs' source for their strange devices would be great. You should also try to keep the Road Hogs from discovering your ruse — we may need to try something like this in the future."

The briefing agent will readily answer questions, but doesn't know anything more than what's already been said.

INSIDE INFORMATION

Players with contacts in the State Troopers will be told that their mission is "crazy" and that they should "make sure their wills are made and their insurance is paid up" before leaving.

Ninja contacts, when asked about the Road Hog territory, will be told, "Pork Land is a dangerous place for a Ninja. If you find yourself there, be prepared to undergo a test of restraint equal to anything you have ever seen."

Highway Engineers who make inquiries will find that they can get a pre-Death map of the Road Hog area (called "Oregon") for $100. This provides important information on Back Roads and reduces the characters' chances of getting lost.

GAME MASTER INFORMATION

The player characters should be provided with as many Road Hog weapons and vehicles as necessary (see below for specifics). This should be no more than one car (assigned to three characters) and one motorcycle each, for the rest of the group.

That address, 111 Washington, is the location of a large warehouse/garage. A fleet of 6, sixteen-wheeler trucks (standard Semi-Truck, no vehicle armor, Speed Class 8, driver equipped with .45 Pistol, guard armed with 5.56mm Assault Rifle) are based here. There are 60 mutant dogs (*all* dogs) who serve as guards, drivers, and warehouse managers. Only a select few Road Hogs know about this place.

Every week, 4 of the trucks are used in a convoy that travels 550 miles north and 80 miles east to a secret air base. The air base is manned by 24 mutant dogs, 12 guards, 2 aircraft mechanics, 2 automotive mechanics, 2 air traffic controllers and 6 Canine Rangers. Large, unmarked, cargo planes bring in assault rifles (usually 1,000), ammunition (48 crates of 288 clips each), 24 motorcycles, 2 cars and a special briefcase with coded communications for the Road Hog leader (Catsblood).

Once the characters get to Pork Land, all this will be fairly easy to discover. The difficult thing will be *getting* to Pork Town . . .

GM Tip: It's a good idea to get some road maps of the northern California, Oregon and Colorado areas. A decent road atlas is as close as your local library.

ENCOUNTERS

The following are all potential run-ins. The GM may, of course, skip over or simplify any of these steps.

Step 1: Getting There is Half the Fun. First the fake Road Hogs must go far to the east, through either the Imperium of Prairie Dogs or through the Stainless Steel Stallion Territory. Considering they look like Road Hogs, this means a certain amount of native resistance.

The trip north will be through Free Cattle Territory. The Free Cattle will be hostile to Road Hogs, but don't have vehicles with anywhere near the speed needed to stop the characters.

Cutting back west into Road Hog lands is where things get dangerous again. Road Hogs are very territorial and they will stop and question any strangers. A story about coming from the far north and making "a wrong turn somewhere" should serve the characters well.

Step 2: In the vicinity of the Road Hog camp, they'll start seeing patrols who will guide them right to the center of the camp. They will be welcomed, and questioned only to the extent of — "so, where are you boys from?" The characters will find the Road Hogs to be boisterous, loud, obnoxious and pushy. Fights will start over anything trivial, and will often end in bloodshed (fights to the death are relatively rare, about 10%). The camp is in a captured farm where the Road Hogs are using (and destroying) the house, barn and outbuildings.

Optional: Some of the farm family may still be alive. Since being held captive by Road Hogs is no picnic, the characters may feel moved to secretly help them.

Step 3: *Catsblood*, leader of the Road Hogs, will make a speech in front of the assembled crowd as bonfires burn. He will announce that the Road Hogs will attack a Stallion camp the following morning. The crowd will respond enthusiastically. The characters will be slapped on the back, offered terrible booze (smells terrible!), and offered bets on who'll kill more of the enemy. Later that evening, a mutant Bat will approach the group and ask them — "you guys wanna' be in the front line assault or you wanna' ambush the suckers, whatever suckers try ta' get away?"

Step 4: The Stallion target is a half-finished, walled fortress. About 200 Stallions will be defending against over 1400 Road Hogs.

If the players opt to be in the front assault they'll be assigned with charging through the gaps in the wall. Every player character will have to endure four rifle shots (+1 to Strike) and two arrow shots (+3 to Strike) *without a Dodge* before they make it inside the compound. Once inside, each character should be assigned an individual combat. This can be either with weapons or hand-to-hand. The fighting will be over very quickly, no possibility of a second fight.

If the characters choose to ambush the fleeing Stallions, they'll be lying in wait along a roadside. At some point, from 2-12 Stallions will come by on Dirt Bikes; usually 2 mutant animals to a bike. The characters will then be responsible for chasing down and killing the Stallions. Note that *other* Road Hogs are in the area and letting the Stallions go will be noticed.

Step 5: After a rowdy celebration and an invitation to the "victory parade", about 300 Road Hogs will head off to Pork Land. The trip will take two days (most of the Road Hogs will want to stop every hour for "refreshments"). Pork Land itself will be an incredibly rowdy town. There are bars everywhere, and each character should be challenged to a fight, at least, once.

Step 6: Investigating 111 Washington reveals a combination warehouse/garage with two large doors big enough for Semi-Trucks. The whole area is surrounded by a chain link fence topped with barbed wire. Mutant Dog guards in Road Hog outfits are on duty at all times, and will turn away anyone trying to get in, saying — "nobody comes in. Orders from Catsblood himself!" Since they're actually *New Kennel troops*, working for the *Empire of Humanity*, they wouldn't let in Catsblood himself. Characters with Ninja, digging, or other covert skills, should be able to check out the area. See *After the Bomb* for details on New Kennel and the Empire.

Step 7: The day after the characters arrive in Pork Land there will be a convoy to the secret air field. Characters could stowaway on the empty trucks or follow in their own vehicles. If the player characters are discovered, the dogs will use the radios in the trucks, or the air base radio, to alert the Road Hogs.

Step 8: Getting back to Americorp can be as easy as simply driving back, or as difficult as being chased all the way. It all depends on whether or not the character's identity is ever discovered.

NPC CHARACTERS

Typical Stainless Steel Stallion Vehicle:

Dirt Bike: 75 S.D.C.; no vehicle armor or weapons
Speed Class: 6 (Maximum 132mph/Cruise 90mph)
Fuel Efficiency Modification: 60mpg

Typical Stainless Steel Stallion: Roll percentile for type, 01-20, Horse; 21-30, Cow; 31-35, Pig; 36-50, Deer; 51-60, Pronghorn; 61-65, Prairie Dog; 66-75, Buffalo; 76-100, Random Animal. Typically, they have Rifles (5D6 damage, single shot), and ancient, hand-to-hand weapons. About 15% will be 6th level Bow Experts.

ROAD HOG

Typical Road Hog: The characters will be running into a *lot* of Road Hogs. Roll percentile for type: 01-25, Pig; 26-35, Vulture; 36-45, Dog, 46-100, Random Animal. On the average, they'll be well armed, with at least +3 to Strike, Parry, Dodge and Damage. Average Size Level: 11, with 30 Hit Points and 48 S.D.C. Roll for animal. About 30% will have special, mutant animal powers; only 5% will have animal psionics.

VEHICLES AND WEAPONS

The following items are of origin unknown to the mutant animals of the West Coast (actually made in the *Empire of Humanity* on the East Coast – see After the Bomb). About one out of four Road Hogs have one of the Assault Rifles. The motorcycles make up about 20% of the Road Hogs entire fleet, and the cars are fairly rare with less than 500 in existence. The Empire of Humanity is supplying the Road Hogs to subvert the West Coast, mutant animal societies, making it easier for eventual conquest. The Empire of Humanity is a fanatical, human society (affiliated with the dogs of New Kennel who serve as their pawns in a greater scheme) dedicated to destroying ALL mutant animals.

Road Hog Assault Rifle

5.56mm, 4D6 Damage, 1,200ft Range
Clips are 30 rounds each.
Equipped with Unknown Sighting Device:
The weapon gives off a soft, "beeping" noise when this device is turned on. The "beep" becomes more rapid as the weapon is aimed at a living being or directly at an engine. +3 to Strike.

Road Hog High Tech Motorcycle

Base S.D.C.: 180
Vehicle Armor: A.R.: 17; S.D.C.: 900
Speed Class: 14 (Maximum 210mph/Cruise 100mph)
Fixed Forward Mount Assault Rifle: 5.56mm, 4D6 Damage, 800ft
Driver Console equipped with Deluxe Engine Readout
Unknown Diagnostic Computer Readout:
Mysterious device that does the equivalent of an auto mechanic's diagnosis at 92%. Displays vehicle problems within 2 Melee Rounds. Also displays of sustaining damage or malfunction.
Radar Display with no outward antenna — 2,500ft Range
Unknown Fuel Efficiency Device: Runs at 320mpg
Oil Slick: Good for a single charge.
Description: Massive Street Cycle with oversized tires, strange white armor and digital displays that glow yellow.

Road Hog High Tech 2-Door Sedan

Base S.D.C.: 600
Vehicle Armor: A.R.: 17; S.D.C.: 1800
Crew Compartment Armor: A.R.: 17; S.D.C.: 900
Speed Class: 18 (Maximum 300mph/Cruise 120mph)
Twin, Fixed, Forward Mount Assault Rifle: 4D6 Damage; 800ft
Gun Ports Mounted: 1 Right, 1 Left, 2 Rear, 1 Right Front
Driver Console equipped with Deluxe Engine Readout
Unknown Diagnostic Computer Readout:
Mysterious device that does the equivalent of an auto mechanic's diagnosis at 92%. Displays vehicle problems within 2 Melee Rounds. Also displays of sustaining damage or malfunction.
Radar Display with no outward antenna — 4,000ft Range
Unknown Fuel Efficiency Device: Runs at 110mpg
Unknown Computer/Robotic Auto-Pilot Device
Americorp scientists are baffled by this control. All the driver has to do is flip the switch marked "Automatic" and the vehicle starts to drive itself. It will avoid obstacles, dodge collisions at a +4, and do Control Rolls at 80% (standard penalties apply).
Single, Rear Mounted Turret:
Armor: A.R.: 17, S.D.C.: 550
Energy Cannon: 5D6 Damage, 450ft Range
1 Shot/Melee Round; Maximum/30 Rounds
Aiming Mechanism: +3 to Strike (see Rifle)
Description: Sleek car with gull-wing doors, strange white armor and console displays that glow yellow. Seats two (bucket seats) in crew compartment and one in weapon turret.

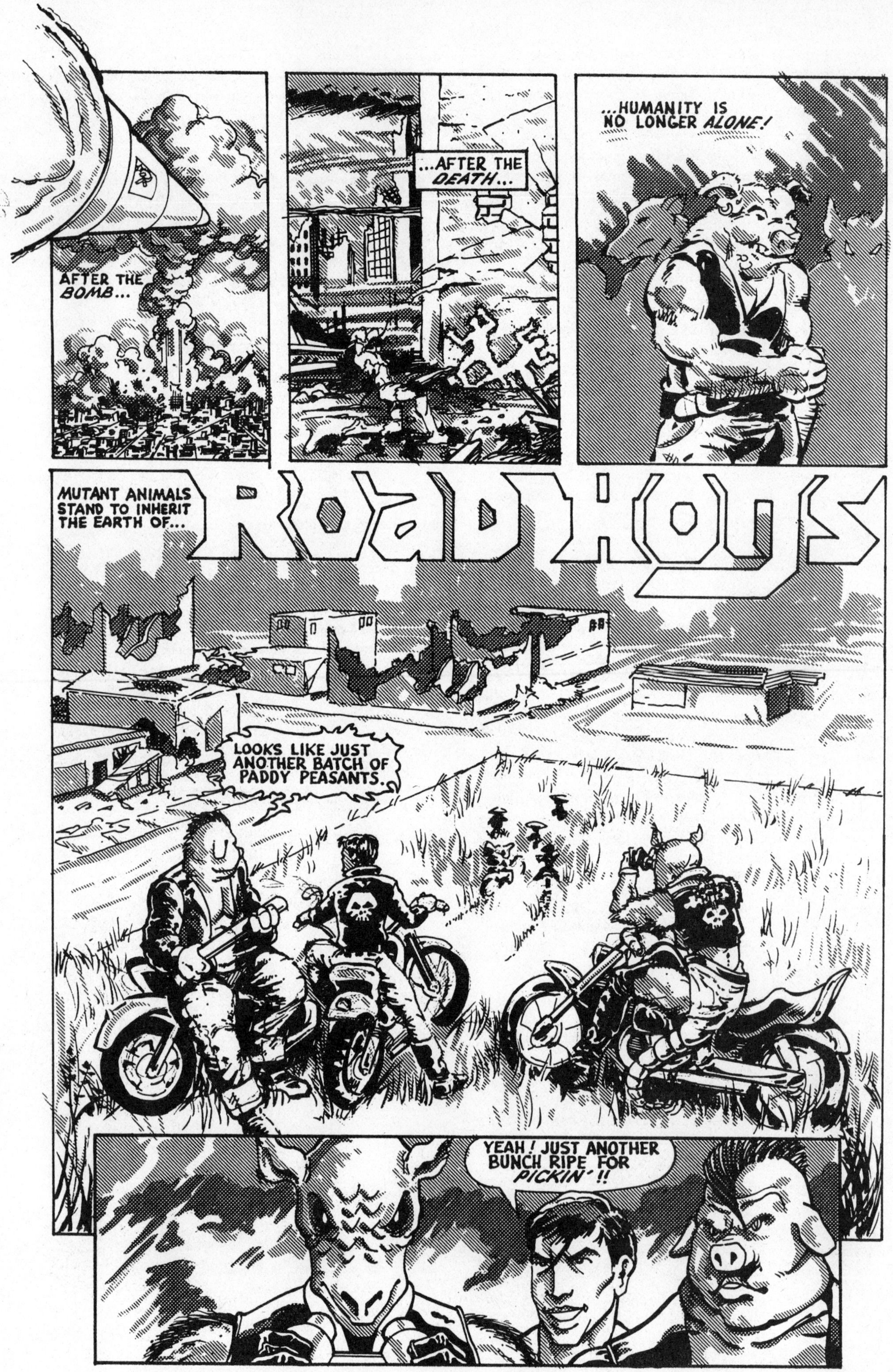

MUTANT ANIMALS STAND TO INHERIT THE EARTH OF...

ROAD HOGS

LOOKS LIKE JUST ANOTHER BATCH OF PADDY PEASANTS.

YEAH! JUST ANOTHER BUNCH RIPE FOR *PICKIN'*!!

SO, DO YOU DIRTBAGS-- OOF!
WATCH YER LANGUAGE, DUMMY!
SORRY. DO YOU FARMERS HAVE ANY GUNS?
GUNS! Y'KNOW--SHOOTERS, BANG-BANGS? ANY WEAPONS? ANY BULLETS?
OH, YES! WE KEEP THEM ON DISPLAY IN THE TEMPLE.
UNDER GUARD?
WELL, SURE-- OLD WHISKERS KEEPS THE CHILDREN AWAY...
THEY'RE DANGEROUS! WE HAVE TO MAKE SURE NOBODY TOUCHES THEM.
REALLY?
GREAT! THAT MEANS--
WELL, WE'VE REALLY GOT TO BE GOING!
BUT YOU WILL COME BACK IN THREE DAYS FOR OUR FEAST?
YES, WE WANT TO BRING ALL OUR FRIENDS!!
WELL, HURRY BACK!
WELL, IT'S ALL SET NOW.

THINK WE'LL BE ABLE TO TAKE 'EM ?
Teenage Mutant Ninja TURTLES

THEY HAVE NO DISCIPLINE. THEY WILL BE NO THREAT.

"...LATELY HIS GREAT AGE HAS BEEN SHOWING."
MIKE ?

I HATE TO DISTURB SENSEI...

THROUGHOUT THE PEASANT VILLAGE THE WORK BEGINS...
--UNTIL...
SO YOU THINK THIS IS A *TRAP*?
ABSOLUTELY. THOSE WERE NOT THE HANDS OF A FARMER--HE REGULARLY PRACTICES WITH A STAFF OF SOME KIND.
A WARRIOR BORN AND BRED.
HMM...NO MATTER.
WE'LL TEACH THESE PEASANTS THAT TRICKERY IS USELESS AGAINST *ROAD HOGS !!*
YOU, NED, BERNIE AND I WILL ATTACK FROM THE REAR WHILE THE REST GO IN THE FRONT WAY.

UH OH!

WHA--?

UH OH

BOOBY-TRAP!

ALL OF YOU--
STAY SHARP!

YOU SCUM HAVE TERRORIZED YOUR LAST VILLAGE!
LET'S TAKE 'EM DOWN.

YOU CAN *TRY*, SWEETHEARTS, YOU CAN *TRY*!

OOF!
FOOLS! I'LL NOT BE DEFEATED SO EASILY!

I CAN HANDLE THIS GUY!

UNNH!

CRACK

POW

SENSEI..?
COME ON, OLD ONE--I'LL MAKE TURTLE SOUP OUT OF YOU!
HAH! YOU MISSED!
PERHAPS...
...PERHAPS NOT.
CLEAN THIS MESS UP FOR ME, OKAY, MIKE?

PEOPLE, POWER AND POLITICS

Political change through time

A Study in Development
Modules 3 & 4

Robert Ellis

Stanley Thornes (Publishers) Ltd

Artwork by Mike Parsons, Barking Dog Art

First published in 1995 by:
Stanley Thornes (Publishers) Ltd
Ellenborough House
Wellington Street
CHELTENHAM GL50 1YD
England

ISBN 0 7487 14995
A catalogue record for this book is available from the British Library.

Typeset by Tech-Set, Gateshead, Tyne & Wear
Printed and bound in Great Britain at The Bath Press, Avon

Other books in the series
A Study in Depth, Modules 1 & 2
A Study in Depth, Modules 3 & 4
A Study in Development, Modules 1 & 2
A computer program (with Teacher's Guide) accompanies Depth Module 2.

Contents

Introduction

This volume is one of four written for the Cambridge A-level History Project syllabus, *People, Power and Politics*. It is the second of two written to accompany the Development Study, *Political change through time*, while another two accompany the Depth Study, *Was there a mid-seventeenth-century English Revolution?* One of the principal aims of the Project is to develop understanding of what history is and what is involved in the study of history. To this end, all four volumes contain sections explaining historical concepts and techniques. However, *People, Power and Politics* is a syllabus about history, not the philosophy of history. The sections of this volume dealing with concepts and techniques provide advice about how to explain historical situations and occurrences, how to construct developmental accounts, and how to use evidence to formulate and test hypotheses about the past. The remainder of the volume provides the material from which explanations and accounts are to be constructed and hypotheses formulated and tested.

Modules 1 and 2 of the Development Study are contained in another volume which should be studied before addressing this one. Module 1 looks at broad sweeps of history covering many centuries in order to identify patterns of change and development in the nature and exercise of political power in Britain. A brief account of the development of the powers of the monarchy and of parliament is provided in the context of which you are asked to evaluate the significance of such events as the Norman Conquest, the political and religious reforms of the 1530s, the Glorious Revolution of 1689, the accession to the throne of George I and the First World War. Module 2 deals with developments from prehistory to the present day and enables you to construct accounts of change in different strands of British political history. It also explores the causes of change and development.

This volume comprises Modules 3 and 4 of the Development Study. Module 3 shows how alternative lines of development can be constructed depending on whether you focus on the exercise of power by 'those who rule' (as in Module 2), reactions to the exercise of power by 'those who do not rule', or different strands within those accounts. It also employs case studies on the Black Death and on popular radicalism in the nineteenth century. These show how the temporal and spatial perspectives within which accounts are constructed, and the purposes and assumptions of the historians who construct them, influence the nature of the resulting accounts, and how alternative lines of development can be combined into more complex accounts of change over time. Module 4 continues to examine how conflicting developmental accounts might be reconciled, but it also asks you to transfer what you have learned about patterns of change and development in British political history to the sphere of Russian history. It considers two of the most popular explanations of the development of Russian political institutions and practices over the last eleven centuries, and asks whether or not it is possible to reconcile these competing explanations and what role the Russian Revolutions of 1917 play within them. The Development Study ends with a unit that considers, in the context of both Russian and British history, the influence of the age in which they live on historians' interpretations of the past.

Acknowledgements

This volume is the result of extensive trials of teaching materials in over 80 schools and colleges throughout the country between 1988 and 1992. The author owes an enormous debt of gratitude to all the teachers and students involved in the pilot phase of the Cambridge History Project for their input to the development of the Project and, above all, for their enthusiasm.

Special thanks are due to Denis Shemilt and Peter Lee for conceiving the Project and for guiding it to fruition; to the University of Cambridge Local Examinations Syndicate for funding and support; to Alan Kelly, my predecessor as Executive Director, for co-ordinating the production of the trial materials and for overseeing the development of the Project until the end of 1989; to Humberside LEA for releasing Alan Kelly on secondment; and to the following for their major contributions to the trial materials on which this present volume is based:

Frances Blow
Peter Butterworth
Andy Cummings
Alan Kelly
Charles Maltman
Denis Shemilt.

I would also like to thank Graham Berry for reading and commenting on the manuscript, and Judith Harvey and Barry Page of Stanley Thornes (Publishers) Ltd for their advice and patience during the writing of this volume. While the help and support of those mentioned and of others were invaluable, responsibility for any errors or shortcomings lies entirely with the author.

Robert Ellis, 1995

The author and publishers are grateful to the following for permission to reproduce copyright material:

Illustrations (numbers refer to sources unless stated otherwise)

Module 3
Bodleian Library 52; Cambridge University Collection of Aerial Photography 25; Camera Press 84; Communist Party Library 77; Derby Local Studies Library 171, 172; English Heritage 107; Fotomas Index 43, 51, 53, 58, 69, 70, 152, 167; Hulton-Deutsch Collection 118; Mansell Collection 14, 20, 59, 60, 79, 81, 92, 127, 130; Popperfoto 83; Royal Archives © 1995 Her Majesty the Queen 169; Weidenfeld Archives 76.

Module 4
ET Archive 5; Mary Evans Picture Library 6, 74; Fotomas Index 54, 76; Hulton-Deutsch Collection 3, 79; David King Collection 103, 107, 109; Mansell Collection 55, 63, 81; Novosti 36, 42, 68, 105, 111 (both); Popperfoto 133; Society for Cooperation in Russian and Soviet Studies 4, 48, 59, 100; Weidenfeld Archives 53, 80, 112; Weidenfeld Archives/Victoria and Albert Museum 71.

Text material
Blackwell Publishers for material from A.R. Bridbury, 'The Black Death', *Economic History Review*, 1973, pp.58–91; Cambridge University Press for material from Charles Halperin, 'The Ideology of Silence', *Comparative Studies in Society and History*, 27, 1984, pp.459–66; Channel Four Television for material from Shaun Whiteside, 'Fin de Siècle', a pamphlet written to accompany a television series of the same name, 1992; Victor Gollancz Ltd. for material from E.P. Thompson, *The Making of the English Working Class*, 1968; Guardian News Services Ltd. for material from Francis Fukuyama, 'The End of Hysteria?', *The Guardian*, 15.12.89; and an editorial in *The Guardian*, 22.3.93; Hamish Hamilton Ltd. for material from George Deaux, *The Black Death 1347*, 1969. Copyright © George Deaux 1969; HarperCollins Publishers for material from Philip Zeigler, *The Black Death*, 1969; The Historical Association for material from J.R. Dinwiddy, *From Luddism to the First Reform Bill*, Blackwell Publishers, 1986; James Bolton, 'The Black Death', *The Historian*, Autumn 1993; W.H. Chaloner, review of R.J. White's *Waterloo to Peterloo*, *History*, June 1958,

43:148; and Roger Bartlett, 'Images: Catherine II of Russia, Enlighted Absolutism and Mikhail Gorbachev', *The Historian*, Spring 1991; History Today Ltd. for material from Ronald Hutton, 'Rulers and Ruled, 1580–1650', *History Today*, Sept. 1985, pp. 19–20; C. Durston, 'Phoney War – England, Summer 1642', *History Today*, June 1992, p. 17; Anne Laurence, 'Women's Work and the English Civil War', *History Today*, June 1992, p. 20, 24–5; Marc Raeff, 'Muscovy Looks West', *History Today*, Aug. 1986, pp. 16–20; Sergei Averintsev, 'The Idea of Holy Russia', *History Today*, Nov. 1989, pp. 41–2; Victor Kiernan, 'Marxism and Revolution', *History Today*, July 1991, p. 39; Bill Wallace, 'The Democratic Development of the Former Soviet Union', *History Today*, July 1994, pp. 46–52; John Roberts, 'Goodbye to All That?', *History Today*, Aug. 1991, pp. 40–2; Tony Judt, 'Chronicles of a Death Foretold', *History Today*, Oct. 1991, pp. 48–50; Gareth Stedman Jones, 'The Changing Face of 19th Century Britain', *History Today*, May 1991, pp. 36–9; Peter Clarke, 'Love's Labours Lost', *History Today*, Sept. 1991, pp. 36–8; and Edward Acton, 'From Tsarism to Communism', *History Review*, Dec. 1993, p. 35; Hodder & Stoughton Ltd. for material from Clive Behagg, *Labour and Reform*, 1991; International Creative Management, Inc. on behalf of the author, for material from Francis Fukuyama, 'The End of History', *The National Interest*, Summer 1989. Copyright © 1989 by Francis Fukuyama; Longman Group for material from John Stevenson, *Popular Disturbance in England 1700–1850*, 1992; D.J. Wright, *Popular Radicalism*, 1988; Edward Acton, *Russia* 1986; and Derek Turner, *The Black Death*, 1978; Oxford University Press for material from P.D.A. Harvey, *A Medieval Oxfordshire Village: Cuxham 1240 to 1400*, 1965. Copyright © Oxford University Press 1965; Penguin Books Ltd. for material from Fernaud Braudel, *The History of Civilisations*, trs. Richard Mayne (Allen Lane, The Penguin Press, 1994, first published in France as *Le monde actuel, histoire et civilisations*, Libraire Eugène Berlin, 1963. Copyright © Les Editions Arthaud, Paris, 1987, translation copyright © Richard Mayne, 1994; Reed Consumer Books Ltd. for material from Tibor Szamuely, *The Russian Tradition*, Martin Secker & Warburg Ltd., 1988; and T. Williamson and E. Bellamy, *Property and Landscape*, George Philip Ltd., 1987; Routledge for material from Dr. Michael Reed, *Georgian Triumph 1700–1830*, Routledge and Kegan Paul, 1983; and Harold Perkin, *The Origins of Modern English Society 1780–1880*, 1969; M.E. Sharpe Inc. for material from L. Zakharova, 'Autocracy, Bureaucracy and the Reforms of the 1980s in Russia', *Soviet Studies in History*, Spring 1991, p. 6–33.

Every effort has been made to trace all the copyright holders but if any have been inadvertently overlooked the publishers will be pleased to make the necessary arrangement at the first opportunity.

Module 3: Alternative lines of development

UNIT 3.1

REACTING TO POLITICAL POWER

Introduction: Alternative accounts

As its title indicates, this Module focuses on the production of *alternative* lines of development. It begins by looking at how alternative developmental accounts can be produced of the reactions of ordinary people in Britain to the exercise of political power during the last thousand years. These alternative accounts are the result of asking and answering questions about different aspects of change and development in the rights and powers of ordinary people. The accounts that are produced can be regarded not only as alternatives to each other (i.e. alternative accounts of the development of how people have reacted to the exercise of political power), but also as alternatives to the accounts of the exercise of political power produced in Unit 2.2.

The remainder of the Module comprises two case studies. The first invites you to consider how alternative significances might be attached to the Black Death in accounts of political development, according to whether it is considered in the context of a shorter or longer period of time and whether a British or European perspective is employed. The second provides alternative accounts of political radicalism and the widening of the franchise during the nineteenth century, and asks you to assess the extent to which the differences between the accounts stem from the different assumptions held, purposes pursued, questions asked and definitions employed by historians.

However, before we consider how alternative lines of development can be produced and justified, we need to be absolutely clear about what we mean by the word 'alternative'. The *Shorter Oxford English Dictionary* defines it, in its adjectival form, as meaning 'of two things, such that one or the other may be chosen, the choice of either involving the rejection of the other'. Thus, a motorist approaching a T-junction may take one of two alternative directions. He may turn left or he may turn right, but he may not do both simultaneously. Similarly, if one historical account claims that the Privy Council was the creation of Thomas Cromwell and another claims that it did not come into existence until after Cromwell's death, we must choose between them because they are mutually exclusive. We cannot accept them both without first modifying one or both of them.

It should be clear from this that we are not interested here in accounts that are merely 'different'. It would be possible to produce two accounts of the development of women's rights, one of which argues that the political rights of women have made considerable progress since they first acquired the right to vote in county council elections in 1888, while the other claims that their industrial rights did not really begin to improve until the Trades Union Congress demanded equal pay for equal work in 1942 and the 1944 Education Act provided free secondary education for girls on the same terms as boys. These accounts would be different, but they would not be mutually exclusive. It would present absolutely no difficulty to synthesize them into a single account in which developments in the political rights of women originated in the late nineteenth century, but developments in their industrial rights did not begin until much later.

The main distinction, then, is that 'different' accounts may complement each other and may be capable of integration into a single multi-strand account without surrendering any of their former identity or integrity; whereas 'alternative' accounts are necessarily in some degree of competition or conflict with each other and cannot be integrated into a single account without modifications to one or both of them, or an explanation of why the conflict is more apparent than real.

There are many reasons why different historians may produce alternative accounts of the same events. Some of these reasons have to do with the nature of the past and of the surviving evidence, while others have more to do with the nature of historians' activities.

The nature of the past

The past is so vast an area that historians have to cut it up into manageable portions in order to understand it. This dissection of the past is usually accomplished in three dimensions: those of theme, space and time. When a historian undertakes research, the first tasks are to identify the theme or issue that will constitute the subject of that research and to determine the time period and geographical area within which it will be undertaken. The production by different historians of competing or conflicting accounts can often be attributed to variations in the theme or issue, or in the temporal and spatial contexts within which they are operating. It can also result from the complexity of the past and from the difficulties inherent in trying to identify the currents of development within a particular historical theme.

1. Themes and issues

The past does not come neatly wrapped in packages labelled 'political history', 'economic history', 'the consequences of the Norman Conquest' or what have you. In the words of F.W. Maitland, 'such is the unity of history that anyone who endeavours to tell a piece of it must feel that his first sentence tears a seamless web'. Nevertheless, it is the task of the historian to identify strands or themes within that seamless web and to examine them closely in the hope that such an examination will improve our understanding not only of that particular strand, but also of the entire web.

Historians define their themes and issues in many different ways, seeking to answer a wide variety of questions about the past. As we have noted elsewhere, there are 'truffle hunters', who conduct diligent investigations into the minutiae of history, and 'parachutists' whose gazes sweep lightly over vast historical panoramas. Within and overlapping each of these broad categories there are other differences. For example, some historians are interested in political history, others in industrial archaeology or in social, economic, religious, military or diplomatic history, or in some arcane subdivision of one of these themes. The accounts produced by historians pursuing these interests will differ because the themes and issues that they are researching are different: they are asking different questions about different aspects of the past. Since such accounts do not necessarily compete or conflict with each other, they are not necessarily alternative. They only become alternative accounts if they cover the same events, themes or issues and interpret them in different ways that are, or at least appear to be, mutually exclusive. Some of the ways in which they might interpret the same themes in different ways are outlined below in the section entitled *The nature of historians' activities*.

2. The temporal context

Historians study their themes and issues within defined periods of time, and the location and extent of the period a historian chooses will influence the account that is produced. An account of the development of the Church in England between 1066 and 1399 will be different from, but not alternative to, a similar account covering the years from 1399 to 1529. However, an account of the development of the English church from 1066 to 1399 may well be an alternative to an account from 1066 to 1529 *for the time period that the accounts have in common with each other*. The conflict between the accounts might result from the longer time span of the second account allowing an interpretation of developments before 1400 that would not be appropriate to an account ending in 1399 because it rests on an interpretation of occurrences that took place after that date. This idea should already be familiar to you because, in Unit 1.5, you considered the differing, and perhaps alternative, significances that might be attached to the Glorious Revolution and the accession of George I in the context of developments between 1660 and 1760, and then again in terms of developments between 1660 and 1830.

3. The spatial context

Many historians have produced histories of individual villages, towns or regions; still more have written accounts of the history of nations and states, while others have widened their horizons to take in whole continents or even the entire world. The accounts written by these historians differ from each other, but are only likely to be in competition or conflict when they address the same theme within the same time period, but come to different conclusions. Thus, alternative accounts might cover the same theme or issue within different but overlapping geographical areas. For instance, one account might trace the development of the diocese of Lincoln, another the ecclesiastical history of England and a third the place of England in the development of the Church in Western Europe. The effect of different geographical contexts on the interpretation of historical developments will be investigated further in Unit 3.2, where the significance of the Black Death is considered in the context of local, national and international developments.

4. The complexity of the past

It is important to recognize that historical development does not flow neatly and evenly in one direction. Like a stream or river flowing to the sea, sometimes it flows quickly, sometimes slowly; in some places it maintains a steady course, in others it meanders; in some places the current is strong and steady, but often it is subject to eddies, undertows and cross-currents. In other words, the flow of history is complex and the task of recognizing and describing variations in the pace and direction of change is difficult. Consequently, it is hardly surprising that historians' interpretations of the past do not always concur with each other. However, this does not mean that one is right and that another is necessarily wrong. Where the views of two historians conflict, it is likely that both interpretations will contain some merit (otherwise it is doubtful whether they would have got into print), but that they have laid different degrees of emphasis on different aspects of a complex picture, or that one will have seen one part of the picture more clearly, whereas another will have interpreted other aspects of it more successfully. Since this is so, rather than simply adjudicating between alternative accounts of the past, we should identify the nature of the conflict between the accounts and attempt to reconcile it. This might be achieved be recognizing that historical events can sometimes have consequences that are almost diametrically opposed one to another. For example, one of the outcomes of the parliamentary reform legislation enacted between 1832 and 1928 was to increase the participation of the individual in politics by introducing universal suffrage and abolishing the property qualification for MPs. However, mass participation in politics led to better organized political parties with improved electioneering techniques that had the effect of virtually eliminating independent MPs from parliament. Thus, in one direction individual participation in politics was increased while in another it was decreased as a consequence of the same body of legislation. While these may appear to be alternative interpretations of the significance of electoral reform, they are, in fact, two facets of the same account, an example of the cross-currents that crop up so regularly in history.

The nature of historians' activities

The purpose of history is to enquire into the past, and, since the past is many-faceted, the ways in which it can be interpreted vary considerably. The nature of a historian's activity depends to a considerable extent on the task that is being undertaken. For example, someone who is engaged in ascertaining the nature and extent of Ranterism in England during 1650 and 1651 will need to interpret the writings of Ranters such as Coppe and Clarkson, together with the anti-Ranter tracts published at that time, in the context of wider knowledge of the social and political climate and of contemporary attitudes and beliefs (see Depth Study, Unit 3.3). On the other hand, such careful documentary analysis would be totally inappropriate to an account of the development of monarchy in Britain from prehistory to the present day, not only because there will be no documentary evidence for the earliest period, but also because the sheer scope of the undertaking is too large for an historian to be able to analyse sources so thoroughly. In this case, the historian must rely to a considerable extent on interpretations of evidence provided in the works of other historians specializing in particular periods in order to make the task manageable. One further example will suffice to indicate something of the range of historians' activities. A historian investigating the development of agriculture in Britain since the Norman Conquest will need to use both documentary source material and the detailed work of other historians on particular periods, but will also need to use other forms of evidence, particularly statistical evidence about such things as crop yields, which might be compiled and examined using a computer database, and fieldwork to interpret evidence in the landscape of former agricultural practices.

Not only are different techniques more or less appropriate to different types of historical investigation, they can also lead to the production of accounts that might appear to be in conflict with one another. Alternative accounts, however, rarely result purely from the employment of different techniques: other factors that may come into play include the nature of the questions that historians are seeking to answer, the assumptions that they make, the interpretations they place on the evidence and the definitions of key concepts that they employ.

1. *Asking questions*

The questions that historians ask can have a considerable bearing on the way that they interpret the evidence. If two historians are researching the same general topic, the Glorious Revolution for example, they may come to entirely different conclusions because of the different questions they are trying to answer. One might ask how effective the revolution was in achieving its political aims and conclude that it was spectacularly successful because a Catholic king was deposed, Protestantism was protected and the ability of the monarch to act independently of parliament was restricted severely. Another might ask how the revolution affected the power of the monarch and deduce that, provided he was willing to work with parliament, virtually all of his existing powers remained intact, while some, such as his ability to wage war against an adversary as powerful as Louis XIV's France, were enhanced considerably.

2. *Making assumptions*

Historians cannot question everything simultaneously. Theoretically, a historian who seeks to provide a full explanation of why something happened in the past should identify the direct causes, explain how those causes came about, then explain the causes of the causes and so on *ad infinitum*. In reality, of course, this is impossible; so historians must make assumptions. They must assume that certain things in history are true without testing them in order to concentrate the their attention on testing other things. This is like the mathematicians or economists who hold certain things constant in order to investigate the effects of particular variables in which they are interested.

The assumptions historians make can have a considerable effect on their conclusions. For instance, a historian who assumes that the Celtic British were a barbarous and backward race might interpret the Romanization of Britain as the introduction of beneficial social, cultural and political changes which advanced the development of the native population. On the other hand, a historian who assumes that Celtic Britain already contained a distinctive and highly developed culture and society might see Romanization as the destruction of one civilization and its forcible replacement by an alien culture imposed by military might (see Depth Study, Unit 1.1, Sources 30, 31 and 40).

3. *Interpreting evidence*

You should already be very familiar with some of the methods historians use to interpret evidence and to construct and test hypotheses on the basis of that evidence. Little needs to be added at this point, but it should be recognized that alternative accounts can stem from alternative interpretations of evidence, either because the evidence itself is equivocal or because it can be interpreted in differing historical contexts that enable different conclusions to be drawn from it.

4. *Defining terms*

One of the main reasons why historians disagree with one another and produce alternative accounts of the past is because when they appear to be describing or explaining the same thing they are not always doing so. Often this is because they are using the same terms but defining them differently. Let us consider the question 'How important was the Bill of Rights of 1689 in transferring power to the people?' One historian might interpret 'the people' as meaning those who participated actively in politics (i.e. the gentry and nobility); another might see the term as denoting the forty-shilling freeholders and urban citizens who were entitled to vote; while another might define the term more literally as encompassing the whole adult population. Clearly, the first historian is likely to identify a greater transference of power to 'the people' in 1689 than the last. The term 'power' is open to even more different definitions than 'the people'. It could mean the legal powers as laid down in the Bill of Rights itself; it could be interpreted as the actual power resulting from the new circumstances created by the enactment of the Bill of Rights, which was probably somewhat greater than that specifically conferred by the Bill itself; it could also be seen as the implications and potentialities of the Bill which led to further changes in the balance of power within the country during the eighteenth century. These definitions deal with the nature of power, but historians might also define it in terms of its scope. One might interpret it as the power to govern, another as the power to influence those who govern, a third as the power to restrict the freedom of action of those who govern, a fourth as the power to resist those who do not govern according to the rules, and a fifth as a combination of some or all of these definitions. It will be obvious that the way in which historians define both 'power' and 'the people' will have an important bearing on the way in which they answer the question.

Before embarking on the construction of developmental accounts of the powers of 'those who do not rule', let us consider briefly the effects of the nature of the past and the nature of historians' activities on subject matter with which you should already be familiar. In Unit 1.4, Geoffrey Elton put forward the thesis that there was a 'Tudor Revolution in government', a view that found favour with many historians but was contested strongly by others. Some at least of the reasons for the alternative interpretations of the significance of the 1530s put forward by these historians can be attributed to factors referred to on the previous four pages.

Question

1. Read the alternative accounts of the significance of the 1530s for the political development of England put forward by Geoffrey Elton (Unit 1.4,

Source 114) and G.L. Harriss and Penry Williams (ibid. Sources 118–9). To what extent would you regard the conflicts between these accounts as the result of

(a) the nature of the past?

(b) the nature of historians' activities?

Markers for change

The markers for change introduced in Unit 1.1 proved useful in the construction of developmental accounts in Modules 1 and 2. By answering the questions posed by the markers you will have produced accounts which will certainly have been different from one another and will probably have been in competition or conflict, at least in part. However, these markers were devised for the construction of developmental accounts related to the exercise of political power by 'those who rule'; they have little relevance to 'those who do not rule'. For instance, the marker 'Who makes the rules?' specifically excludes those who do not rule. Therefore, for the purposes of this module, we will need to adapt the markers so that they enable us to trace developments in the composition and activities of those who react to, rather than exercise, political power.

The markers that will be employed when tracing the development of the rights and powers of ordinary people are:

- What rights and powers do ordinary people possess?
- Who exercises the power to protest?
- Why and over what issues does protest occur?
- What methods are employed by protesters?
- How effective are protesters in achieving their aims?

The first unit enables you to employ these new markers for change to help you construct alternative accounts of the powers of ordinary people to protest when those who exercise power act in ways that they dislike or resent.

The rights and powers of ordinary people

Refusal, riot, revolt and rebellion

At the beginning of the eleventh century, Ælfric, the abbot of Eynsham, wrote that 'the throne stands on these three supports: those who work, those who fight, and those who pray'. 'Those who fight' were the earls and thegns, and after the Norman Conquest the barons and knights, who rallied to the king's standard when he summoned them and who protected and administered their own districts at other times. Together with the priests and bishops, they comprised an élite that shared with the king in the exercise of power. The development of their powers has been the subject of much of Modules 1 and 2. However, little has been said so far about the third support of the throne identified by Ælfric, 'those who work'. From the medieval peasant to the factory worker of the Industrial Revolution and beyond, these people, the vast majority of the population, were the primary producers on whom the economic well-being of the country rested, yet throughout most of British history they have been largely without a voice in government. An apt description of them is 'those who do not rule': they have been affected by political power, but they have not exercised it.

Or have they? Even those who have few legally constituted rights possess certain latent powers. There is the power to say 'no', the power of bloody-minded intransigent resistance to unpopular measures, such as the refusal of increasing numbers of peasants – after the Black Death produced an acute shortage of labour – to perform boon work on the demesne farm of the lord of the manor. If enough people adopt such tactics of passive resistance, there is little that the authorities can do about it. One of the most striking examples of the power of passive resistance and refusal to co-operate with the authorities was the campaign organized by Gandhi against British rule in India, which contributed significantly to the British decision to grant independence to that country in 1947.

Then there is the power to protest peacefully, employing whatever means are at the disposal of the protesters short of violence. Sporadic isolated protest can be easily ignored, but when the protesters are more organized and persistent they can sometimes cause those who hold the reins of power sufficient inconvenience or embarrassment to have an effect. Among the clearest examples of this have been the various forms of industrial action undertaken by trade unionists to secure improved pay or conditions of work, or to protect existing arrangements. While rarely achieving complete success, industrial action has frequently forced employers, including the government, to compromise.

There is also the power to protest violently by means of riot or revolt. The difference between riots and revolts is not clear-cut, but riots have tended to be localised, often spontaneous reactions against unpopular measures, lacking clear-cut aims and often without identifiable leaders. For instance, in 1607 there was serious rioting in three Midland counties against the enclosure of common land by the Earl of Lincoln and several members of the local gentry. In this case, the riots achieved results in that James I appointed a commission of enquiry which upheld the rioters' complaints and fined the culprits. However, such a successful outcome was by no means the rule. Revolts often affected a larger geographical area than riots, although difficulties of communication before the twentieth century meant that they tended to be regional rather than national in scope. They tended to have identifiable, often charismatic, leaders who organized their supporters with clearly articulated aims. One of the most famous instances, the Peasants' Revolt of 1381, is dealt with in greater detail on pages 11–14. At this point, suffice it to say that it displayed all the classic characteristics of a revolt: it was regional rather than localised, affecting Kent and Essex most severely, but also Norfolk, Suffolk, Cambridgeshire, Hertfordshire and elsewhere; it had identifiable leaders, of whom John Ball, Wat Tyler and Jack Straw were the most well-known; and it had a list of demands that included the abolition of the poll tax, of the ecclesiastical hierarchy, of villeinage and of the payment of manorial dues and the introduction of fixed rents for land.

There is considerable overlap between revolts and rebellions but, whereas the former were often peasant insurrections, the latter tended to be led by, and pursued goals formulated by, disaffected members of the political élite. While they were frequently supported by many of 'those who do not rule' and pursued aims designed to appeal to them, these aims were usually the first to be sacrificed if the rebels achieved some degree of success. A typical rebellion was the Pilgrimage of Grace in 1536, which affected large parts of the north of England and was widely supported by peasants. Their grievances were included alongside those of the gentry and churchmen in the Pontefract Articles (Source 34) issued by the rebels. However, the rebellion was led by members of the gentry and lesser nobility, such as Robert Aske and Lord Darcy, and there is little doubt that, had the rebels succeeded, their grievances would have stood a greater chance of being redressed than those of the peasantry.

The possibility that ordinary people might refuse to co-operate, or engage in riot, revolt or rebellion, led the authorities to take precautions against such behaviour, which often included repression to prevent protest and reprisals that made examples of those who transgressed the law. However, the latent power of ordinary people also gave them influence among those who wielded authority over them. Thus, lords of medieval manors used manorial courts not only to enforce their will, but also to redress local grievances. They also involved the peasantry in the definition and implementation of customary law by empanelling juries of villeins. Similarly, many modern employers have included representatives of the workforce in their management structure in the hope that the opportunity to exert influence will avert industrial conflict.

It is probable that popular protest has existed in some form or other for as long as political power has existed. Once some people began to exercise power over others, those who were on the receiving end of this power were likely to express resentment when the actions of those in power conflicted with their interests. If this resentment became sufficiently strong, it was likely to be translated into action. In many cases, the disturbances that ensued were no doubt fomented, orchestrated and led by disgruntled members of the political élite or displaced former members of that privileged section of society, but not always. For instance, a serious slave revolt in ancient Rome that began in 73 BC was led by the gladiator, Spartacus.

In constructing accounts of change and development in the rights and powers of ordinary people, we shall focus on the period from 1066 to the present day. This is for the purely practical reason that evidence of popular protest before the Norman Conquest is virtually non-existent and evidence of the rights and freedoms of the Anglo-Saxon peasantry is by no means plentiful. The post-Conquest era has been broken down into three chronological periods, each with accompanying questions designed to help you identify changes and developments within and between the periods. The questions will enable you to compile relevant notes that can be used at the end of the section to construct developmental accounts covering the entire period related to the markers for change identified earlier in the unit.

From the eleventh to the fifteenth century

Questions

2. (a) What rights and freedoms did ordinary people possess under the feudal system as it operated during the twelfth and thirteenth centuries?

(b) How had these rights and freedoms changed by the end of the fifteenth century? SC. 8

3. (a) What sorts of people took part in popular protest during the Middle Ages?
   (b) Why and over what issues did they protest?
   (c) What methods were employed by the protesters?
   (d) How successful were the protesters in achieving their aims?
4. What changes and continuities can be detected in the nature of popular protest during the Middle Ages?

Despite the scarcity of evidence, we can be confident that popular protest did exist in Britain before the Norman Conquest, although probably not on the scale that it was later to assume. Two main reasons can be advanced for the greater levels of protest that can be detected after 1066. Firstly, Anglo-Saxon society was more fluid and contained clearer vestiges of the kinship and tribal organization from which it evolved than the Norman society that was superimposed on it. Secondly, the Norman Conquest imposed a foreign ruling élite on England who had no racial ties with the peasantry, who had different attitudes and customs from the Anglo-Saxon earls and thegns who preceded them, and who were viewed long after 1066 with the smouldering resentment reserved by subject peoples for those who have forced them into subjection. An example of this resentment sparking off violent action by ordinary people occurred in Durham in 1069.

Source 1

From Simeon of Durham, *History of the Church of Durham*, c.1096.

William was patient with the men of Northumbria for a long time. In the third year of his reign, he appointed a certain Robert, surnamed Cumin, to govern them....The earl was one of those who rewarded their followers by allowing them to plunder and kill, and he had already killed many of the church's peasants. So the earl entered Durham with 700 men, and they treated the citizens as if they were enemies. At first light, the Northumbrians banded together, broke in through all the gates, ran pell-mell through the city, and killed the earl's men....A considerable number [of Normans] still survived, and they defended the door of a house where the earl lodged, and held it securely against the attacks of the assailants. They, on their part, tried to set fire to the house....The house had been fired and continued to blaze. Those who were inside died; some were burnt and some were killed as soon as they crossed the threshold. So the earl was put to death with all but one of his men.

This may have been an unplanned riot or it may have been part of a co-ordinated rising that was crushed by William at York later that year. Either way, Simeon's account depicts the oppressed and resentful inhabitants of Durham taking matters into their own hands when one of their principal oppressors came among them. However, such action could, and often did, lead to terrible repercussions. *The Anglo-Saxon Chronicle* reports that shortly after the murder of Earl Robert at Durham, 'Earl Gospatric with the Northumbrians' joined other Anglo-Saxon earls, including Edgar and Waltheof, and a force of Danes led by King Swein in storming York, burning it to the ground and 'slaying many hundreds of Frenchmen'. William reacted swiftly, recapturing York and defeating the rebels. The severity of the reprisals, which have become known as the 'Harrying of the North', was described in graphic detail by Orderic Vitalis.

Source 2

From Orderic Vitalis, *Ecclesiastical History*, c.1114–41. Despite his Anglo-Norman parentage and education in a Norman monastery, Orderic was horrified at the severity with which William treated the northern peasantry in 1069.

He cut down many in his vengeance; destroyed the lairs of others; harried the land, and burned homes to ashes. Nowhere else had William shown such cruelty....He made no effort to restrain his fury and punished the innocent with the guilty. In his anger, he commanded that all crops and herds, chattels and food of every kind should be brought together and burned to ashes with consuming fire, so that the whole region north of the Humber might be stripped of all means of sustenance. In consequence, so serious a scarcity was felt in England, and so terrible a famine fell upon the humble and defenceless populace, that more than 100,000 Christian folk of both sexes, young and old alike, perished of hunger.

Such was the severity of this Harrying of the North that 20 years later, when the Domesday Book was compiled, many of the villages were described as being 'waste'. As Tom Williamson and Liz Bellamy explain in Source 3, the Domesday Book also provides valuable evidence about the rights and responsibilities of peasants in the late eleventh century and about the manorial system that governed their lives. Further evidence about the services expected of and the financial burdens heaped upon the peasants or serfs is provided by Edmund King in Source 4.

Source 3

From T. Williamson and E. Bellamy, *Property and Landscape* (George Philip, 1987) pp.32–7.

Domesday Book describes a landscape divided up into basic tenurial units known as 'manors'. Each was under the control of a manorial lord who drew an income from the renders of the peasants who lived within it. Domesday classifies these peasants in various ways.…There were freemen, sokemen, villeins, bordars, cottars and slaves. Different combinations of these groups are found in the entries for different Domesday manors and, as is clear from the later documents, each of them had a particular set of obligations to their lord.

Freemen and sokemen were defined as free, while villeins, bordars and cottars can best be described as 'semi-free' and were subject to certain constraints. These semi-free tenants were particularly dependent on their manorial lords. For instance, they were not allowed to grind their own grain, but were obliged to take it to the lord's mill. They had to pay a fine when they inherited their farm, and on occasions like the marriage of their daughters. Above all, they had to render labour services to their lord.

The villeins were the most substantial farmers of the semi-free tenants.…Bordars and cottars were lesser men, smallholders and part-time labourers. Below these classes were the unfree, or slaves. Their numbers were fast declining in the late eleventh century, and it was not long before they disappeared altogether, becoming bordars and cottars as they received small quantities of land.

Freemen and sokemen had to pay dues and rents to their lords, but as free tenants they were not usually subject to labour services. This did not mean, however, that they were necessarily wealthier than the semi-free tenants, for the distinction between the two groups was tenurial rather than economic. Many villeins were richer and worked larger holdings than the neighbouring freemen.…

Apart from payments made to the lords, farmers also had to render various taxes and services to the state. These were not imposed through the manorial structure, but through a separate system of extortion based on an administrative unit called the 'vill'. Each vill was made up of a number of holdings, and the farmers within it had to carry out duties delegated by central government, as well as pay the onerous land-tax known as the geld.

Source 4

From Edmund King, *England 1175–1425* (Routledge and Kegan Paul, 1979) pp.50–1.

The chief disability of peasant servitude was to perform agricultural services for the landlord free of charge, as a condition of tenure.…On top of this basic service between lord and man, there were drafted other and heavier obligations, which took their pattern from the 'incidents' [legal burdens] of feudal tenure imposed on the higher ranks of society. An aid, or tallage, was sometimes taken: on some estates, this was a heavy, annual tax on the peasantry. Invariably there would be the equivalent of a 'relief', a fine upon entry to an unfree holding. These fines, adjusted to the size of holdings and to the new tenant's capacity to pay, could be very heavy indeed. On top of this there were numerous petty and irregular fines, for fornication, for unsatisfactory ploughing, for permission to have your sons educated.

In the light of the restrictions and burdens placed on the lives of the peasantry, it is hardly surprising that some of those in the upper echelons of society pitied them, as did Pope Innocent III (Source 5). But pity rarely extended to action to alleviate their condition. Nevertheless, as Williamson and Bellamy explain in Source 6, medieval peasants were not entirely without rights or the means to influence their masters.

Source 5

A sympathetic view of the condition in which most serfs lived, from Pope Innocent III, c.1160–1216.

The serf serves: he is terrified with threats, wearied by forced services, afflicted with blows, despoiled of his possessions; for, if he possesses nought he is compelled to earn; and if he possesses anything he is compelled to have it not; the lord's fault is the serf's punishment; the serf's fault is the lord's excuse for preying on him.…O extreme condition of bondage!

Source 6

From T. Williamson and E. Bellamy, *Property and Landscape*, pp.41–3.

Medieval villagers were able to exert a certain amount of influence over the way that they were treated by their lords. A thirteenth-century villein was theoretically tied to the manor of his birth. He could be sold by one lord to another, arrested and imprisoned without trial and was generally devoid of rights of self-determination. However, although individual villeins may have been subjected to this arbitrary and tyrannical treatment, it rarely happened to entire communities. In practice the power of the lords was limited by their financial dependence on the peasant community. The lords could not afford to antagonize the farmers of the villages, because arbitrary or unpopular action on their part could lead to disputes, non-co-operation, legal actions, or even a rent strike. Some historians have suggested that disputes between lords and their tenants occurred as often in medieval society as industrial disputes do today.

This may be an overstatement, for then as now many people were prepared to accept extreme inequalities of power and wealth as part of the natural order of things. Nonetheless, disputes were certainly more common than one might expect, and in the Middle Ages as today they were frequently stimulated by attempts to overturn a customary way of doing things. Trouble could arise, for example, when the lords tried to introduce any reduction in the rights and benefits of the community. Thus in 1291:

> 'All the villeins of the township of Broughton...went away from the great harvest boon, leaving their work from noon till night...giving the malicious and false cause that they did not have their loaves as large as they were accustomed formerly and ought to have them.'

Such disputes could involve individuals as well as groups of tenants. In 1288, for example, in the village of Shillington in Bedfordshire, the son of Hugh Walter lay at the head of a strip at harvest and impeded the work of the lord. This was presumably an early form of passive resistance, for which the protester received a fine of 6*d*. at the manorial court. In 1282 the whole of the vill of Abbots Langley in Hertfordshire was fined 18 shillings by the manorial court for failing to come to the Abbot's harvest with 36 sickles. Moreover, many of the communities engaging in such acts of defiance seem to have been highly organized....Led by their reeve, the villeins of Stoughton in Leicestershire raised the money to hire a lawyer to represent them in the royal courts against attempts on the part of their lord to increase labour services....

Some disputes ran for years, like that between the abbots of Halesowen in the West Midlands and their tenants. This continued on and off from 1243 to 1327, and involved numerous proceedings in the royal courts, royal inquests and a petition to the king as well as more violent confrontations. In 1278 the Bishop of Worcester ordered the excommunication of all those who had physically attacked the abbot and his monks at Beoley....The lot of the medieval peasant may not have been particularly enviable, but material deprivation was not necessarily accompanied by a lack of any power of self-determination.

The customs of the medieval village were usually defined by the manorial court. This dealt with minor criminal and civil offences, determined the means by which land could be sold or inherited, dictated agricultural practices and set the number of days to be worked and the amounts of money to be paid by tenants. It settled the balance of power in the community by establishing both the status of tenants and the relationship between the tenants and the lord.

The court was not simply an instrument of feudal oppression. It was also a system of self-regulation run by the community. The court was presided over by the steward, who was the lord's representative, but the jury was made up of villeins. They not only judged the facts of each case, but articulated the customs of the manor on which their judgments were based.

Rights the peasants certainly possessed, but taking action to protect those rights when they were infringed could be a hazardous undertaking. As Source 7 illustrates, if the lord of the manor was determined to exercise his authority, there was little that the peasantry could do to protect themselves, even when they were in the right.

Source 7

From an entry in *The Ledger Book of Vale Royal Abbey* for 1336, recording a conflict over feudal services between the abbot and the villagers of Darnall and Over in Cheshire.

Be it remembered that in the year 1336...the villeins of Darnall and Over conspired against their lords, the abbot and convent....Sir Hugh de Fren, then justiciar of Chester, came to a place which is called Harebach Cross, at which a great number of villeins had taken refuge together, and they had laid a serious complaint against the said abbot, [declaring] that, whereas they were free and held their lands and tenements from aforetime by charter of the Lord the King, the abbot, contrary to his customs hitherto observed in his manor of Darnall, had put them in close confinement in shackles, as though they were villeins, and forced them to serve him in all villein services....

At length the bondmen, finding no other place in which they might be longer concealed, returned to the abbot their lord, submitting themselves and their goods to his grace, and the abbot put them all in fetters as his bondmen. And so it came to pass that, touching the holy gospels, they all swore they were the bondmen of the abbot and the convent, and that they would never claim their freedom against them, and their successors. And for many Sundays they stood in the choir, in the face of the convent, with bare heads and feet, and they offered wax candles in token of subjection.

Conflicts over feudal rights such as that between the Abbot of Vale Royal and the peasants of Darnall and Over were commonplace, as were bread riots in times of famine and high prices. Tax revolts also occurred from time to time. One of the earliest to be recorded began in London in 1194 when a levy was imposed to raise the ransom needed to free Richard I, who had been imprisoned by the Duke of Austria. William FitzOsbert led a campaign against the unfair way in which the aldermen of London administered the levy, complaining that it fell more heavily on the poor than on the wealthy merchants. Mass meetings took place at the folkmoot near St Paul's, and one such meeting in 1196 was broken up by armed men on the orders of the Archbishop of Canterbury. FitzOsbert and nine others claimed sanctuary in the church of St Mary-le-Bow, but the

Archbishop ordered the church to be set on fire. As they fled from the flames, FitzOsbert and his friends were arrested. They were sentenced to death and executed a few days later.

One group of ordinary people whose rights need to be considered separately are women. However restricted the rights of ordinary men were in medieval England, the rights of their wives and daughters were even more limited, since they were legally subject to their menfolk. Anglo-Saxon women had rather more in the way of rights and freedoms than their Norman counterparts, but even they were unable to represent themselves in courts of law (Unit 1.3, Sources 102 and 104). The status of Norman women was eroded by the feudal system, under which land tenure was based on military service from which women were excluded, and by the teachings of the Church, which regarded women as deceitful and likely to tempt men to sin, in the same way that Eve had tempted Adam in the Garden of Eden. Consequently, church law regarded women as subject to their husbands and specifically permitted wife-beating.

Virtually the only women to be educated were nuns, and even they had no influence over the administration of the Church. Wealthy women often managed estates during the absence of their husbands on military or other forms of service and poorer women managed their husbands' homes and worked in the fields. Some worked in skilled trades, but restrictions on such employment became ever tighter. They received lower wages than men and, in periods of unemployment, they were accused of worsening the problem by reducing the employment prospects for men. In 1461, the burgesses of Bristol tried to curb unemployment in the cloth industry by decreeing that 'no person of the said craft of weavers from this day forward may set, put or hire his wife, daughter or maid to such occupation...upon pain of [a fine]'. However, women did not always accept such restrictions submissively: they were quite capable of protesting, and even rioting, when they felt that their livelihoods were threatened. In 1455, female silk workers marched through the streets of London protesting against the importation of foreign silks which they claimed was damaging their trade.

Women were not even free to marry without restrictions. Ordinary women had to seek the permission of the lord of the manor to marry and a fee had to be paid to him before the marriage could take place. Heiresses could own land in their own right if they were unmarried or widowed, but once they married their estates became the property of their husbands. Consequently, an heiress was much sought after and her marriage was usually arranged by the king or a powerful magnate in return for a payment from her future husband (Unit 1.3, Sources 105–7).

Throughout the thirteenth and fourteenth centuries, the feudal system continued to develop in response to changing circumstances. Initially, economic factors worked in favour of the lords of the manor and led to a reduction in the rights and freedoms of the peasants, but a move in the opposite direction can be detected from the early fourteenth century that gained considerably in momentum after the Black Death reduced the population by about a third during 1348–9.

Source 8

From T. Williamson and E. Bellamy, *Property and Landscape*, pp.72–3, 78 and 87–8.

From the late twelfth century the manorial lords became increasingly involved in the farming of their demesne land. They resumed control of those lands which had been leased out in the previous century, and at the same time increased the exactions on their villeins. Heavier labour services were introduced....At the same time, significant changes were taking place in the legal status of villeins. They were increasingly regarded as totally unfree, so that they were unable to bring cases against their lords in the royal courts. Any dispute had to be settled within the manorial court, from which villeins had no recourse to any higher authority. Thus they were prevented from contesting the increasingly onerous burdens placed upon them....

From the middle decades of the thirteenth century there was an important change in the legal tenets surrounding enclosure with the passing of the Statute of Merton in 1236. This statute was an attempt to limit disputes over the enclosure of common land, by empowering lords to enclose manorial waste provided they left sufficient pasture for the requirements of their free tenants – in other words, it enshrined the rights of free tenants in national law. But it also marked a significant decline in the independence of the villeins, for it made no provision for compensation in cases where they lost their customary rights....Before the passing of this act, free tenants seem to have been able to oppose any unilateral enclosure of the waste by appealing to the royal courts. After 1236, however, it was legally recognised that the lord of the manor was the ultimate owner of the commons....

Although the population decline [resulting from the Black Death] caused some economic contraction, the cake did not shrink anything like as fast as the population. With fewer people, land and food were abundant and labour was scarce. The situation experienced in the early medieval period was therefore in many ways suddenly reversed and as a result there were fundamental changes in the structure of English society. The Black Death profoundly affected the relationship between landlord and peasant....

The demise of large sections of the labour force strengthened the hand of those who survived in the years following the onslaught of the disease. As peasants capitalized on rising wage rates and falling rents, there was a great increase in the geographical mobility of the labouring population. Villeins were still in theory tied to the manors of their birth, but in practice they could move if they wished. The lords of manors into which they moved would not have readily turned them away. They needed the income from their rent rolls, and were quite prepared to turn a blind eye to breaches of manorial discipline in order to attract tenants to their holdings.

At the same time the lords found it increasingly difficult to compel their villeins to perform their customary dues and services. The balance of power had shifted away from the lords and the villeins were not slow to take advantage of the new situation....But the lords did not take the new power of the labourers lying down. They sought to legislate against it, and in 1351 the Statute of Labourers was passed. This was a rearguard action which attempted to control wages, and to restrict geographical mobility. It totally failed to achieve anything of the kind. The economic cards had, for the time being, played into the hands of the workers....There was a gradual slackening of the chains of villeinage. The old form of personal servitude came to an end, although it was eventually replaced by inequalities that were unrestrained by the power of custom.

Some aspects of this analysis of the development of feudalism have been challenged by other historians, most notably the assertion that the Statute of Labourers was totally ineffective. From the wording of the Statute [see Unit 3.2, Source 103], it is clear that an earlier Ordinance of Labourers passed in 1349 was almost totally ignored by the peasants, probably with the active connivance of many landowners who were desperate to attract peasants to their manors, even at the cost of higher wages and freedom from feudal services. The failure of the 1349 Statute stands as clear evidence of the power that the peasants possessed when enough of them refused to comply with the rules made by their masters. However, the Statute of 1351 must have had at least some effect. Otherwise, it would not have caused such resentment among the populace and neither would it have been an important grievance contributing 30 years later to the outbreak of the Peasants' Revolt, as the chronicler, Froissart, among others, claimed it to be.

Source 9

From Jean Froissart, *Chronicles*. Froissart (c.1337–1410) was from Hainault, a duchy straddling the modern border between France and Belgium. He probably received the information for his account of the Peasants' Revolt when he visited the court of Richard II in 1395.

In England, as in other countries, it is usual for the nobles to exercise great authority over the commons and to hold them in a state of serfdom; that is to say, as serfs they are compelled by law and custom to labour on the lords' lands....Thus the noblemen and prelates are served by them, and specially in the counties of Kent, Essex, Sussex and Bedford. The unhappy people of these counties began to stir, because they said they were kept in great bondage, and in the beginning of the world, they said, there were no bondmen, wherefore they maintained that none ought to be in bondage now...which, they said, they would no longer suffer, for they would be all one, and if they laboured or did anything for their lords, they would have wages for it as well as other men.

And of this opinion was a foolish priest in the country of Kent called John Ball, who had often been imprisoned by the Archbishop of Canterbury on account of his impassioned preaching in the villages after mass on Sundays....'Good people', he would say, 'nothing can go well in England, nor ever will do, until all goods are held in common, until there is neither villein nor nobleman, until we are all one. We all come from one father and one mother, Adam and Eve: so what makes them our masters? They wear silks and velvet furred with squirrel and ermine while we wear poor cloth. They have wine, spices and good bread, but we eat rye and chaff and have water to drink. They live in fine manors and dwelling houses, while we sweat and toil in the fields in the wind and rain; and it is our labour that maintains their estates. They call us 'serf' and beat us if we do not hasten to serve them, and we have no overlord to complain to, no one to listen to us or do us justice. Let us go to the king, he is young; let us explain our condition to him and tell him that we want it changed, or else we will change it ourselves. If we go together, all manner of people that are now in bondage will follow us with the intention of being made free; and when the king sees us, we shall have some remedy, either by fairness or otherwise.'

John Ball's teaching was well-known to many of the common people in the city of London, who were envious of wealthy and aristocratic men and were beginning to say among themselves that the kingdom of England was badly governed and that it was being robbed of its silver and gold by those who called themselves noble.

They spread the word to the men of Kent, Essex, Sussex, Bedford and the neighbouring districts, who rose and began to make for London. There were a good sixty thousand of them under one principal captain, a man called Wat Tyler, together with his comrades Jack Straw and also John Ball....On Monday 10 June in the year 1381, these people left their homes and set out to go to London to talk to King Richard and be made free.

While Froissart was probably right in regarding villeins' demands for freedom from bondage as a major cause of the Peasants' Revolt, it cannot provide a sufficient explanation by itself. If it could, one would have expected the revolt to have broken out soon after 1351, when the Statute of Labourers was passed laying down additional penalties for peasants who attempted to evade their feudal obligations and attempting to hold down wages to the levels that were paid before the Black Death. The Peasants' Revolt of 1381 was a serious disturbance in which large numbers of ordinary people made common cause and it sent shock waves through the political establishment. Such an occurrence could not have taken place without other causes. Sources 10, 11 and 12 identify some of those causes and emphasize the particular importance of the poll tax, without which it is unlikely that the revolt would have taken place, at least in the form and at the time that it did.

Source 10

From J.L. Bolton, *The Medieval English Economy 1150–1500* (Dent, 1980) pp.215–6.

The kindling for a general peasant revolt was there in the 1370s, and the resistance was for the first time born of hope, not of despair. The basic relationship between land and people had at last changed. Social and economic freedom now seemed a practical possibility and this is what the peasants demanded at Mile End in 1381: an end to villeinage, free rents at 4*d*. [2p] an acre and freely negotiable wage labour contracts. Rebellion might have come in any year after about 1377 and to understand why it did not come until 1381 the Revolt has to be set firmly in its political background. By the 1370s English politics had turned sour. Edward III was in his dotage, his eldest son, Edward the Black Prince, was sick with the illness that was to kill him in 1376. The French war was going badly: it cost a great deal but the government appeared to be unable to protect even the South Coast. There had been outright attacks on the king's ministers in the Good Parliament of 1376 and discontent smouldered during the unpopular regency of John of Gaunt after Edward III's death in 1377. To general political unrest must be added anti-clericalism. The resentment of the Church's wealth permeates the works of Chaucer and Langland. An heretical movement, Lollardy, inspired partly by John Wyclif, was growing in strength. The Lollards demanded the disestablishment of the Church and the redistribution of its property. Such ideas had a wide popular appeal as can be seen in the fundamental cry of the rebel priest John Ball,

When Adam delved and Eve span
Who was then a gentleman?

Yet what finally set off the revolt was the weight of taxation.

Source 11

From Charles Poulsen, *The English Rebels* (Journeyman, 1984) pp.9–11.

The cost of the war, soon to be known as the Hundred Years War, was more than the nation could bear.... The king and his new parliament were desperate for money; even the crown jewels had been pawned. They thought up the novel idea of a poll tax – a personal tax on every individual in the country.... A levy of one groat [about 1.25p] was made on everybody over fourteen years old, male or female, rich or poor. The proceeds were quickly spent on the war or absorbed by corruption, and were followed by a 'graduated' poll tax. And in the year 1380, in a move suggested by Simon Sudbury, Archbishop of Canterbury, a new poll tax of three groats [about 5p] per head over the age of fifteen was levied. There was a maximum payment of twenty shillings from men whose families and households numbered more than twenty, thus ensuring that the rich paid less than the poor. Three groats was a considerable sum for a working man – almost a week's wages. A family might include old persons past work and other dependants, and the head of the family became liable for three groats on each of their 'polls'....

The tax was to be collected at source by commissioners sent out by the county authorities.... Before the commissioners arrived there were often mass desertions from the villages and boroughs.... Out of £100,000 expected by Archbishop Sudbury, now also Chancellor of England, a mere £22,000 was brought in. The government, aware of the widespread evasion, decided to send again to the towns and villages, but this time with escorts of armed men.... The taxes due were to be collected under threat of force and imprisonment.

On 30 May 1381, Thomas Bampton, commissioner for the collection of poll tax, rode into the Essex town of Brentwood, accompanied by several clerks and a small armed escort. He called on the people of the villages of Fobbing, Corringham and Stanford-le-Hope to appear before him to pay their due taxes. They appeared, about a hundred strong, refused point-blank to reply or to pay, and stoned the commissioner's party out of the town.... All over Essex and across the Thames in Kent, the commons left their villages and assembled with what weapons they could arm themselves.... The immediate steps were to settle accounts with the feudal landowners. Monasteries, abbeys, the houses of repressive landlords were attacked, the records and charters of labour and other dues dragged out and burnt.... Along with these old parchments disappeared, it was hoped, the oppressions of serfdom and villeinage.... Little mercy was shown to clerks and lawyers, who were regarded as the main enemies of the commons, as it was they who operated the old laws, taxes and dues.

Source 12

From John Thomson, *The Transformation of Medieval England 1370–1529* (Longman, 1983) pp.26–7.

Undoubtedly taxation provided the occasion for the Peasants' Revolt....This was prompted by the costs of war – indeed since the renewal of the conflict with France in 1369 there had been several major fiscal exactions, of which the three poll taxes were the last....The taxation in itself, however heavy, could hardly have sparked off so violent a conflagration if conditions had not been appropriate for it. One may eliminate famine as a possible underlying cause of discontent, as the harvests in the five years before 1381 were at least average and sometimes good. The demands made by the rebels provide the clearest guide to their grievances, and according to the *Anonimalle Chronicle* those put forward by the Essex men at Mile End on 14 June were that they should be allowed to seize and punish traitors, and that no man should be made a serf nor do homage or any type of service to a lord in return for land; instead they should hold it at a rent of 4*d*. an acre. This suggests that grievances were both political and social. Significantly, on the following day at Smithfield, after the deaths of Sudbury and Hales, there seem to have been no further demands concerning 'traitors', but further ones about social and legal status, that there should be no lordship apart from the king's, and that the Church should be disendowed.

The tax revolt spread rapidly across south-east England. Rebels from Kent, Essex and elsewhere converged on London, led by Wat Tyler, Jack Straw and John Ball. The rebels declared their loyalty to the young King Richard, but were determined to punish those they held responsible for the poll tax and others who had incurred their wrath. Chief among these were the king's uncle, John of Gaunt, and Archbishop Sudbury of Canterbury, the architect of the poll tax. Sympathetic Londoners admitted the rebels to the city where they rapidly took control. John of Gaunt's Savoy palace was burnt, legal records at the Temple and Lincoln's Inn were destroyed and prisoners were released from the Fleet and Newgate prisons, but it seems that sufficient discipline was maintained to ensure that there was little or no looting. Powerless to disperse the rebel peasants, the king agreed to meet them at Mile End, where he accepted all their demands and his officials drew up charters granting them freedom, abolishing serfdom and pardoning them for acts committed during the revolt.

Source 13

From an account in the *Anonimalle Chronicle* of the demands put forward by Wat Tyler at Mile End and accepted by Richard II.

He asked that there should be no law in the realm save the law of Westminster...and that no lord should have lordship except civilly, and that there should be equality among all people save only the king, and that the goods of Holy Church should not remain in the hands of the religious...that clergy already in possession should have a sufficient sustenance from the endowments, and the rest of the goods should be divided among the people of the parish... and all the lands and tenements now held by [bishops] should be confiscated, and divided among the commons....And he demanded that there should be no more villeins in England, and no serfdom or villeinage, but that all men should be free and of one condition.

Flushed with success, Tyler and his followers dragged Archbishop Sudbury out of the Tower of London and executed him. Along with Sudbury died, among others, Robert Hales, the Treasurer, who was reviled as 'Hob the Robber', and John Legge, who was responsible for administering the poll tax. After this, many returned home, unaware that the king had no intention of honouring the promises made at Mile End. A hard core, led by Tyler, remained and held a second meeting with the king at Smithfield, where they demanded a complete reform of the law and of the Church. What happened next is not entirely clear. It was claimed by members of the royal entourage that Tyler behaved insolently towards the king and went to draw his dagger; others alleged that members of the royal party had come to the meeting intending to murder Tyler. Whatever the truth of the matter, he was knocked from his horse by William Walworth, the mayor of London, and killed. The young king then rode over to the truculent peasants, pacified them by announcing that he would be their new leader, and persuaded them to return to their homes, promising that the charters of freedom they had been granted would be honoured.

Source 14

A composite illustration of the Peasants' Revolt, 1381, showing, on the left, the murder of Wat Tyler while talking with Richard II and, on the right, the king addressing the rebels

As the peasants began to return home, the government was quick to seize the initiative. Many leaders, including Jack Straw, were rounded up and summarily executed before they had a chance to leave London. Peasant risings elsewhere in the south-east and East Anglia were ruthlessly suppressed and many rebels were tried and executed, among them John Ball.

The Peasants' Revolt had revealed both the strength and weakness of the power of direct popular action. The government had been powerless to resist a large force of peasants determined to achieve specific political goals, but the peasants in their turn had proved incapable of maintaining their cohesiveness over a long period of time. Sooner rather than later, they had to return to their villages to gather the harvest without which they would have faced starvation during the coming winter. Once that happened, the government reasserted its authority and exacted retribution. Not surprisingly, the freedom granted by Richard II at Mile End to villeins and serfs was revoked almost immediately. As the Parliament Rolls for 1381 make clear, the political élite was not prepared to relinquish rights from which it gained considerable economic benefit.

Source 15

From the Parliament Rolls for 1381.

The king commanded Sir Richard Scrope, the newly created chancellor [to explain to parliament] the repeal made [by the king] of the grant of freedom and manumission [replacement of labour services with money rents] to the serfs and villeins of the land. It was...asked of all those present in full parliament whether this repeal pleased them or not....And they – that is to say, the prelates and lords, as well as the commons – humbly besought our lord the king that these manumissions and enfranchisements, thus made and granted through coercion, to their disinheritance and the destruction of the kingdom, should be quashed and annulled by the authority of this parliament, and that the said repeal should be affirmed as well and justly made.

Source 16

From John Thomson, *The Transformation of Medieval England 1370–1529*, p.31.

The sudden collapse of the rising leaves one final question: did the revolt play any significant part in the development of English society in the following decades? The general view is that it was basic economic forces rather than the events of 1381 which brought about the end of villeinage....Alone among recent writers, Hilton suggests that the rising may have deterred the ruling class from further local attempts at repression [R.H. Hilton, *Bondmen Made Free*, pp.213–2]....Certainly the suppression of the rising did not eliminate peasant unrest, although this reverted to being a purely local phenomenon, and in general to taking less violent forms. The most obvious casualty of the rising was the poll-tax, which was abandoned as a future source of revenue.

Contemporaneous with the Peasants' Revolt were the first stirrings of the Lollard movement, which was to plague the English Church for the next 150 years. The Lollards were followers of the teachings of John Wyclif, an Oxford theologian who criticised the wealth, greed and corruption of the Church, rejected the doctrine of transubstantiation and declared that papal decrees were only valid if they conformed to the Scriptures. He argued that people should live their lives according to the teachings of the Bible and that Church practices not specifically sanctioned by the Bible should be abolished. He encouraged people to read the Bible for themselves rather than relying on priestly interpretations, and translated it into English in 1382. These teachings met with predictable opposition from the Church, but he was protected by a powerful patron, John of Gaunt, and his views quickly attracted a sizeable following throughout the country.

Source 17

Extracts from the writings of John Wyclif, 1320–84, whose ideas inspired the Lollards.

A. Jesus Christ was a poor man from his birth to his death, shunning worldly riches. The Pope at Rome, by contrast, from the time of his birth until he dies, tries to be worldly rich....Christ was the humblest of men, but it is said that the Pope is the most proud man on earth: he makes lords kiss his feet whereas Christ washed the feet of his apostles....Bishops and priests with all their deans and officials should not tax the poor people, for this is worse than common robbery....It seems to true men that tenths or tithes should be divided between priests and other poor men who are feeble or lame or blind....

Then there are the services of the Catholic Church....These are sung in trilled notes by large choirs, to hinder men from understanding the meaning of what was sung....Fools value these services more than the commandments of God and the study and teaching of Christ's Gospel.

B. Confession that man makes of sin is made in two manners. Some is made only to God truly by heart or mouth. And some confession is made to man, and that may be in many manners; either openly and generally, as men confessed in the old law; or privately and whisperingly as men confess nowadays....It seems that [private confession] is not needful, but brought in of late by the devil; for omniscient [all-knowing] Christ used it not, nor any of his apostles after. And if it were needful to man, Christ would have used it or taught it....And thus it seems to many men that Christian men might well be saved without such confession; as they were before Pope Innocent, and thus it seems presumption of this pope to make this law.

Although Wyclif died in 1384, his followers continued to preach and embellish his message. Their opponents christened them 'Lollards' because they said that they mumbled incoherently. Itinerant Lollard preachers travelled around the country finding receptive audiences among a populace that resented paying tithes to a Church that seemed more concerned with wealth than with piety. Bishops and monastic houses were among the largest landowners in England and had a reputation for being even stricter than lay landowners in extorting labour services from their villeins and serfs. You will note that calls for ecclesiastical reform featured prominently among the demands of the participants in the Peasants' Revolt (see Sources 10 and 13).

Source 18

From the *Chronicle* of Henry Knighton, a monk at Leicester Abbey, c.1382.

The believers of these doctrines grew in number until they filled the whole kingdom....A great number of people were foolishly deceived and drawn to their sect. They wore, for the most part, clothes of russet, showing outwardly the simplicity of their hearts, so they could begin their work of teaching and sowing their mad doctrine....Over half the population of the country were won over to their sect....They thought and preached that they alone were good men and worthy of God: those who observed the ancient and firm doctrine of the Catholic Church they declared to be sinners.

Knighton exaggerated when he claimed that over half the population was won over by the Lollards, but they certainly attracted a great deal of support from all sections of society. The Church's hostility to the Lollards, expressed so forcefully by Knighton, led to the passing of various punitive measures against them, but it was not until the failure of an ill-judged rebellion led by Sir John Oldcastle in 1414 that the power of the Lollards was broken.

Source 19

From an Act passed in 1401, entitled 'On the Burning of Heretics'.

Many false persons do maliciously preach and teach these new doctrines against the holy Catholic Church; they make and write books, they wickedly instruct the people and stir them to rebellion....From henceforth, therefore, no one within the realm shall presume to preach openly without a licence from a bishop; no one shall make or write any book contrary to the Catholic faith, nor hold schools; anyone possessing books of such wicked doctrines shall deliver them to the local bishop within forty days. And if any persons be convicted of acting against this law, the severest penalty may be pressed against them; they shall be burnt before the people in a public place, so that their punishment shall strike fear into the hearts of others, so that no wicked doctrines may be tolerated.

Source 20

The execution in 1417 of Sir John Oldcastle, who had led an unsuccessful Lollard revolt three years earlier

Oldcastle's rebellion brought home to many that Lollardy posed a political as well as a religious threat to the stability of the country. Consequently, support from among the gentry and nobility ceased abruptly, but the movement continued to find adherents among peasants and artisans throughout the fifteenth century. The repression that followed the rebellion weakened the Lollard movement and drove it underground, but did not kill it. The movement began to experience something of a revival in the early fifteenth century, when significant pockets appeared in various parts of the country, including Berkshire, Kent, Essex and Coventry. In 1521, Bishop Longland rounded up 400 Lollards in Buckinghamshire, of whom four were executed, while the recantation of John Croft in 1505 [Unit 1.4, Source 124] testifies to the presence of a group in Herefordshire, and suggests that Lollard views had changed little since they were first expounded over a century earlier. Many of their opinions about the greed and corruption of the Church and about predestination were later to be shared by the continental reformers, Martin Luther and John Calvin, and, after the Reformation in England, Lollardy merged into the wave of Protestantism that engulfed the country.

The inability of the authorities to eradicate Lollardy illustrates certain essential differences between religious and political dissent among the populace. Religious dissent was not proceeded against with as much vigour as political protest unless it threatened the stability of the state, in which case it became political. Secondly, heretical religious beliefs were more difficult to counter because those who held them were often willing to suffer martyrdom rather than conform to Church orthodoxy. Even their deaths strengthened their cause by acting as an example to others. Furthermore, while political action by ordinary people could only be of short duration because it required mass participation, efficient organization and took people away from their work, religious protest was able to sustain itself over long periods of time because it took the form of individual conviction and belief, required little or no organization and did not need to distract people from earning their livelihood.

The lives of medieval peasants were harsh and short. They worked hard in all weathers; they lived in inadequate housing which, for the poorest, was often little more than a one-room hut; their diet was monotonous and lacking in nutrition; in times of crop failure many of them starved to death; they had to pay rents to the lord of the manor, tithes to the Church and taxes to the crown; and on top of all this, many of them had to perform labour service and pay feudal dues. For the most part, they submitted to all this because of the time-honoured belief, strongly reinforced by the Church, that everyone's place in the social hierarchy was divinely ordained and that it was a sin against God as well as a crime against the state to challenge the established order. Nevertheless, from time to time a combination of circumstances arose that galvanized people into violent protest. As we have seen, one such occasion was the Peasants' Revolt of 1381; another was the Kentish Rebellion led by Jack Cade in 1450. Whereas the Peasants' Revolt was primarily a reaction against economic measures such as the poll tax and the Statute of Labourers, Cade's Rebellion was more overtly political in origin, stemming from the misgovernment of Henry VI.

Source 21

From A.L. Morton, *A People's History of England* (Lawrence and Wishart, 1948) pp.122–3.

The general discontent aroused by this misgovernment had found expression in the Kentish revolt led by Jack Cade...[which] was a genuinely popular rising...against the misgovernment of the great nobles. It was a very different movement from that of 1381. Serfdom was now almost extinct, and in Kent had long been extinct. The demands of the rebels, set out in the 'Bill of Complaints and Requests of the Commons of Kent', are wholly political in character, while the composition of Cade's army, which included many squires and well-to-do people as well as peasants and labourers, was far wider and more varied than that of the earlier rising. The main grievances listed were the inclusion of 'persons of lower nature' in the King's Council, the mismanagement of the French war...and the rigging of elections. The rebels demanded that the Duke of York and his party should be brought into the Council and the followers of Suffolk should be dismissed and punished.

Early in 1450 a strongly Yorkist parliament had met and impeached Suffolk, who was banished. On his way to Calais he was seized by sailors on board ship, beheaded and his body thrown on Dover beach. This murder was the signal for revolt and on 1 June an army of 50,000 men from all parts of Kent marched on Blackheath to place their demands before the Council.

They were refused a hearing and a royal army moved out to Greenwich against them. They retired in good order to the wooded country around Sevenoaks. A panic then seized the government. Its army melted away and Cade's followers entered London, where they had many supporters, on 2 July. Lord Saye, one of the most unpopular ministers, and Crowemer, sheriff of Kent, were captured and executed. The rebels kept good order and there was little looting, but this restraint soon created a real problem. To feed so large an army demanded considerable funds and Cade proposed to levy the rich London merchants for this purpose. They had hitherto supported the rebels, sharing the general hatred of the government, but now they began to wonder what this popular army would do next.

On 5 July they suddenly seized London Bridge, shutting off Cade and his men, quartered in Southwark, from the city. All next day a battle was fought for the bridge, but the rebels were at last driven back. On the 6th, while they were disheartened by this reverse, envoys from the government came offering a free pardon to all and promising to consider their demands. They dispersed, only Cade and a few of his fellows remaining in arms. Cade was hunted down and killed and in a judicial progress through Kent, known as the 'harvest of heads', many of the most active rebels were executed.

Source 22

From David Cook, *Lancastrians and Yorkists: The Wars of the Roses* (Longman, 1984) pp.18–20.

At the end of May...large numbers of Kentish peasants assembled in the Ashford area and marched to Blackheath. The rising spread to Essex and contingents came from there. In these early stages the peasants were well-ordered, showing a firm leadership and a strong common purpose.... The rebels demanded that [the Duke of] York and other members of the wider royal family, such as the Dukes of Buckingham and Exeter, should be given their rightful position on the royal Council....

A striking characteristic of the rebellion was the production of well-publicised manifestoes, incorporating a skilful mixture of national and local grievances. It is clear that the Kentishmen regarded themselves as petitioners backing up the demands of parliament, rather than rebels. Political reform was their desire, not revolution. They affirmed their loyalty to Henry VI and attacked his 'evil' advisers for monopolising royal patronage and ruling oppressively. The specifically Kentish grievances were a microcosm of the general political *malaise* [disorder]. They were dominated by the activities of the household officials in the area, principally Lord Saye, Treasurer of England, and his son-in-law, William Crowemer....

The rebels entered the city, but despite Cade's good intentions the peasant army soon degenerated into a looting and burning mob. Saye and Crowemer were taken from the Tower and executed. The unrest was now beginning to spread. In Wiltshire, another household official, William Aiscough, Bishop of Salisbury, was dragged from a church and beheaded. Mobs also threatened the Bishops of Lichfield and Norwich.

How much Cade and his supporters achieved is difficult to say. In the immediate and literal sense they attained some of their objectives. Saye, Crowemer, Aiscough and other hated royal officials were dead. However, in the short term, the Duke of York and other members of the wider royal family continued to be excluded from the King's Council and the misgovernment of Henry VI not only continued but worsened. In the summer of 1453 and again in the autumn of 1455, the king suffered bouts of mental illness that rendered him incapable of governing. On each occasion, York was appointed as Protector, exercising royal power on the king's behalf, only to lose office as soon as Henry recovered. This deepened the divisions between the Yorkists and the Lancastrians and they were soon at war with each other. The Duke of York was killed at the Battle of Wakefield in 1460, but his son defeated the Lancastrians at Towton the following year and was crowned Edward IV. The first ten years of Edward's reign were spent consolidating his position, which was only finally secured with the defeat of the Lancastrians at Barnet and Tewkesbury, and the death in captivity of Henry VI. Only then could Edward begin to provide the sound government for which Cade's rebels had petitioned 20 years earlier.

The Peasants' Revolt in 1381 and the Kentish Rebellion in 1450 mark an important stage in the development of protest by ordinary people. No longer was peasant protest purely local, directed against the authority of the lord of the manor and his manorial court, or artisan protest against the authority of the borough corporation. These two revolts showed that, when the circumstances were right, peasants and artisans from large areas were capable of combining in pursuit of political goals including demands for the reform of government. Henceforth, demands for reform and the issuing of manifestoes were to become a common feature of the uprisings that occurred at irregular intervals over the next two centuries. In some cases, the demands pursued by the peasantry displayed a degree of sophistication, especially when their leaders were educated but disaffected members of the political élite. However, without such leadership peasant rebels often displayed extreme political naïveté.

Source 23

A revolt against Edward IV occurred in the West of England in 1462. The following words were uttered at their subsequent trial by peasants who took part in the revolt.

We commons have brought King Edward to his prosperity in the realm of England, and if he will not rule as we will have him rule, as able we were to make him king, as able we be to depose him and put him down and bring him there as we found him.

As these rebels found to their cost, peasants could only dislodge a king when they acted in concert with powerful nobles. Without that alliance, they could shake the tree, but they could not bring it down, and their fate was likely to be death at the hands of the executioner.

From the late fifteenth to the eighteenth century

Questions

5. What changes and developments in the rights and freedoms of ordinary people took place between the fifteenth and the eighteenth centuries?

6. What developments took place between the fifteenth and the eighteenth centuries in:
   (a) the sorts of people who took part in popular protest?
   (b) the issues over which they protested?
   (c) the methods they employed?
   (d) the ability of protesters to achieve their aims?

By the end of the fifteenth century a revolution had taken place in the countryside. The feudal manors of the early Middle Ages with their demesne farms worked by villeins and serfs had almost vanished. In their place had evolved a patchwork system in which lords of the manor farmed their estates using hired labourers or rented them out to tenants; freeholders owned their own farms – the more prosperous of them evolving into yeomen; copyholders rented small-holdings – often on insecure and unfavourable tenures; and wage labourers worked for the gentry, yeomen or freeholders who would employ them. Individual ownership was developing at the expense of communal rights. While the rights of those who owned land grew and were protected by the increasing volume of land law, those of landless labourers diminished with the decline of the manorial courts that had afforded some minimal protection for their customary rights. Litigation in the common law courts was beyond the means of most people below the rank of yeoman and, in any case, was likely to be unsuccessful when pursued against a member of the gentry from whom the magistrates and judges were drawn. If landless labourers had few rights, most women had even fewer.

Source 24

From S. Bindoff, *Tudor England* (Penguin, 1964) pp.28–9 and 37–8.

In Tudor England, as in England down to very recent times, the inequality which affected the largest number of people was not a social, but a sexual one. The woman of the time, whatever her rank in society, was treated as an inferior being, and her freedom of action was restricted at every turn. Prior to marriage she was an infant, to be watched over by parent or guardian. Her marriage which was normally a business arrangement in which she had no say whatever…submerged her legal personality in that of her husband. Only as a widow could she hope to enjoy something approaching equality with man in the disposal of her person and property….

Certain things we can say about [customary tenants – the majority of the rural population]. The great majority of them had already achieved personal freedom, and were no longer beholden to anyone save the king. In the generation before 1485 the king's courts had even shown a disposition to extend their [recognition]…of the customary tenant's rights as a person to his rights in [the holding of] his land. This was a development which, if persevered in, might have immeasurably strengthened his security of tenure. But the courts did not persevere in it, and although the Tudors brought some cases [before] their new Courts of Star Chamber and Requests, the common lawyers' failure to handle them was in the long run to prove fatal. Thus protected…solely by the 'custom of the manor' from arbitrary interference with the terms of his tenure, the customary tenant was ill-placed to resist a grasping landlord's demands for 'improved' rents or [entry] fines…for the compulsory substitution of leases for existing tenures, or for any other devices by which the increased value of the holding might be transferred to the lord's pocket; while he and his fellows were seldom able to prevent those enclosure operations which made it difficult, or impossible, for them to go on making a living out of their holdings.

The changes in the economic structure of the countryside altered the nature of peasant protest. No longer were the principal grievances to do with labour services and money rents. The former had largely died out with the achievement of the latter. The new economic climate was one which encouraged landowners to seek a better income from their land. Arable farming was costly, labour intensive and, at a time of falling food prices, less profitable than formerly. On the other hand, sheep farming was becoming increasingly attractive because wool prices were high and labour costs low. Large tracts of land could be managed by just two or three shepherds. Consequently during the late fifteenth century, and even more during the sixteenth and seventeenth centuries, manorial lords began to enclose common land, which they came increasingly to regard as theirs by right, with the result that villagers lost the right of pasturage that for the poor was essential to their precarious existence. In more extreme cases, whole villages were depopulated as landowners turned the land over to sheep pasture and evicted the peasants.

Source 25

All that remains of the village of Burston in Buckinghamshire, depopulated in 1488 when John Swafield enclosed the land for grazing and evicted sixty inhabitants. As a result of Swafield's action, the value of the land rose from just over £13 to £40 per annum.

Thomas More, later to become chancellor to Henry VIII and to be martyred for his religious beliefs, was one of relatively few among the propertied classes who cared about, and could see clearly the effects that unjust enclosures could have upon, the poor.

Source 26

From Thomas More, *Utopia*, 1516.

Your sheep that used to be so meek and tame, and so small eaters, now...have become such great devourers and so wild, that they eat up...the very men themselves. They consume...whole fields, houses and cities.... Therefore that one covetous and insatiable cormorant may...enclose many thousand acres of ground together within one pale or hedge, the husbandmen be thrust out of their own....They must needs depart away, poor wretched souls, men, women...children, widows...and their whole household....Away they trudge...out of their...houses, finding no place to rest in....All their household stuff...they are constrained to sell it for a thing of nought. And when they have wandered abroad till that be spent, what can they do else but steal, and then justly...be hanged, or go begging. And yet then also they are cast in prison as vagabonds, because they go about and work not.

By no means all enclosures were for the purposes of grazing. Many of them were concerned with the pursuit of more efficient and profitable arable farming. Many also were uncontentious, but, as Thomas More has shown, others had serious consequences for the livelihoods of the poorest and most vulnerable elements in society. Consequently, enclosure was the most frequent cause of peasant unrest during this period. As Source 27 illustrates, the government was aware of the problem and tried to prevent its worst abuses, but its measures were directed more towards reducing vagrancy than alleviating the plight of those adversely affected by enclosures. Besides, the legislation did little to stem the tide of rural depopulation.

Source 27

From the preamble to an Act against enclosure of land, passed in 1489.

Great inconveniences daily doth increase by desolation and pulling down and wilfull waste of houses and Towns within this...realm, and laying to pasture lands which customarily have been used in tillage, whereby idleness – the ground or beginning of all mischiefs – daily doth increase, for in some Towns two hundred persons were occupied and lived by their lawful labours, now be there occupied two or three herdsmen and the residue fallen to idleness; the husbandry, which is one of the greatest commodities of the realm, is greatly decayed; churches destroyed; the service of God withdrawn; the bodies there buried not prayed for...; the defence of this land against our enemies outwards feebled and impaired; to the great displeasure of God, to the subversion of the policy and good rule of this land.

Since legislation tended to be ineffective, peasants frequently resorted to direct action in the form of anti-enclosure riots and, somewhat surprisingly in view of the expense involved, to litigation in the courts of law. As Brian Manning and Ronald Hutton illustrate in Sources 28 and 29, anti-enclosure riots were particularly prevalent during the 1530s and 1540s and again during the early and mid-seventeenth century. Hutton also argues that the rioters were often successful and that, even when they were not, they tended to be treated leniently by the courts.

Source 28

From Brian Manning, *Village Revolts* (Oxford, 1988) pp.31–2.

Anti-enclosure riots were the most typical and widespread manifestations of agrarian protest in early modern England and Wales. Although such disturbances had occurred during the medieval period, the riotous levelling of hedges became especially prevalent during the 1530s and 1540s....Enclosures of land for both pasturage and tillage had been undertaken since the beginning of English agriculture and did not usually cause conflict....But the rapid increase in population in the early sixteenth century pressed hard upon the available supply of land. The necessity of increasing the food supply speeded up the process of enclosure and the introduction of new methods in agriculture and thus altered the familiar patterns of land use in many local communities. The many changes taking place in rural English society are reflected in the increased number of enclosure disputes between c.1530 and 1549. Considering the tension bred thereby, the social relationships between landlords, farmers, smallhold tenants, landless labourers and rural artisans could hardly remain unaffected.

Source 29

From Ronald Hutton, 'Rulers and Ruled, 1580–1650', in *History Today*, September 1985, pp.19–20.

Official treatment of leaders of riots varied according to the reasons with which they had incited their mobs to rise. If they had attacked the misconduct of individuals, then they were usually rebuked and often bound over to keep the peace....If they had denounced the political and social order, then they were executed as rebels....Rioting could never be commended by magistrates, but they tacitly recognized that it had value in exposing weaknesses in the social order as long as the social order itself was not under attack. It is notable that areas of the country in which the populace did not organize itself for grain riots were also those which suffered longest from famines....

[Although the crown often sympathized with anti-enclosure rioters and sometimes took action to punish enclosers, as in the Midland riots of 1607 referred to on page 6,] there remain some spectacular cases in which the crown was united with nobles and gentry in violent confrontation with commoners....One was set in the Fens, the marshes dividing the Midlands from East Anglia. During the 1620s and 1630s a number of people who owned land there, from Charles I downward, commenced drainage projects to increase the agricultural yield of the area and thereby their own, and the realm's, wealth. These destroyed the traditional pastoral economy, and the commoners, led variously by minor gentry, freeholders and people of lesser status, reacted by destroying the new works and taking the issue to law. They lost the legal actions, and the rioters were fined and gaoled. When the central governent collapsed in 1640–2, the drainage works were demolished again, only for the new regime to attempt to restore some of them. Further sporadic rioting followed, until in the 1660s schemes to compensate the local people were implemented. In some districts the works had not been restored, and no new projects were attempted anywhere....

Even more striking are the simultaneous events in the royal forests of Wiltshire and Dorset. Here, the government of Charles I attempted, as in the Fens, to combine personal and national enrichment by having the land enclosed and divided up for agricultural improvement. In this case, the crown took care to reconcile local opinion to the change, by giving all who owned land, including small-holders, a stake in it. What it did not take into account was that the forest contained a large population of landless people who lived by cottage industry employing forest products as raw materials. These, the 'dregs' of rural society, could find nobody more important to espouse their cause than a few very minor gentry. Yet when enclosure began, they resisted it ferociously, rioting in one forest, encouraging outbreaks in others as the news spread. Even when the militia and cannon were employed, the combined forces of local and central government required years to suppress and punish them. During the next thirty years most of them proceeded, like the Fenlanders, to destroy the 'improvements' anew every time that the attention of the central government was distracted. In some cases, as in the Fens, they were eventually pacified by being awarded compensation. In others, the enclosures seem never to have been restored.

In these regions, therefore, ordinary people fought for their interests, without hesitation, with considerable self-organization, and with a tenacity that spanned generations, when every authority to which they had been accustomed to defer was ranged against them. Yet in the process, they took precautions to preserve the existing social and political order. None of them spoke against its fundamental characteristics. In most cases they took as a leader the person who possessed the highest social status among them.

In focusing on popular protest, we must be careful not to give the impression of a society in perpetual turmoil. Tudor governments did not possess military forces that could be used to maintain order, but they had something more effective: a generally accepted belief reinforced by Church doctrine, which persuaded ordinary people to accept as natural enormous inequalities in wealth, social position and political power. The religious foundation for this acceptance by the poor of their inequality was the doctrine of the Great Chain of Being, summarized by Sir John Fortescue in Source 30 (see also Depth Study, Module 1, p.49).

Source 30

From Sir John Fortescue, *The Governance of England*, c.1471. Fortescue had been Chief Justice under Henry VI.

God created as many different kinds of things as he did creatures, so that there is no creature that does not differ in some respect superior or inferior to all the rest. So that from the highest angel down to the lowest of his kind there is absolutely not found an angel that has not a superior and inferior; nor from man down to the meanest worm is there any creature which is not in some respect superior to one creature and inferior to another. So that there is nothing which the bond of order does not embrace.

However, it was not just the Great Chain of Being that enabled Tudor governments to maintain law and order. The country was governed efficiently and fairly by the standards of the age: there was a progressive system of taxation, whereby the rich paid most and the poorest paid nothing; there was an effective system of poor relief which provided help for the starving during periods of famine or economic depression; and verdicts when people were charged with serious offences were determined not by magistrates or judges, as in many European countries, but by juries drawn from men of the same social rank as the accused. Thus, while there was social inequality, the English governmental and judicial systems were not particularly oppressive.

The rights and status of women in society changed little during the sixteenth and early seventeenth centuries. A sixteenth-century lawyer claimed that 'every woman is a sort of infant...[whose] husband is her prime mover, without whom she cannot do much at home, and less abroad'. As Joyce Youings explains in Source 31, women possessed some rights, and were not averse to using the power of protest on occasion, but heiresses were in a particularly vulnerable position, and few can have been as fortunate as Margaret Kebell in having their grievances redressed by the king.

Source 31

From Joyce Youings, *A Social History of England in the Sixteenth Century* (Fontana, 1984) pp.124–5.

It was rare for women to appear as plaintiffs in the courts, especially if married, because they had nothing [i.e. no property] to lose....Almost immediately after the Statute of Wills of 1540 had enabled men to [bequeath] the greater part of their land by will, another statute denied to married women, along with idiots and infants under the age of 21, the right to [bequeath] any land....'The good nature of a woman', wrote Sir Thomas Elyot in 1531, 'is to be mild, timorous, tractable, benign, of sure remembrance, and shamefast'. Not all early Tudor women were, of course, such mild creatures, but when in 1536, on the occasion of the pulling down of the rude loft in St. Nicholas Priory at Exeter, a crowd of women caused something of a riot, the main instruction to those appointed to carry out an enquiry into the disturbance was to discover whether these were not in fact men dressed up as women. It was when widowed that women really came into their own....Compared with their opportunities when first married, they had considerable freedom as widows....Until they remarried, as they usually did, widows carried on farming, and in the towns they were found running workshops and businesses, even being admitted in their own right to guilds and companies (though never to governing bodies or to office) and being assessed for tax. But any wealthy woman, whether widow or unmarried heiress, was at grave risk of abduction in a society whose law gave her husband complete control of all her property, real and personal. The statute of 1487 'against taking away of women against their wills' was little more than a restatement of existing law, intended not so much for the protection of women as for the maintenance of law and order. The case of Margaret Kebell, a 25-year-old widow, abducted from her uncle's house in Staffordshire at six o'clock in the morning by Roger, son of Sir Henry Vernon, accompanied by some 120 armed men, serves to underline the deficiencies of the common law in such matters. Although pursued by her formidable mother and her fiancé, Ralph Egerton, Margaret was carried off into Derbyshire where the Vernons were powerful landowners and there married, under threat, to Roger Vernon. What followed is not entirely clear, but Margaret succeeded in bringing her husband and his accessories before the Court of King's Bench in London. Owing to legal technicalities, this got her nowhere, but she later managed to gain audience with the king himself at Greenwich and the matter came before the Council in Star Chamber. Justice was now done, the Vernons were heavily fined, and Margaret was eventually freed to marry the patient Ralph.

The principal cause of discontent among ordinary people during the early Tudor period was taxation. The old system based on fifteenths and tenths was gradually being superceded by a new system of subsidies, which, because they were more efficient, bore more heavily on the tax-paying public. Twice during Henry VII's reign the levying of subsidies led to rebellion and on each occasion the rising was firmly suppressed. The first occurred in Yorkshire in 1489, where the Earl of Northumberland, who was charged with collecting the subsidy in the county, was murdered by an angry mob at Topcliffe near York. General rioting followed, but was firmly and effectively dealt with by forces under the command of the Earl of Surrey, and the Yorkshireman subsided into sullen quietude.

The second rising took place in 1497 and was caused by Henry VII levying by far the heaviest taxation of his entire reign to protect the north of England from an anticipated invasion from Scotland in support of the impostor, Perkin Warbeck. This provoked a rebellion among the independent and parochial Cornishmen, who resented paying taxes towards the defence of what to them seemed to be almost a foreign country. Writing 80 years later, Raphael Holinshed summarized the grievances of the Cornish rebels.

Source 32

From Raphael Holinshed, *Chronicles of England, Scotland and Ireland*, 1577.

These unruly people, the Cornishmen, inhabiting a barren and unfruitful country, resented that they should be so grievously taxed and burdened by the King's council....Flammock and Joseph [the local leaders] exhorted the local people to put on harness [military equipment] and not be afraid to follow them in that quarrel, promising not to hurt any creature, but only to see those punished that procured such taxes to be laid on the people.

The rebels marched to London – a remarkable feat in itself and indicative of their strength of feeling. Along the way, they gained an additional leader, the impoverished nobleman, Lord Audley, and eventually encamped just outside the capital at Blackheath, 15,000 strong. The Londoners manned their defences, the king despatched an army to deal with the threat and the rebellion came to a predictable end. One notable feature of Holinshed's description of the defeat of the rebels [Source 33] was the leniency shown by the authorities, who executed only the three leaders, Audley, Flammock and Joseph.

Source 33

From Raphael Holinshed, *Chronicles of England, Scotland and Ireland*, 1577.

The city was in great fear...[because] the rebels were encamped so near the city, every man getting himself to harness and placing themselves some at the gates some on the walls, so that no part was undefended. But the king delivered the city of that fear....There were slain of the rebels which fought and resisted above 2,000 men and taken prisoner an infinite number, and among them the blacksmith [Joseph] and the other chief captains, which were shortly after put to death.

While tax revolts could only end in failure, passive resistance sometimes succeeded in alleviating the tax burden. If small groups of people refused to pay, they could be coerced, but when enough people refused, the authorities were virtually powerless. In 1513, parliament voted Henry VIII a subsidy and a fifteenth and tenth in the same year, not long after a previous tax had been collected. Many communities in the impoverished north of England pleaded that they were unable to pay this additional burden and refused to do so. There seems to have been some truth in their claim and the king granted a petition from 19 Yorkshire towns and villages exempting them from payment.

Even higher taxes were collected between 1523 and 1525, on top of which Cardinal Wolsey sent out commissioners to collect an 'Amicable Grant' which the historian, A.F. Pollard, has called 'perhaps the most violent financial exaction in English history'. It was a tax of one-third on the goods of the clergy and one-sixth on those of the laity. Large areas of south-east England refused point-blank to pay, claiming that they lacked the money with which to do so. In the face of such widespread resistance, the king could do little other than revoke the Amicable Grant. This had a significant effect on his foreign policy, forcing him to abandon his ambitious, expensive and unpopular schemes to dominate Europe.

Between 1536 and 1549 there were three major rebellions in England in which ordinary people banded together with members of the gentry, nobility and Church. Each of these rebellions was directed by disaffected members of the political élite who pursued their own aims, but they would not have received widespread support among the politically excluded elements of society unless at least some of these aims had struck a sympathetic chord among the populace, and if they had not included among their demands the redress of grievances felt by ordinary people. Added to the issues of taxation and enclosure, which we have already seen were capable of fomenting popular protest, was the new ingredient of opposition to the religious reforms initiated by Tudor monarchs.

The first of these rebellions was the Pilgrimage of Grace, led by the lawyer, Robert Aske, which took hold of most of northern England during 1536. It occurred at a time when heavy taxation following bad harvests was coupled with resentment at the work of commissioners sent out by Henry VIII to supervise the dissolution of the smaller monasteries. Many of the gentry who led the Pilgrimage were relatives or tenants of the Earl of Northumberland, the most powerful landowner in the north, but out of favour at court. Robert Aske was his legal adviser. It has been argued that the rebellion was secretly incited by Northumberland and other discontented nobles to restore their political fortunes and reinstate Mary as heir to the throne, from which Henry VIII had disinherited her because of her continued allegiance to Rome. Aske recognized the need to attract and retain support among both the gentry and the masses. Thus the Pontefract Articles, which enumerated the rebels' demands, reflected the concerns of the various groups that participated in the rebellion.

Source 34

From the *Pontefract Articles*, 1536.

1. To have the heresies of Luther, Wyclif [and other continental and English religious reformers] and such other heresies of Anabaptism...annulled and destroyed.
2. To have the supreme head of the Church...restored unto the see of Rome....
3. That the lady Mary may be made legitimate and the former statute therein annulled....
4. To have the abbeys suppressed to be restored unto their houses, land and goods....
8. Lord Cromwell, the Lord Chancellor, and Sir Richard Riche to have condign punishment, as the subverters of the good laws of this realm and maintainers of the false sect of those heretics [the Protestant reformers]....
11. Reformation for the election of knights of the shire and burgesses, and for the uses among the lords in the parliament house after their ancient custom.
12. [The Act] for enclosures and intakes [see Source 26] to be put in execution, and that all intakes and enclosures since 1489 to be pulled down except mountains, forest and parks.
14. To be discharged from the fifteenth and taxes now granted by Act of Parliament....
17. That all recognizances [fines], statutes, penalties new forfeited during the time of this commotion may be pardoned and discharged....

18. The privileges and rights of the Church to be confirmed by Act of Parliament....
20. To have the statute that no man may will his lands [the Statute of Uses: see Unit 1.4, Source 184] to be repealed.

The rising began as a peasant riot at Louth in Lincolnshire in October 1536 and soon spread to Yorkshire, Westmorland, Cumberland and elsewhere, acquiring gentry leaders as it did so. Aske stressed the religious nature of the rising and referred to the rebels as 'pilgrims'. So effective was the maintenance of discipline and order that only one man was killed by the rebels – the hated Dr Raynes, chancellor to the Bishop of Lincoln. The king sent the Duke of Norfolk to suppress the rebellion, but Norfolk found his forces vastly outnumbered and decided that it would be more prudent to negotiate than to fight. On the king's behalf, Norfolk promised the rebels a general pardon and a free parliament to consider their grievances. Aske was convinced that he had won and the rebels dispersed. However, neither Norfolk nor Henry had any intention of honouring the promises made. Sir Francis Bigod, almost alone among the Pilgrimage's leaders, did not believe that the government's pledge of a free pardon would be honoured. In January 1537, he organized a minor rising in East Yorkshire, which failed dismally and ended with his flight and subsequent capture. In February, the Cumberland peasants, having lost patience with the local gentry, launched an unsuccessful attack on Carlisle. These two incidents gave the king a pretext to break his word in respect of a general pardon and to launch a savage reprisal. Martial law was declared in Cumberland, where many commoners were hanged, while the gentry leaders, including Aske, were rounded up, sent for trial in London, and then executed.

The important new element introduced by the Pilgrimage of Grace was in religion. Protest had taken place over religion before, the Lollards being a case in point; but Henry VIII, by breaking the Church's ties with Rome, created a dilemma in the minds of Englishmen who were loyal to their king, but also retained their traditional allegiance to the Pope as the head of the Catholic Church. Robert Aske attempted to resolve this dilemma by declaring his loyalty to the king while at the same time seeking to reverse his religious policies, and paid with his life for his temerity. However, this did not prevent others from claiming that, while violent resistance to the crown was wrong, it could not be right to accept laws made by kings when they ran counter to the law of God.

Source 35

From Henry Brinkelowe, writing under the pseudonym of Roderick Mors, *The Complaynt of Roderyck Mors*, c.1542.

Inasmuch as there is no power but of God, and whensoever any person be grieved, oppressed, or over yoked, they must resort unto the higher powers for remedy, which be ordained of God only for the same cause; and inasmuch as the Council of Parliament is the head Council of all realms, for it, being done with the consent of the King, what laws soever be made thereby, being not against the Word of God, we be bound to observe them. And though they be against God's Word, yet may we not bodily resist them with any war, violence or insurrection, under pain of damnation. But now, contrariwise, as we may not resist the power of a prince, even so may we not observe nor walk in his wicked laws, if he make any against God's word, but rather to suffer death: so that we may neither observe them nor yet violently resist them in that case.

The problem of loyalty to the crown clashing with religious conscience surfaced again in the Western Rebellion which came to a head in Cornwall and Devon in 1549. Protector Somerset and Archbishop Cranmer had driven through a Protestant reformation on behalf of the young king, Edward VI. The bible and prayer book were translated from Latin into English and the new translations were ordered to be used in all churches. Catholic practices were abolished and all images and statues were removed from churches. The strength of the opposition that the people of Devon and Cornwall felt towards these innovations is revealed clearly in the manifesto they drew up outside the walls of Exeter. Of the 16 demands made in this manifesto, only one concerned a grievance that was not of a religious nature.

Source 36

From the manifesto drawn up by the Western rebels while beseiging Exeter in 1549.

1. We will have the general counsel and holy decrees of our [Catholic] forefathers observed...and whosever shall gainsay [deny] them, we hold them as heretics.
2. We will have the laws of our sovereign Lord King Henry VIII concerning the Six Articles to be in use again....
3. We will have the mass in Latin as was before, and celebrated by the priest....
7. We will have holy bread and water made every Sunday..., images to be set up again in every church, and all other ancient old ceremonies used heretofore by our mother the holy Church.
8. We will not receive the new service because it is but like a Christmas game, but we will have our old service...in Latin not in English, as it was before. And

so we the Cornishmen (whereof certain of us [speak only Cornish and] understand no English) utterly refuse this new English.

Apart from Humphrey Arundell, who held estates near Bodmin and was chosen by the common people to lead them, the Western Rebellion attracted hardly any gentry support. The rebels marched east and beseiged Exeter for six weeks before forces under the command of Lord Russell came to the city's rescue, defeating the rebellion at Clyst St Mary and again at Sampford Courtney, after which the rebellion collapsed. The rebels had never had a chance of reversing the English Reformation, but it did cause the government some anxious moments, not so much because it was a serious threat in itself, but because it coincided with the outbreak of war against France and with the occurrence of Kett's Rebellion in Norfolk.

The rebellion in Norfolk was totally different in aims and character from that in the south-west. It began as an anti-enclosure riot in the village of Attleborough and soon spread throughout Norfolk and to large areas of Suffolk. It was essentially a revolt of the common people against the East Anglian gentry and nobility, with enclosures, high rents and over-grazing of the commons by the sheep flocks of the gentry to the detriment of the rights of ordinary people as the main grievances. Far from opposing the government's Protestant religious reforms as the Cornishmen had done, the Norfolk rebels positively welcomed them, demanding that their children be taught the principles of the Protestant religion contained in the new Book of Common Prayer and that ministers who could not preach should be deprived of their livings. The suggestion that parishioners might choose the replacement for an inadequate minister was revolutionary and was an early precursor to the demands of the Independents in the mid-seventeenth century.

Source 37

From Kett's *Demands Being in Rebellion*, 1549.

1. We pray your grace...that from henceforth, no man shall enclose any more....
3. That no lord of any manor shall common upon [share the use of] the Commons....
5. That reed ground and meadow ground may be at such price [rent] as they were in the first year of King Henry VII [1485]....
7. That all bushels [measures of grain] within your realm be of one size, that is to say,...eight gallons.
8. That priests or vicars that be not able to preach and set forth the word of God to his parishioners may be thereby put from his benefice, and the parishioners there to choose another, or else the patron or lord of the town....
11. That all freeholders and copyholders may take the profits of all commons, there to common, and the lords not to common nor take profits of the same.
14. That copyhold land that is unreasonably rented may go as it did in the first year of King Henry VII, and that at the death of a tenant or on a sale, the same lands to be charged with an easy fine [entry fee to the next tenant]....
16. That all bond men may be made free, for god made all free with his precious blood shedding....
20. That every proprietory parson or vicar having a benefice of £10 or more a year shall...teach poor men's children of their parish the book called the catechism and the primer [the Book of Common Prayer].

Led by Robert Kett, a tanner and local landowner, the rebels marched on Norwich, setting up a camp on Mousehold Heath, just outside the city, in July 1549. Three other such camps were established, one in Norfolk and the other two in Suffolk, but the largest and most disciplined was at Norwich, which was captured by the rebels a week later. Protector Somerset sent the Marquis of Northampton to crush the rebellion, but his army was routed by the rebels. However, a larger force raised by the Earl of Warwick broke the rebellion despite fierce resistance by Kett and his followers. Kett escaped but was later captured and executed, as were between 50 and 300 of his followers (estimates vary). Although the rebels suffered inevitable defeat, their uprising was not without effect, particularly in slowing down the rate of enclosures in East Anglia.

Kett's Rebellion was somewhat untypical of mid-sixteenth-century uprisings in the degree of emphasis it placed on social and economic grievances and in the Protestantism of the rebels, but in other respects it shared the characteristics of Tudor rebellions identified by Anthony Fletcher in Source 38. There were two more major uprisings in the 20 years following 1549: Wyatt's Rebellion in Kent during 1554 and the Northern Rebellion of 1569. Both were instigated by disaffected members of the ruling élite in pursuit of political and religious goals: the former reacting against Mary Tudor's decision to marry Philip II of Spain and the latter in support of the Catholic Mary Queen of Scots in the reign of Elizabeth. Although each attracted a degree of popular support, the rank and file rebels were drawn almost exclusively from the tenants and estate workers of the dissident nobles and gentlemen. After 1569, major rebellions became something of a rarity. Paul Slack (Source 39) argues that this was due to changes in the economic and social structure of England, and to an increasing tendency among the gentry and nobility to settle their differences in the courts. Peasant revolts also came to an end, although localised popular riots against injustice and food shortages continued to occur during times of hardship (Source 40) and were often successful (Source 41).

Source 38

From Anthony Fletcher, *Tudor Rebellions* (Longman, 1983) pp.101–2.

What then were the patterns and themes of the rebellions of the sixteenth century? They have the character of demonstrations. They were pursued with varying degrees of order and organization according to the capability of the gentry leadership and the emotional force of the issues involved. On the whole, Tudor rebellions were remarkably non-violent....Only one clear theme of national significance ran through the rebellions. This was the opposition of a conservative and pious society to the English Reformation....The rebels were parochial because local chantries, shrines and monasteries were of more significance to them than new statements of faith from London. In most cases they tried to besiege the provincial capital, for example Exeter, Carlisle or Norwich. And their agrarian grievances took their distinctive form from the character of particular farming regions.

Tudor rebellions then were essentially the responses of local communities to local grievances. The main thing they had in common was their provincialism. The Levellers took up this provincial thinking in the 1640s. Their third *Agreement of the People* called for the abolition of the law courts in London and the substitution of regional courts administered by locally elected sheriffs and JPs. An examination of the programme of the Levellers, in the light of late medieval and Tudor rebellions, reveals that there was also a persistent egalitarian tradition from 1381 to 1649. The ideas of John Wyclif and John Ball were submerged for much of the Tudor period because social equality was identified with anabaptism and was thus hated and feared. Egalitarianism [equal rights] emerged occasionally though with startling and dramatic force. The tensions of 1549 brought it to the surface....It was the belief in equality based on the Christian view of the brotherhood of man that caused Rainsborough to make his famous claim at the Putney Debates in 1647 on behalf of the freedom and rights of the poorer members of society [see p.28].

Source 39

From Paul Slack, 'A Divided Society', in C. Haigh (ed.), *The Cambridge Historical Encyclopedia of Great Britain and Ireland* (Cambridge, 1985) p.186.

[In the second half of the sixteenth century] the amount of naked violence fell, as property-owners fought out their disputes in the courts and took the law less often into their own hands. The business of every court in the land expanded enormously between 1500 and 1625. Rebellion also ceased, partly because of the military decline of the magnates, partly because of the disappearance of the peasantry who once led it. The last major peasant revolt was that in Norfolk in 1549; the last serious provincial rebellion was the Rising in the North twenty years later. Despite the poverty, popular dissidence and crime to which contemporaries were so sensitive, the country was in some obvious respects more orderly in 1625 than it had been in 1450.

Source 40

From Anthony Fletcher, *Tudor Rebellions*, pp.100–1.

'There is nothing will sooner lead men into sedition', Lord Burghley said, 'than dearth of victual' [shortage of food]. Although the years 1595–8 saw no major rebellion, it can be argued that this was one of the most insecure periods of Tudor government....There was a crisis of subsistence: a dramatic inflation of prices and a disastrous drop in wages led to starvation and weakened resistance to infection....

In 1596 there was a rising in Oxfordshire based on the villages of Hampton Gay and Hampton Poyle, which had been much enclosed by local gentry. The plan, until the ringleaders were arrested by the Lord Lieutenant, was to seize arms and horses from the houses of the gentry and join the London apprentices who were rumoured to have rebelled. In Norfolk in 1597 the commons assembled near Lynn and forcibly unloaded a barge laden with corn bound for Gainsborough. At Canterbury the same year the commons of the poor suburb or St Dunstans, unable to obtain food, stopped two carts carrying corn on Watling Street, after hearing rumours that it was being exported to France.

Source 41

From K. Wrightson, *English Society 1580–1680* (Hutchinson, 1982) p.179.

Riot posed no lasting threat in a society in which few men imagined any alternative form of social order. It did however play its part in the establishment of the terms on which the common people gave their assent to the existing structure of authority. There was a strong element of negotiation in the tradition of riot which both rioters and the governing classes understood. Riot was less a form of self-help than a way of demanding that certain legitimate rights of the common people be respected and that the authorities live up to the standards of their own paternalistic rhetoric. Surprisingly often, it worked.

Poverty and economic distress were the principal causes of popular disturbances during the late sixteenth and early seventeenth centuries. Famine stalked the land in years when the harvest failed, provoking food riots and increasing the numbers of vagabonds and beggars roaming the country in search of food and work. Fear of the threat that these 'masterless men' posed to the fabric of a society in which everyone was supposed to know their place led to the passing of legislation that placed responsibility for poor relief on the parish where the person was born. 'Vagabonds and rogues' were to be apprehended and returned to their own parishes, receiving a whipping in each parish through which they passed on their journey home. The Elizabethan system of poor relief alleviated the worst of the suffering, but vagrancy remained a problem [see Depth Study, Unit 1.1, Sources 19–23 for further evidence of this].

Source 42

From John Pound, *Poverty and Vagrancy in Tudor England* (Longman, 1971) pp.51–3.

Hunger [caused by successive harvest failures, especially between 1594 and 1597] was the driving force behind the disturbances, so vividly described by Edward Hext in his letter to Lord Burghley [Depth Study, Unit 1.1, Source 23], and also accounts for the considerable increase in the number of vagrants in these years. All too often it coincided with, or led to, plague....

The sheer weight of evidence had compelled the government to realise that there were many thousands of men, both in urban and rural areas, who were unemployed through no fault of their own, and that in future adequate provision would have to be made for these as well as for the old, the incapacitated and the unrepentantly vagrant. Not altogether surprisingly, in view of the recent dearth of corn, attacks were made again on enclosures....After considerable discussion, no less than seventeen separate bills were introduced, of which eleven dealt specifically with the problem of poor relief.

During the upheavals of the mid-seventeenth century the lower orders took an unprecedented role in the affairs of the nation. Increasing levels of literacy, the translation of the Bible and Prayer Book into English, and Puritanism, with its emphasis on preaching and Bible-reading, all encouraged ordinary people as never before to think for themselves on matters of religion. When Charles I's religious policies provoked political opposition from parliament, it became almost inevitable that the common people, especially those in London, would become embroiled in the conflict. Membership of Puritan congregations began to increase during the 1630s and sympathetic crowds attended the official mutilation of Prynne, Burton and Bastwick in 1637, many dipping their handkerchiefs in the victims' blood as though they were martyrs. Later in 1637, Jenny Geddes initiated a riot in St Giles' Church, Edinburgh, by hurling a stool at the head of the minister when he tried to read from the new Prayer Book that Laud had imposed on the Scots. Rioting against the English Prayer Book spread to churches throughout lowland Scotland, leading to the drawing up of the Solemn League and Covenant and the outbreak of the first of two Bishops' Wars aimed at reversing the Laudian religious reforms north of the border (see Depth Study, Unit 1.2, pp.62–3). In London, an indignant mob attacked Lambeth Palace, the London residence of Archbishop Laud.

Since religion and politics were so closely interrelated in the mid-seventeenth century, it was inevitable that ordinary people, concerned about the direction that government religious policy was taking, would become increasingly critical of other aspects of Charles I's government. A London mob, possibly instigated by John Pym and his parliamentary colleagues, bayed outside the Palace of Whitehall for the blood of the Earl of Strafford in May 1641, and probably pressurized the king into signing his death warrant. Huge crowds cheered at Strafford's execution on Tower Hill a few days later (Depth Study, Unit 2.1, Source 12).

While the events that precipitated the Civil War were played out in parliament and in the councils of the king, they occurred against a background of, and were undoubtedly influenced by, a welter of petitions from the counties and riots and demonstrations in the capital.

Source 43

A procession of Buckinghamshire petitioners en route to present a petition to parliament, 11 January 1642

The issue of abolishing episcopacy was first introduced into parliament as a result of a 'Root and Branch' petition presented by the citizens of London and was reinforced by petitions from a number of different counties. When Charles I appointed the disreputable Sir Thomas Lunsford as Lieutenant of the Tower, this was interpreted by many as the prelude to a royalist coup against parliament. The resulting riots forced the king to rescind the appointment, but did little to conciliate the mob. The impeachment by parliament of 12 bishops in December 1641 and the subsequent passing of the Bishops' Exclusion Bill were direct consequences of anti-episcopal rioting, which had prevented the bishops from attending the House of Lords. When the bishops felt it safe to return to parliament, they demanded that all measures enacted in their enforced absence should be regarded as invalid, and it was this demand that provided Pym and his colleagues with the excuse they desired to impeach them.

If the years leading up to the outbreak of the Civil War provided ordinary people, especially in London, with opportunities for greater involvement in the affairs of the nation, the war itself increased those opportunities still further. Petitions were presented and demonstrations were held with increasing frequency in support of one policy or another, but most often in favour of peace. It should come as no surprise that peace was the foremost priority for the vast majority of ordinary people because the privation and distress caused by the English Civil Wars, as with all wars, bore most heavily on those whose subsistence was most precarious. Although the extent of the suffering caused by the war is the subject of much dispute among historians and was unevenly distributed across the country, there can be little doubt that for some the destruction and economic dislocation of war, added to the bad harvests of the mid-1640s, caused real privation. The popular disturbances unleashed by this distress fuelled fears among the landowning élite that the traditional social order and their privileged place within it were under attack.

Source 44

From C. Durston, 'Phoney War – England, Summer 1642', in *History Today*, June 1992, p.17.

As the summer months [of 1642] progressed, more and more people found that the war ceased to be merely a menacing prospect and became instead a disruptive reality which intruded upon their normal domestic lives in a variety of disturbing ways....Perhaps even more alarming for the gentry and aristocracy was the gradual breakdown of the traditional social order in the localities based on deference and obedience. Early in the summer Charles had warned his opponents that if they continued to provoke a conflict they might unleash a social revolution which would 'destroy all rights and properties, all distinctions of family and merit'. Over the next few months events began to bear out this analysis. Throughout the country crowds peopled by those Richard Baxter referred to as 'tied mastiffs, newly loosed' began to petition, demonstrate and riot, sometimes verbally and physically attacking the wealthy, and destroying or confiscating their property. Violent street politics was already a well established feature of life in the capital, but such activity was now exported to hitherto quiet rural communities. Some of the most serious incidents occurred in Essex and Suffolk. During late August a large mob attacked the houses of Sir John Lucas and the Catholic Countess of Rivers, plundering or destroying their contents, attacking household servants and threatening their owners. Such rural *jacqueries* [peasant risings] raised the ominous spectre of wholesale social upheaval.

The collapse of censorship in early 1641 opened the floodgates to a torrent of pamphleteering, both religious and political, during the next 20 years. Religious sects began to flourish during and after the First Civil War, from the relatively acceptable Baptists and Congregationalists to the morally abhorrent Ranters, the socially feared Quakers and the politically dangerous Fifth Monarchists. As Puritanism had done since Elizabeth's reign, these sects attracted much of their support from the lower strata of society, particularly the skilled artisans. Other groups, such as the Levellers and the Diggers, espoused programmes that were more political than religious, demanding a revolutionary restructuring of the social, economic and political life of the country. Even more than the radical religious sects, their support tended to be drawn mainly from among urban artisans. The Leveller programme had little to offer agricultural workers, and the Digger phenomenon was too brief and their proposals too radical to attract more than a tiny handful of adherents. The conservatism of the countryside during times of radicalism in London and other urban centres has been a recurrent theme in English history. For instance, it can be detected in the support for Chartism in the nineteenth century and for left-wing socialism in the twentieth.

For fuller accounts of the development of radical religious and political groups during the English Revolution, of their degree of support among ordinary people, of the methods they employed in an attempt to influence the government, and of their stubborn resistance in the face of persecution, especially in the case of the Quakers, you should refer to Module 3 of the Depth Study.

Particular attention should be paid to the role of the parliamentary army in the development of radicalism. Cromwell's policy of recruiting men of religious conviction, who had engaged in the war 'upon a matter of conscience' and who knew what they were fighting for, created a more disciplined fighting force, but it also created an entirely new phenomenon: a thinking army. They had religious and political goals of their own, as Richard Baxter (Source 45) and the authors of *The Case of the Army Truly Stated* (Source 46) make clear.

Source 45

From *The Autobiography of Richard Baxter*. As a moderate Puritan minister, it was natural that Baxter would disapprove of the religious radicalism that affected much of the parliamentary army, especially since his *Autobiography* was not written until after the Restoration.

When the court newsbook [a Royalist news-sheet] told the world of the swarms of Anabaptists in our armies, we thought it had been a mere lie....But when I came to the army, among Cromwell's soldiers, I found a new face of things which I never dreamed of. I heard the plotting heads very hot upon that which intimated their intention to subvert both Church and state. Independency and Anabaptistry were most prevalent....

I perceived that they took the king for a tyrant and an enemy, and really intended absolutely to master him or ruin him; and that they thought...they might kill him or conquer him; and if they might conquer, they were never more to trust him than he was in their power....They said, what were the Lords of England but William the Conqueror's colonels, or the barons but his majors, or the knights but his captains? They plainly showed me that they thought God's providence would cast the trust of religion and the kingdom upon them as conquerors....They most honoured the Separatists, Anabaptists and Antinomians.

Source 46

From *The Case of the Army Truly Stated*, 1647. This pamphlet was allegedly written by five army Agitators, but the Leveller, John Wildman, is generally regarded as having played a significant part in its authorship.

The army took up arms, in judgment and conscience, for the people's just rights and liberties and not as mercenary soldiers, hired to serve an arbitrary power of the state, and...they proceeded upon the principles of right and freedom and upon the law of nature and of nations....

It is now many months since the army declared...that they would insist upon the people's interest....And yet no relief for the people in any of their oppressions, by arbitrary powers, Monopolies, injustice in the proceeding at Law, Tithes, Excise, etc. is effectually procured....We wish therefore that the bowels of compassion in the whole army might yearn towards their distressed brethren, and that they might with one consent say each to the other, come let us join together speedily to demand present redress for the people's grievances, and security for all their and our own rights and freedoms as Soldiers and Commoners.

When, after the Civil War, it appeared that these goals were being thwarted by parliament, the army rank and file showed confidence and determination in pursuing demands for religious toleration, the payment of arrears due to them, the enactment of a bill of indemnity absolving them from punishment for any acts committed during the war, the dissolution of the Long Parliament and the calling of a general election. They elected Agitators to represent their views in the General Council of the Army and in the Putney Debates; they pressurized their leaders after the Second Civil War into purging parliament and executing the king; they propounded programmes of political, social, economic and legal reform; and they organized rendezvous to demonstrate support for their aims.

The ease with which the army leaders were able to overawe the discontented rank and file at Ware and defeat them at Burford should not blind us to the influence that the Agitators were able to wield earlier, most notably during the Putney Debates, where the moderate generals were undoubtedly on the defensive against a confident and articulate group of Agitators. It was during these debates, in October 1647, that Thomas Rainsborough claimed 'that the poorest he that is in England hath a life to live as the greatest he; and therefore...every man that is to live under a government ought first by his own consent to put himself under that government; and I do think that the poorest man in England is not at all bound in a strict sense to that government that he hath not had a voice to put himself under'. Such democratic views sent shivers of alarm through the entire political élite, including Cromwell, Ireton and the other army leaders, and explain their determination to reassert their authority over the rank and file and to purge the army of Leveller influence.

There is no doubt that the collapse of censorship in 1641 played an important part in politicizing the army. The flood of unlicensed pamphlets published during the 1640s enabled radical religious sects and political reformers, most notably the Levellers, to appeal directly to all who could and would read their literature. They found their most receptive audiences among the middle and lower ranks of the army. The influence of the radical religious sects and of the Levellers is explored in detail in Module 3 of the Depth Study and therefore will not be enlarged upon here. However, their impact in both the short and the longer term is of vital importance to the development of radical protest in England. The religious sects, particularly those that survived the persecution of the Restoration years, such as the Quakers and the Baptists, broke for ever the religious monopoly of the state Church. This was achieved not by riots, rebellions or demonstrations, but by a simple and stubborn refusal to renounce sincerely held beliefs in the face of an intermittent, but at times virulent, official persecution. The Levellers, with ideas that included widening the franchise, reforming the law and abolishing tithes, were ahead of their time, as were the small Digger group led by Gerard Winstanley, who advocated a form of communism (Source 47). However, the emergence of such groups marks the genesis of popular reform movements with coherent and positive political agendas. While they were of short duration, the memory of them lingered on and provided inspiration for sturdier and more vibrant reform movements to emerge in the late eighteenth and early nineteenth centuries.

Source 47

From Gerard Winstanley, *The Law of Freedom in a Platform*, 1652. (For further information on the Diggers and their beliefs, see Depth Study, Unit 3.1, Source 23).

When mankind began to buy and sell, then did he fall from his innocence; for then they began to oppress and cozen [cheat] one another of their creation birthright. As for example: if the land belong to three persons, and two of them buy and sell the earth and the third give no consent, his right is taken from him, and his posterity is engaged in a war....Therefore this buying and selling did bring in, and still doth bring in, discontent and wars....And the nations of the world will never learn to beat their swords into ploughshares, and their spears into pruning hooks, and leave off warring, until this cheating device of buying and selling be cast out among the rubbish of kingly power.

'But shall not one man be richer than another?' There is no need of that; for riches make men vain-glorious, proud, and to oppress their brethren; and are the occasion [cause] of wars. No man can be rich, but he must be rich either by his own labours, or by the labours of other men helping him. If a man have no help from his neighbour, he shall never gather an estate of hundreds and thousands a year. If other men help him to work, then are those riches his neighbours' as well as his; for they may be the fruit of other men's labours as well as his own.

There seems to have been a significant difference between the reactions of ordinary people in the towns and cities to the upheavals of the Civil Wars and the reactions of those living in the countryside. While many of the former imbibed the political ideas of the Parliamentarian army, which they joined in considerable numbers, and of the Levellers, the vast majority of the latter tried, not always successfully, to avoid all contact with the war and the political ideas that it generated. In some areas, towards the end of the war, they formed groups of 'clubmen' (Source 48) with the intention of keeping both warring factions out of their counties, by force if necessary. Although the existence of the clubmen indicates a desire for neutralism, the activities of these groups were sporadic and ineffective, due no doubt to the inherent contradiction of seeking to use force to keep themselves out of the conflict.

Source 48

From Yves-Marie Bercé, *Revolt and Revolution in Early Modern Europe* (Manchester University Press, 1987) pp.168–9. (For further details of the aims and activities of the clubmen, see Depth Study, Unit 4.1, Sources 20–2).

The seventeenth century revolution was overwhelmingly foreign to the rural world. The communist agrarian policy of the Diggers was the work of an urban sect. The tenants and labourers of the countryside remained passive from 1640 to 1652, avoiding recruitment by the different armies, and confining themselves to self-defence reactions and to meetings of clubmen in the final years of the civil war.

The upheavals of the Civil Wars and Interregnum provided an unprecendented opportunity for women to play a more active role in the political life of the nation, especially in the peace movement during the First Civil War (Source 49) and as members of radical sects, some even becoming preachers. However, such activity was not generally welcomed (Sources 50–1), was of short duration, and did nothing in the long run to improve the status of women in society.

Source 49

From a letter written by Thomas Knyvett in August 1643, informing his wife, who was at home in Norfolk, of disturbances outside parliament. A women's peace demonstration was held on 8 August and the women returned in larger numbers the following day intent on throwing Pym and other parliamentary leaders into the river. Mounted troopers were summoned to disperse the demonstrators and in the ensuing mêlée a number of demonstrators were killed or injured.

We had fair hopes on Saturday last of some overture for peace. Six propositions drawn up by the Lords were sent down to the House of Commons....The consideration of them, after a great debate, was voted to be referred till Monday. Monday morning being come, there came down a great concourse [gathering] of people out of the city, and filled all passages [at Westminster], crying to the Lords and Commons 'No peace', 'Remember the late oath and covenant', 'We'll die in the cause' and such like acclamations, that would have made any honest peaceable spirit's heart have bled. That night it was carried by the majority against these proposals. Tuesday morning [8 August] a multitude of women came and made an outcry for peace. Some verbal satisfaction they had, and no hurt was done that day. This day [9 August] they came again in a far greater number, and fell to be more unruly, which occasioned a sadder spectacle, divers men and women being slain by the trained guard.

Source 50

From Anne Laurence, 'Women's Work and the English Civil War', in *History Today*, June 1992, pp.20 and 24–5.

Brilliana, Lady Harley of Brampton Bryan, is one of the best known of several valiant women famous for defending their husband's castles during the English Civil War. It is known that women petitioned parliament and took part in other forms of demonstration, often to try to stop the war, to secure pensions as war widows, or for the release of their husbands from gaol....Something is known, too, of the secondary effects of the Revolution upon women's lives: how they played an important part in the radical religious congregations of the 1640s and 1650s....

Women's petitioning was regarded by men in two ways, according to whether it was being done for or against them. It seems generally to have been regarded as appropriate for widows to petition for pensions and other women for relief for disabled or imprisoned husbands. But where their demands had a political content, petitioning seems to have been regarded as an unsuitable activity for women. The Leveller wives were energetic petitioners for their husbands' release from gaol but did not miss the opportunity to make political demands as well. A member of the House of Commons sent away Elizabeth Lilburne and her companions in 1649 telling her that it was not for women to petition, they should stay at home and wash the dishes....

It is clear that women were involved in the war effort, in particular in providing goods and services to the armies and in running estates and businesses in the absence of husbands. The war provided many women with the opportunity to exercise initiative in public in ways which had not been possible in peacetime. But there seems to have been little long-term benefit for working women or change in attitudes to women's public activity. Indeed, there seems to have been a reaction against women's participation in, for example, religious life....So whilst modern wars may be seen to promote women's emancipation, it is possible to argue that in the long term the English Civil War limited, rather than expanded, the opportunities open to them.

Source 51

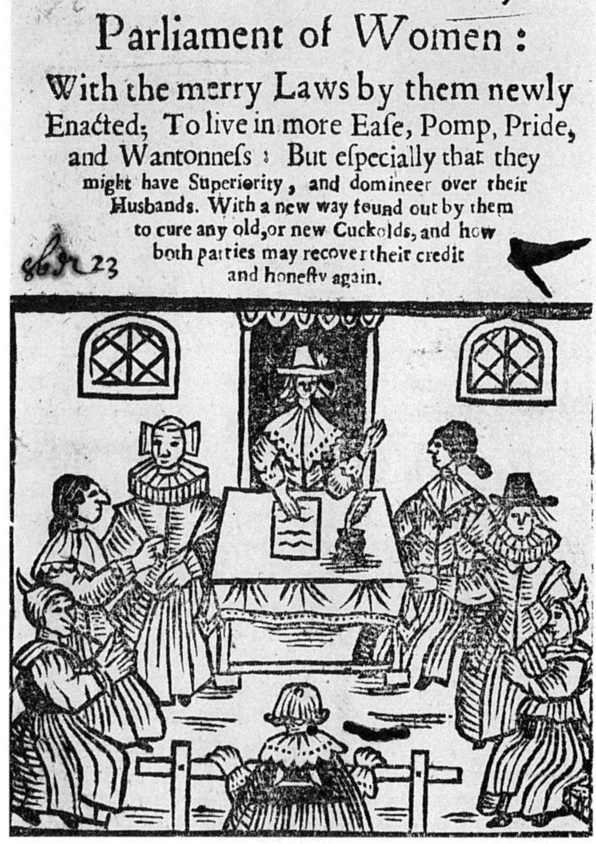
THE

Parliament of Women:

With the merry Laws by them newly Enacted; To live in more Ease, Pomp, Pride, and Wantonness: But especially that they might have Superiority, and domineer over their Husbands. With a new way found out by them to cure any old, or new Cuckolds, and how both parties may recover their credit and honesty again.

The title page from The Parliament of Women, *a pamphlet published in 1646 satirizing the more active role in public life played by women during the Civil War*

The restoration of the monarchy in 1660 was brought about by elements of the political élite, among whom George Monck, Edward Hyde and the Presbyterian MPs Monck enabled to resume their seats in the Long Parliament played crucial roles. However, the London mob, which had frequently influenced events by its unruly demonstrations during the previous 20 years, did so again in 1659 and 1660 to significant effect. Serious anti-army riots in December 1659 among the London apprentices, reported by Thomas Rugg in his *Diurnal* (Depth Study, Unit 2.5, Source 151), contributed to the downfall of the Committee of Safety; while the increasing opposition of the Londoners to the Rump in the ensuing months strengthened Monck's hand when he decided to readmit the secluded members as a prelude to the dissolution of the Long Parliament and the calling of fresh elections. Samuel Pepys recorded in his diary in February 1660 that 'boys do now cry 'Kiss my Parliament' instead of 'Kiss my arse', so great and general contempt is the Rump come to among all men'. A few days later, Pepys noted being able to see 31 bonfires at one glance from the Strand bridge and that everywhere people were roasting 'rumps' of beef to express their contempt for the Rump Parliament.

Source 52

A seventeenth-century playing card depicting the 'roasting of the Rump' in February 1660

The century after 1660 witnessed a predictable reaction against the excesses of popular political activity, as the landowning élite sought to ensure that the threat of social revolution, so narrowly averted during the 1640s and 1650s, did not return to menace them again. In this they were helped considerably by an upturn in the economy: the steep rise in population and inflation which had made the first half of the seventeenth century a period of severe distress for the poor came to an end in the 1650s and was followed by a period of stable population and prices, increasing agricultural output and rising prosperity for ordinary people (see Depth Study, Unit 1.1, pp.25–9).

While riots and popular demonstrations became less frequent, religion in particular was still capable of harnessing popular emotions and prejudices to direct action. The conversion of James, Duke of York, to Catholicism, together with the open practice of Catholicism at court, led to a wave of anti-Catholic hysteria which was given form and substance by Titus Oates' revelations in 1678 of what he claimed to be a Popish Plot to kill the king and place James on the throne. Encouraged, intentionally or otherwise, by Shaftesbury and the Whigs, who mounted a determined but unsuccessful campaign to exclude James from succession to the throne, London mobs attacked Catholics, organized pope-burning processions (Source 53) and demonstrated in favour of the Exclusion Bills that Shaftesbury forced through parliament and tried to pressurize the king into signing.

Source 53

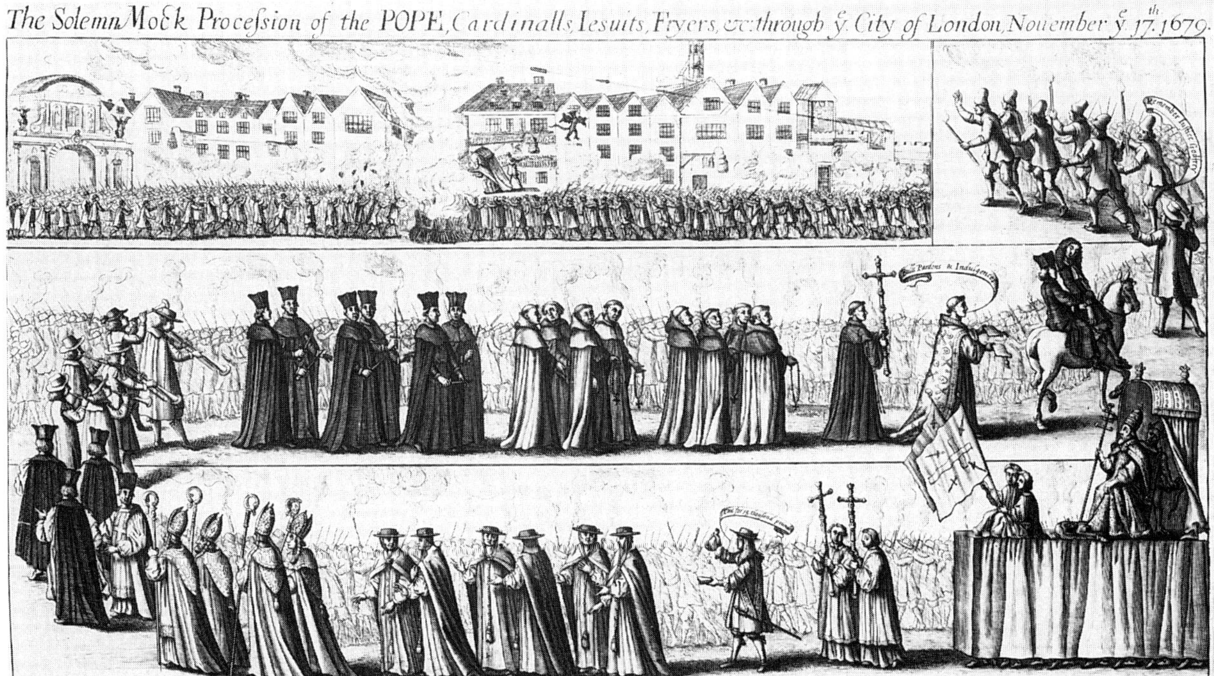

A pope-burning procession, 1679

The failure of the Exclusionists to bar James from the succession to the throne and his subsequent coronation as James II in 1685 brought about the last major armed uprising in England, Monmouth's Rebellion. The Duke of Monmouth, an illegitimate son of Charles II, claimed that he was legitimate and therefore the rightful king. It is unlikely that many of the thousands of West Countrymen who flocked to his banner when he landed in Dorset in 1685 believed in his legitimacy; more important to them was his Protestantism. Although he assembled an army of over 6,000, mostly artisans and agricultural workers, his force was poorly armed and failed to attract the support from the gentry and nobility that was essential if he was to succeed in overthrowing the king. The rebellion also suffered from incompetent and indecisive leadership and was brought to a predictable end at the Battle of Sedgemoor, the last battle to be fought on English soil. Monmouth was executed, despite grovelling pleas for clemency, and Judge Jeffreys presided over a vindictive orgy of reprisals, sentencing over 1,300 to death and many more to be sold into slavery in the West Indies. The viciousness of Jeffreys' 'Bloody Assizes' contributed to the unpopularity of James II and to his downfall three years later.

The accession of William and Mary can be seen as a watershed in the involvement of ordinary people in direct political protest. Previously in their riots, rebellions and protests, they had sought the leadership of disaffected members of the political élite. After 1689, however, a new degree of co-operation and trust developed between the king and parliament, so that henceforth political conflict was fought out at court and in parliament between rival factions vying for royal favour and electoral support, depriving rebels of their traditional leaders. Apart from a brief period in the early 1700s when Henry Sacheverell raised the cry of 'the Church in danger', religion became less important politically during the eighteenth century and lost its ability to unite gentry, nobility and commoners in rebellious defence of cherished Protestant beliefs. The political élite also closed ranks to ensure that 'those who do not rule' had little opportunity to use the power to protest to influence those in authority. Nevertheless, as H.T. Dickinson explains in Source 54, the populace retained a latent power which they were capable of employing when sufficently roused.

Source 54

From H.T. Dickinson, 'The Precursors of Political Radicalism in Augustan Britain', in C. Jones (ed.), *Britain in the First Age of Party* (Hambledon, 1987) pp.81–2.

Direct involvement in elections, pressure groups...and borough politics was largely confined to the middling orders. Only occasionally did political activity of this kind involve the poorer sections of society. Nevertheless, the lower orders did engage in direct action which proved capable of influencing the political decisions of the governing élite. In numerous crowd demonstrations the poor revealed...a capacity for effective collective action, though they never developed a coherent [theory of revolution]. Most riots were caused by social and economic grievances but the poor did occasionally involve themselves in disputes which raised wider political issues. They rioted in 1688–9 in support of the Glorious Revolution and they rioted in 1710 and 1715–16 when they identified the Court Whigs with the unpopular monied interests. The poor did not expect to control who would govern them, but they were prepared to take direct action in order to restrict how the ruling oligarchy should exercise its authority.

One way in which the government sought to prevent popular protest was by muzzling the press (Source 55), which had exerted increasing influence since the appearance of a spate of anti-Laudian pamphlets during the 1630s, and which was blamed, with considerable justification, for fomenting popular disorders during the 1640s and 1650s and again during the Exclusion Crisis. Public resentment against attempts to prevent press reporting and criticism of parliamentary debates and government policies was widespread (Source 56), and attempts to restrict public access to political news were largely unsuccessful. However, government fears of the dangers of emotive, rabble-rousing political journalism were shown to be well-founded when, in 1763, John Wilkes published in his newspaper the *North Briton* an attack on the King's Speech at the opening of parliament, which made reference to the recently concluded Peace of Paris, ending the Seven Years' War (Source 57). Wilkes' brand of journalism had already won him considerable popularity among the London mob, who held large unruly demonstrations in support of 'Wilkes and Liberty' following his arrest on charges of seditious libel.

Source 55

From entries in the House of Commons' Journal in 1694 referring to the illicit reporting of parliamentary debates.

21 December. A complaint being made to this House that Dyer, a News Letter writer, has presumed in his News

Letter to take notice of the proceedings of this House; Resolved, that the said Dyer be summoned...to attend this House...to answer the said complaint.

22 December....Ordered, that the said Dyer be brought to the Bar and, upon his knees, reprimanded by Mr. Speaker for his great presumption....Resolved, that no News Letter writers do, in their letters or other papers that they disperse, presume to intermeddle with the debates or any other proceedings of this House.

Source 56

From a letter to an MP written in 1697.

Sir, according to your commands, I here present you with those reasons that oblige me to oppose the restraining of the Press, as inconsistent with the Protestant religion and dangerous to the liberties of the nation....The greatest enjoyment that rational and sociable creatures are capable of is to employ their thoughts on what subject they please, and to communicate them to one another as freely as they think them; and herein consists the dignity and freedom of human nature, without which no other liberty can be secure. For what is it that enables a few tyrants to keep almost all mankind in slavery but their narrow and wrong notions of government? Which is owing to the discouragement they lie under of mutually communicating, and consequently of employing, their thoughts on political matters....The arts of state, in most countries, being to enslave the people or to keep them in slavery, it became a crime to talk, much more to write, about political matters: and ever since printing has been invented, there have been in most places state-licensers, to hinder men from freely writing about government; for which there can be no other reason than to prevent the defects of either the government or the management of it from being discovered and amended.

Source 57

From John Wilkes, the *North Briton*, No. 45, 1763.

I am sure all foreigners, especially the King of Prussia, will hold the minister in contempt and abhorrence. He has made our Sovereign declare: 'My expectations have been fully answered by the happy effects which the several allies of my Crown have derived from this...treaty. The powers at war with my good brother the King of Prussia have...been induced to agree to such terms of accommodation as that great Prince has approved; and the success which has attended my negotiations has...diffused the blessings of peace throughout...every part of Europe.' The infamous fallacy of this whole sentence is apparent to all mankind....No advantage has accrued to that magnanimous Prince from our negotiations, but he was basely deserted by the Scottish Prime Minister [the Earl of Bute].

After the affair of the *North Briton* had died down, popular demonstrations and riots in support of Wilkes erupted once more in 1768 during the 'Middlesex Election' crisis, when Wilkes was elected as MP for Middlesex and the king persuaded parliament to refuse him the right to take his seat (see Development Study, Unit 1.5, p.126). The involvement of the populace in elections, even though they had no right to vote, became commonplace by the eighteenth century and was a corollary of the changing relationship between election candidates and the voters (Source 58). Once candidates began to court the electorate, the non-voting populace had a role to play that included boisterous demonstrations by supporters in favour of their candidate (Source 59), violent disruption of the meetings of opposing candidates and intimidation of voters.

Source 58

A cartoon drawn in 1780 contrasting the relationship between electors and election candidates in 1580 and 1780. On the left, a reluctant sixteenth-century gentleman is requested by the electors of his county to represent them in parliament. On the right, a dandy and a businessman bribe electors to vote for them.

Source 59

A detail from William Hogarth's satirical engraving, The Election, *c.1740, showing a candidate and his supporters being impeded by a busker*

The property-owning classes tried to maintain a tight control over the populace through the influence of squire and parson, backed up by repressive measures such as the Game Laws, the Riot Act of 1715 and the Waltham Black Act of 1723 which increased substantially the number of offences for which capital punishment could be inflicted. Nevertheless, it would be an exaggeration to describe eighteenth-century England as a peaceful and orderly society. Mob violence and rioting was a regular occurrence as ordinary people continued to mount spirited defences of their interests on occasions. However, unrest tended to be localized, of brief duration and the aims of the rioters were usually limited to redressing specific grievances and injustices. Only occasionally was unrest widespread and even more rarely did it pursue overtly political goals.

The most common causes of disturbances were food shortages, recruiting, enclosures and turnpikes. Of these, food riots were the most frequent. There was nothing new about protests against the scarcity and high prices of basic foodstuffs; such disturbances had occurred since the beginning of the sixteenth century, if not earlier. However, the eighteenth century saw a dramatic increase in their frequency and a change in their nature. While privation continued to affect ordinary people in years of poor harvest, the threat of starvation had receded and consequently riots were less likely to be desperate reactions against famine, and tended increasingly to be concerned with lowering prices and preventing food from being shipped to other areas. National waves of food rioting occurred in 1709–10, 1727–9, 1739–40, 1756–7, 1766–8, 1772–3, 1783, 1795–6, 1799–1801, 1810–3 and 1816–8, and local disturbances were even more frequent. The rioters were much more likely to be the urban poor than the rural poor, since the latter had easier access to food supplies. The riots usually had limited aims such as the seizure and enforced sale of foodstuffs at 'fair' prices, forcing dealers and local authorities to reduce prices, and attacking mills and warehouses when they failed to do so. In most cases, disturbances were surprisingly orderly, with virtually no loss of life, and were often successful in forcing price reductions. In some areas, the local authorities were clearly in sympathy with the rioters. By the early nineteenth century, the incidence of food riots was in steep decline as trade unionism and political organization among ordinary people began to gain ground, leading to more frequent demands for improved pay and conditions of work, accompanied by strikes and other forms of industrial action.

The recruiting riots began in 1757 following the passing of a Militia Act which introduced a system of recruitment for local militias whereby a proportion of the able-bodied men of each parish was selected by drawing lots and required to serve for a period of three years. Riots broke out in many counties with the aim of preventing the implementation of the new method of recruitment and met with some success. In some areas the local gentry refused to implement the Act in the face of strong public hostility and by 1759 only half of the projected number of troops had been selected. Recruiting riots continued intermittently in some counties until the end of the century, sometimes occasioning loss of life. The worst incident occurred in Northumberland in 1761 when a crowd of 5,000 forced the abandonment of the selection process at Morpeth and then marched to Hexham, where they were fired on by the Yorkshire Militia causing over one hundred casualties, of whom about half were fatal.

Anti-enclosure riots were nothing new and it is hardly surprising that quite a number occurred during the second half of the eighteenth century, since the incidence of enclosures was greater then than at any other time in history. More than 2,000 Enclosure Acts were passed between 1750 and 1800 and there were countless private agreements to enclose. In view of the rate of enclosure at this time, what is striking is not the opposition to enclosure but its comparative rarity. Ordinary people were not opposed to enclosures in principle, but took action on those occasions when they felt a sense of injustice at the loss of customary common grazing rights or felt that the allocation of enclosed land was being carried out to their detriment.

Turnpike roads with their frequent toll-gates were resented as an indirect form of taxation and in some areas were believed to contribute to increasing the local prices of food and other goods. As with enclosure riots, the incidence of anti-turnpike disturbances, which usually amounted to the destruction of turnpike houses and toll-gates, was small in comparison to the number of roads built. Nevertheless, there were some serious outbreaks of violence between 1725 and 1750, especially in Gloucestershire, Herefordshire and West Yorkshire.

Apart from the London demonstrations in support of 'Wilkes and Liberty', the main politically motivated risings in the eighteenth century were the 1715 and 1745 Jacobite Rebellions and the Gordon Riots of 1780. In the Jacobite Rebellions, the peasantry of the Scottish Highlands joined their clan chiefs in supporting the abortive claims to the throne of James Edward Stuart, the 'Old Pretender', in 1715 and of his son, 'Bonnie Prince Charlie', in 1745. The Gordon Riots of 1780 were the most serious civil commotion to occur in England during the last 300 years. Lord George Gordon, president of the recently formed Protestant Association, incited anti-Catholic riots in London in an unsuccessful attempt to force the government to rescind the Catholic Relief Act passed two years earlier in 1778. The rioting lasted for more than a week with the authorities powerless to bring it under control until more than 10,000 troops were drafted into London for the purpose. By the time order was restored, 300 people had lost their lives and property worth more than £100,000 had been destroyed.

Source 60

The burning of Newgate Prison during the anti-Catholic Gordon Riots, 1780

While the Gordon Riots were the most serious upheaval in eighteenth-century England, they took place against a backdrop of lawlessness that the authorities were often hard pressed to keep under control, as Roy Porter argues in Source 61. The fact that control was ultimately maintained was due to the survival of deeply ingrained beliefs in deference and the existing social and political order (Source 62), and to the rioters' concern with opposing unpopular change and injustice within the existing system rather than demanding changes to the system itself.

Source 61

From Roy Porter, *English Society in the Eighteenth Century* (Penguin, 1982) pp.113–20.

Recent historians...have dynamited the idyll of Georgian harmony....Crime was rife and could be bloody....There was a continual hubbub of verbal violence: newspapers, cartoons, and street ballads attacking their targets with scabrous insults; political sermons thundered from pulpits...and crowds often took the law into their own hands. Brothels were rifled by disgruntled punters, homosexuals stoned to death in the pillory....Crowds, often led by women, would break in to stop farmers and dealers selling corn above fixed prices...or would attack mills and granaries, sometimes wielding firearms, to prevent grain being bulk-shipped elsewhere in times of local shortage. Bread and food riots were endemic, not least because they were successful. In 1740 disturbances paralysed Norwich for five days over the price of mackerel. Bloody food riots in Somerset and Wiltshire in 1766–7 involved attacks on stores and looting: 3,000 troops were sent in. Turnpike gates, hated as a new concealed tax, were rooted up....Strikes for higher wages and machine-breaking to halt the installation of new technology were commonplace....Over 400 labour disputes have been recorded during the century....Fear of popery sparked the Gordon Riots in London in 1780....The city lay paralysed in the hands of the crowd for a week; £100,000 of damage was done to property (ten times as much as in Paris throughout the French Revolution) before troops restored order at the cost of 290 citizens' lives....

Alarm was well founded, partly because the fabric of law enforcement was patchy. Most parishes boasted only an amateur constable or two: aided by community vigilance these could cope with petty crime but not with disturbances. Faced with disaffection, mayors and JPs sometimes trembled to act....In any case they lacked disciplined, readily mobilized forces, for there was no national police to summon....

Yet the political fabric – much abused, pulled, torn, tattered, and patched – was never ripped up. If the sociopolitical nation really had been verging on anarchy or revolution, the Jacobite rebellions of 1715 and 1745, or the Gordon Riots, would have sparked explosion. But crypto-Jacobite sympathies – though widespread – did not lead to people taking up arms in England; the Gordon Riots did not spread beyond London or become a general cause, and most radical bodies of the 1790s such as the Friends of the People (1791) and the London Corresponding Society (1792) expected to carry the day through reason.... Piecemeal violence never turned into general insurrection.

Why? One reason for this was the particular protocol of rioting. Protesters' aims were usually concrete, defensive, and limited, such as the restoration of long-standing wage-rates or rights of way. Their appeal was to a traditional order, to be restored by society's traditional leaders. The crowd did not want to direct the grain market itself, still less abolish private property in grain; it wanted magistrates to enforce the regulatory statutes....And once a mob had aired its grievances – uprooted a toll gate, destroyed a recruiting office – it dispersed.

Source 62

From John Stevenson, *Popular Disturbances in England 1700–1832* (Longman, 1992) pp.320–2.

Politically, it can be argued that much eighteenth-century protest was ultimately deferential. Apart from those elements in the early part of the century which were explicitly Jacobite, participants in the disturbances either expressed no political feelings at all or affirmed their loyalty while protesting against specific grievances. Mobs who acted against dissenters, Catholics and other minorities often claimed to be doing so on behalf of 'Church and King'. Handbills and anonymous letters often ended with a 'loyalist' slogan and there was even an occasion when food rioters, having concluded the unloading of a barge, gave a rendition of 'God Save the King'....

Riots, however, were frequently the arena in which the gentry were reminded forcibly of their obligations....The scarcely veiled and sometimes openly revealed point that the country could only be governed short of a reign of terror by the compliance of the governed was one of the ways in which riots and disturbances re-negotiated relations between the elements of eighteenth-century society....What was often striking was the way in which the boundaries of legality were often stretched or broken with only little retribution on the part of the authorities....

There were limits to the deference shown by English 'mobs'....The beliefs that Englishmen were not 'slaves'...and were possessed of a 'birthright' were frequently articulated in slogans, handbills, and popular rhymes, and appear often to have been derived from the religious and constitutional struggles of the seventeenth century. Appeals were commonly made to the 'Norman Yoke' and the 'Golden Age' of Alfred and Saxon Democracy, to the memory of Cromwell and the dismissal of the Rump, and the Whig martyrs, Sidney and Russell [executed after the discovery of the Rye House Plot in 1683].

Religion lost much of its potency as a political issue during the eighteenth century, although it would be a gross exaggeration to suggest that it became unimportant. Attendance at Anglican service on Sundays, or indeed at any kind of religious service, was no longer compulsory and many ministers complained of falling congregations and worsening morals. Nevertheless, prejudice against Catholicism was still fierce enough to generate an incident such as the Gordon Riots, and opposition to Protestant nonconformity, although often muted, remained strong. In times of stress, Quakers, Unitarians and other nonconformists were sometimes attacked as scapegoats for a variety of ills. The group that elicited the most divergent reactions was the newly emergent Methodists. Their doctrine that even the poorest and humblest were important in God's eyes attracted widespread support among ordinary people, but their practice of preaching in the open air, the socially disruptive belief that people were equal before God and the jealousy of Anglican ministers led many local gentry and clergy to incite crowds to disrupt Methodist meetings and attack their preachers.

Source 63

From Michael Reed, *The Georgian Triumph 1700–1830* (Routledge and Kegan Paul, 1983) pp.22–6.

It is...possible to exaggerate the spiritual [apathy] of the eighteenth century. On 2 April 1739 John Wesley preached his first open-air sermon to an assembly in Bristol. His message of salvation for all those who would put their faith in Christ, no matter how poor or ignorant, had an enormous impact. The social and ecclesiastical 'establishment' found his emotional methods distasteful, his theology distasteful, even impertinent, and, even more important, the large crowds that he attracted, composed as they were of labourers, were seen as a threat to social order....To the poor agricultural labourer, collier or handloom-weaver he brought hope, and with it the right and the obligation to belong to the local societies that sprang up all over the country, but more especially in the industrial areas of Yorkshire, Durham, Derbyshire, Staffordshire and South Wales.

From the Industrial Revolution to the twentieth century

Questions

7. How have the Industrial Revolution and developments during the nineteenth and twentieth centuries affected the rights and freedoms of ordinary people?
8. What developments took place between the eighteenth and twentieth centuries in:
   (a) the sorts of people who took part in popular protest?
   (b) the issues over which they protested?
   (c) the methods they employed?
   (d) the ability of protesters to achieve their aims?

One of the most fundamental changes to have affected the lives, rights and powers of ordinary people was the transition during the late eighteenth and early nineteenth centuries from small-scale cottage industries to production based on large factory units, together with the urbanization, mechanisation and improvements in power and transport that are known collectively as the Industrial Revolution.

Source 64

From Michael Reed, *The Georgian Triumph 1700–1830*, pp.129–31, 153–5, and 215–9.

The family and household were of basic importance not only to the social organisation of eighteenth-century Britain, but also to its economic organisation. They constituted the basic unit of industrial and manufacturing enterprise no less than of husbandry and agriculture, which is why such enterprises were very small in scale....It was the household that was the basic unit of manufacture, with very many of the actual manufacturing processes being carried out in workshops which were physically part of the house of the craftsman or artisan who performed them.

But the craftsman did not work alone. The labour of wife and children made as important a contribution to family prosperity as that of husband. Moreover, their contribution is to be found across the entire spectrum of economic activity, including manual labour of the heaviest kind in agriculture and mining....Much production...was carried out at home, in conditions of heat, noise and squalor that are almost impossible now to re-create. The low level of technology meant that long hours of work were necessary before even a modest reward could be earned....The domestic craftsman was supplied with his raw materials, and frequently also with his tools, and the finished goods were bought from him by someone who is probably best described as a dealer....

The normal manufacturing enterprise for much of the eighteenth century was domestic and small-scale. The journey to work was the exception, and buildings devoted solely to industrial and commercial purposes were unusual. This is why the large-scale enterprises which did slowly appear during the course of the eighteenth century seemed so astonishing and so extraordinary to contemporaries....Coalbrookdale, where there were several industrial plants in close proximity to one another, was considered one of the wonders of Europe....

The increasing scale upon which water power was utilised, and then its gradual replacement by steam power, wrought the most profound changes throughout the entire fabric of eighteenth-century Britain. The domestic basis of manufacture was slowly broken down as more and more machinery was concentrated under one roof, although it had by no means entirely disappeared by 1830. Mechanisation came first to the spinning of cotton. The resulting bottleneck in weaving brought a period of unparalleled prosperity to the domestic handloom weaver and it was the 1820s before this began to be seriously threatened.

As manufacture ceased to be domestic in its organisation so the structure of the family and household was changed. Apprentices disappeared, and servants became exclusively domestic in their functions and a symbol of middle-class prosperity rather than assistants in small-scale manufacturing processes. The demand for female labour in the cotton mills brought considerable change to family structure. It became quite common for an elderly relative to be taken into the family to act as a child-minder whilst the mother went out to work....

Machinery may have been taken out of the home, but those who worked in the new factories had to be housed close by because their own means of reaching the factory was by walking. Workers' housing in semi-rural surroundings was fairly satisfactory, at least to contemporaries, largely because there was little overcrowding. It was only when factories began to be built in close proximity in towns and on the coalfields that rows upon rows of mean streets and courts appeared, creating conditions of gross overcrowding which were exacerbated by the total lack of sanitation engineering from which all suffered to a greater or lesser extent. It is the 1790s before conditions become so bad that they begin to impinge upon the consciousness of contemporaries and then only in the most rapidly growing industrial towns....

The transport system of eighteenth-century Britain was slow, cumbersome, expensive, unreliable and uneven.

Indeed to call it a system at all is to suggest that it possessed uniformity, cohesion and central direction, whereas these were the very things which it lacked. The coming of the railway in 1830 brought a smoothness, efficiency and speed to transport which make it almost impossible for generations living in a post-railway age to appreciate what had gone before....

If the rural and urban landscapes of Britain in 1830 had changed dramatically since 1714 [as a result of the agrarian and industrial revolutions] then in comparison the institutions guiding the relationships of the men and women who inhabited these landscapes had changed remarkably little. The formal structures of political power in Britain showed almost no signs of change between 1714 and 1830, although it was becoming very clear to many people that change was both long overdue and very necessary....Similarly, there had been very little change in the institutions of local government. Counties were still administered by justices of the peace, who were still drawn almost exclusively from the landed gentry....County justices of the peace were gradually deprived of many of their administrative functions during the course of the nineteenth century, beginning with the Poor Law Amendment Act of 1834, but it was 1888 before elected county councils were created to take their place. The administration of English and Welsh boroughs...also remained unchanged throughout the period....

Many old social ties were broken down by the drift of population into towns, although kinship networks remained important for recruitment into factories. In the countryside enclosure was undoubtedly a contributory factor to the pauperisation of the agricultural labourer from the 1790s, and the night sky over south-eastern England was ablaze with burning ricks in the autumn of 1830 as the Captain Swing riots released pent-up resentment....

Although the social structure of Britain remained, formally at any rate, almost unchanged, the 1790s and succeeding decades saw a greater, more radical and more popularly based questioning of the whole fabric of society than had taken place in Britain since the period of the Commonwealth in the seventeenth century. This popular radicalism was feared because of its associations with the French Revolution, and for much of the period of the Napoleonic Wars almost every suggestion for reform, however mild, was condemned out of hand as savouring of Jacobinism. Nevertheless this radicalism was one of the contributors to the quickening of social awareness that is also discernible from the 1790s as the grim problems created by industrialisation became more and more apparent.

It was almost inevitable that fundamental changes in the economic structure of Britain without corresponding changes in its social and political systems would lead to the emergence of new forms of protest more radical in nature, pursuing more coherent political aims and employing more sophisticated techniques than those that were characteristic of the pre-industrial age. The Industrial Revolution created both the need for reform, as the standard of living fell for those housed in the tightly packed back-to-back dwellings of the new industrial towns, and the means by which more effective agitation for reform could take place. People living and working in close proximity to each other could be organized more effectively than those dispersed more widely in the mainly rural economy that had prevailed until the mid-eighteenth century, and improvements in transport, especially the development of speedy and efficient railway communications, made possible for the first time the development of national trade union and reform movements and provided ordinary people with more ready access to national news.

Two main categories of protest movement can be discerned during the late eighteenth and early nineteenth centuries. One looked back to a mythical golden age of rural harmony and found its expression in blind destructive protest against industrialization and against innovation that threatened the traditional livelihoods of ordinary people. The other, which was eventually to dominate as people came to recognize that the march of progress could not be halted, accepted the changes and sought improved living and working conditions and increased political rights for ordinary people. Typical of those in the first category were the Luddites, the followers of 'Captain Swing' and the Rebecca rioters.

Luddism originated in the stocking industry of Nottinghamshire, Derbyshire and Leicestershire in 1811–12 and subsequently spread to the Yorkshire woollen and Lancashire cotton districts. Letters and proclamations began to appear bearing the signature of the apparently fictitious 'Ned Ludd', 'King Ludd' or 'General Ludd' and threatening to wreck new machinery that was held responsible, at least in part, for the unemployment, short-time working and wage reductions in the textile industries during the latter years of the Napoleonic Wars.

Source 65

From a letter sent to the owner of a Huddersfield woollen mill, 1812.

Sir, Information has just been given in that you are a holder of those detestable Shearing Frames, and I was desired by my men to write to you, and to give you fair warning to pull them down....If they are not taken down by the end of next week, I shall send one of my lieutenants with at least 300 men to destroy them, and furthermore take notice that if you give us the trouble of coming thus far, we will increase your misfortune by burning your buildings down to ashes, and if you...fire at any of my men, they have orders to murder you and burn all your housing....*Signed by the General of the Army of Redressers, Ned Ludd.*

At the height of the disturbances in Nottinghamshire, Derbyshire and Leicestershire, more than a thousand stocking frames were destroyed in at least 100 separate attacks, prompting the government to draft 2000 troops to the area to restore order. This was the largest force ever deployed in England to deal with a local disorder. In Yorkshire, the most serious incidents were the attack by 150 armed men on William Cartwright's mill in Spen Valley in April 1812, during which two Luddites were killed, and the murder of the mill-owner, William Horsfall, near Huddersfield a fortnight later. Following these incidents, 64 people were tried for murder, 17 of whom were hanged. The worst incidents in Lancashire also occurred in April 1812, culminating in the destruction of Burton's Mill at Middleton, during which several rioters were killed and wounded by soldiers who tried unsuccessfully to protect the mill. Although the authorities were somewhat slow to act, by the end of 1812 order had been restored in all the areas affected by Luddism. Minor outbreaks occurred again in 1814 and 1816, but the relatively short duration of the Luddite phenomenon may well owe much to the early stirrings of trade unionism and the use of strike action as more positive and effective means of influencing employers.

Machine-breaking was also a feature of the 'Captain Swing' riots that broke out in Kent in 1830 and spread rapidly across much of southern and eastern England, although in this case the wrath of the rioters was directed against the introduction of agricultural machinery, especially threshing machines. Population growth and innovations in farming methods had been gradually lowering rural living standards for decades, but it was the distress caused by the poor harvest of 1830 that fanned seething resentment into violent action. While there were other grievances, such as low wages, the payment of tithes and the introduction of cheap Irish labour, the use of agricultural machinery leading to a reduction in manpower on farms was the principal grievance, and threatening letters signed by the mythical 'Captain Swing' (Source 66), rick-burning and the destruction of machinery were the main forms of protest employed. Stationing troops in the affected areas was sufficient in most cases to bring the disturbances to an end, and by 1832 the riots had virtually ceased. Almost 2,000 people, mainly agricultural labourers, were tried for their part in the disturbances, of whom 19 were executed, over 600 imprisoned and almost 500 transported to penal colonies in Australia.

Source 66

this is to inform you
what you have to underg[o]
Gentelmen if providing you
Dont pull down your mas-
chines and rise the poor
mens wages the maried
men give tow and six
pence a day a day the
singel tow shilings or we
will burn down your
barns and you in them
this is the last notis
from [illegible]

A 'Captain Swing' letter, 1830

Neither the Luddites nor the Swing rioters achieved anything more than venting their frustrations on a few luckless factory-owners and farmers, but the Rebecca rioters achieved more tangible results from their violent protests against toll-gates in south-west Wales during 1839–42. The rioters, led by a man dressed as a woman and calling himself 'Rebecca', were protesting against the increasing number of turnpike toll-gates and high tolls, especially on lime. After the destruction of the new workhouse at Narberth and a toll-gate at Efailwen in 1839, the riots ceased until 1842–3, when turnpike gates were destroyed through much of south-west Wales. The most serious incidents occurred in June 1843 at Carmarthen and in September at Hendy (Source 67). The death of the aged female gate-keeper in the incident at Hendy lost the Rebecca rioters public sympathy and the disturbances ended as suddenly as they had begun. Although a small number of rioters were imprisoned or transported, an Act passed in 1844 reorganized the turnpike trusts and reduced the tolls on lime by half.

Source 67

From Joseph Irving, *Annals of Our Time*, 1869.

June 10, 1843. Disturbances at Carmarthen by 'Rebecca and her Daughters'. They marched through the town about 1,000 strong, took possession of the workhouse, and remained till the afternoon, when they were broken up by a troop of dragoons sent from Cardiff, and eighty of them taken prisoners. The following evening another mob assembled, Rebecca being on horseback in full attire. They set out for St. Clears; there they demolished the turnpike gate. This destruction of turnpike gates by bands of disguised Rebeccaites continued for months to almost a nightly occurrence in different parts of South Wales....

September 10, 1843. Rebecca and her followers murder an old woman, keeper of a tollgate. Government offer a reward of £500 for the discovery of the ringleaders, and afterwards appoint a Special Commission to inquire into the operation of the Turnpike Laws in Wales.

The origins of popular agitation *for* reform in the interests of ordinary people as opposed to agitation *against* reforms that damaged their interests can be traced to the demonstrations in support of John Wilkes in the 1760s (Unit 1.5, pp.126 and Unit 2.2 pp.234–5). In insisting that the election of Wilkes as MP for Middlesex be accepted as valid despite all the efforts of the king and parliament to prevent it, the Middlesex voters and the demonstrators who thronged the streets of London championing Wilkes's cause were campaigning for recognition of MPs as genuine representatives of their constituents. This, together with the democratic ideas unleashed by the American Revolution, fuelled demands for parliamentary reform from radical groups such as the Society for Constitutional Information founded by John Cartwright in 1780, which pressed for reforms including manhood suffrage, annual parliaments and the abolition of rotten boroughs.

Source 68

From a *Declaration of those Rights of the Commonalty of Great Britain, without which they cannot be Free*, a pamphlet distributed by the Society for Constitutional Information c.1782.

It is declared,

First, That the government of this realm, and the making of laws for the same, ought to be lodged in the hands of King, Lords of Parliament, and representatives of the whole body of the freemen of this realm.

Secondly, That every man of the commonalty (excepting infants, insane persons and criminals) is, of common right, and by the laws of God, a freeman, and entitled to the full enjoyment of liberty.

Thirdly, That liberty, or freedom, consists in having an actual share in the appointing of those who frame the laws, and who are to be the guardians of every man's life, property, and peace: for the all of one man is as dear to him as the all of another; and the poor man has an equal right, but more need, to have representatives in the legislature than the rich one.

Fourthly, That they who have no voice nor vote in the electing of representatives, do not enjoy liberty, but are absolutely enslaved to those who have votes, and to their representatives.

The causes of reform and of lower-class radicalism received a further impetus from the French Revolution which broke out in 1789. Many reformers welcomed the revolution in France, but public opinion among the middle and upper classes turned sharply against it when the revolution degenerated into a violent and bloody onslaught against the French aristocracy. In England, reformers were characterized as revolutionaries in disguise (Sources 69 and 70). Measures were passed banning the newly emerging trade unions (Source 71) and severe restrictions were placed on groups like the London Corresponding Society, which was founded in 1792 by a group of artisans led by Thomas Hardy and demanded 'an equal representation of the whole body of the people'. Two years later the Habeas Corpus Act was suspended and in 1797 a mass meeting of the London Corresponding Society was forcibly broken up by police and troops, leading to the banning of the Society and the arrest and imprisonment of its leading members.

Source 69

'Death or Liberty', a cartoon from 1819 equating radical reform with revolution. Radical reform wearing a mask and the trappings of the French Revolution is seen as a threat to both life and liberty. The lion of loyalty rushes to the rescue of ravished Britannia.

Source 70

'A Radical Reformer', a cartoon from 1819. Radical reform, represented as a guillotine, pursues Lords Londonderry, Eldon and Liverpool and the Prince Regent

Source 71

From the Combination Act, 1800.

Be it therefore enacted from and after the passing of this Act that all contracts, covenants and agreements whatsoever...between any journeymen manufacturers or workmen...for lessening or altering their usual hours of time or working, or for decreasing the quantity of work...or for preventing or hindering any person or persons from employing whomsoever he...shall think proper to employ in his...manufacture, trade or business...are hereby declared to be illegal, null and void.

Despite the best efforts of the authorities to stamp out radical political activity among the lower strata of society, both during and after the Revolutionary and Napoleonic Wars against France, the reformist seeds sown by Wilkes and the American Revolution and watered by the French Revolution and Thomas Paine's *The Rights of Man* continued to flourish. Blind reactionary protest against unpopular innovations, of which the Luddite machine-breaking riots were one of the last serious outbreaks, gave way to more rational and clear-sighted reform programmes with coherent agendas of demands to improve the political, social and economic position of ordinary people. Of these, the most important were the trade unions and the Chartists. The former with their strikes and early attempts at collective bargaining with employers, and the latter with their six demands for parliamentary reform, their newspapers and their mass rallies and petitions, showed that not only was the focus of popular agitation changing but its methods were also becoming more varied and sophisticated.

Source 72

From J.R. Dinwiddy, *From Luddism to the First Reform Bill* (Blackwell, 1986) pp.19–20, 24–9, 33–5, 37–8 and 43–4.

The democratic agitation of the period of the French Revolution reached its first peak in 1792, the year which saw the publication of the second part of Thomas Paine's *Rights of Man* [Unit 1.5, p.129], the revolution of 10 August in Paris, and the first substantial working-class organizations devoted to the cause of parliamentary reform in Britain. There was a second peak during the subsistence crisis of 1795, but at no stage in these years did the movement attract *mass* support....After 1795, public agitation for reform encountered almost insuperable obstacles: in particular, the repressive legislation passed by Pitt's government [Unit 1.5, p.129 and Sources 295–6], and the waves of loyalist sentiment which were aroused, especially in 1796–8 and 1803–5, by the threat of a French invasion....It was only after the Battle of Trafalgar, which reduced the pressure for national unity by removing the danger of invasion, that there was a gradual revival of public interest in reform. This was fuelled by resentment at the high level of wartime taxation....

After the end of the war, there was a dramatic extension of working-class interest in political reform. The economic depression of 1816–17...was particularly resented because people had hoped for better things when peace eventually came....From November 1816, when [William] Cobbett began republishing the leading article of his *Weekly Political Register* as a separate twopenny pamphlet, the message that parliamentary reform was the key to an improvement in the condition of the people was being transmitted directly to a large working-class audience. Samuel Bamford wrote later in his *Passages in the Life of a Radical* that in the winter of 1816–17 Cobbett's writings were being read in nearly every cottage in south Lancashire and the east Midlands. 'Their influence was speedily visible; he directed his readers to the true cause of their sufferings – misgovernment; and to its proper corrective – parliamentary reform. Riots soon became scarce, and from that time they have never obtained their ancient vogue with the labourers of this country'....

It is not difficult to understand why a predominantly working-class movement for reform should have chosen universal suffrage as its principal goal....It is harder to...explain why working men in the post-war years should have become so receptive to the message of Cobbett and others that the 'proper corrective' for their sufferings was *political* reform. Part of the answer must lie in the failure or ineffectiveness of other strategies. Direct action had been tried with very little positive result. Luddism, suppressed in 1812, was briefly revived in Nottinghamshire and Leicestershire in 1816, but was again suppressed with the help of several executions. It had never had much success....The year 1816 also saw an outbreak of fierce agrarian rioting, prompted by high food prices and unemployment, in East Anglia; and this too was crushed with some severity....The alarms created by the French Revolution and Painite radicalism had hardened the attitudes of the propertied classes towards popular violence....

By contrast, peaceful methods of collective bargaining, focused on wages rather than prices, were being more widely used in the early nineteenth century. The fact that, between the passage of the Combination Acts in 1799–1800 [Source 71] and their repeal in 1824, trade unions were illegal...did not prevent the continuation of their long-term growth. Indeed in a number of industries...conditions of high demand and full employment produced a marked strengthening of trade unionism during the Napoleonic Wars....Nevertheless, there were a number of factors...which limited the scope and effectiveness of trade union action as a means of protecting living standards. The most important underlying factor was the almost permanent surplus of labour which existed in many areas as a result of the high rate of population growth....There can be no doubt that many workers turned to parliamentary reform because of their weakness in the industrial sphere, and because they believed that state power was contributing to that weakness when it could be used to protect them....

There was one evil which *all* supporters of radical reform hoped that it would relieve: the burden of taxation....Unlike other causes of distress – such as harvest-failure, or a disappointing level of foreign demand for British manufactures, or the population growth...– the fiscal burden could be squarely attributed to the government and the legislature....

The vast popular meetings which were held by radicals in places such as Spa Fields in London, Newhall Hill outside Birmingham, and St Peter's Fields, Manchester, were an innovation for which precedents could hardly be found....When parliament treated large-scale petitioning with indifference, the methods adopted by the radicals for enforcing attention to their demands became more threatening and hovered on the edge of illegality. In the spring of 1817 there was an abortive mass march from the north west to London to present petitions to the Prince Regent in person (the March of the Blanketeers), and in August 1819 there were drilling parties on the moors of south Lancashire in preparation for the great demonstration with drums and banners in St Peter's Fields, Manchester. When the authorities responded to radical agitation by passing repressive legislation, as they did in March 1817 and December 1819, or by taking physical action against the crowd at 'Peterloo', the leaders of the movement were able to heighten their rhetoric and invoke the right of resistance to oppression....

Yet, however much radical orators and journalists might claim that the government had overstepped the bounds of constitutional propriety and thereby legitimized resistance, it was extremely difficult to mount such resistance in practice. One of the most basic problems was lack of arms....The working population as a whole had very little access to weapons....Some ultra-radicals nurtured the dream of an uncontrollable 'general rising', perhaps in support of some sensational coup: Thistlewood and his colleagues in the Cato Street Conspiracy of February 1820 hoped that a collective assassination of the cabinet would excite this kind of popular response....In the post-war years there were at least two efforts to arrange a co-ordinated rising in the provinces, one in the north and midlands in the early summer of 1817, and one in the northern counties and the west of Scotland in the spring of 1820. But as soon as radical agitation became conspiratorial, it became vulnerable to penetration by spies....The post-war radical movement was never highly organized; and when the agitation went underground...it was extremely difficult to establish effective communications among scattered groups of conspirators. The tiny attempts at insurrection which did take place, such as those at Pentrich in Derbyshire in June 1817 and Grange Moor near Huddersfield in April 1820, seem to have been undertaken by people who believed that similar groups would be rising simultaneously elsewhere, when in fact action in other places had been called off....

The leading journalists...did not on the whole set a revolutionary tone. Papers such as Cobbett's *Register* and the *Black Dwarf*...did play a central part in co-ordinating the public reform movement. They acquired a national circulation such as no radical paper of the 1790s had achieved, and by disseminating ideas and reports of meetings they gave radicals all over the country a sense of participation in a widespread campaign. But the characteristic style of the radical press in the Regency period was more satirical than violent....

After 1820 a number of factors combined to dampen radical agitation. One, probably the most important, was a markedly improved economic climate, which lasted – apart from a sharp recession in 1826 – until towards the end of the decade. Another was repression....Hunt, Knight, Bamford, Wooler and even Burdett were among those who suffered terms of imprisonment. And even more efficacious than prison sentences in reducing the strength and influence of the radical press was the Publications Act of 1819 (one of the Six Acts), which imposed a stamp duty of 4*d*. on all periodicals with any political content which were published more frequently than once a month and sold for less than 6*d*. Radicalism in the broad sense did not by any means die out in the 1820s, but it became rather disjointed....

[The radical journalist, Francis Place,] did not believe that trade union activity could do much to improve the remuneration of working men. It is somewhat ironic, therefore, that Place should have been the individual most responsible for what seems in retrospect the most notable landmark of the 1820s in labour history: the repeal of the Combination Laws in 1824....The 1820s saw a strengthening of trade unionism and inter-trade alliances, helped after 1824 by the emergence of a legal trade union press.

Source 73

From John Stevenson, *Popular Disturbances in England 1700–1832*, pp.324–5.

There is clear evidence of the development of more organized and permanent means of articulating grievances and presenting demands....The rise of the reform movement depended on the development of middle and lower-class organizations and the methods of effective agitation, notably the press, petitioning, and peaceful meetings and demonstrations. The growth of trade unionism...also illustrates the increasing emphasis on more effective and more permanent forms of organization. This process was by no means simple, but there was a growing reliance by both middle and lower-class groups on peaceful and orderly methods of protest....Popular radicals were often aware that whatever the frustrations and difficulties of gradualism, they had more to lose from violence and its subsequent repression than from broadening the basis of support and relying on the education of opinion. One result was that reformers were forced to concentrate on developing legal and peaceful methods, ones which it was hoped would...influence ministers to concede. These tactics appeared to have triumphed in 1832, where they had failed earlier.

Source 74

From D.G. Wright, *Popular Radicalism* (Longman, 1988) pp.21–2.

Although organizations of labouring men to secure higher wages or better conditions existed long before the Industrial Revolution, there began in the 1790s a tradition of working-class radicalism which was partly inspired by the outbreak of the French Revolution, while drawing at the same time on an English radical tradition dating back to the seventeenth century. This popular radical tradition increased in strength and appeal, though not at an even rate, during the first half of the nineteenth century. In an important sense, the study of this tradition is the study of the prehistory of the Chartist movement, when the world's first national labour movement appeared in Britain. Furthermore, this popular radical tradition was based on growing class consciousness, even if it were confined to specific sectors of the total workforce. Much of this radicalism was directly concerned with trade issues and the defence of livelihoods against the forces making for proletarianization; but there was at the same time a growing tide of popular opinion aimed at procuring a more democratic constitution and a state machine less firmly in the grasp of property-owning élites. It was a movement which governments between 1793 and 1820, and again in 1829–32 and 1838–48, saw as constituting a revolutionary threat which placed established institutions and the social order in jeopardy....

The fact that working and middle-class radicals were often able to combine in a common cause, such as mounting pressure for a Reform Bill after 1829..., did not preclude that the two movements possessed some distinct aims and tactics. When working-class radicalism reached its climax in the first phase of Chartism in 1839–40, accompanied by a considerable amount of arming and drilling, middle-class radicals either kept their heads well down or restricted themselves within the narrow confines of the Anti-Corn Law League....

After 1848, working-class consciousness was admittedly more subdued, as distinct working-class radicalism seemed almost to disappear. But...both the consciousness and the radicalism were still present, if rather more subtle in both approach and tactics; only seriously being weakened in the years between the 1867 Reform Act and the socialist revival of the 1890s.

Source 75

From recollections of an old Chartist quoted by Frank Peel in *The Risings of the Luddites, Chartists and Plugdrawers*, 1888, p.328.

The settled conviction of the Chartists was that bad trade, dear living, and all their misfortunes rose from bad laws, and that if only they could get votes and send men of their own to parliament they would so order matters that a reign of peace and plenty would at once be inaugurated.

Source 76

From an 1846 edition of The Northern Star, *a Chartist newspaper founded in 1837 which achieved a large circulation*

Source 77

The Chartists carry the Great Petition to the House of Commons, 1842

It has been noted elsewhere that the Chartists did not directly achieve any of their six demands, but that five of them were granted during the 70 years following the demise of Chartism in 1848. While the politicians who abolished the property qualification for MPs in 1858, passed the Secret Ballot Act in 1872, redistributed parliamentary seats in 1885, introduced payment for MPs in 1911 and gradually extended the franchise until universal manhood suffrage was achieved in 1918 would not have accepted that any of these reforms owed anything to Chartist agitation, it is undeniable that the Chartists brought these issues to the forefront of public attention and kept them there for over ten years. By their mass petitions and demonstrations, they left the government in no doubt about the potential power of ordinary people when enough of them felt sufficiently strongly about an issue. Thus, while they failed in the short term, in the longer term the Chartists played an important part in creating the conditions in which reform became seen as necessary, if not entirely desirable, by a majority of the political élite.

As Source 78 illustrates, ordinary people were involved in the electoral process long before they gained the right to vote, and elections were frequently riotous affairs. However, the introduction of secret voting in 1872 and the passing of the Corrupt Practices Act in 1883, which made the use of bribery, threats and unfair influence at elections illegal, largely eliminated the violence and enabled ordinary people to participate in the electoral process in a more peaceful and constructive manner.

Source 78

An account of riots at the municipal elections in Blackburn in 1868, during which rival mobs destroyed the committee rooms of each candidate. From the *Annual Register*, 1868.

A cart of stones was kept in readiness by the blue and orange [Tory] party, and a crowd of women kept supplying them with missiles. Most of the rioters were armed with picking sticks....All along the pavement streams of blood were flowing, and the sickening sight of men with blood flowing from their heads and faces met one at every turn. The police charged the mob with drawn cutlasses and truncheons, committing great havoc; but they did not succeed in restoring even comparative quiet for a long time....Business was interrupted at the polls for hours.

Source 79

Secret voting at Taunton following the passing of the Ballot Act in 1872

While the enfranchisement of the lower orders increased their power and forced politicians to address issues of concern to them, such as health, housing, education and living standards, the traditional political élite was in no mood to relinquish its monopoly of power. The development of party organizations by the Conservative and Liberal Parties, which began soon after the passing of the 1832 Reform Act, was primarily a response to the increase in the electorate and the need to win its support without losing control of the reins of government. It was not until the Labour Party was formed at the beginning of the twentieth century that substantial numbers of ordinary people began to enter parliament. The strength of the Labour Party lay in the financial and electoral support it received from the trade unions and in its claim to represent the interests of ordinary people in a much more direct way than the Conservative and Liberal Parties had ever done.

Source 80

Labour's Long Road to Citizenship. From Clive Behagg, *Labour and Reform: Working-Class Movements 1815–1914* (Hodder & Stoughton, 1991) p.1.

The metaphor most often used to describe the development of working-class movements in the nineteenth and early twentieth centuries is that of a journey or, more evocatively, a 'march'. The journey runs from a point around 1815, where workers find themselves without the means to defend their way of life, possessing neither the vote nor the right form of trade unions. They travel slowly and with many setbacks to a point in the early twentieth century when, having achieved both the vote and legal status for their unions, working people become full political members of a mature industrial nation, a situation exemplified in the growing strength of the newly formed Labour Party.

The right to vote conferred an important political right on ordinary men and women. Henceforth, they could no longer be described accurately as 'those who do not rule' because, at least once every five years, they participated directly in the election of the government, a fact which governments could never entirely ignore in the years between elections. Nevertheless, this did not mean that more direct ways of influencing the government were abandoned. On the contrary, they became more important and the methods employed became more diverse during the twentieth century. Suffragettes demonstrated the power of mass demonstrations, civil disobedience and the value of headline-grabbing activities such as going on hunger strike when in prison. Trade unions showed how industries could be disrupted by concerted strike action and they almost brought the entire country to a standstill during the General Strike of 1926. However, the limits of their power were exposed by their inability to maintain the unity of the strike, largely due to insufficient funds to support the strikers for a long period of time, and the strike ended in failure.

Source 81

A Punch *cartoon commenting on the failure of the 1926 General Strike*

The press and, more recently, broadcasting have played increasingly important roles in informing and moulding public opinion. The first daily newspaper, the *Daily Courant* was produced in 1702, to be followed by *The Times* in 1785 and the *Guardian*, formerly the *Manchester Guardian*, in 1821. However, the readership of these papers was drawn from the educated and propertied classes. Cobbett's weekly *Political Register* and the Chartist *Northern Star* catered to a radical audience during the first half of the nineteenth century, but it was not until 1896 that the first mass circulation national daily newspaper, the *Daily Mail* was published, followed within eight years by the *Daily Express* and the *Daily Mirror*. By the 1930s, total sales of national daily newspapers exceeded ten million copies a day, but competition was already emerging from radio and television, which began broadcasting in 1922 and 1936 respectively. While newspapers, radio and television have increased the political awareness of the public and kept it informed about important issues, they have also been used to manipulate political opinion by means of advertising and newspaper campaigns, supporting or opposing particular policies or politicians. Thus, the media has at one and the same time increased the power of the general public by keeping it informed of current developments and, in the case of most newspapers, attempted to manipulate it in pursuit of their own political goals.

Source 82

From D. Butler and D. Stokes, *Political Change in Britain* (Macmillan, 1974) p.419.

The monopoly of a partisan press, weakened by the coming of radio, was broken completely by television, which for the mass of the people became the prime source of political information....There can hardly be any doubt that this revolution in the media helped to prepare the way for the much more fluid changes of party preference in recent years....The years just after television had completed its conquest of the national audience were the years in which the electoral tides began to run more freely.

Political protest movements learnt much from the campaign led by Gandhi in India for independence from Britain, which was finally achieved in 1947. His policies of passive resistance were emulated by, amongst others, the Campaign for Nuclear Disarmament (CND), which was founded in 1958 and used 'peace marches' and 'sit-down demonstrations', blocking roads to win publicity and cause disruption without using violence. Other organizations have followed CND in using non-violent protest to achieve their ends. In the early 1990s an unpopular 'poll tax' was introduced to finance local government, and spawned demonstrations throughout the country. So widespread was the refusal to pay that the government had no choice but to abandon the tax and replace it with a fairer Council Tax.

Other forms of protest have often been more violent. From the late 1960s to 1994, when a fragile ceasefire was declared, Catholic and Protestant paramilitary organizations in Northern Ireland each used systematic violence and intimidation to try to achieve their aims. The Irish Republican Army (IRA) murdered Protestants and members of the security forces, and planted bombs in city centres and elsewhere in both Northern Ireland and mainland Britain; Ulster loyalist groups retaliated by murdering Catholics. Neither, however, made any political progress as a result of their violent activity. Nor have those who have resorted to violence elsewhere in Britain. The suffragettes, for example, only achieved the vote after renouncing violence.

During the 1980s, there were riots in a number of inner city areas, including Brixton in London, Toxteth in Liverpool and St Paul's in Bristol. These riots were a reaction against inner city deprivation and are a reminder that the violent protest against injustice, so common of the period up to the early nineteenth century, has not entirely disappeared in favour of more organized and articulate forms of protest.

Source 83

The first 'Aldermaston March' from London to the weapons research establishment at Aldermaston in Berkshire, 1958. The march was organized by the recently formed Campaign for Nuclear Disarmament.

Source 84

The aftermath of the Toxteth riots in Liverpool, 1982

Throughout this unit, we have explored the capacity of ordinary people to protest and rebel against authority, but we should not lose sight of the fact that people only tend to take such action when provoked by deprivation or by strong convictions. As Asa Briggs explains in Source 85 and the cartoonist Pont gently mocks in Source 86, the average English man and woman has been, and to a large extent remains, conformist, deferential to those in authority and a lover of order.

Source 85

From Asa Briggs, 'The English: Custom and Character', in R. Blake (ed.), *The English World* (Thames & Hudson, 1982) pp.250–2.

[The Frenchman, Hippolyte] Taine described England as haunted, in contrast with France, by the ghosts of the feudal spirit: 'The lord provides for the needs of his dependant, and the dependant is proud of his lord'....During the middle years of the nineteenth century, when Taine was writing, the great landed estate was still an economy and a society in itself. Despite fears expressed during the successful fight to repeal the Corn Laws (1846), the position of the aristocracy and gentry remained exceptionally strong....

It is not only deference which has often been singled out as an English trait. Another related feature has received equal attention – the Englishman's natural sense of order. As recently as 1955, Geoffrey Gorer in his book *Exploring English Character*, describes the English people as 'among the most peaceful, gentle, courteous and orderly populations that the civilized world has ever seen'....The generalization had not always stood before 1955, as Gorer recognized. The English did not enjoy their 1955 reputation in the Middle Ages, in the Tudor period or in the seventeenth or eighteenth centuries. There was little evidence of a natural sense of order in the London riots of 1736, 1768 and 1780 which gave London the reputation of being more turbulent than Paris....Gorer...[believed] that there was a big change in Englishmen's attitudes to 'order' in the mid-Victorian years...[partly due to] Methodism, which set out to appeal to the 'low' as well as the 'high' [and] could generate change from within: in particular, it could convert the 'wicked' into the 'respectable'....As far as public life was concerned...'there does seem to have been this remarkable transition from the Roaring Boys to the Boy's Brigade, from John Bull to John Citizen'.

It is notoriously difficult to locate precisely in time shifts in attitudes and values: and Gorer's middle years of the nineteenth century, quieter though they were in domestic history than the preceding and later years...are also associated with one of the most strident displays of English nationalism during the Crimean War. If crime rates were falling – and the statistics are controversial – there was still no shortage of violence. Nor did John Bull ever completely change into John Citizen: indeed, it required the Education Act of 1870 and the new Board Schools to help form John Citizen....What seems likely is that the mid-nineteenth-century changes...make a new kind of national and individual character necessary. Industry had to become a matter of habit and routine…: it depended for its performance on punctuality, regularity and discipline. Self-help had to be extolled along with the gospel of work and the belief in thrift….Much of this was new. In the eighteenth century, work was irregular and often undisciplined, particularly before the move from the home to the factory….

In order that the change might take place smoothly, it was obviously more desirable to develop new attitudes, and the character traits that went with them, by implanting them from within rather than by imposing them from without. The policeman and the judge were to be necessary agents in the process, and respect and deference were to be accorded to them, but in the first resort at least the actual transformation of character was in the hands of other agencies – schools, particularly Sunday Schools…, and publicists, most of whom had 'risen in society' themselves'….

Yet there was increasing suspicion among social critics…that the degree of conformity being demanded was too great, and in the same year as Samuel Smiles's *Self-Help* (1859), John Stuart Mill published his famous essay *On Liberty* in which he complained of the 'increasing inclination to extend unduly the powers of society over the individual'….He was more concerned with the pressures of society than the controls of the state, for in England, he believed, 'from the particular circumstances of our political history, the yoke of opinion is perhaps heavier, that of law…lighter than in most other countries of Europe'. It was not that individual Englishmen were losing their freedom to the state: they were rather losing their individuality to the society and the culture.

Source 86

The British Character: Exaltation of Freedom, *a 1946 cartoon by 'Pont' gently mocking the British businessman who, despite his considerable freedom of thought and action, imposes numerous constraints upon his own behaviour*

Why have reactions to the exercise of political power changed over time?

The questions and material in the previous section enabled you to construct accounts of developments in the power of ordinary people to protest against, resist and sometimes overturn the policies of those in power over them. You have identified continuities and changes in the types of people who have engaged in popular protest, in the issues over which protest has taken place, in the methods that protesters have employed and in the degree of success they have achieved. It is almost impossible to consider the nature of change without paying some attention to the reasons why change has taken place. There is a great deal of evidence in Sources 1–86 and the accompanying narrative regarding the causes of change and development in the powers of ordinary people to protest against and influence the ways in which political power has been exercised. This section enables you to analyse and establish connections between that evidence so as to draw conclusions about the factors that have encouraged and inhibited change in the way that ordinary people have reacted to the exercise of power. In this final section of Unit 3.1, you are asked to consider four questions about the causes of change and development in the power of 'those who do not rule'. Since much of the material on pages 5–48 provides evidence that can be used to answer these questions, little new evidence will be included here. It is expected that you will utilize evidence from earlier sections to help you answer the questions.

Questions

9. Why have the types of people who participate in protest changed over time?
10. Why have the causes of popular unrest and the issues over which people protest changed?
11. Why have the methods they employ changed?
12. Why have protesters' prospects of success changed over time?

These are questions about why change and development has taken place and are therefore similar in nature to the questions with which you will be more familiar, about why events happened or actions were taken. To answer them, you will need to consider how different factors interacted to bring about the type of development highlighted in each question. This will involve demonstrating that different factors play different roles in the explanation of change: for instance, some factors affect the power of ordinary people directly, while others affect their power indirectly; some influence people's outlook and beliefs whereas others influence the conditions under which they live; some increase or decrease the power of protesters, while others strengthen or weaken the ability of the authorities to resist them. It is also important to recognize that some factors are more important to the explanation than others and to explain why this is so. It might be argued, for example, that there were a number of factors that brought about the increased political activity of ordinary people during the first half of the nineteenth century, one of which was the Industrial Revolution, but that the Industrial Revolution was more important than other factors such as increased urbanization, depressed living conditions and the development of radical journalism because each of these other factors was in itself a consequence of the Industrial Revolution. Alternatively, it might be argued that the Industrial Revolution was more important than some of the other factors because it was a *necessary cause* while others were not. In other words, if the Industrial Revolution had not occurred as and when it did, it is unlikely that there would have been an upsurge in popular political activity during the early nineteenth century, whereas if radical journalism had not existed then it is unlikely that this would have made very much difference, since the protesters would probably have gained their inspiration from elsewhere.

From the eleventh to the fifteenth century

Even before the introduction of the feudal system in the eleventh century, there was a strict social hierarchy in which each social rank had attached to it certain clearly-defined rights and obligations. The feudal system developed these rights and obligations further by tying them to the tenure of land. The system was reinforced by the Church, which taught that it was part of God's plan that everyone should accept their allotted place in society and behave accordingly. As a result, people were prepared to accept injustices, lack of rights and inequalities in the distribution of wealth as part of the natural order of things. This explains why popular protest during the Middle Ages was less frequent or widespread than might otherwise have been expected and why, when it did occur, it tended to be conservative in nature. Most ordinary people were suspicious of change and wanted to cling to the security of the old ways. Thus, when the king or a local lord introduced changes that they conceived to be to their disadvantage, their resistance was born not only from a natural desire to protect their own interests, but also from an ingrained suspicion of anything new.

In the aftermath of the Norman Conquest, this resistance to change was stiffened by Anglo-Saxon resentment of the Norman conquerors, which led Anglo-Saxons of all social stations to make common cause against their Norman overlords in a series of regional rebellions, of which the Rebellion of the Northern Earls in 1069 (Sources 1 and 2) was the most serious. Such rebellions were doomed to failure and goaded William and his Norman followers into bloody reprisals against nobleman and peasant alike.

As Englishmen came reluctantly to accept that the Normans were here to stay, the temporary unity of interest between the different ranks of society disintegrated. Peasant protests tended to be about economic matters. Some were local grievances against rules imposed by the lord of the manor through his manorial court. Protests of this nature had some prospect of success, since the lord was dependent on the labour of his peasants for his prosperity. Most local grievances were of an economic nature, concerning such matters as conditions of service on the lord's demesne lands or reductions in the size of the standard loaf (Source 6). This reflects the issues that were important in what was primarily a subsistence economy. What mattered above all else to most peasants was that they should have food in their bellies and a roof over their heads. Anything which appeared to jeopardize these fundamental needs was resisted strenuously.

Protests against government action were less common, and those that did occur also tended to be motivated by economic considerations, such as opposition to unpopular taxes. Tax revolts tended to be local or regional rather than national, due to the problems of coordinating action over large areas at a time when communications were slow and difficult. In general, such protests proved futile, but there was a partial exception in 1381, when the Peasants' Revolt (Sources 10–16), led by John Ball, Wat Tyler and Jack Straw, brought about the abandonment of the poll tax as a source of revenue. Although the Peasants' Revolt failed and its leaders were executed, the comparative ease with which the rebels had gained control of London and murdered leading courtiers, including Archbishop Sudbury and Robert Hales, the Treasurer, taught Richard II's government that the wrath of the populace was something that it was perilous to ignore.

Protests by the gentry and nobility were as likely to be political as economic in origin, since struggles for power and influence at court could, and sometimes did, lead to open rebellion by those who were excluded from power. During the reign of Stephen and in the mid-fifteenth century, the factional rivalry boiled over into civil war. Peasants were conscripted into the armies of their lords and masters when they rebelled against the crown or rallied to its defence, but it is doubtful whether many of them either understood or cared about the political issues over which they were fighting.

There was, however, one cause of popular protest that could unite people from all social strata, and that was religion. Leadership of religious protests lay in the hands of educated men from the higher levels of society, but the rank and file were usually well versed in the issues and were willing participants in the opposition organized by their betters. At a time when religion affected almost every aspect of the lives of all people, no matter what their social station, it is hardly surprising that this issue could unite people like no other. The most serious and prolonged religious unrest to afflict medieval England was the Lollard movement (Sources 17–20), which sought to reform Church abuses and make the Bible more accessible to ordinary people. Although its origins lay in the fourteenth-century teachings of the Oxford academic, John Wyclif, and in his illegal English translation of the Bible, its survival into the sixteenth century, despite official persecution, owed much to the simple faith of ordinary people like John Croft (Unit 1.4, Source 124). Nevertheless, deeply ingrained beliefs in social deference ensured that the only major Lollard rebellion, which occurred in 1414, was led by an influential courtier, Sir John Oldcastle.

Not all popular reactions to the exercise of power involved violence. Sources 6 and 7 provide examples of the use of peaceful demonstrations, strikes and passive resistance by peasants who had grievances against their lord. Some of the most effective reactions were characterized by nothing more than a widespread disregard for new and unpopular laws. For instance, an Ordinance of Labourers passed in 1349 to prevent peasants from taking advantage of the labour shortage following the Black Death by demanding higher wages was ignored by so many people that it was almost completely ineffective. A frustrated parliament passed a Statute of Labourers in 1351 which gave the courts wider powers to punish those who sought or agreed to pay inflated wages, but even this was of limited success in the face of the determination of peasants to exploit the advantages that the shortage of labour had unexpectedly thrown in their direction.

The political and economic consequences of the Black Death are explored more fully in the next unit, but it should be noted here that it had important implications for ordinary peasants, because it increased their influence over where they lived and worked and the conditions under which they did so. Whether this influence was an immediate consequence of the tremendous loss of life during the Black Death or a more gradual development as successive waves of plague periodically decimated the population during the second half of the fourteenth century is a matter over which historians disagree. What is not under dispute is the economic advantage surviving peasants gained from the labour shortages created by the epidemic. They were able to demand that labour services on the lord's demesne farm in return for land on which to grow their own crops should be replaced by proper wages and rents, and landowners desperate for labour were in no position to refuse. If they did so, peasants would simply move to another village where the lord was prepared to meet their demands. Thus, the Black Death signalled the beginning of the end of the feudal system. This in turn had an effect on the nature of popular reactions to the exercise of power. Protests against changes introduced by the lord of the manor worsening the conditions of service for his peasants gave way to protests against lords who sought to retain the existing conditions of service for peasants who demanded greater economic freedom. The substitution of a wage economy for a service economy affected the issues over which protests took place – wages and prices rather than conditions of service – and gave the populace more bargaining power because, as long as there was a shortage of labour, they could seek employment elsewhere if they failed to gain satisfaction from their current lord.

From the fifteenth to the eighteenth century

The decline of feudalism gave ordinary people more independence and control over their own lives. They were no longer tied to the land as serfs, but could move around in search of a better master, better pay or improved conditions of work. They also had more freedom to leave the land in search of other forms of work. This freedom was limited by social legislation against vagrancy, by their lack of education and by an economy that provided only limited opportunities for the poor. Nevertheless, a greater sense of independence can be detected among the peasantry from the fifteenth century onwards, and this influenced popular protest during this period.

Many characteristics of medieval popular protest continued to be important until the Industrial Revolution: protest tended to be about social and economic issues rather than political; it tended to be conservative and reactionary, seeking to preserve existing conditions in the face of innovations introduced by the gentry and aristocracy; and it tended to be led by educated men drawn from the ranks of the gentry. However, the gradual replacement of feudalism with a capitalist economy caused changes in the issues over which protest took place. As has already been noted, protests over prices and wages came to replace those over conditions of service. An important factor which contributed to protests over prices and wages was the sustained level of inflation which, between 1530 and 1650, saw prices rise almost twice as fast as wages. In years when inflation was coupled with bad harvests, food riots became common occurrences, but such uprisings tended to be local in character. Also localized were the campaigns against enclosures (Sources 25–9), which deprived villagers of their rights of grazing on common land and, in some cases, led to the forcible depopulation of entire communities. Protest was often violent, but not always: while some enclosures were forcibly torn down, in other cases villagers sought, and sometimes gained, redress through the courts.

Source 87

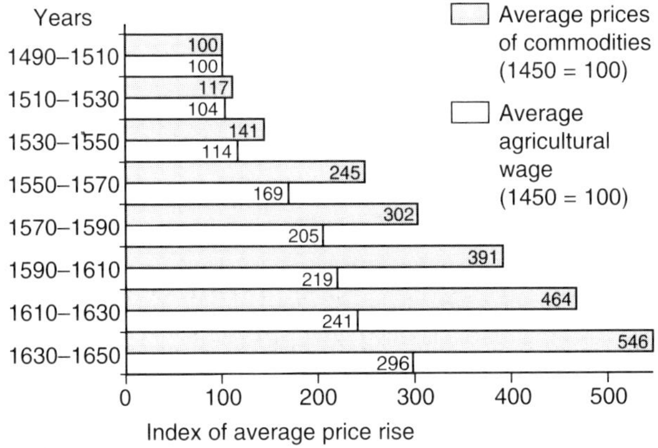

Prices and wages, 1490–1650

While food riots and protests against enclosures tended to be localized, some forms of protest attracted support from a wider area. Inflation and the resultant decline in living standards sometimes sparked off regional protests against unpopular taxation at a time when people were finding it increasingly difficult to pay their contributions. One such instance was the rebellion in Cornwall after Henry VII levied a tax in 1497 (Sources 32–3). The rebels succeeded in marching to London with a force of 15,000 men before they were defeated.

After England broke away from the Roman Catholic Church, popular protest over religious issues became increasingly common. Such protests took various forms, from open rebellion during the Pilgrimage of Grace, the Western Rebellion (Sources 34 and 36) and the English Civil War to defiance of religious legislation by those who joined radical religious sects in increasing numbers from the early seventeenth century.

As Dietrich Gerhard argues in Source 88, religious protest tended to be regional rather than local, because the issues were clear enough and emotive enough to unite people over large areas, despite the poor communications that existed in the sixteenth and seventeenth centuries. However, such protests often combined social and economic grievances with religious issues, as occurred during the Pilgrimage of Grace.

Source 88

From Dietrich Gerhard, *Old Europe: A Study of Continuity, 1000–1800* (Academic Press, 1981) pp.69–70. Gerhard is generalizing about revolts in Europe between the fourteenth and mid-seventeenth centuries.

There can be no doubt that in town and countryside many of the revolts were the result of tensions stemming from economic depression combined with increased taxes required by the central government. The interrelations of simultaneous uprisings, however, were tenuous. They spread over wide areas only in times of deep religious emotion, such as the Hussite movement of the early fifteenth century [in Bohemia] or the great German Peasant War of the Reformation period. A striving for equality as the natural condition of man surfaced in such periods. To a priest in southeast England who was involved in the great revolt of 1381...we owe the often quoted verses, 'When Adam dalf [dug] and Eve span – where then was the gentleman?' Often the grievances were the result of declining prices or increased taxation, governments and indebted landlords made demands that were rightly regarded as legally not justified. Neither class consciousness nor the idea of a new and better order is discernible, however, with the exception of the religiously influenced movements. Most of these revolts were regional; they harked back to the old order, and their demands were strictly traditional. Most striking – and a further proof of the continuity of the old order – is the similarity of causes, demands and goals throughout centuries.

While Gerhard is right to stress the continuity and the importance of tradition in the causes and aims of popular unrest, the gradual introduction of printed ballads and news sheets following the invention of printing during the mid-fifteenth century, coupled with a slow but significant increase in literacy over the next two centuries, enabled ordinary people to become better informed about what was happening outside their immediate vicinity. Without doubt, this contributed to protests on an increasingly wide scale, as men and women recognized that their concerns were shared by people elsewhere. Source 89, a widely circulated broadsheet complaining against the depressed state of the textile industry, was printed in Norwich and Leeds and circulated in textile producing areas as far apart as Yorkshire and Somerset.

Source 89

The Clothiers Delight:

OR, The Rich Mens Joy, and the Poor Mens Sorrow.

Wherein is exprest the craftiness and subtilty of many Clothiers in England, by beating down their Work-mens wages.

Combers, Weavers, and Spinners, for little gains,
Doth Earn their money by taking of hard pains.

To the Tune of, *Jenny come tye me*, &c. *Packington's Pound*, Or, *Monk hath confounded*, &c.

With Allowance, *Ro. L'Estrange.* **By *T. Lanfire.***

Of all sorts of callings that in England be,
There is none that liveth so gallant as we;
Our Trading maintains us as brave as a Knight,
We live at our pleasure, and taketh delight:
We heapeth up riches and treasure great store,
Which we get by griping and grinding the poor.

And first for the Combers we will bring them down,
From Eight-groats a score unto Half a Crown:
If at all they murmer, and say 'tis too small,
We bid them chose whether they will work at all.
We'l make them believe that Trading is bad,
We care not a pin, though they are ne'r so sad:

The Clothiers Delight, *a ballad from a seventeenth-century broadsheet complaining of low wages in the textile industry*

In Source 90, Lawrence Stone argues that the increases in education and literacy levels during the seventeenth century were politically and religiously dangerous. They enabled people to interpret the Bible for themselves, and led many to criticize Church practices and teachings and to join radical sects. It was only a short step from this for ordinary people to begin criticizing the government and to demand political reform as the Levellers did in the aftermath of the English Civil War. The religious and political conflicts of the English Revolution were fuelled by a mass of political and religious pamphlets which helped to mobilize the populace both politically and religiously. Extracts from many of the pamphlets published at that time can be found in Module 3 of the Depth Study.

Source 90

From Lawrence Stone, *The Causes of the English Revolution: 1529–1642* (Routledge & Kegan Paul, 1972) pp.96–97.

It has been argued in the light of the experience of the twentieth century that the combination of factors most likely to lead to revolution is 'rapid increase in the proportion of the population receiving primary education, but a slow rate of percentage change in gross domestic product *per capita*'. But this presupposes a situation in which there is a normal expectation of an improvement of standards of living, which was hardly the case in the seventeenth century. The expansion of literacy was in fact dangerous in another way, because it aroused expectations of political and religious participation and exposed large numbers of humble people to the heady egalitarian wine of the New Testament. Literacy and Puritanism went hand in hand, and the whole Leveller movement, fuelled as it was by pamphlet literature, was only possible because remarkably large numbers of the poor in south-eastern England could now read. If one combines the expansion of higher education with the parallel expansion of secondary education in Latin grammar and of elementary literacy, it looks more and more as if this educational explosion was a necessary – but of course not a sufficient – cause for the peculiar and ultimately radical course the revolution took.

Another factor that played an important part in the development of popular political activity during the 1640s and 1650s was the Parliamentary army. Unhappy about parliament's plans to turn England into a Presbyterian state, and angry about the extent to which their pay was in arrears, the rank and file provided fertile ground for the spread of religious radicalism and of Leveller ideas (Sources 45–6). For a short time, they had the means at their disposal to exert a significant influence on national events. Agitators were elected to represent their views on the army council; they were able to pressurize the generals into holding the Putney Debates; and agitators were among the first to demand that the king be put on trial.

All this was possible because the army brought together large numbers of ordinary men in one place who could discuss their views and organize themselves on a scale that was impossible during peacetime, when they were scattered in small village communities. The only community that had been able to share political opinions and organize protest on this scale during peacetime had been the London mob, which had long had a reputation for political protest. However, neither the London mob nor the rank and file of the army had either the means or the political skill to sustain activity for long enough to do more than inflict a short, sharp shock on the political élite. The Levellers could organize demands for reform but could not bring to bear enough pressure to force the élite to take notice of their demands. The army rank and file could force the generals to take notice of them, but had no means to prevent Cromwell from dispersing the regiments and thus eliminating the danger. When they mutinied at Ware and later at Burford, they had no idea how to carry the protest any further and the mutinies were easily suppressed.

Nevertheless, the experience of the late 1640s demonstrated how large numbers of ordinary people who were in regular and close contact with one another and who shared a common set of goals could pose a serious threat to the political élite. Such a combination, however, was not to reappear until the Industrial Revolution.

During the century after 1660 it seemed in some respects as though the English Revolution had not happened. Popular protest did not seek to reform the franchise, as the Levellers had done, or to abolish tithes, as many religious radicals had done. It fell into the old routine of reacting in favour of traditional methods when unpopular innovations were introduced. The means did not exist to unite people behind any sort of reform programme and the ruling élite, mindful of the lessons learnt during the English Revolution, kept a tight rein on the populace.

However, in one important respect protest initiated by the English Revolution continued and was ultimately successful. Despite persecution by the Anglican Church following the Restoration, radical sects such as the Quakers remained strong. Religious uniformity had been reimposed by law, but it proved impossible to enforce. Consequently, in 1689, the Toleration Act gave legal recognition to something which had been true in practice since the 1640s: that England was no longer a state with a single religion.

In Source 91, John Stevenson argues that deprivation and a sense of injustice were the main causes of eighteenth-century unrest, and that protests tended to be defensive in character. Thus, despite the political turmoil and fervour generated among the populace by the events of the 1640s and 1650s, eighteenth-century protest was little different from protest in the sixteenth and seventeenth centuries: it was essentially defensive in nature, reacting against unpopular innovations.

Source 91

From John Stevenson, *Popular Disturbances in England 1700–1832* (Longman, 1992) p.306–7 and 316.

There is no simple answer to why disturbances occurred at one time rather than another or in some places rather than others....Probably the most persistent attempts have been made to relate popular disturbances to economic factors....T.S. Ashton highlighted the coincidence of popular disturbances and harvest failure in the course of the eighteenth century. E.J. Hobsbawm also attempted to correlate economic fluctuations in the nineteenth century with a wide range of social movements, including not only such things as food riots, but the growth of trade unionism and political militancy....There is no doubt that the relationship between economic hardship and protest is extremely complex. Initially it can be said that many food riots occurred in times of high prices...; with the growth of industrialisation there also appears a rough correlation between periods of trade depression, distress, and unemployment with the incidence of protest and political agitation. Cobbett's dictum that 'I defy you to agitate a man on a full stomach' is almost a cliché and must be respected in the sense that it reflects the experience of many early reformers that periods of distress provided the most fertile soil for the development of mass agitation....

What was often most important was less the absolute level of deprivation than the popular perceptions of status, living standards, or accepted practice; the state of 'relative deprivation' rather than absolute deterioration was crucial in many instances. Carlyle wrote: 'It is not what a man outwardly has or wants that constitutes the happiness or misery of him. Nakedness, hunger, distress of all kinds, death itself have been cheerfully suffered, when the heart was right. It is the feeling of injustice that is insupportable to all men...'. The element of perceived injustice mobilizing discontent operated in many disturbances: food riots tended to occur where malpractice was suspected, attacks on press-gangs for straying outside the customary categories of men to be taken, and machine-breaking attacks against 'unfair' machines or work practices....

The most striking feature of many English popular disturbances was their essentially defensive character. Whether brought about by high prices, recruiting, new machinery, turnpikes, enclosures, Methodist itinerants, or a myriad of other causes, they occurred most frequently as attempts to resist interference or innovation of some kind. In doing so the participants were acting in ways which were not unique to the eighteenth or nineteenth century; many which conform to similar patterns could be found before 1700. Examples of price-fixing riots, collective bargaining by riot, resistance to enclosure, community justice, and many other types [common in the eighteenth century] can be found in early modern England. Although there is a tendency to think of the 'mob' as a peculiarly eighteenth-century phenomenon,...popular direct action to preserve threatened values, community norms or customary living standards certainly had its roots far earlier. Historians now see some of the major episodes of the early modern period, especially the anti-enclosure revolts of the 1620s or the 'Clubmen's' revolt of the Civil War years, as bearing many of the characteristics of [later disturbances].

From the Industrial Revolution to the twentieth century

We have noted in earlier units how the Industrial Revolution, which began in the mid-eighteenth century, transformed England from a rural society of small communities isolated by poor communications into an industrialized and urbanized society in which improvements in transport and communications brought all but the most remote settlements into closer and more regular contact with one another. Working shoulder to shoulder in the new factories, and living side by side in the new towns and cities, the working classes were able to share with one another their dissatisfaction about low wages, long hours, unsafe working conditions, insanitary living conditions and exclusion from the political process.

Initially, these social and economic changes provoked predictable and traditional reactions from the populace: they reacted, often violently, against unpopular innovations. The Luddites attacked the factories and broke the machinery that they blamed for putting them out of work (Source 65); the Rebecca rioters destroyed toll-gates on the new turnpike roads because they resented having to pay the tolls to use the roads. Nevertheless, the scale of the disorders should not be exaggerated. The belief in social deference, which can be traced back to the Great Chain of Being and beyond, was still strong among rich and poor alike, and explains why the majority of the populace accepted the inequalities and injustices of the social and economic system with resignation (Source 62).

However, change can be detected in the nature of popular protest from the mid-eighteenth century. The Wilkes affair (Source 57) demonstrated the increasing importance of the press in informing, moulding and inciting public opinion. Once this was coupled with a rapid and efficient transport network, which began to appear with the expansion of the railways from the 1830s onwards, the conditions existed within which national pressure groups and reform movements could emerge, pursuing coherent sets of objectives (Source 73). Trade unions began to flourish, campaigning for improved pay and working conditions; the Chartist movement emerged as one of the first national organizations to demand and campaign for political rights for the populace (Source 75). It had its own national newspapers (Source 76) and was able to organize massive petitions and demonstrations in pursuit of its goals (Source 77).

The changing economic and social conditions in Britain enabled popular protest to transform its character during the first half of the nineteenth century from mere reactive protest against unpopular innovations to proactive demands for specific and clearly articulated reforms. Improvements in education and literacy levels as the century progressed enabled more and more people to become well-informed politically and provided a sharper focus to their aspirations for social improvements and political reform.

Change can also be detected in the early nineteenth century in the methods employed by protesters. The violence and intimidation employed by food rioters, machine wreckers and toll-gate breakers gave way gradually to the press campaigns, petitions and peaceful demonstrations of Chartists and the strikes of trade unionists. This was due in part to subtle changes in the attitudes of society, which made violent disorder less effective and even counterproductive as a means of protest. However, it was also a result of more effective organization and stronger leadership which was able to sustain political pressure over longer periods of time. Violence had been the principal weapon of people who could not sustain concerted action over long periods of time and who needed to make an immediate impact. Press campaigns, petitions, demonstrations and strikes exerted a more sustained pressure and were evidence of the ability of the new popular political organizations to mount long-term campaigns for improvement.

The gradual widening of the franchise during the nineteenth and early twentieth centuries was in large measure a consequence of industrialization, urbanization and the opportunities for political organization that these processes provided. However, the achievement of the vote caused further changes in the nature, methods and prospects of success of popular political activity. Once the battle for political participation was won, or at least partially won, the issues over which the populace attempted to exert an influence changed from demanding the right to vote to attempts to influence the nature of government policies. Since MPs were now dependent for their seats in parliament on the votes of their constituents, the majority of whom were no longer drawn from the higher echelons of society, the populace became able to bring pressure to bear in more subtle ways. A demonstration of the strength of public opinion, exercised through press and television campaigns, opinion polls, demonstrations or refusal to co-operate was now sufficient in some cases to pressurize the government to think again about unpopular policies. Thus, the poll tax introduced during the early 1990s was withdrawn due to its widespread unpopularity and replaced by the more acceptable council tax.

However, it would be wrong to think that the government is always responsive to such pressure. The Campaign for Nuclear Disarmament began to protest against nuclear weapons in the 1950s (Source 83) and has maintained its pressure on the government ever since, but Britain remains a nuclear power. Similarly, peaceful protest has not entirely replaced violence, as can be seen from the 'troubles' in Northern Ireland and the inner city riots during the 1980s in London, Liverpool and Bristol.

UNIT 3.2

TEMPORAL AND SPATIAL PERSPECTIVES

Introduction

We have seen how alternative developmental accounts can be produced by focusing on different strands in an account and how those strands can be identified by using 'markers for change'. However, there are other possible explanations for the existence of alternative accounts. For instance, accounts may differ because, while they refer to the same events, the significance of those events may be considered from different *temporal perspectives*. This could occur in one of two ways. One account might consider the significance of an event or series of events over a longer period of time than another and this might affect the developmental significance attached to the event or events in each account. For instance, in Unit 1.5 the significance of the Glorious Revolution and of the accession of George I to the British throne was considered first in the context of developments between 1660 and 1760 and then in the context of a longer time period extending to 1830. In an account ending in 1760, the events of 1688–1714 might be interpreted as having established the supremacy of parliament over the monarch and of the Whigs over their political rivals, the Tories; but an extension of the account to 1830 is likely to reveal that, whereas the ascendancy of parliament over the monarch was maintained and strengthened, the dominance of the Whigs over the Tories was only temporary.

Alternatively, an event or series of events might occupy different positions within accounts, appearing early in the time period of one account and somewhat later in another. For example, when considered in the context of developments between 1066 and 1553, the English Reformation carried out by Henry VIII and Thomas Cromwell in the 1530s might be interpreted as the ultimate victory of the English monarchy in a struggle to establish its authority over religion, representing as it did the end of the influence of the Pope over religious affairs in England. However, when considered in the light of developments between 1509 and 1714, the termination of papal authority might be regarded as a less significant consequence of the English Reformation than the increasing influence of parliament over religious policy.

Accounts may also differ because the same set of events is considered from different *spatial perspectives*. For instance, the English Revolution of 1640–60 may appear more significant in the development of English politics than it does in the context of developments in Europe, even allowing for the views of Eric Hobsbawm, Hugh Trevor-Roper, Geoffrey Parker, Jack Goldstone and others that the English Revolution was part of a 'general crisis in Europe' (see Depth Study, Unit 4.2).

It is clear, then, that variations in temporal or spatial perspective can lead to the production of differing accounts, but that does not necessarily mean that these accounts are *alternatives* to one another. For accounts to be alternative, as has been argued earlier, they must not only differ, but also be in some degree of competition or conflict. This must involve more than just competing or conflicting interpretations of a single event; the competition or conflict must extend to substantial elements of the accounts.

In this unit, we will use the Black Death of 1348–9 as a case study and consider how variations in the temporal and spatial contexts within which it is studied can affect the significance attached to it in developmental accounts. We will also consider whether the accounts produced merely differ or whether they can be regarded as genuine alternatives to one another. The unit begins with a brief outline of the Black Death itself and then considers its significance within differing temporal and spatial contexts. Where alternative accounts of its historical significance are identified or produced, consideration is given to the extent to which these competing or conflicting accounts can be reconciled in a single more complex account.

The Black Death: 1348–9

The Black Death, which swept across Europe between 1347 and 1350 and ravaged England during 1348–9, was the most devastating epidemic in recorded history. It is difficult to be certain about the exact scale of the catastrophe, but the historian James Bolton has claimed that 'something like 40 per cent of the English and Welsh population seems to have perished between 1348 and 1350'. It is likely that the death tolls in most other European countries were of a similar order. Such enormous loss of life could not fail to send shock waves through the political, social, economic and cultural fabrics of every country that was affected. However, as we shall see later, the effects of this epidemic were not the same in each country.

The Black Death was a name given later to the most virulent outbreak of what contemporaries called 'the pestilence' or 'the plague'. The most common form of the disease was bubonic plague, the symptoms of which include high fever, swellings in the lymphatic glands (known as buboes), usually occurring in the groin but sometimes in the armpits or neck, haemorrhages under the skin causing dark blotches, and infection of the nervous system which could cause uncontrollable spasms, sometimes known as 'the dance of death'. If the buboes burst, the patient stood a good chance of recovery; if not, he or she usually died in agony within four to seven days. It has been estimated that the death rate among those contracting the disease was between 60 per cent and 90 per cent, probably nearer the higher figure.

Source 92

The dance of death. One of many contemporary illustrations depicting death 'dancing' with its victims. Such images probably originate from the spasms that frequently preceded death from the plague.

Bubonic plague was at its most severe during the spring and summer months, but it was usually accompanied by another variety, pneumonic plague, that was more prevalent in the cold and damp conditions of autumn and winter. Pneumonic plague, which attacks the lungs, was even more deadly than the bubonic variety and was usually fatal within two days. The third and rarest variety, septicaemic plague, was even worse: it attacked the bloodstream and killed its victims within a couple of hours. It was probably septicaemic plague that accounted for those cases where apparently healthy people were reported to have dropped down dead in the street. All three varieties were present during the Black Death, although it seems clear from contemporary descriptions that bubonic plague was the main killer.

While people at the time were all too well aware of the symptoms and dismal prognosis of the disease, they had little idea about what caused it or how to prevent or cure it. Theories about its causes included a 'poisonous miasma' or mist; a punishment from God for human sinfulness; the positions in the sky of the planets Saturn, Jupiter and Mars, and the poisoning of wells by lepers or by the Jews. Doctors offered a variety of preventive medicines – all of them useless. Some advised flight from areas of infection; others abstinence from hard work and sexual intercourse. Attempts to cure the disease were equally unsuccessful. Among the most common were measures to open and drain the buboes, to reduce the fever, or to restore the balance of 'humours' or fluids in the body by bloodletting. The impotence of the doctors was hardly surprising, given the level of medieval medical knowledge, although many did recognize that there was a connection between dirt, lack of hygiene and the disease, and some towns attempted to prevent its spread by cleansing the streets. It was not until 1894 that scientists finally identified the germ that caused the plague and discovered that it was transmitted by the bite of fleas that lived on rodents, especially black rats.

Source 93

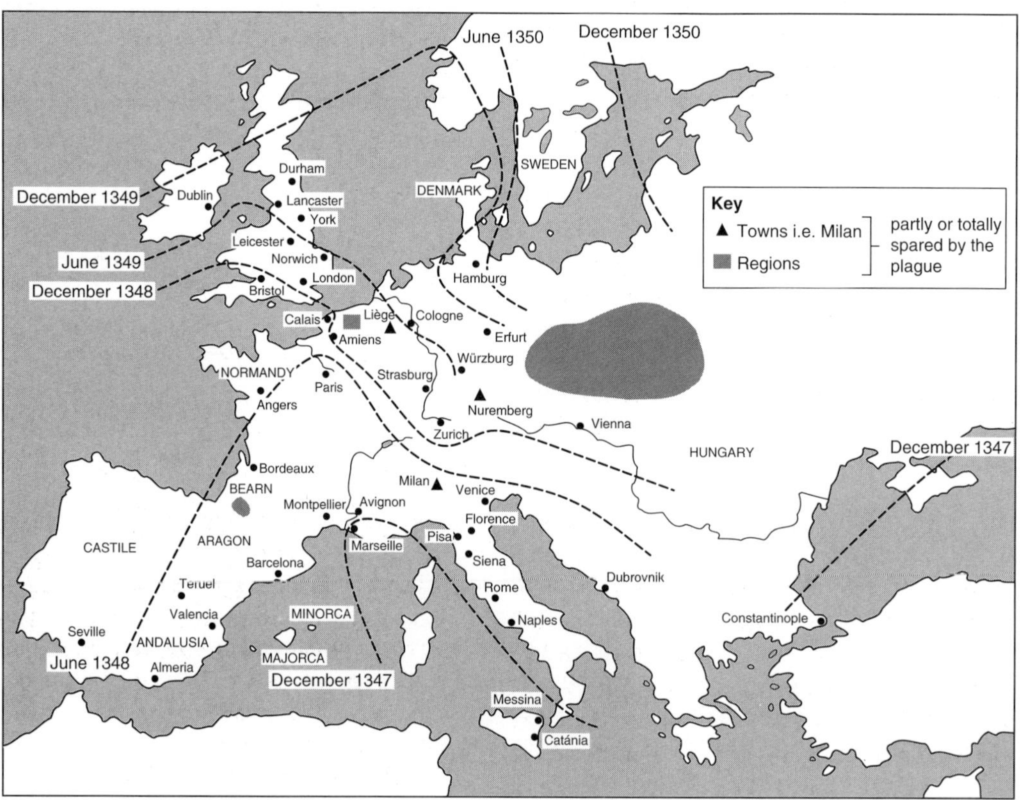

The spread of the Black Death in Europe, 1347–50

Source 94

Three doctors at the bedside of a plague victim, who is pointing to a bubo or swelling in his armpit

The epidemic known as the Black Death began in Central Asia around 1334 and spread west along the trade routes. By 1347 it had reached the coasts of the Black Sea and the eastern Mediterranean, from whence it moved westward and northward infecting the whole of Europe with the exception of a small area in the Pyrenees and a larger area in eastern Europe covering parts of Bohemia, Poland and Lithuania.

The plague reached England in the summer of 1348, apparently from Gascony in southern France, entering the country through a small Dorsetshire port (Source 95). From there it spread swiftly to Bristol and across southern England, reaching London by November, Norwich by January and all but the north of Scotland and north-western Ireland by the end of 1349.

Source 95

From the *Chronicle of the Grey Friars of Lynn* (now King's Lynn) in Norfolk, recording the arrival of the Black Death in England in June 1348.

In the year 1348, at Melcombe in the county of Dorset, two ships, one of them from Bristol, came alongside. One of the sailors had brought with him from Gascony the seeds of that terrible pestilence and, through him, the men of Melcombe were the first in England to be infected.

Since there were no systematic registers of deaths in the fourteenth century, it is difficult for historians to estimate how many died and what proportion of the population this represented. However, it appears that some communities and areas of the country were affected more severely than others. Priests and monks seem to have suffered a higher than average mortality, probably because the former stood a higher risk of infection as they ministered to the sick and dying, while the latter lived in enclosed communities where the disease would spread quickly once it entered a monastery. As one might expect, the death rate was higher in the towns than in the countryside, although many villages in East Anglia, one of the worst affected regions, appear to have experienced rates of 60 per cent or more. London, the largest, unhealthiest and most insanitary city in the country, suffered badly. Somewhere between 40 per cent and 50 per cent of a population of 50–60,000 seem to have died, and civic records suggest a mortality rate of around 290 people a day between June and September 1349.

The fear and horror experienced by those who lived through those years is difficult to imagine, but some idea of the scale of the disaster and its effects on families and communities as far apart as Italy and northern England is conveyed by contemporary writers such as Boccaccio and an anonymous monk from Tynemouth. Such scenes must have been repeated in cities, towns and villages throughout Europe between 1347 and 1350.

Source 96

From Giovanni Boccaccio's introduction to *The Decameron*, written during the 1350s. Boccaccio was an eyewitness to the ravages of the plague in the city of Florence in Italy, and something of his own anguish is conveyed by the following short extract from his account of the effects of the plague on his city.

Tedious were it to recount how citizen avoided citizen, how among neighbours was scarce found any that showed fellow-feeling for another, how kinsfolk held aloof and never met, or but rarely;...brother was forsaken by brother, nephew by uncle, brother by sister and, oftentimes, husband by wife; nay, what is more and scarcely to be believed, fathers and mothers were found to abandon their own children, untended, unvisited, to their fate....Many passed from this life unregarded, and few indeed were they to whom were accorded the lamentations and bitter tears of sorrowing relations....Few also there were whose bodies were attended to the church by more than ten or twelve neighbours, and those not the honourable and respected citizens, but a sort of corpse-carrier drawn from the baser ranks....Nor did the priests distress themselves with too long and solemn a service, but with the aid of the corpse-carriers hastily consigned the corpse to the first tomb which they found untenanted.

Source 97

From a chronicle written by the monks of Tynemouth.

Very many country towns and quarters of innumerable cities are left altogether without inhabitants. The churches or cemeteries did not suffice for the dead, but new places outside the cities and towns were dedicated to that use....And the said mortality was so infectious that hardly anyone remained alive in any house it entered. Hence flight was regarded as the main hope of safety by most, although such fugitives, for the most part, did not escape death but merely obtained some delay in the sentence. Rectors and priests, by the hearing of confessions, were so infected that they died more quickly than their penitents, and parents in many places refused contact with their children, and husband with wife.

Temporal perspectives

In this section, it will be argued that the significance of the Black Death varies according to whether it is viewed in the context of a shorter or a longer period of time and according to whether it occurs towards the beginning or towards the end of that period of time.

Question

1. What significance should be attached to the Black Death in the context of developments in the political, social and economic power of ordinary people between 1066 and 1400?
2. How far does the Black Death assume a different significance when it is considered in the context of developments in the power of ordinary people between 1300 and 1700?
3. (a) To what extent are the accounts produced in answer to Questions 1 and 2 in conflict with each other?

   (b) Is it possible to reconcile the conflicts between these accounts? If so, how?

If we are to consider the significance of the Black Death in the context of political, social and economic developments in England, then it is important to understand the nature of medieval England and of the developments that were taking place within it. Medieval institutions and methods of government have been traced in some detail in Unit 2.2, and the effects of government on ordinary people and their reactions to it have been considered in Unit 3.1. Broadly speaking, for at least two centuries before 1348, England had been a feudal country in which peasants performed labour services on the lord of the manor's demesne farm in return for land on which they could grow sufficient crops for their own consumption and, in good years, a small surplus that could be sold in the local market.

This feudal system was seriously dislocated by the enormous loss of life caused by the Black Death. Shortage of labour meant that fields were left untilled, livestock untended and landowners short of tenants and farm workers. Villeins and other peasant farmers were able to take advantage of this situation by demanding the right to pay money rents in lieu of the irksome labour services, by demanding wages for work on the demesne farm, or, in the case of those already paid a wage, demanding an increase. If their demands were not met, they could move to another manor where desperate lords were willing to offer better terms. Thus, mobility of labour increased, wages rose and labour services gave way increasingly to paid employment.

These developments had already begun before 1348, but the catastrophic plague epidemic dramatically accelerated the pace of change. What is not clear is whether the Black Death of 1348–9 was sufficient on its own to bring about these major changes which heralded the ultimate extinction of feudalism in England, or whether it was the cumulative effect of successive plague epidemics which returned every few years from 1361 until the end of the century and beyond. Between 1348 and 1350, it must have seemed as though the entire manorial system, on which the political, social and economic structure of medieval life rested, was in the process of collapse. However, there is some evidence to suggest that there was sufficient over-population before 1348 for the country to weather the demographic storm and to begin to recover during the 1350s. No such reserve of labour existed when later outbreaks of plague occurred and it has been argued that it is only when the effects of these later epidemics are taken into account that the full significance of the Black Death can be appreciated.

Philip Ziegler, in Source 98, emphasizes the stability of the manorial system in England in the mid-fourteenth century and its ability in the short term to recover from the Black Death, but argues that in the longer term the effects were much more significant. On the other hand, Derek Turner, in Source 99, sees little difference between the shorter and longer-term consequences of the plague, claiming that it had an immediate and lasting impact.

Source 98

From Philip Ziegler, *The Black Death* (Collins, 1969) pp.120 and 137–8.

The England of 1348, politically and economically, was not in so frail a state as some of the countries on the mainland of Europe. Indeed, viewed from France, it must have seemed depressingly prosperous and stable....One of the most striking features of the Black Death in England...is the way in which communal life survived. With his friends and relations dying in droves around him, with labour lacking to till the fields and care for the cattle, with every kind of human intercourse rendered perilous by the possibility of infection, the medieval Englishman obstinately carried on in his accustomed way. Business was very far from being as usual, but landlord and peasant alike did their best to make it so....

The Englishman's reaction, or lack of reaction, was a victory for the system under which he lived. It can be argued that, in the long term, the Black Death struck a fatal blow at the manorial system and heralded the end of the Middle Ages. Be that as it may, in the short term the Black Death provided an impressive tribute to the system's strength and to the readiness of the Englishman to accept the security which it offered and the limitations which it imposed.

Source 99

From Derek Turner, *The Black Death* (Longman, 1978) p.32.

Many families suffered disaster but many others were able to start building up their fortunes by renting or buying land cheaply. Some families were turned out of their homes to make way for the great new sheep pastures that the lords made in parts of England, but there were new opportunities for families to make a living by becoming weavers of woollen cloth. Hard-working and go-ahead tenants found that it suited them to pay a money rent for their land instead of working on their lord's farm because, with fewer workers about, wages went up....Quite often those who were living on poor land or had a bad landlord could do better for their families by moving to another village which had been badly hit by the Black Death. Before 1348 most ordinary people had about the same amount of land and wealth.

After the Black Death there came to be less equality but more opportunity. Many, through bad luck or bad management, got poorer. Others, who were lucky, hard-working, ambitious or clever became richer.

The contemporary significance of the Black Death is undeniable. William of Dene and Henry Knighton were just two of many contemporary observers who bore witness to the disruption of agricultural production, prices and the labour market caused by the high death toll. From Knighton's account it seems that at the time of the Black Death there was also 'a great pestilence among the sheep'.

Source 100

From the chronicle of William of Dene, a monk from Rochester in Kent. The reference to more than a third of the land lying idle is almost certainly an exaggeration, but it testifies to serious economic dislocation during and immediately after the Black Death.

To our great grief, the plague carried off so vast a multitude of people of both sexes that nobody could be found who would bear the corpses to the grave....There was so marked a deficiency of labourers and workmen of every kind at this period that more than a third of the land in the whole realm was let lie idle. All the labourers, skilled or unskilled, were so carried away by the spirit of revolt that neither King, nor law, nor justice, could restrain them.

Source 101

From the chronicle of Henry Knighton, canon of Leicester Abbey, who was a boy at the time of the Black Death and wrote his chronicle around 1382.

In this year [1348] there was a great pestilence among the sheep everywhere in the kingdom, so that in one place more than 500 sheep died in one pasture, and they became so putrid that neither beasts nor birds would touch them. And because of the fear of death there were low prices for everything....For a man could have one horse which was before worth 40*s*. [£2] for one half a mark [33p]....And sheep and cattle wandered through fields and among crops and there was no one who was concerned to drive and collect them, but an unknown number died in ditches and hedges throughout every region for lack of herders. For there was such a lack of servants and helpers that there was no one who knew what he ought to do....

The workers, nevertheless, were so elated and contrary that they did not heed the mandate of the king [prohibiting higher wages] but if anyone wanted to hire them, he had to give them what they desired; either lose their crops and fruit or grant the selfish and lofty wishes of the workers.

The authorities did not surrender to the newfound economic power of the peasantry without a fight. Although the Ordinance of Labourers passed in 1349, at the height of the epidemic, failed in its aims of forcing wage levels back down to their pre-plague level and preventing servants leaving their masters in search of more lucrative employment elsewhere, the Statute of Labourers enacted in 1351 appears to have been more successful in stabilizing both wages and, as Source 104 illustrates, prices.

Source 102

From the Ordinance of Labourers, 1349. This attempt to force wages down to the levels that had pertained before the Black Death proved unsuccessful and led to the passing of the Statute of Labourers in 1351.

That every man and woman of our realm of England, of what condition he be, free or bond,...if he is in suitable service...he shall be bound to serve him who so shall require him; and take only the wages, livery or salary which were accustomed to be given in the places where he owes to serve [in 1347], or five or six years before....And if any such man or woman, being so required to serve, will not do this..., he shall be taken...and committed to the next jail....

If any reaper, mower, or other workman or servant...retained in any man's service, do depart from the said service without reasonable cause or licence before the term agreed, he shall have the penalty of imprisonment....That no man pay or promise to pay any servant any more wages, liveries or salary than was accustomed as afore is said.

Source 103

From the Statute of Labourers, 1351.

Whereas, to curb the malice of servants who after the pestilence were idle and unwilling to serve without securing excessive wages, it was recently ordained by our lord the king, with the assent of the prelates, nobles and other men of his council, that such servants, both men and women, should be bound to serve in return for the salaries and wages that were customary in those places where they were obligated to serve during 1347....And whereas our lord the king has now...been given to understand that the said servants have no regard for the said ordinance, but, to suit their ease and their selfish desires, refrain from serving their lords or other men unless they receive double or triple that which they were accustomed to have in 1347 and earlier, to the great damage of the lords and the impoverishment of all men of the said commons, who now pray for remedy of these matters. Therefore,...the following measures are ordained and established to curb the malice of the said servants. [There follows a list of punishments for servants who leave their masters without permission or who demand higher wages, and for landlords who entice servants away from other lords or pay excessively high wages.]

Source 104

Years	Price per quarter (13 kg) varied between
1347–8	5*s*. (25p) and 8*s*. 8*d*. (43p)
1348–9	3*s*. 6*d*. (17p) and 6*s*. (30p)
1349–50	6*s*. 8*d*. (33p) and 9*s*. (45p)
1351–2	14*s*. (70p)
1355	5*s*. (25p) and 8*s*. (40p)

The price of wheat around the time of the Black Death in Hampshire and Somerset

The extent to which the Statute of Labourers achieved its aims is, however, a matter of dispute among historians. Some, like Williamson and Bellamy (Source 105) and Thorold Rogers (referred to in Source 111) regard it as no more successful than the Ordinance that preceded it and claim that during the second half of the fourteenth century the economic advantage was so much with the peasantry that many landlords gave up the struggle to farm their demesnes and rented them out to tenants. Others, such as Philip Ziegler (Source 111) argue that it must have been at least partly successful in restoring the old order because wages and prices fell back during the 1350s, if not to their pre-1348 level, at least to well below their high points in 1348–9. Furthermore, they argue, the fact that labour services and low wage rates were a source of grievance during the Peasants' Revolt in 1381 suggests that the Statute of Labourers must have had some effect.

Source 105

From T. Williamson and L. Bellamy, *Property and Landscape* (George Philip, 1987) p.88.

The demise of large sections of the labour force strengthened the hand of those who survived in the years following the onslaught of the disease. As peasants capitalized on rising wage rates and falling rents, there was a great increase in the geographical mobility of the labouring population....At the same time the lords found it increasingly difficult to compel their villeins to perform their customary services. The balance of power had shifted away from the lords and the villeins were not slow to take advantage of the situation. Furthermore, as the profits from agriculture slumped, many lords got out of demesne farming as rapidly as they could by leasing out their demesne lands and thus had less need of labour.

But the lords did not take the new power of the labourers lying down. They sought to legislate against it, and in 1351 the Statute of Labourers was passed. This was a rearguard action which attempted to control wages, and to restrict geographical mobility. It totally failed to achieve anything of the kind. The economic cards had, for the time being, played into the hands of the workers, and in the short term it was the peasants and labourers who gained from the social upheavals of the fourteenth century....

Villeins now had much greater choice over where they would farm. They could easily take up tenements on land where the rent was low or the soil good, and desert the poor soils or high rents of their home. Thus on areas of marginal land, such as the sandy Brecklands of Norfolk, and the Wolds of Yorkshire and Lincolnshire, there were extensive desertions in the fourteenth and early fifteenth centuries, and these areas are dotted today with the earthworks and sometimes the crumbling churches of these deserted medieval villages.

Contemporary writers and historians alike have made the link between the Black Death and the large number of villages throughout England that were depopulated in the following decades. Few, if any, villages were wiped out by the plague, but it contributed to the abandonment of villages in two ways. Firstly, the shortage of labour helped to persuade many landlords to abandon labour-intensive arable farming and convert their lands to sheep pasture. Since sheep require few shepherds, unwanted peasants were expelled from their homes and villages were either destroyed or left to decay. Secondly, the high mortality of the Black Death left many vacant tenancies. The more attractive tenancies on fertile land were often filled by families moving out of villages on the margins of production, which became deserted. By no means all these desertions occurred immediately after the Black Death. Some villages did not succumb until well into the fifteenth century, while others were deserted before 1348. However, in most cases, villages became depopulated as a result of successive waves of famine and plague and the increasing profitability of livestock over arable farming.

Source 106

From the chronicle of Henry Knighton, c.1382.

After the aforesaid pestilence, many large and small buildings in all the cities, boroughs and villages collapsed and were levelled with the earth for lack of inhabitants; likewise many villages and hamlets were deserted. No house was left in them for everyone who had lived in them had died, and it was probable that many such villages were never to be inhabited again.

Source 107

Hound Tor, Dartmoor: a medieval village that was deserted during the late fourteenth century

Source 108

From Christopher Dyer, 'A Deserted Village – Upton in Gloucestershire', in Edmund King, *Medieval England* (Phaidon Press, 1988) p.201.

Upton began to decline by 1299, when three tenants had taken over neighbours' holdings that had formerly been held as separate units....The famine of 1315–17 and the plagues of 1349 and 1361–2 made vacant holdings available in other villages, and people were glad to move to larger places with more facilities. They shook off their servile status, which in theory tied them to their lord, and gained their freedom by migration....Desertion was apparently complete by 1383. The village and its fields became a sheep pasture, served by a sheepcote [pen] nearby. From the late fifteenth century, 'Upton Wold' was leased to graziers who kept enough sheep to pay a rent of £9. 6*s*. 8*d*. [£9.33] from their profits. All over England, 3,000 villages were being deserted in the period 1320 1520, reflecting not just the fall in population, but also the vulnerability of corn-growing peasant communities; the future lay with the large-scale farmers who took over the empty lands.

One should not think in terms of clear-cut divisions between short and long-term consequences of the Black Death, as the evidence in respect of the depopulation of villages illustrates. Rather, we should think in terms of a continuum in which a gradual extension of the time period alters, sometimes subtly, the significance which we attach to the event. This is demonstrated in Source 109, where James Bolton, despite dividing the consequences into two separate time periods, sees considerable overlap between the significance accorded to the Black Death in each. It is also implied by A.R. Bridbury and Philip Ziegler in Sources 110 and 111, both of whom stress the cumulative effect of successive outbreaks of plague rather than identifying the first epidemic, the Black Death, as the principal agent of change.

Source 109

From James Bolton, 'The Black Death', in *The Historian*, Autumn 1993, pp.6–7. In this extract, the author assesses the shorter and longer-term consequences of the Black Death.

The Consequences: 1350–75

By any standards, medieval or modern, this was a catastrophe which brought chaos to England. Fields lay untilled and livestock untended, commerce was at a standstill and no wool could be exported. Courts could not be held nor records kept, the dead could scarcely be buried except in common graves and labour was in such short supply that the crown had to hurry through first the Ordinance (1349) and then in 1351 the Statute of Labourers to try to peg wages at pre-plague levels and enforce contracts so that landlords could continue the cultivation of their estates. Depopulation on this scale should have led to a radical shift in the economy, to a world turned upside down where the poor labourer was now a man much sought after, where the authority of lords, lay and ecclesiastical, was challenged at every level.

All this, indeed, was to happen, but not at once, and here lies the paradox of the first plague. If we look forward no more than five or six years to the mid-1350s, we see a country where the pre-plague pattern of society, and more importantly economy, had swiftly reasserted itself. New tenants had been found for vacant holdings in the countryside, and lordship over men and women, in all its various forms, manorial and non-manorial, was still exercised in much the same way as it had been before 1348. The ranks of regular and secular clergy were filled, and wool exports reached again the levels of the late thirteenth century....Yet if we look ahead a further 20 years to the mid 1370s we see all the signs of substantial and what was to prove sustained change, well into the fifteenth century. In the countryside peasant holdings were falling vacant and staying vacant and land was beginning to go out of use on a large scale which, in a subsistence economy, is always the sign of falling population. More significantly, all over the country, but particularly in the Midlands, whole villages were being deserted. Only three or four were completely depopulated by the plague, most villages instead dying a long, slow death. They were mainly on poor soils, where peasants held their land on unfavourable terms. Now they could move away, to seek better land and better status elsewhere, and they did. Indeed, there was an increasing mobility in society generally.... Along with that mobility, partly caused by it and partly the result of an increasing awareness that the advantage now lay with the tenant, and not the lord, came increasing difficulties in enforcing manorial discipline, difficulties which were to be one of the main causes of the Peasants' Revolt. In towns the trends are more contradictory, with a degree of false prosperity, lasting perhaps until the 1420s,...concealing underlying problems caused by population decline....

The Consequences: 1375–1500

Why then was this apparent recovery followed by long-term demographic decline so that, as the accompanying graph shows, there were probably no more people in England in 1500 than there had been in 1200 and, looking further ahead, not as many in 1600 (c. five million) as there had been in 1300, with some historians arguing that the population did not again reach late thirteenth-century levels until about 1750.

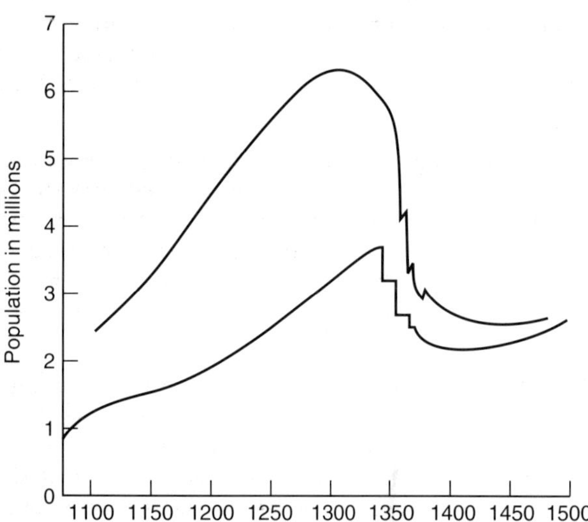

Possible maximum and minimum population estimates for England, 1100–1500. The upper graph is the more acceptable of the two (permission Economic History Society).

To the first part of the question – Why was there a fairly rapid recovery after the catastrophe of 1348–50, but then a sharp decline in the population over the next quarter of a century? – there is a fairly easy answer. England was probably overpopulated, in relative terms, in 1348 and the first plague clearly made it possible for an underclass, who had neither land nor jobs, to move forward and step into dead men's shoes, to fill vacant holdings and to repopulate towns. More important, modern epidemiologists tell us that one major natural disaster, such as the plague, does not of itself cause permanent demographic decline. In an underdeveloped rural society it will release land, improve economic prospects and encourage an earlier age of marriage, so that more children are born of the marriage. The population will replace itself, and even grow, and that seems to have been the case in the 1350s. But if one disaster is followed by a regularly recurring series of similar disasters, then demographic downturn is likely, because the systematic and cumulative reduction in the number of survivors results in fewer and fewer children to replace those who have died. That is what seems to have happened between 1350 and 1375. Plague had come to stay, in reservoirs in town and countryside. In 1361–2 there was a second severe national outbreak, called by the Anonimalle and Meaux Abbey chronicles 'the plague of children' and by Walsingham a great pestilence which affected men more than women, both of which observed phenomena would have had severe consequences for the reproductive cycle. In 1369 there was a third outbreak of plague, in 1375 a fourth, so that by the late 1370s prices for agricultural produce fell in response to severely reduced demand, and wages rose, both in money and real terms, owing to a shortage of labour – trends which were to persist until the end of the Middle Ages.

Clearly, recurrent outbreaks of plague had caused cumulative population decline by the late 1370s..., but why there was not then a sustained recovery, as land became readily available and standards of living rose, rather than continued demographic stagnation, has become...the subject of a lively debate. Some historians believe that recurrent outbreaks of plague...acted as a constant brake on recovery. They point to further national epidemics in 1390, 1400, 1407, 1413, 1434, 1464, 1471 and 1479, with frequent and ill-recorded outbreaks at other times and a severe famine with disastrous short and long-term consequences in the north in 1438–9....So, it is argued, although plague may have been less virulent after 1350,...recurrent mortality crises meant that after the mid-1370s the population barely replaced itself. Other demographic historians see the problem as more complex, however, suggesting that there was also a lowering of the fertility rate and that appallingly high death rates were accompanied by stagnant or low birth rates. They offer a variety of explanations for this phenomenon, but most interestingly a later age of marriage due to the new opportunities for young women at a time of labour shortages which allowed them to preserve their independence....There may also have been an imbalance between the numbers of males and females in the population...for both contemporary chronicles and modern medical evidence suggest that males were more susceptible to plague than females.

In Source 110, A.R. Bridbury argues that the social and economic consequences of the epidemic of 1361–2 were more profound than those of the earlier epidemic of 1348–9 when viewed against trends in prices and wages. From 1264 to 1309, prices fluctuated about a level which was low by subsequent standards but was consistent with a cycle of harvest surpluses and failures. In 1310 they began to rise, reaching spectacular peaks during the famine caused by the harvest failures of 1315 and 1316. Prices fell back somewhat after 1316 but remained high until 1334, after which there was a period of good harvests and low prices until the Black Death. Between 1351 and 1376, prices were generally higher than they had ever been, though the peaks of 1370–1 were lower than those of 1316–7. The first really good harvest for thirty years occurred in 1378, after which prices began to fall and continued to do so into the next century.

From 1290 to 1378, wages tended to rise and fall broadly in line with fluctuations in prices, but thereafter wages rose steeply without being accompanied by an increase in prices. Thus, for the first time in the century, agricultural wage-earners experienced a noticeable improvement in their standard of living.

Source 110

From A.R. Bridbury, 'The Black Death', in *The Economic History Review*, 1973, pp.583–91.

With the arrival of the Black Death wages rose once more. Contemporary outcry prepares one for a truly spectacular rise. But the figures do not tell a story which is in any way consistent with the volume of the outcry. Wages certainly rose, and sometimes rose sharply. But wage-rates did not soar. After the first shock of the pestilence was over, what was most remarkable about the wage-rates was the way in which they drifted steadily upwards, particularly in the sixth and seventh decades of the century, and continued to do so even in the fifteenth century....

If these figures are to be trusted, demesne farmers were undoubtedly paying more for labour after the Black Death than ever before. The rise in wages meant that demesne farmers who were very dependent upon wage labour, as many were, could not make profits which were commensurate with the prices they were getting...but even those demesne farmers who had to watch their wage-bills found that the rise in wages was not sharp enough to eat into profits....

The second pestilence arrived in 1361 and persisted throughout the winter in certain parts of the country. It or something else certainly upset price levels, for famine prices prevailed in 1362, 1363, 1364, and even in 1365. If the price index is rightly linked to the plague epidemics, then plague left a far deeper mark in 1361–2 than it did when it first devastated the country in mid-century. High prices rose to a peak in 1370 when prices were higher than they had ever been except for the terrible years of 1316 and 1317. Then came the harvest of 1375. It was the best for twenty-six years. And it was a portent. A new age of low prices began. And for the first time in the fourteenth century, money wages did not conform to the movement of prices....

[Bridbury goes on to argue that it was this fatal split between prices and wages after 1375, rather than accumulated difficulties since 1349 as is often supposed, which caused demesne farmers to clamour for stricter enforcement of the Statute of Labourers of 1351 in an effort to hold down wages. This, in turn, contributed to the outbreak of the Peasants' Revolt of 1381. It also hastened the eventual collapse of the manorial system, because wage-rates continued to rise and prices continued to fall. And this process was of far greater long-term significance than the crisis of mid-century because there was no longer a surplus of population to fill vacant tenancies.]

The result of these dramatic changes in the relationship of wages to prices was to ruin demesne farming. The records are full of it. They make sombre reading. In earlier periods, before the Black Death as well as after it, when the records told of unfilled vacancies and terms offered which were unsatisfactory from the landlord's point of view, they did not necessarily tell of a countryside from which the life was ebbing away. By the late fourteenth century that is exactly what they do. By then, as never before, they are full of despondent reckonings of [unpaid] rents, abandoned holdings, and demesne farms surrendered to tenants on almost any terms they cared to offer. The big demesne farmers who had weathered so many storms could not weather this one. For them it was the end. And their failure is at once reflected in the movements of prices and wages and explained by them....

All our difficulties with the evidence disappear if we take it that the immensely heavy mortality caused by the Black Death was quite incapable of altering the social and economic relationships of the community...because so much of the population was surplus by the fourteenth century that the early famines and the mid-century pestilences were more purgative than toxic....

The chief economic problem of the fourteenth century remains a population problem even when we have shifted it from mid-century to the 'seventies....Moreover, changes which continued for so many years that the relationships of wages to prices were not stabilized until the second or third decade of the fifteenth century presuppose a series of epidemic diseases which overwhelmed the recovery powers of the population as [it was once thought] the Black Death did.

Source 111

From P. Ziegler, *The Black Death*, pp.240–59.

'The year of the conception of modern man was the year 1348, the year of the Black Death' wrote the German historian, Friedell, in 1927. It was as significant a phenomenon as the Industrial Revolution, claimed G.M. Trevelyan in *English Social History* [1942]....The classic exposition of the Black Death's role in England as a social force of the first importance comes from that great medievalist Thorold Rogers, writing in 1866....'The effect of the plague', he wrote, 'was to introduce a complete revolution in the occupation of land'. His contention...was that commutation, that is to say the substitution of wages and rent in monetary terms for the labour services owed by the villein to the lord, was already well advanced by the time of the Black Death. The sudden disappearance of so high a proportion of the labour force meant that those who already worked for wages were able to demand an increase while those who had not yet achieved this status agitated to commute their services and share in the benefits enjoyed by freemen. If the landlord refused, conditions were peculiarly favourable for the villein to slip away and seek a more amenable master elsewhere.

The landlord was thus in a weak position. Finding himself forced to pay higher wages and obtain lower prices for his produce because of the reduced demand, he increasingly tended to break up his demesne and let it off for a cash rent to the freemen or villeins of his manor. But he did not succumb without a fight and Parliament came to his rescue with legislation designed to check increased wages and the free movement of labour. The landlords sought to put back the clock and not only to hold on to the relatively few feudal services which still existed but to exact others which had been waived in the period before the Black Death while labour was cheap and plentiful. The result was resentment on the part of the serfs which simmered angrily for thirty years and finally erupted in 1381 in the shape of the Peasants' Revolt....

[At this point] it would be useful to restate three general considerations....The first of these is that the damage done by the epidemics of bubonic plague during the fourteenth century was cumulative. The epidemic of 1348 was certainly the most devastating...but further outbreaks occurred in 1361, 1368–9, 1371, 1375, 1390 and 1405. On the whole these were progressively less violent but the second epidemic of 1361, by any standards other than those of the Black Death, was catastrophic in its dimensions....Whenever, therefore the question arises of the responsibility of the Black Death for any marked change in England...unless the comparison is strictly between the period before 1348 and the period between 1351 and 1361, then two and not one epidemics have to be taken into account. If the comparison is made with some date near the end of the fourteenth century [or later] then the problem of responsibility becomes still more difficult to resolve since three, four or more epidemics had, by then, taken their toll, as well, of course, as all the other factors which may have contributed to the transformation....

The second point to remember is that the decline in the economy had already set in well before 1348....For at least 25 years before the Black Death, exports, agricultural production, the area of cultivated land and possibly also the population had all been shrinking. In assessing the baleful effects of the Black Death these earlier difficulties must never be forgotten. Continued deterioration in the state of England – and, indeed, of Europe – would have been likely, even if it had never occurred.

Thirdly..., the economic impact of the Black Death was to some extent blunted by the fact that England...was grossly over-populated....This led to chronic under-employment rather than unemployment....

Bearing these factors in mind, it remains to consider whether the Black Death did indeed bring about as fundamental a revolution in land tenure and social organization as has been suggested. There is...much that is incontestably true in the thesis. Among the phenomena which Thorold Rogers noted as being particularly relevant were the rise in the level of wages and of prices and the greatly increased mobility of labour....'The immediate effect of the Plague', wrote Rogers, 'was to double the wages of labour; in some districts to raise the rate even beyond this'....Professor Rogers and other proponents of his theories are also undoubtedly right in saying that prices of agricultural products fell steeply during and directly after the Black Death; thus making still more troublesome the life of the landlord....

The proof that labour was on the move is provided by the energetic efforts which the government made to check it. The Ordinance of Labourers of 1349 and the Statute of Labourers in 1351 were a direct attempt to prevent workmen transferring their loyalties from one employer to another....'The Statute of Labourers', wrote Dr. Putnam, 'must be regarded...as proof that radical changes had occurred, ushering in a new era'. Perhaps the most radical of these changes was the new desire, even determination, on the part of the medieval labourer to have a say in deciding his terms of employment and to seek his fortune elsewhere if such a right were denied him....The landlord – unable to hire labour except at greatly increased wages, unable to get a good price for his products or to buy what he needed for the farm except at exorbitant cost, unable to enforce his manorial rights because his villeins fled when he attempted to – was sorely tempted to abandon the struggle altogether. His remedy was to let off the demesne to the tenants for a cash rent in units small enough for them to farm themselves....It would be hard to find an age in which the change was more fundamental. The pattern of several centuries was breaking up; not only the pattern of society but the set of men's minds as well....

Dr. Levett has provided the weightiest evidence against the presentation of the Black Death as a watershed in English social history. She has shown that, on many of the manors of the Bishop of Winchester, commutation was hardly known before the Black Death and that there was remarkably little change introduced in the years immediately afterwards.... Her statistics are impressive, but against them it can be contended that the experience of manors belonging to rich, powerful and conservative churchmen need not necessarily be applicable even to other manors in the same neighbourhood, let alone to the country as a whole....

In some parts of England, therefore, the Black Death was a sharp stimulus to rapid and lasting commutation of manorial services, in others it gave rise to much commutation but the landlords were able to check the process and more or less restore the *status quo*, in yet others it had little perceptible effect on the manorial structure and, finally, in a few it impelled the landlords into a reaction which sought to resurrect labour services that had long been suffered to fall into disuse. The more prosperous and stable manors were the least affected; where the land was poor, the landlord ineffective, or the disease raged with especial violence, then the consequence was likely to be a rapid growth in commutation....However, it is reasonable to contend that commutation was well known in most parts of England before 1348, and that the Black Death did no more than accelerate, though often violently accelerate, an established and, in the long run, inevitable progress.

What of the other economic and social effects of the Black Death which Thorold Rogers maintained did so much radically to change the manorial system and lead towards the Peasants' Revolt? Wages and prices of manufactured goods certainly rose sharply after the Black Death, but this rise was not maintained. Nor was the fall in the value of agricultural products. Almost all the examples cited to illustrate the dramatic effects of the plague can also be used to show how quickly the effects passed. But for the most part they did not pass altogether. Particularly in the case of wages a very real advantage was won and retained by the labourer in almost every part of England....Prices of agricultural produce seem on the whole to have more than regained their level within a year or two of the end of the plague....The price of manufactured goods, on the other hand, dropped back a little from the abnormally high level of the years of the Black Death and immediately after but still remained well above the pre-plague average....

Again and again in the patchwork of horror stories which composes our knowledge of the Black Death one of the most striking features has been the speed of recovery shown by the medieval community....Yet it would be a mistake to suggest that this was an easy or painless process, or that all areas recovered completely....England had consumed her fat and it was going to be far more difficult for it to recover a second time if any fresh strain were imposed. Such a strain was to be imposed with the second epidemic of bubonic plague in 1361....Obviously by 1361 the children of the post-plague years were not yet competent to undertake the work done by their deceased uncles and cousins, but numerically at least the recovery had begun. It was only after 1360, and still more in the last quarter of the fourteenth century, that depopulation began substantially to change the face of England....

Rogers is surely justified in his belief that the Black Death was a stimulus towards greater mobility of labour and hence towards the disintegration of the manorial system. But the legislation which this new mobility provoked to counter it went far towards nullifying this result. For a long time it was accepted doctrine that the Ordinance of Labourers and the subsequent Statute of Labourers were dead letters from the start; ignored by the labourers and treated with indifference or contempt even by the employers themselves....It is hard to reconcile this doctrine with the facts. The object of the statutes was to pin wages and prices as closely as possible to pre-plague figures and thus to check the inflation that existed in the England of 1349–51....The result is self-evident. Within a few years wages and prices had fallen back; not indeed to the pre-plague level, but at least to a point well below their maximum. Governmental action cannot be given all the credit for this; it is probable that there would anyhow have been a reaction once the immediate shock of the Black Death had worn off. But equally it seems unreasonable to dismiss as a total failure legislation which, in fact, achieved most of what it set out to do....For the most part the statutes did not operate to make the labourer worse off than he had been before, but they cut off a line of advance towards a new prosperity which had been opened by the plague. The fact that they were largely successful was an important factor in the compound of national issues and local grievances which was eventually to give rise to the Peasants' Revolt....

Because the Black Death was not an immediate cause of the Peasants' Revolt, it does not follow that it should not bear a large share of the responsibility. If there had been no plague it is arguable that the circumstances which so disturbed society in 1381 would eventually have arisen. The breakdown of the structure of a society can never be painless and, by the second half of the fourteenth century, the disintegration of the manorial system was inevitable and already well advanced. But the Black Death immeasurably aided the process....[According to Dr. Levett] 'the Black Death did not...cause the Peasants' Revolt or the breakdown of villeinage, but it gave birth, in many cases, to a smouldering feeling of discontent, an inarticulate desire for change, which found its outlet in the rising of 1381'....The Black Death did not initiate any major social or economic trend but it accelerated and modified – sometimes drastically – those which already existed....The Black Death was a catalytic element of the first order, profoundly altering the economic and social forces on which it operated. Without it the history of England and of Europe in the second half of the fourteenth century would have been very different.

Ziegler's characterization of the Black Death as 'a catalytic element of the first order, profoundly altering the economic and social forces on which it operated' suggests that we should regard 1348–9 as a turning point in the development of wages, prices and patterns of employment in England, and perhaps we should. However, analysis of fluctuations in wool production, prices and wages over long periods of time (Sources 112–4) might suggest different interpretations. The decline in the export of raw wool which began early in the fourteenth century does not appear to have been much affected by the Black Death, but the export trade in woollen cloth began almost immediately afterwards and may have resulted partly from the conversion of unprofitable demesne farms into sheep pasture. The 1350s marked the birth of a cloth industry which grew steadily until it came to dominate English exports from the fifteenth to the eighteenth century.

Source 112

	Exports of raw wool	Exports of cloth (raw wool equivalent)
1281–90	26,856	
1301–10	34,493	
1311–20	30,686	
1321–30	25,268	
1331–40	29,569	
1341–50	22,013	
1351–60	32,655	1,267
1361–70	28,302	3,024
1371–80	23,241	3,432
1381–90	17,988	5,521
1391–1400	17,679	8,967
1401–10	13,922	7,651
1411–20	13,487	6,364
1421–30	13,696	9,309
1431–40	7,377	10,051
1441–50	9,398	11,803
1451–60	8,058	8,445
1461–70	8,237	7,667
1471–80	9,299	10,125
1481–90	8,858	12,230
1491–1500	8,149	13,891
1501–10	7,562	18,700
1511–20	7,634	20,388
1521–30	4,990	20,305
1531–40	3,481	23,424

Exports of English cloth and raw wool, 1281–1540. Events such as the Wars of the Roses (1455–71) had a short-term impact on the volume of trade without seriously affecting the general direction of the trend.

The graph of consumer prices (Source 113) illustrates clearly how the significance of an event can vary according to the time period within which it is considered. Looked at in the context of developments between 1264 and 1375, the plague appeared to play a major role in reversing the downward trend in prices that had followed the high point reached during the famine years of 1315–6. Extend the time period to 1500 and the Black Death appears less significant because the price rise is revealed to have been temporary. Extend the period again to 1700 or later and the significance of the epidemic is reduced still further in comparative terms, because the sustained inflation which began in the early sixteenth century, caused by a rapid rise in population and changes in agriculture, is shown to be of greater and more lasting significance.

Source 113

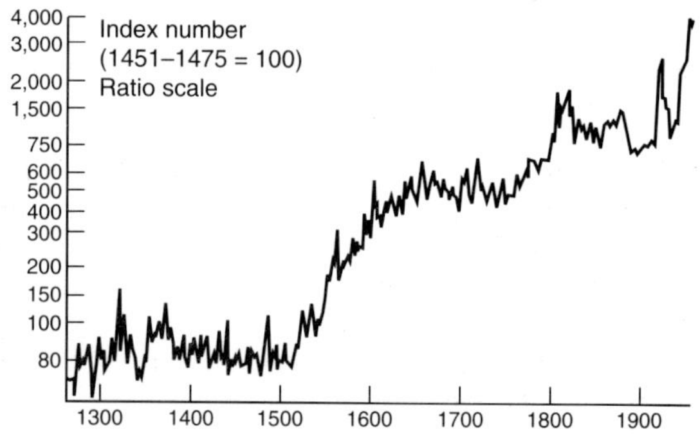

Consumer prices in England, 1264–1954

Real wages (i.e. wages adjusted to take account of the cost of living) tended to move in inverse directions to prices. The impact of the Black Death on real wages was less clear and immediate than it was on prices, but the effects were more long-lasting. The rise in real wages began before 1348, and so was not due entirely to the effects of plague, but increased more rapidly as successive epidemics created labour shortages. The significance of the higher wage levels of the fifteenth century is revealed even more clearly by extending the time period to 1900, because it was only in the late nineteenth century that real wages once again reached fifteenth-century standards.

Source 114

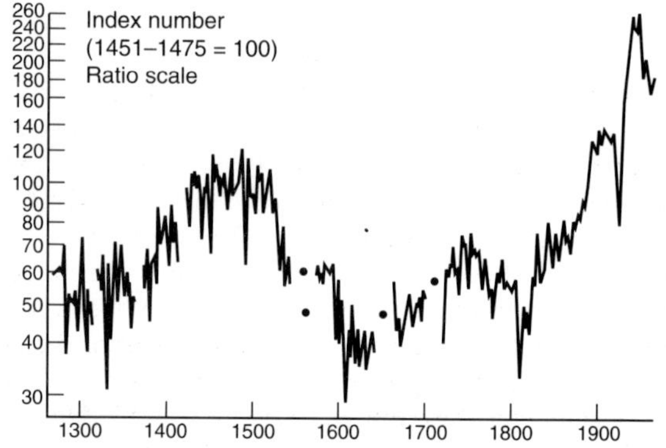

Real wages of English building craftsmen, 1264–1954

The long view of trends in prices and wages reveals, in each case, only three or four major directional changes. One of these certainly occurred in the latter part of the fourteenth century and was a response, at least in part, to the severe population losses associated with the sequences of harvest failures, famines and epidemics in the early and middle years of the century. Historians in search of 'the end of the Middle Ages' have been attracted to the period between the Black Death and the end of the century as a point at which acceleration occurred in the transformation of medieval society.

Source 115

From H.O. Meredith, *Outlines of the Economic History of England* (Pitman) pp.79–83.

At the beginning of the reign of Edward I (1272) the fusion of Norman and Saxon elements in the population was incomplete. Royal power and justice bound together districts and towns which had hardly yet felt their common interests. At the end of the sixteenth century a keen sense of national unity pervaded all parts of the country and all classes....

The whole structure of industry is changed in this transition. In agriculture, production for the market has largely increased at the expense of subsistence farming. Correspondingly in the towns the multiplication of specialised employments has proceeded....Hence a continued division of trading and productive functions; the growth on the one hand of an army of wage-earners, on the other of a number of capitalist distributers and entrepreneurs....

Breaches in the isolation of individual manors and towns were made possible by, and in turn demanded an increase in, the economic functions of the central government. In many matters which could be left to the manorial custom or municipal regulation in the twelfth and thirteenth centuries, national treatment came to be required, or at least national supervision of the local authority. The need was met by the development of the legislative power of Parliament and the executive and administrative duties of the Justices of the Peace....

The course of the movement lies concealed beneath a series of conspicuous accidents....Commencing with the Black Death, in the middle of the fourteenth century, we pass to the Hundred Years' War, the war between Lancaster and York, the enormous expansion of sheep farming, the discovery of the new World and the Cape route to the east, the dissolution of the monasteries, the debasement of the currency, and the fall in the value of silver. Each of these events in turn found out weak points in the old order, or warped the development of the new from lines which might otherwise have been followed. After each shock the crumbling fragments settled to a new equilibrium, soon again to be disturbed. As always in human history, the part played by conscious deliberation and concerted action was small.

The influence of the Black Death is especially noteworthy in the rural districts. It turned the slow decay of the manorial system into rapid dissolution. It threw the economic system of manorial farming, the social system of customary regulation into like confusion, and made their permanent maintenance impossible. Every side of the subsequent economic development can be traced back before the disaster, and though progress in each particular was hugely accelerated, the change was not a revolution. But in regard to customary regulation something comparable to a geological fault perceptibly marks off the period before the plague from the period which followed it. In the former period the manorial court is still the centre of interest, in the latter the Crown and Parliament regulate the main conditions of human life.

Other historians have agreed with Friar Wadding (Source 116) in seeing the Black Death as contributing to a sustained decline in the quality of the clergy and respect for the Church. Philip Ziegler (Source 117) has even argued that it helped to create conditions that were to lead ultimately to the English Reformation.

Source 116

From P. Wadding, *Annales Minorum*. Wadding was a Franciscan friar, who blamed the laxity and decline of his own order on the Black Death.

It was because of this misfortune [the Black Death] that the monastic Orders, in particular the mendicants [orders who, like the Franciscans, supported themselves by begging], which up to this date had been flourishing, both in learning and in piety, now began to decline. Discipline became slack and faith weakened, both because of the loss of their most eminent members and the relaxation of rules which ensued as a result of these calamities. It was in vain to look to the young men who had been received without proper selection and training to bring about a reform since they thought more about filling up the empty religious houses than about restoring the lost sense of authority.

Source 117

From P. Ziegler, *The Black Death*, pp.269–70, 273 and 278.

The priests suffered and died at the side of the laity; were always, indeed, among the most likely victims. Yet the slender evidence that exists shows that they lost popularity as a result of the plague. They were deemed not to have risen to the level of their responsibilities, to have run away in fear..., to have put their own skins first and the souls of their parishioners a bad second....One of the most perplexing features of the Black Death is the reconciliation of this criticism with the outstandingly high mortality amongst priests....

It does not seem that the new recruits who took the place of the dead were spiritually or, still more, educationally, of the calibre of their predecessors. During and immediately after the plague the usual rules governing the ordination of priests were virtually abandoned....Henry Knighton referred to such recruits disparagingly: 'a very great multitude of men whose wives had died of the pestilence flocked to Holy Orders of whom many were illiterate and no better than laymen except in so far as they could read though not understand'....

The monasteries, on the whole, were still worse affected [by the plague] than the clergy. Including monks, nuns and friars the total population of the religious houses in England shortly before the Black Death had been something near 17,500. Not far short of half these appear to have perished in the two years of the epidemic....The blow to the prestige and power of the monasteries did not stem only from their dwindling membership. The enormous number of chantries endowed in parish churches during and immediately after the Black Death inevitably detracted from the significance of the monasteries in the eyes of the people.

The Black Death did not cause the Reformation; it did not stimulate doubts about the doctrine of Transubstantiation [the belief that the bread and wine in the mass were transformed into the body and blood of Christ]; but did it not cause a state of mind in which doctrines were more easily doubted and in which the Reformation was more immediately possible?...Wyclif was a child of the Black Death in the sense that he belonged to a generation which had suffered terribly and learned through its sufferings to doubt the premises on which its society was based. The Church which he attacked was a victim of the Black Death because of the legion of its most competent and dedicated officers who had perished and, still more, because of the honour and respect which it had forfeited in the minds of men. The Church continued as an immensely potent force in the second half of the fourteenth century but the unquestioned authority which it had been used to exercise over its members was never to be recovered.

Spatial perspectives

In this section, the effects of viewing the impact of the Black Death within different spatial contexts will be considered. First, the consequences of the epidemic for certain local communities will be compared with its consequences for England as a whole. Then the consequences for England will be compared with those for other European countries, especially Italy and Germany. It must, however, be borne in mind that what we are interested in is the developmental significance of the Black Death. Therefore, whatever the geographical context, the significance of the epidemic must be considered over a relatively long period of time.

Local significance

Questions

4. To what extent was the impact of the Black Death on the local communities examined in this section similar to and different from its impact on England as a whole?
5. Do the differences identified in answer to Question 4 require a reassessment of the national impact of the Black Death? Explain your answer.

The local impact of the Black Death varied considerably from one community to another. Some, such as Ashwell (Source 118), were almost annihilated; others, for example Norwich, suffered severe loss of life; while still others escaped relatively lightly. Source 119 uses examples from Cambridgeshire to illustrate the enormous variation in the effects of the plague on villages in close proximity to one another.

Source 118

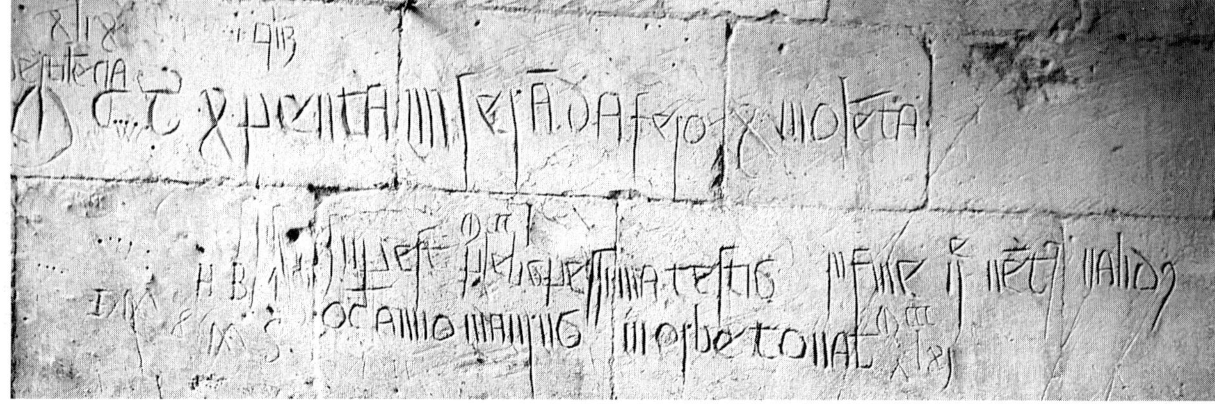

An inscription in Latin cut into the stone wall of the village church at Ashwell in Hertfordshire in 1350. The inscription translates as 'Wretched, terrible, destructive year; the remnants of the people alone remain'.

Source 119

From Philip Ziegler, *The Black Death*, pp.176–8 and 185–6. In this extract, Ziegler considers some of the effects of the Black Death on East Anglia.

Norwich, the second city of the kingdom, lost more than half its population and not only never recovered its position in relation to the rest of England but, in absolute terms, had barely regained its vanished citizens by the end of the sixteenth century. Though the whole of Bishop Bateman's diocese [of Norwich] may not have suffered as much as its capital...it seems certain that the death rate in East Anglia was well above the national average..., but the incidence of the plague seems to have been even more erratic than in other parts of England. Within a radius of ten miles of Cambridge 35 out of 50 tenants died on the Crowland manors at Oakington, 20 out of 42 at Dry Drayton, 33 out of 58 at Cottenham and yet at the manors of Great Shelford and Elsworth...there is no evidence that the Black Death had any effects at all....

The chronicler of Louth Park, the great Cistercian abbey, 25 miles north-east of Lincoln,...[recorded that] 'in many places not even a fifth part of the people were left alive'....No rural economy, however resilient, could recover quickly from devastation on this scale. All generalizations are dangerous, but at least it can be said with confidence that the wapentakes [areas into which northern counties were divided] at the southern end of the Lincolnshire wolds, 'the classical district of ruined churches and lost village sites', were left entirely desolate. Centuries were to pass before any serious recolonization took place....Fifteen villages in Lincolnshire vanished directly after the Black Death or within a decade or two of its visitation. Probably all of them were thinly populated and economically weak...but, in most cases, it must have been the plague which applied the *coup de grâce*.

Source 120 is an account of the effects of the plague on the manor of Witney, near Oxford, which belonged to the Bishop of Winchester. The manor consisted of three villages – Crawley, Curbridge and Hailey – with a combined population of between 450 and 500. Each contained part of the lord's estate [the demesne] and the rest of the land was rented out to 80 or 90 tenants, each of whom in return had to work unpaid for three days a week on the demesne. In the years before 1348 the lord could expect to make a profit of about £30 a year from his farms and receive about £90 a year rent from his tenants.

Source 120

From Derek Turner, *The Black Death*, pp.26–7.

No less than 59 tenants, about two-thirds, died during the year [1349] and very few tenants could be found to replace them....The profits of the farms fell to £3 in 1349 and £4 in 1350. The large number of deaths helped to balance this because when a tenant died a tax in money or goods called a heriot was paid to the lord from his property. So in 1349 the lord received £30 in fines. Nevertheless, the whole profit from the manor in 1349 was only half of what it had been the year before. In the next few years things got worse rather than better.

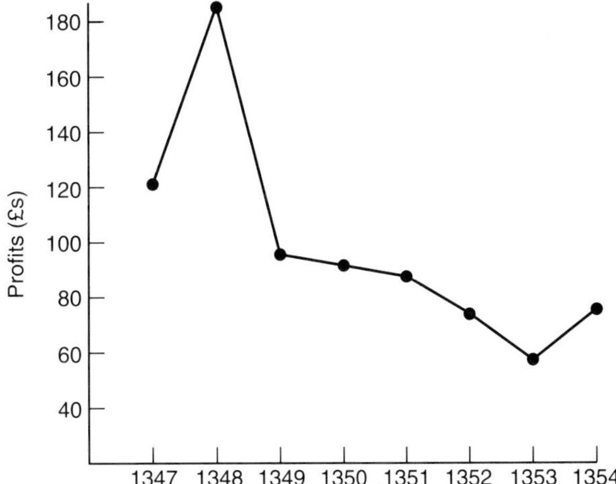

Manor of Witney profits 1347–54

Gradually a few more tenants came forward, but only on condition that they did not have to work on the lord's demesne. As a result the lord for the first time had to start paying people to work for him.

Year	Number of people who came to harvest (unpaid)	Money paid in wages to reapers
1348	121	None
1349	60	£3.10*s*. (£3.50)
1350	28	£5.10*s*. (£5.50)

Manor of Witney harvest figures 1348–50

By 1376, the bishop had reduced arable farming activities on the manor substantially and had doubled his numbers of sheep. In 1377 he decided to stop farming the demesne altogether and let out the whole manor, except for the sheep pastures, to William Gilles for £11 a year. As a result of these changes, the manor profits by 1377 were £115, about the same as the average annual profit in the 1340s.

However, it would be wrong to assume that what happened at Witney was typical of the effects that the plague had in manors all over the country or even all over Oxfordshire. Derek Turner illustrates this using the example of Brightwell, an Oxfordshire village which also belonged to the Bishop of Winchester. During the 1340s it had about 400 inhabitants, including 66 tenants who paid rents amounting to £80 a year.

Source 121

From Derek Turner, *The Black Death*, pp.28–30.

When the Black Death arrived [in Brightwell] only 19 tenants died, less than a third, and all were replaced within two years, apparently without any difficulty. The profit of the manor dropped much less [than at Witney].

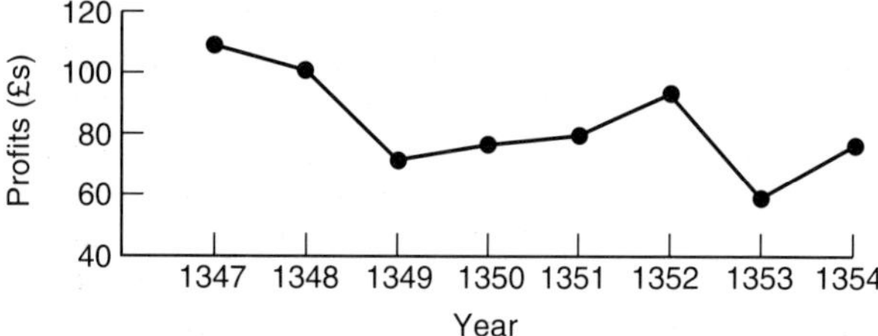

Manor of Brightwell profits 1347–54

From the lord's point of view, the death of perhaps 100 people from the Black Death made very little difference to the manor. The position of the tenants did not change very much either. In 1377 many were still forced to work unpaid on the demesne.

Other variations in the effects of the plague on local communities are revealed in Sources 122–5.

Source 122

From Edmund King, *Medieval England* (Guild Publishing, 1988) p.199.

In the spring of 1349, men sowed crops that they would not reap. At Warboys in Huntingdonshire, eight main holdings and ten cottages were left vacant by the plague, and the landlord was able to sell the corn growing on them....Life went on. The greater number of holdings were occupied again within a matter of months. There was still a pool of heirs, blood relations, if not sons and daughters, available in well-populated villages to take up land. But it was soon drained. And as it was soon drained, the nature of the village came to change. Men would no longer take up land on the old terms. In particular, they declined to take up land that was burdened with labour services [unpaid work on the lord's estate].

Source 123

From Philip Ziegler, *The Black Death*, pp.143–6. The extract examines the effects of the plague in Oxfordshire.

Common tradition in England ascribes to the Black Death the responsibility for the disappearance from the map of many villages, leaving the church, usually the only solidly constructed building, as a solitary monument to the past. Certainly the Black Death helped the process of depopulation and so weakened many communities that they were unable to survive the economic and social fluctuations of the next two centuries. But very few villages can be shown to have been finally and completely deserted as a direct result of the Black Death. One of the exceptions was the Abbot of Eynsham's manor of Tilgarsley [in Oxfordshire] where the collectors of the lay subsidy reported in 1359 that it was not possible to gather the tax because nobody had lived in the village since 1350. There is no reason to think that Tilgarsley was either rich or thickly populated before the Black Death, but the fact that the tax was fixed at 94*s*.10*d*. suggests that the community was reasonably prosperous, or at least far removed from starvation.

Another Eynsham manor, that of Woodeaton, went near to sharing the fate of Tilgarsley....[In 1349] 'scarce two tenants remained in the manor and they would have departed had not Brother Nicholas of Upton, then Abbot,...made an agreement with them and the other tenants that came in afterwards'. The bargain which the Abbot struck, giving the tenants a somewhat higher rent but less arduous feudal services, is an interesting example of the methods to which landlords were to have recourse in the years following the Black Death. He was only partly successful. By 1366 there were 27 tenants in the village, but six cottages still stood vacant.

At Cuxham, some seven miles south of Thame,...by 1360 the lord had given up any attempt to farm the manorial demesne and was seeking to put all his land out to rent....

One moral to be drawn is that it is dangerous to generalize even about relatively small areas – one village may suffer disastrously; another, only a mile or two away, escape virtually unscathed.

Source 124

From P.D.A. Harvey, *A Medieval Oxfordshire Village, Cuxham 1240–1400* (Oxford, 1965) pp.44, 55, 72–3, 78–9, 84–6, 94–5, 135–7 and 152–3. The village was part of the estates belonging to Merton College, Oxford.

[In Cuxham] the Black Death did not lead to an increase in the area of demesne;...by May 1355 all the holdings which had come into the lord's hands in 1349 had been let out to new tenants....Thus, despite the apparent evidence to the contrary, the amount of arable in demesne remained constant throughout this period....The abnormal labour conditions after the Black Death led to the introduction of new forms of contract for threshing, now for the first time performed almost wholly by hired labour....

The records...show Robert Oldman [the reeve of Cuxham who was a victim of the Black Death] as a man of substance, holding a position of responsibility and trust...and it is perhaps typical that his last hours were spent in making up the [demesne] accounts....Robert Oldman's first two successors [his son John and Thomas at Green] seem likewise to have fallen victim to the plague, but in the next ten years the demesne was successively in the hands of at least seven officials; one, William de Elmden, had charge of another manor as well. The difficulty of finding a suitable manager seems one reason why the College let the demesne from 1359 onwards....

The dislocation and shortage of labour caused by the Black Death is reflected in the payment of 1*s*.0*d*. to the *famuli* [demesne servants] between April and June 1349 to encourage them to do the lord's business the better, and two years later, in the cost of putting up stocks for recalcitrant workers, as required by the Statute of Labourers. It appears more directly in larger wages, especially in the first year or so after 1349 and in many vacancies and changes among the *famuli*. In 1357–8 the bailiff's expenses in making an agreement with a new shepherd, John Leeflyf, came to 7*s*.3*d*., besides part of his wages in advance, but the next year he recorded the cost of having John Leeflyf excommunicated for breaking his oath – presumably by failing to stay the stipulated term. Maybe the difficulty of securing a shepherd led to the sale of the demesne flock that year....

The effects of the Black Death are clear; labour services virtually ceased, and the amount spent on hired labour rose to about £10 a year, while, probably because of the difficulty of finding *famuli*, the total work they performed gradually fell by nearly a half during the ten years after 1349. The same table shows that the period 1293–1349 was one of maximum cultivation of the demesne; the total work done seems to have risen slightly between 1276 and 1293, and it certainly declined sharply after the Black Death, for the rise in labour costs must be taken into account. It is not clear whether this contributed to the decrease in crop-yields in this decade nor how far both contributed to the College's decision to lease the manor, but the possible connection cannot be ignored....

Before the Black Death the recorded profits ranged from £25 to £65, and averaged just over £40. As would be expected, they declined after 1349; the only year for which a figure is given, 1354–5, sets them at £10.13*s*. The rent at which the manor was set to farm [i.e. leased] in 1361–8 was £20 a year; in 1395–1401 it was £18.10*s*., and in 1401–5 £20 again. For the rest of the fifteenth century the rents recorded vary from £13.8*s*.8*d*. in 1425–34 to £18.2*s*. in 1449–52....

The effects of the Black Death at Cuxham were immediate and lasting. Nearly thirty years later, in March 1377, the Poll Tax return lists only 38 inhabitants over fourteen years old, one third of its probable population in 1348. But the immediate mortality may have been even greater. Of the twelve villeins of Cuxham in January 1349, not one was alive at the end of the year; of the eight cottagers only four can be shown to have survived until 1352....

	1276–7	**1293–4**	**1323–4**	**1343–4**	**1348–9**
Customary labour:					
No. of days worked	818	1,223	1,379½	1,252½	1,052½
Value	£4.8*s*.2*d*.	£6.12*s*.10½*d*.	£7.9*s*.9*d*.	£6.17*s*.1*d*.	£5.17*s*.1*d*.
Famuli:					
No. of days worked	2,490	2,080	2,080	2,080	2,005
Unskilled hired labour:					
Payments in cash	£4.19*s*.1¼*d*.	£2.16*s*.11*d*.	£3.2*s*.4*d*.	£3.15*s*.9*d*.	£2.7*s*.6½*d*.
Payments in corn	3 quarters 7 bushels	2 quarters 2 bushels	1 quarter	2½ bushels	1 bushel

	1349–50	**1350–1**	**1353–4**	**1357–8**	**1358–9**
Customary labour:					
No. of days worked	205	25	43	55	57
Value	—	—	—	—	—
Famuli:					
No. of days worked	1,899	2,073	1,464	1,300	1,150
Unskilled hired labour:					
Payments in cash	£12.12*s*.8½*d*.	£6.16*s*.4*d*.	£9.9*s*.3*d*.	£7.11*s*.4*d*.	£7.10*s*.9*d*.
Payments in corn	—	5 quarters 6 bushels	—	19 quarters 2 bushels	9 quarters 1 bushel

1 bushel = 8 gallons (36.4 litres) 1 quarter = 8 bushels (290.9 litres)

Work performed on the demesne, 1276–1359

In March 1352 its consequences were still fully apparent. Nine of the thirteen half-virgates [areas of land equal to about 15 acres] were without a tenant, and so were two cottages....It was...the Black Death that began the decline of the group of homesteads along the stream north-west of the present village – though it was probably not until the sixteenth century that the entire group was deserted. In some of the neighbouring villages and hamlets the Black Death had led to the abandonment of tenements on a larger scale. [Beresford, *Lost Villages of England*, pp.159–60, attributes the depopulation of Standhill in Pyrton (a neighbouring village) directly to the Black Death; from the list he gives of depopulated villages in Oxfordshire it seems possible that the decline of Easington and of Golder in Pyrton also began at this time]....By May 1355, however, tenants had probably been found for all the vacant holdings [in Cuxham]. The new villeins all seem to have come from outside Cuxham....Probably the College was meeting the same difficulty in its tenants at Cuxham as in its bailiffs; they were men from outside, who took the tenements because they were offered at advantageous terms, but who, having no particular ties with Cuxham or the College, simply abandoned them when they saw a chance of greater advancement elsewhere....

From 1322 until 1351 Cuxham can have seen little of its rectors. Two, John de Waneting and Robert de Tring, were successive wardens of the College, to whom the living of Cuxham was merely a subsidiary emolument [income]; the third, Walter de Burton, during his seven years as rector of Cuxham was a canon and subdean both of Wells and of York....To all three the Bishop of Lincoln gave licence for study or non-residence, and the care of the parish must have been delegated to a chaplain....In 1351 a change occurred. The new rector, William de Elham, had been a fellow of Merton for fifteen years, and when he was admitted to the living was second Bursar; but he seems to have given up his position in the College, and to have lived in the parish....Perhaps the College, beginning to experience the difficulties in managing the demesne that followed the Black Death, felt it advisable to have an experienced and reliable representative living in the village; ten years later he became the lessee of the manor.

Source 125

From Philip Ziegler, *The Black Death*, pp.200–1. In this extract Ziegler compares the effects of the Black Death on England and Wales.

The effects of the Black Death in Wales seem to have been very similar...to the effects in England. The decay of the manor and the manorial system was the immediate and permanent consequence of the plague....The lords of the manor renounced the farming of the manorial demesne and began to let it out at the best rent they could get. The principle of bondage thenceforward played a far less significant part in the social structure of the manor. The system, in short, broke down because of the shortage of labour and the improved bargaining position of the villein.

All these phenomena were recorded in England too. But in the latter country so many qualifications have to be made to allow for the history of the previous decades [and] for regional variations...that any generalization is open to destructive criticism. In Wales the scope for generalization is greater. Partly the reason for this is geographical: the area was smaller and more homogeneous; variations therefore were less. But the nature of the manorial system in Wales ensured that it would bear the imprint of the plague in a way much more clear-cut and decisive than its English counterpart. On the one hand the seeds of decay, which were already beginning to corrupt the English system, long before the plague added its contribution, had by 1349 hardly affected Wales. Any change which did take place at this period can therefore be attributed with greater confidence to the plague. On the other hand, since the manorial system in Wales was younger and more fragile, it succumbed more rapidly to the blows which it received in 1349. In Wales the Black Death accomplished in a year or two a revolution which in England was worked out over the whole of the fourteenth century....

The generalization so often made and so often disputed in the case of England – that the Black Death was directly responsible for the ending of the manorial system – can with greater confidence be applied to Wales.

European significance

If the Black Death marked the end of the manorial system in Wales and contributed to its decline and eventual extinction in England, the same cannot be said for most of the rest of Europe. In many countries, it was not until the agricultural and industrial revolutions of the eighteenth and nineteenth centuries that the manorial system finally disappeared. This was only one of the differences between the effects of the Black Death on England and Wales and its effects on continental Europe, but, as Sources 126–35 demonstrate, there were similarities as well as differences in the experience and consequences of the plague on each side of the English Channel.

Question

6. In what ways were the shorter and longer-term consequences of the Black Death for continental Europe similar to and different from its consequences for England and Wales?

Source 126

From Philip Ziegler, *The Black Death*, pp.30–5.

During the eleventh, and even more the twelfth and first half of the thirteenth centuries, Europe had enjoyed a period of massive and almost unbroken economic growth....Land in the valleys of the Rhine and the Moselle was worth seventeen times as much at the end of the thirteenth century as it had been at the start of the tenth, yet the old customary rents remained substantially unchanged. Colonization, that is to say the capture of virgin lands from hills, fens and forests, went on apace. By 1300, in Central and Western Europe, the amount of land under cultivation had reached a point not to be matched for another 500 years. The primary driving force behind the new colonization was...pressure of population on existing resources. By the middle of the thirteenth century Europe was becoming uncomfortably overcrowded....In the whole of Western Europe, villages grew into towns, and cities of 10,000–20,000 inhabitants were no longer freakish rareties....As the population soared, more and more mouths had to be filled, and the gap between production and demand grew ever wider....

The climate played a major part in the mischief seventy or eighty years before the Black Death. The intense cold led to a striking advance of the glaciers, polar as well as Alpine....The cultivation of cereals in Iceland and of the vine in England was crippled and virtually extinguished; wheat-growing areas were reduced in Denmark and the Uplands of Provence. The most grave consequence was a series of disastrous harvests. There were famines in England in 1272, 1277, 1283, 1292 and 1311. Between 1315 and 1319 came a crescendo of calamity. Almost every country in Europe lost virtually the whole of one harvest, often of two or three....Cannibalism was a commonplace; the poor ate dogs, wrote one chronicler, cats, the dung of doves, even their own children. Ten per cent of the population of Ypres died of starvation. Nor was this the end: 1332 was another disastrous year for the crops and the period between 1345 and 1348 would have seemed uniquely unfortunate in any other century.

Before the Black Death, therefore, most of Europe was in recession....The prices of agricultural produce were falling: agriculture was no longer the easy road to prosperity which it had been for the past 200 years. To what extent this recession was reflected in a drop in the population can only be guessed at. Famines on the scale which Europe had endured must at least have checked the hectic growth of the previous two centuries...but there is little or no evidence of serious depopulation....

At the middle of the fourteenth century, therefore, chronic over-population was rendering intolerable the existence of many, if not a majority of Europeans....Slicher van Bath [a modern economic historian] attributed the high death rate of the Black Death largely to the prolonged malnutrition which was the consequence of over-rapid growth....All that can be said with confidence is that, in many parts of Europe in the twelfth and thirteenth centuries, the population had grown with unusual speed; that this growth was a factor of importance, though by no means the only factor, which led to general malnutrition; that malnutrition was a contributory reason for the high death rate of the plague years; and that, as a result of the plague, the population was reduced to more easily manageable proportions.

Source 127

The burial of plague victims at Tournai in Flanders in 1349

As Sources 128–9 illustrate, the effects of the Black Death on the Italian city states varied from one to another but, whereas in England the consequences of the disease affected the feudal manorial system on which government and power were based, in some Italian cities the plague had a more direct effect on the system of government itself.

Source 128

From Derek Turner, *The Black Death*, pp.39 and 63–4. The extract compares the impact of the plague on two Italian cities, Orvieto and Florence.

Orvieto in 1346 was quite a happy and prosperous place. There were only 15,000 inhabitants compared with Florence's 90,000, but it was able to do well from its good position on the busy trade routes....[After the Black Death] Orvieto never recovered its former prosperity and independence. It came under the rule of the popes and when two rival popes were chosen, it...became a battleground. In the siege of 1380, 3,000 people were killed. By 1400 there were less than half the number of people in the town than there had been a hundred years before. Certainly the Black Death had a lot to do with this collapse....A combination of a fierce war, near famine and the Black Death so shocked the Orvietans that they lost the will to win back their former prosperity and independence.

In Florence an even greater proportion of the people died than in Orvieto....Yet by 1400 Florence was more powerful and prosperous than ever before. In the town records of Orvieto the Black Death is constantly used as an excuse for the city's decline from its former glory. The Florentines soon put the Black Death out of their minds and got on with rebuilding their fortunes to new heights. Between 1400 and 1500 Florence became probably the most important city in Italy, a centre of trade, banking and the arts.

Source 129

From Philip Ziegler, *The Black Death*, pp.59–60. The extract assesses the effects of the Black Death on the Italian city of Siena.

Siena is an example of a city which, superficially, recovered quickly from the Black Death but, in reality, suffered economic and political dislocation so profound that things were never to be the same again.…What was left of the old oligarchy [ruling élite] gained enormously through inheritances from their dead relations and the accumulation of power in fewer hands.…The remnants of the oligarchy had not been the only group to profit financially from the epidemic. A class of new rich arose and wished to play the part in the city's government to which they felt the length of their purse entitled them. But their pretensions met with a chilly response. No concessions were made to meet them and harsh sumptuary laws [laws about the clothing that could be worn by different ranks of society] were passed to curb the ambitions of those who affected the trappings of a higher station than their birth and education justified. Meanwhile the poor, among whom the disease had raged the worst, often found that they had lost even the little which they had once possessed. The gap which divided them from their luckier neighbours grew ever wider.

By the time of the Black Death, the Government of Nine had ruled Siena without serious challenge for some seventy years. A few years later it seemed successfully to have weathered the storm and to have launched Siena on another era of stable prosperity. Yet in 1354 it fell. It can be argued that this was not a direct consequence of the plague but, equally, it is certain that the Black Death…'was instrumental in creating demographic, social and economic conditions that greatly increased opposition to the ruling oligarchy'.…It is important to bear in mind the lesson of Siena: that a patient has not necessarily recovered because his more obvious wounds are healed.

In Germany, as Philip Ziegler explains in Source 131, a combination of the Black Death and the weakness of the Church brought forth the Flagellant movement, in which participants travelled around the country scourging [whipping] themselves, hoping to atone for the sinfulness of man which they believed had led God to inflict the punishment of the plague. However, the Flagellants were a short-lived phenomenon that was quickly suppressed by the Church and by secular rulers. Of more lasting significance was the persecution of the Jews which also resulted from the Black Death and was at its most virulent in Germany, although it began in France.

Source 130

A Flagellant procession in which people whipped themselves and each other. They believed that the Black Death was a punishment from God and that by punishing themselves they might gain God's forgiveness.

Source 131

From Philip Ziegler, *The Black Death*, pp.86–111.

The details of the daily horrors [of the Black Death in Germany] are very similar to those in the cities of Italy and France.…One point of difference is the abnormally large number of churchmen who died during the epidemic.…Therefore, the German Church found itself short of personnel in 1349 and 1350. One result was a sharp increase in plural benefices [churchmen holding more than one parish]. In one area, between 1345 and 1347, 39 benefices were held by 13 men. In 1350–52 this had become 57 benefices in the hands of 12 men. Another was the closing of many monasteries and parish churches; a third was the mass ordination of young and often ill-educated and untrained clerics. As a sum of these factors, the German Church after the Black Death was numerically weaker, worse led and worse manned than a few years before.…The many benefactions which it received during the terror ensured that its spiritual and organizational weakness was matched by greater financial prosperity, a disastrous combination which helped to make the Church despised and detested where formally it had been loved, revered, or at least accepted. By 1350 the Church in Germany had been reduced to a condition where any energetic movement of reform was certain to find many allies and weakened opposition.…

The Black Death in Germany is of peculiar interest since that country provided the background for two of its most striking and unpleasant by-products: the pilgrimages of the Flagellants and the persecution of the Jews. The Flagellant movement, even though it dislocated life over a great area of Europe, and at one time threatened the security of governments, did not, in the long run, amount to very much....

The 'Brotherhood of the Flagellants', or 'Brethren of the Cross' as the movement was called in 1348, traditionally originated in Eastern Europe...but it was in Germany that the Flagellant movement really took root....The Flagellant movement, at first at least, was well regulated and sternly disciplined. Any new entrants...had to promise to scourge themselves thrice daily for 33 days and 8 hours, one day for each year of Christ's earthly life, and were required to show that they possessed funds sufficient to provide 4*d.* for each day of the pilgrimage to meet the cost of food. Absolute obedience was promised to the Master and all the Brethren undertook not to shave, bathe, sleep in a bed, change their clothes or have conversation or intercourse with a member of the opposite sex....Ecclesiastics had no pre-eminence...and the leaders of the movement prided themselves upon their independence from the church establishment....

As this side of the movement's character attracted more attention, so a clash with the Church became inevitable. Already the claim of the Masters to grant absolution from sins infringed one of the Church's most sacred...prerogatives....The German Flagellants took the lead in denouncing the hierarchy of the Catholic Church...and cases were heard of Flagellants interrupting religious services, driving priests from their churches and looting ecclesiastical property....

As they trekked from plague centre to plague centre, often bearing infection with them to those they were supposed to help, it was inevitable that many of their older members should perish, including the responsible leaders who had set the standards for the rest. To make up numbers, pilgrims were recruited less remarkable for their piety....Little by little the more respectable citizens of Europe began to look with diminished favour on their turbulent visitors.

Up to the middle of 1349, the Flagellants had things pretty much their own way. Central and southern Germany was their favoured hunting ground but they spread freely over Hungary, Poland, Flanders and the Low Countries....However, in Italy they made little impression....In France they were beginning to gather popular support when Philip VI, showing unusual determination, prevented their penetrating beyond Troyes....They are only known to have held one ceremony in London...[where] they seem to have met with indifference or even hostility and were rapidly deported as unwanted guests.

But the turning point came with the declaration of war by the Church....On 20 October 1349, a papal Bull was published...denouncing the Flagellants for the contempt of Church discipline which they had shown by forming unauthorized associations....All bishops were ordered to suppress the pilgrimages....The Brethren of the Cross 'vanished as suddenly as they had come, like night phantoms or mocking ghosts'. The movement did not die, indeed it was still to be encountered in the fifteenth century, but as a threat to society...it had effectively ceased to exist....

When ignorant men are overwhelmed by forces totally beyond their control and their understanding, it is inevitable that they will search for some explanation within their grasp. When they are frightened and badly hurt they will seek someone on whom they can be revenged....The Jews were not the only candidates as victims [but they were the main ones]. In large areas of Spain the Arabs were suspected of playing some part in the propagation of the plague...but it was the leper who most nearly rivalled the Jew as popular scapegoat....

In Germany, and to some extent also in France and Spain, the Jews provided the money-lending class in virtually every city – not so much by their own volition [wish] as because they had been progressively barred from all civil and military functions, from owning land or working as artisans. Usury was the only field of economic activity left open to them; an open field, in theory at least, since it was forbidden to the Christian by Canon Law....In much of Europe the Jew dwindled to a small money-lender and pawnbroker. He acquired a large clientèle of petty debtors so that every day more people had cause to wish him out of the way....The Jew had become a figure so hated in European society that almost anything might have served to provoke catastrophe....

The Black Death concentrated this latent fear and hatred of the Jews into one burning grievance which not only demanded vengeance but offered the tempting extra dividend that, if the Jews could only be eliminated, then the plague for which they were responsible might vanish too....The first cases of persecution seem to have taken place in the south of France in the spring of 1348, and, in May, there was a massacre in Provence. Narbonne and Carcassone exterminated their communities with especial thoroughness....In Basle, all the Jews were penned up in wooden buildings and burned alive....[In Germany] in November 1348 the Jews were burnt at Solothurn, Zofingen and Stuttgart; in December at Landsberg, Burren, Memmingen, Lindau; in January, Freiburg, Ulm and Speyer....In February it was the turn of the Jews at Gotha, Eisenach and Dresden; in March, Worms, Baden and Erfurt....

Why the persecutions died down temporarily in 1349 is uncertain....But the blame for the renewal of violence must rest predominantly with the Flagellants....In July 1349, when the Flagellants arrived in procession at Frankfurt, they rushed directly to the Jewish quarter and led the local population in wholesale slaughter. At Brussels the mere news that the Flagellants were approaching was enough to set off a massacre in which, in spite of the efforts of the Duke of Brabant, some 600 Jews were killed....On the whole the rulers of Europe did their best, though often ineffectively, to protect their Jewish subjects. Pope Clement VI in particular behaved with determination and responsibility....He published Bulls condemning the massacres and calling on Christians to behave with tolerance and restraint. Those who joined in persecution of the Jews were threatened with excommunication....

In England there were said to be isolated prosecutions of Jews on suspicion of spreading the plague but no serious persecution took place. It would be pleasant to attribute this to superior humanity and good sense. The substantial reason, however, was rather less honourable. In 1290, King Edward I had expelled the Jews from England. Such few as remained had little money and were too unobtrusive to present a tempting target....

The persecution of the Jews waned with the Black Death itself; by 1351 all was over....The Jews had already learned to expect hatred and suspicion and the lesson was not one which they were to have much opportunity to forget. But the massacre was exceptional in its extent and in its ferocity; in both, indeed, it probably had no equal until the twentieth century set new standards for man's inhumanity to man. Coupled with the losses caused by the Black Death itself, it virtually wiped out the Jewish communities in large areas of Europe. In all, 60 large and 150 smaller communities are believed to have been exterminated and 350 massacres of various dimensions took place.

Although a large number of churchmen died in England as well as in Germany, the effects were different. In England, the popularity of the Church did not suffer to the same extent as it did in Germany, and 'pluralities', where one priest held two or more parishes, decreased in England, whereas they increased on the continent.

Source 132

From Philip Ziegler, *The Black Death*, pp.272–3.

It would not have been surprising if the dearth of priests [in England] had led to more cases in which a single parson held two or more benefices but, though this seems to have been the result in certain continental countries, in England the 'great increase in the practice' to which Gasquet referred did not take place. On the contrary the evidence points, if anything, to the existence of less pluralities after the Black Death than before it.

We should avoid generalizing too much about the effects of the plague on Europe in general. As Gerhard and Bean argue in Sources 133–4, the impact varied from country to country and region to region. Gerhard, in particular, stresses the differences between England and western Europe, where it contributed to the decline of serfdom and the manorial system, and eastern Europe and the Baltic states where serfs became tied more closely to manorial estates.

Source 133

From Dietrich Gerhard, *Old Europe: A Study of Continuity, 1000–1800* (Academic Press, 1981) pp.66–7.

The turn to a market economy, for meat as well as for wool and hide production, led to stock raising on a large scale. Its social effect was detrimental to the peasantry. In England complaints about sheep driving the farmers from the land were to be heard in the fourteenth and sixteenth centuries....Less publicized was the same process in southern Italy....Not everywhere did the extension happen at the expense of arable crops. In Italy and in south-eastern France the nonfertile areas used by semi-nomadic ranchers expanded.

Property changes on a large scale in eastern Europe were related to grain production. In contrast to western and central Europe, since the fifteenth century the exploitation of the demesne (manorial land) by peasant labour became ever more stringent. On the large landholdings in eastern Germany, Poland and the Baltic countries the peasants were increasingly tied to the soil. The lord's concern for profits from the export of grain and naval stores was a major cause of the debasement of the peasantry, leading to various types of serfdom.

Source 134

From J.M.W. Bean, 'The Black Death: the Crisis and its Social and Economic Consequences', in D. Williman (ed.), *The Black Death: the Impact of the Fourteenth-Century Plague* (University of New York, 1982) pp.23 and 28–9.

The Black Death in Western Europe has not escaped attempts to scale it down. Nevertheless it has survived, on the whole, remarkably well as one of the great events and turning points in European history since the fall of Rome....

Historians' discussions of the economic effects of the Black Death fall into two categories: local studies of death rates on the one hand, and, on the other, wide-ranging interpretations which speak of a global death rate and seek to place the crisis in the setting of a declining European economy over a period of one and a half centuries....If we are to engage in some tentative generalizations...it is best to do so within the framework of regional comparisons....If inland Tuscany suffered marginally less from the Black Death than other areas of Western Europe, does not this fact offer us some insight into its economic situation in the late fourteenth and fifteenth centuries? According to some authorities Milan suffered less than other Italian cities. Does this statement help us to understand Milanese power under the last Visconti and the Sforzas? Does Bohemia's exemption from the ravages of the Black Death help to explain its comparative prosperity in the reign of Charles IV of Luxembourg? Similarly, the comparative immunity of the hinterland of Antwerp must have provided a labour supply which assisted that area's economic growth over the next century and a half.

Finally, we should bear in mind that the Black Death did not *cause* changes on its own. George Deaux (Source 135) cautions us that it merely contributed, along with other factors, to the development of medieval political, social and economic systems. Nevertheless, the contribution made by the Black Death *was* significant.

Source 135

From George Deaux, *The Black Death* (Hamish Hamilton, 1969) pp.205–10, 213 and 216–7.

The Black Death did not bring the Middle Ages to an end; it did not cause the decline of chivalry or feudalism; it did not hasten in the Renaissance; nor did it cause the rise of nationalistic spirit, humanism, science, the passion of exploration, realism in literature, national languages, or the democratization and secularization of society which we associate with the period that followed it. The Black Death did not bring about these developments in precisely the same way that no other single event caused them. Great revolutions in institutions, values and cultures are invariably the product of long and complex processes of change, and it is simplistic to assign to any one event, no matter how momentous, the full responsibility for such change....Even the decline in population during the fourteenth century, which it would seem absolutely safe to declare to be an effect of the plague, had, in fact, begun earlier in the century and may have been a natural response to the rapid rise in population during the thirteenth century....

In some areas of the arts, the plague had an unquestionable effect....The Black Death permanently interrupted the building of the Duomo at Siena and the church of St Nicholas in Yarmouth. But there is no such general certainty about its effect upon the art of building. The Cathedral of Milan, one of the most glorious of all Gothic churches, was begun shortly after the plague. The building of St Stephen's Chapel in Westminster and the completion of the Abbey cloisters seem to have proceeded without interruption and with no change of style. In England, it is possible that the change from the Decorated to the Perpendicular style of architecture was in some part due to the lack of builders after the plague....Examples of the change can be seen in the nave and cloisters of Canterbury Cathedral and in the west front of Winchester Cathedral....

One of the most important things to happen in the fourteenth and fifteenth centuries was the emergence of a national language in England, France and Italy. The development of English, at least, was due in part to the effects of the Black Death. After the Norman Conquest, French had gradually become the dominant language in England until ultimately nearly everyone who wrote, framed public policy, or expressed public thought, did so in French....English continued to be spoken in a variety of dialects in the villages, and many townspeople were bilingual, but the upper classes used French almost exclusively. Most of the education was in the hands of the clergy, and since many Frenchmen had been put in charge of monasteries and of parishes, French spread generally throughout the educated of the nation. Inevitably the languages became fused. English took to itself French words and syntax, and French, especially after the loss of Normandy, began to be changed for lack of any standard of purity to limit corruption. In such a situation, English, which as the native tongue was continually being purified while French became more corrupted, would ultimately have triumphed as the national language. But the change was accelerated by the Black Death. The plague had carried off many of the monks and nuns who had done the teaching, and their replacements were often poorly trained and almost always of native stock. The result was that English grammar began to be taught more and more widely....Even as early as 1362 English had taken the place of French to the extent that parliament was opened in that year with a speech in English....

The triumph of the vernacular [the native language] in England produced important changes in literature and paved the way for Chaucer and Langland. But one should not forget that England has a rich literature in Old and Middle English dating from long before the Black Death....In Italy, as well, the fourteenth century saw a flowering of vernacular literature. Boccaccio's *Decameron*, one of the great monuments of Italian literature, was written between 1348 and 1353 and there is no question about the influence of the Black Death upon that work; but Dante's *Divine Comedy* had been completed a quarter of a century before the plague. In fact, the vernacular literature of Italy went into sharp decline after the Black Death. Petrarch abandoned Italian to write...in Latin, and his influence led Boccaccio to forsake the vernacular as well....In France the schools suffered as they had in England, and Guillaume de Nangis wrote that after the plague 'few were found who could or would teach children the rudiments of grammar in houses, cities or villages'. The growth of the vernacular in France is indicated by the fact that the king, Charles V, had translations of classical works prepared for himself and his kinsmen....

During the Black Death many men feared that the end of the world was upon them. When the plague was over, many acted as if the old world had, in fact, ended. In all the arts and sciences men struck out for new worlds. And some actually set out in boats to find them. One of the most important developments of the fifteenth century was the development of new navigational techniques, the exploration of new trade routes to the East, and the discovery in actual fact of a new world. One wonders if somewhere in the impulse to find new frontiers was not buried the recollection that the old trade routes had been avenues by which the plague came into the old world....

Joy in life and interest in this world were apparent not only in the scientists, scholars and artists who survived the Black Death. Less well documented but just as real was the release of life force in simple men....The dour moralists of the age were right: men did not learn to be modest and contrite [sorry for their sins] from the agony they had suffered; they learned to be joyful and defiant....

After the death and the suffering, the social, political, economic and spiritual disruption of those few years, what lasting effects did the Black Death have upon the course of human history?...No great institutions collapsed as a result of the Black Death; no national boundaries changed; after a brief interruption, economic, political, religious and even cultural life went on very much as before. The trouble with such a view is not that it is wrong – for surely it is right – but that it is beside the point....The Black Death was not primarily a disaster endured by great men or institutions. It was a tragedy of ordinary men. As such, the story of the Black Death is not a story of economic and political events. It is only partially a story of change. As a tragedy of the poor, the under-privileged, the unpretentious, the weak, it is a story, not of change, but rather of endurance....It is the story of the preservation of institutions, more than of their destruction, of the reassertion of values after temporary demoralization.

Cross-currents in history

One thing that will almost certainly have emerged from the study of this and earlier units is that historical development is not a smooth and even-paced journey from a point of origin to a predetermined goal. The pace and direction of change can vary suddenly or a line of development can veer gradually from its original path into a new channel. Change can also be intentional, unintentional or even both at the same time. For instance, the increase in real wages in the second half of the fourteenth century was intended by the wage-earners who were determined to exploit the advantage given them by the shortage of labour, but it was resisted fiercely by many manorial lords, who enforced as vigorously as they could the Statute of Labourers. As has been noted earlier, there are frequent eddies and cross-currents in the flow of history, such that the consequences of an event such as the Black Death may appear contradictory. At one and the same time, the shortage of labour brought about by successive waves of plague improved the employment prospects of agricultural wage-earners, but deprived many of their homes and livelihoods as their former masters turned demesne farms into sheep pasture.

The eddies and cross-currents in historical development are revealed even more clearly when different accounts are produced relative to local, national and European spatial contexts. In some cases, the accounts will merely differ: for instance, the weakening of the Church, the Flagellant movement and the persecution of the Jews were important consequences of the Black Death in Germany, but made no impact on England. In others, the accounts will be in direct conflict or competition: as with the contribution of the plague to the decline of the manorial system in England and to the strengthening of it in eastern Europe.

Since none of these consequences is demonstrably incorrect, we must reconcile or explain away the conflicts between them by showing how the Black Death could have simultaneous yet apparently contradictory consequences, sometimes in the same country or area, or even more so between one country or region and another.

Question

7. (a) What cross-currents and contradictory consequences resulted from the Black Death?
   (b) How can these cross-currents and contradictions be reconciled within a single, complex developmental account?

UNIT 3.3

THE PURPOSES AND ASSUMPTIONS OF HISTORIANS

Introduction

In the previous unit, we considered how different temporal and spatial contexts can influence the historical significance attached to events, but these are only two of a number of factors that affect the accounts historians produce. Any historical account is necessarily a selection from and interpretation of the surviving evidence from the period under consideration. The selection, marshalling and interpretation of evidence in order to construct and justify a coherent historical account depend to a very considerable extent on the purposes and assumptions of the historian producing the account.

It will be obvious that two historians studying different strands of history will offer different accounts because their purposes differ. We would not expect someone tracing the rise of the Labour Party in the early twentieth century to produce a similar account to someone tracing the decline of the Liberal Party during the same period. Undoubtedly, there will be some overlap between the accounts because the rise of the Labour Party contributed to the decline of the Liberal Party and vice versa, but there will also be elements in one account that will be absent from the other and elements common to both that will play different roles in each. For instance, while the introduction by the trade unions of the political levy was vital to the development of the Labour Party, it plays little part in any account of the decline of the Liberal Party; and, although the splits in the Liberal Party between the Lloyd George and Asquith factions may appear in both accounts, they will play different roles and assume different degrees of importance in each.

What may be less obvious is that historians studying the same strand of history within the same temporal and spatial contexts may also be pursuing different purposes or basing their accounts on different assumptions, and that this may be responsible to a considerable extent for the competition or conflict between their accounts.

This unit examines the different purposes and assumptions underlying accounts of the creation and politicization of the English working class during the nineteenth century, and how these purposes and assumptions have affected the accounts that the historians have produced. Some historians, such as Edward Thompson, have sought to explain the politicization of the working class in terms of its ability to organize radical action to confront, challenge and force change upon the political élite. Others, such as Harold Perkin or John and Barbara Hammond, have set out to show how the working class became assimilated peacefully into the political nation. These differences in aim and purpose rest on different assumptions. Thompson, influenced by the writings of Karl Marx, assumed that political progress could only take place as a result of class conflict, whereas liberal (sometimes known as Whig) historians such as the Hammonds assumed that co-operation rather than conflict was the norm in inter-class relations during the nineteenth century. Consequently, the Hammonds' accounts, in *The Skilled Labourer* and other works, were predicated on the assumption that large-scale popular insurrection in the early nineteenth century was improbable and that such risings as did occur were the work of an unrepresentative 'lunatic fringe', an assumption criticized by Thompson in *The Making of the Working Class*, where he claims that in the conditions that existed during the early nineteenth century, 'it might appear more surprising if men had not plotted revolutionary uprisings than if they had'.

Before embarking on a study of different historians' interpretations of the politicization of the working class, an important note of caution should be sounded. Some students may be tempted to adopt the sweeping and false generalization that both Marxist and 'liberal' historians are politically biased and that therefore one cannot believe a word they say. This, of course, is absurd: all historians hold assumptions and beliefs – conscious or unconscious, political or otherwise – that influence their interpretations of the past. It is precisely these different assumptions and beliefs, and the purposes that spring from them, that lead historians to look at the past from different perspectives and to illuminate it in different ways. Thus, we should not dismiss, say, Marxist historians as 'biased', but recognize that they have enriched our understanding by looking at the past in a different way from other historians, focusing attention on previously neglected areas of research such as the Diggers in the seventeenth century and radical fringe movements in the nineteenth.

In any case, it is not the historian that we should be testing, but specific arguments that he or she has advanced. As with any historian, the arguments put forward by Marxists and liberals will contain some elements with which their colleagues readily concur and others that are more contentious. In order to determine the validity of any particular statement made or hypothesis formulated by a historian, whether Marxist, liberal or otherwise, it must be tested for consistency with the available evidence, especially that evidence which originates from the period about which the historian is writing. Bearing this in mind, let us consider how and when the working class emerged in Britain and the different explanations that have been put forward by Marxist and liberal historians to account for its politicization.

The politicization of the working class

The working class as an entity emerged as a direct result of the Industrial Revolution. Previously, in an economy that was primarily rural and characterized by small units of production in a country with poor communications and no more than a fledgling media, the opportunities for direct communication between working people in one area and another were strictly limited. Without such contacts the emergence of a working-class consciousness and culture was impossible. As Thomas Carlyle noted at the time (Source 136) and D.G. Wright has summarized more recently (Source 137), the mechanization, urbanization and improvements in communication brought about by the Industrial Revolution dealt a severe blow to the paternalism and deference that had governed for centuries the relations between different strata of society; they tended to polarize relations between rich and poor and to create circumstances in which a self-conscious working class could emerge, with its own social, economic and political aspirations.

Source 136

From Thomas Carlyle, *Signs of the Times*, 1829.

Were we required to characterize this age of ours by any single epithet, we should be tempted to call it...the Mechanical Age. It is the Age of Machinery, in every outward and inward sense of that word; the age which, with its whole undivided might, forwards, teaches and practises the great art of adapting means to ends. Nothing is now done directly, or by hand....Our old modes of exertion are all discredited and thrown aside. On every hand, the living artisan is driven from his workshop, to make room for the speedier inanimate one. The shuttle drops from the fingers of the weaver, and falls into iron fingers that ply it faster....What changes too, this addition of power is introducing into the Social System; how wealth has more and more increased, and at the same time gathered itself more and more into masses, strangely altering the old relations, and increasing the distance between the rich and the poor.

Source 137

The Creation of the English Working Class. From D.G. Wright, *Popular Radicalism* (Longman, 1988) pp.3–5.

No serious historian...denies that a working class, as a descriptive category for people who existed by selling their labour power, came into existence during the late eighteenth and early nineteenth centuries. From about the middle of the eighteenth century, English society was increasingly transformed by a series of virtually simultaneous revolutions: demographic, transport, agrarian, industrial. A sustained increase in population began around 1740, whereby the 5 million people in England and Wales in 1700 rose to $7\frac{1}{2}$ million in 1780, 9 million in 1801, 18 million in 1851 and 26 million in 1881. Such unprecedented growth involved a massive increase in the supply of labour; during the first half of the nineteenth century the labour force more than doubled. It also meant a vastly increased number of people to feed, clothe and house....It is important to bear in mind that a good deal of economic growth occurred before the advent of the factory system on any scale. Factories only became dominant in the second half of the nineteenth century. Indeed, the initial impact of the Industrial Revolution, with only limited application of steam power, was to expand both the numbers and the output of hand-workers in the domestic and small workshop system, workers who continued to outnumber factory operatives until at least 1851.

Between 1700 and 1880 the most significant change in the structure and scale of the labour force was the shift away from agriculture into manufacturing....In many sectors of the capital goods industry, the expansion of the labour force was accompanied by an increase in the unit of production and the number of workers on each site: in shipyards, mines, quarries, ropeworks, glassworks and brickyards. Technological innovation in these sectors was limited....So far as consumer goods industries were concerned, the bulk of the workforce remained outside the factory system, which as late as the mid-nineteenth century predominated only in the manufacture of cotton and worsted cloth....Machine operatives in factories were therefore only a relatively small minority of the total workforce as late as 1851....

As in the eighteenth century, industrial production involved the employment of a great deal of female and child labour, with women concentrated in the lighter branches of industry and excluded from the workshop craft trades. On the other hand, it is doubtful whether the Industrial Revolution meant any significant increase in the female proportion of the workforce, given the ubiquity [large numbers] of women workers in the pre-1780 economy. Child labour is more problematic....The 1851 census figure of about a third of children aged under fifteen engaged in paid employment is probably a considerable underestimate, omitting the many children who assisted adult workers or were employed in household production.

Industrialization in Britain took place alongside a process of very rapid urbanization. Only London had a population over 50,000 in 1750; but by 1851 there were 29 towns over 50,000 and 9 with over 100,000, while London's population had increased to $2\frac{1}{2}$ million....A large proportion of the working population had to adjust not only to industrialization, but also to the manifold problems of urban existence, including intense overcrowding and horrific sanitary conditions. The increasing concentration of the workforce in urban areas obviously acted as a stimulant to working-class radicalism; Marx himself argued that urban proximity of work and residence was a major precondition for the emergence of a self-conscious and militant working class.

Socialist and liberal interpretations

We have already noted that the assumptions and purposes of historians affect their interpretations of the past, and this is particularly true in respect of the emergence and politicization of the working class. Historians concerned with nineteenth-century constitutional history, even when considering the development of parliamentary democracy, often make scant reference to the development of working-class radicalism. For instance, many underplay the importance of working class agitation in creating the circumstances in which parliament felt compelled to pass the 1832 Reform Act. As Palmerston put it at the time [Unit 1.6, Source 309], the Act sought to 'strengthen the ties which bind together the middle classes and the aristocracy' in the hope of isolating and weakening working-class radicalism.

It is not by chance that the first historians to rescue working-class radicalism from this neglect were left-wing Liberals writing in the early twentieth century, such as John and Barbara Hammond, who were influenced by the determination of the 1906–14 Liberal government to improve the plight of the rural and urban poor. Nor is it a mere coincidence that Edward Thompson, the historian who has done more than anyone else to focus attention on the politicization of the working class, was a Marxist. Political considerations undoubtedly influenced the questions that these historians asked, but the answers that they put forward were based on sound historical research and were justified by detailed reference to contemporary documentary evidence. While it would be naïve, blinkered and insulting to dismiss such scholarly research as mere political propaganda, it is important to recognize how their political viewpoints have influenced the questions these historians have asked and the interpretations that they have offered.

Question

1. (a) What differences do John Kenyon, Clive Behagg and J.R. Dinwiddy identify in Sources 138–40 between the liberal and Marxist interpretations of class relations in the nineteenth century?

   (b) How, according to Kenyon, Behagg and Dinwiddy, do the interpretations of class relations put forward by Marxist and liberal historians affect their accounts of the 'journey' of the working class towards citizenship?

Source 138

From John Kenyon, *The History Men* (Weidenfeld & Nicolson, 1983) pp.239–40.

The stance adopted by the Webbs, the Hammonds, Tawney and other associates of the London School of Economics in its early years can best be described as left-wing Liberal....The Hammonds were typical of this middle-class clique devoted to practical philanthropy and higher thought....Their joint labours produced two huge studies of working-class conditions before and during the Industrial Revolution, *The Village Labourer* (1911) and *The Town Labourer* (1917). These were works of serious and painstaking research, but they were equally tracts for the time, provoked by the rural destitution that was the concern of all Liberal governments from the 1890s onwards, as well as the violent industrial unrest which reached a climax in 1911–12....

The Hammonds did not take it upon themselves to judge capitalism; like Tawney at this stage they accepted it, for good or ill, as the prevailing economic system, though they were hopeful of reforming it. Their argument was that the sordid and inhumane origins of the present system had left a mark on it which was still evident in current practice....[In] *The Town Labourer*, the Hammonds had the backing of a large section of early Victorian opinion, not least Frederick Engels's. They argued that the working class had never participated in the huge profits accruing from the Industrial Revolution; not only had their living standards fallen disastrously in the new slums of the factory towns, but the amount of real money at their disposal had also declined. They did not suggest that this was the result of a conscious policy on the part of the managerial classes, but they did indict them for moral blindness and a crying lack of social responsibility.

After the war the Hammonds went on to publish *The Skilled Labourer* (1919) and *The Rise of Modern Industry* (1925). But their whole thesis, in so far as it affected the factory worker, was vigorously rebutted by John Clapham in the first volume of a comprehensive *Economic History of Modern Britain*, published in 1926. Clapham reacted strongly against what he regarded as left-wing denigration of the achievements of the Industrial Revolution, and though he admitted that the comparatively sudden concentration of large numbers of families in the new towns had placed them in sub-standard living conditions, he brought statistical evidence to bear which showed that their standard of living in terms of purchasing power and real wages had markedly increased. This was the beginning of the great 'Standard of Living' debate, which ranged to and fro, from generation to generation, over the next forty years and beyond, until the original combatants, Clapham and the Hammonds, were almost forgotten. On the whole, in the profession the 'optimistic' or 'acceptive' school of thought may be said to have prevailed, but the general public have been left with the idea that the Industrial Revolution was a period of callous exploitation – a thesis transmitted to a wider public still in socialist histories like *The Common People 1746–1938* by G.D.H. Cole and Raymond Postgate....This was part of a conscious attempt to provide a historical background for the Labour Party, and led in addition to an increasing preoccupation with the Levellers. The Tories could keep Pitt and Burke, Labour had Lilburne (and Wat Tyler).

Source 139

From Clive Behagg, *Labour and Reform: Working-Class Movements 1815–1914* (Hodder and Stoughton, 1991) pp.12–4.

Historians disagree over the implications of class divisions for the process of historical change. For example, given that classes existed, were they necessarily forever in conflict? The nineteenth-century political thinker, Karl Marx, argued that they were. He identified class conflict as growing logically out of the nature of capitalist society. Employers made their profits by exploiting labour and therefore the interests of the two classes were doomed always to be at odds. At its simplest, when wages went up profits went down, and this polarity of interests produced a necessarily hostile relationship between the two groups. Following this, Marxist historians, such as Edward Thompson and Eric Hobsbawm, have explored those areas of conflict between the classes as the most significant for historical analysis.

Alternatively, some historians share the view of many contemporary observers, that relationships between workers and employers were always at least potentially harmonious, since an industrial society could operate to the benefit of both groups. High profits meant increased investment, more jobs and higher wages, so conflict was not inevitable. Where it occurred it was not a product of the system, but rather the impact of other influences, perhaps economic crisis, or war, or simply misunderstandings that could be rectified by better education. These liberal historians tend to stress the points of mutual agreement between the classes as the really important moments in any historical period. Presenting this approach in his book, *The Origins of Modern English Society 1780–1880*, Harold Perkin argues that by the mid-Victorian period the relations between the classes were 'those of a familiar kind of marriage in which the partners cannot live without bickering but are perfectly aware that apart they cannot live at all'.

The significance of this difference of interpretation for an understanding of the period 1815–1914 relates primarily to the issue of exactly how much political solidarity and enthusiasm the working class displayed at any given moment. Liberal historians stress the fragmentation of the working class, sometimes preferring the term 'working classes'. They point out that this social group consisted of a variety of trades spread over a wide area and such disparity prevented any common view being either held or expressed. Trade unions, with their concern for the members of one trade, are generally cited as an example of this sectionalism. Where wider protest movements emerged, such as Chartism, they are seen by liberal historians as being more regional than national expressions. The failure of such movements is seen as proof that they lacked any class consciousness.

Historians on the political left argue that, despite the differences of regions and trades within the working class, it was still united by a common experience of industrialization. Working people were tied together by exploitation at work, material deprivation, political exclusion and the hostility of the law to their organizations. Movements such as Chartism are seen as evidence of this universal perception of society, held throughout by the working class. Trade unions, though concerned with the interests of particular trades, still brought a common class consciousness to bear on their members' problems. Wider organizations such as Chartism and the Labour Party, it is argued, were the expressions of a growing sense that those who shared this common experience and consciousness should band together to improve their position.

Returning to our original image of labour's achievement of citizenship as a journey [Unit 3.1, Source 80], how do these two, very different interpretations map out the itinerary? Left-wing historians see this as a perilous journey, with each mile travelled at huge cost. Hard won gains could easily be lost since the terrain remained hostile. Thus trade unions had to win the fight for their legality not once but three times, in 1824, 1875 and 1906. Male suffrage, rejected in 1839, 1842 and 1848 was apparently gained in 1884. But the vote was deliberately given in such a way that, in practice, large numbers of working men remained outside the electorate until 1918.

From a liberal perspective, however, each gain represented a step towards a more rational society based on consent and understanding (and a private enterprise economy). The Chartists, it is argued, simply wanted too much too soon. Change came gradually and was conceded as people demonstrated their readiness for citizenship. This produced a gradual and fairly smooth transition to a modern society in a series of well-defined steps marked by the Reform Acts of 1832, 1867, 1884, 1918 and 1928.

Source 140

From J.R. Dinwiddy, *From Luddism to the First Reform Bill* (Blackwell, 1986) pp.35–6.

One needs to ask how widespread and serious the will to revolution was. Historians have differed widely on this question. J.L. and B. Hammond, 'New Liberals' of the early twentieth century,...regarded the working-class movements of the early nineteenth century as basically constitutionalist and non-violent. They tended to attribute what insurrectionary episodes there were to a handful of hotheads, under the influence of *agents provocateurs*, and they maintained that there was no justification for the repressive measures which governments of the time adopted against popular agitation. This interpretation accorded with that put forward in the early nineteenth century by Whig politicians such as H.G. Bennett, and by the respectable radical Francis Place....On the other hand, the interpretation of the 'New Left' historian E.P. Thompson in *The Making of the English Working Class*...is very different. Whereas the Hammonds, he says, tended to start their research with the assumption that it was highly unlikely that English working men engaged in serious revolutionary conspiracies, he considers that in view of the conditions of the time it would have been more surprising if they had *not* done so. He believes that there *was* a strong revolutionary element in working-class agitation; and he writes of a 'secret revolutionary tradition', a continuous strand of underground politics, running from the 1790s through to the post-war period....

Research carried out by Thompson, or inspired by his example, has shown that in some places insurrectionary plotting did take place in the years 1817–20, and that it cannot simply be attributed to the instigation of spies....It is clear that in certain communities where artisan groups faced a steady deterioration of income and status...people could be persuaded by local militants to take the very large step from disaffection into rebellion; and although only a few hundred men actually took this step, many more in the same or similar environments may have seriously contemplated it. However, it is possible that those who *were* in such environments – marked by a fair degree of politicization, a strong sense of communal solidarity, and sharply declining prospects – overestimated the number of people in the country at large who shared their anger and aspirations.

E.P. Thompson and Harold Perkin are referred to in the sources you have just read as having made significant contributions to our understanding of the politicization of the working class, the first from a Marxist standpoint, the second from a liberal point of view. Sources 141 and 142 contain extracts from their work. R.J. White, another respected historian of this period, begins with different purposes and assumptions (Sources 143–4). While recognizing how the varying purposes and assumptions of these historians have influenced them to produce competing interpretations, you should also be aware of the considerable amount of common ground that exists between the accounts. However, as has been stressed earlier, the validity of the accounts can only be determined by judging their consonance with available contemporary evidence. Therefore, once you have completed Question 3, evaluating the provided hypotheses against the evidence contained in Sources 145–70, you might also like to consider the extent to which the interpretations offered by Thompson, Perkin and White in Sources 141–3 are consistent with that evidence.

Question

2. (a) What purposes and assumptions can be detected underlying the accounts produced by E.P. Thompson, Harold Perkin and R.J. White in Sources 141–3?

   (b) How have these purposes and assumptions influenced each historian's interpretation of the rise of the working class?

Source 141

From E.P. Thompson, *The Making of the English Working Class* (Pelican, 1968) pp.11, 604, 629–30, 646–8, 656–9, 781–2, 887–9 and 903.

In the years between 1780 and 1832 most English working people came to feel an identity of interests as between themselves, and as against their rulers and employers. This ruling class was itself much divided, and in fact only gained in cohesion over the same years because certain antagonisms were resolved (or faded into relative insignificance) in the face of an insurgent working class. Thus the working class presence was, in 1832, the most significant factor in British political life....

Luddism lingers in the popular mind as an uncouth spontaneous affair of illiterate handworkers, blindly resisting machinery. But machine-breaking has a far longer history....Although related to this tradition, the *Luddite movement* must be distinguished from it, first by its high degree of organization, second, by the political context within which it flourished. These differences may be summed up in a single characteristic: while finding its origin in particular industrial grievances, Luddism was a *quasi-insurrectionary movement*, which continually trembled on the edge of ulterior revolutionary objectives. This is not to say that it was a wholly conscious revolutionary movement; on the other hand, it had a tendency towards becoming such a movement, and it is this tendency which is most often understated....

The two most important studies of Luddism are those of the Hammonds and of Darvall. *The Skilled Labourer* is a fine book; but the chapters on Luddism read at times like a brief prepared on behalf of the Whig opposition, and intended to discredit the exaggerated claims made by the authorities as to the conspiratorial and revolutionary aspects of the movement. The role of spies and of *agents provocateurs* is emphasised to the point where it is suggested that there was *no* authentic insurrectionary underground and no evidence of delegates passing between the counties....Authentic Luddism (it is implied) was without ulterior aims, and was either a matter of spontaneous riot (Lancashire) or an action with strictly limited industrial objectives (Nottingham and Yorkshire).

F.O. Darvall, in his *Popular Disturbances and Public Order in Regency England*, follows most of the Hammonds' judgements. 'There is no evidence whatever,' he declares flatly, 'of any political motives on the part of the Luddites. There is not one single instance in which it can be proved that a Luddite attack was directed against anything deeper than disputes between masters and men, between workmen and their employers. There was not a single Luddite...against whom a charge of treason was advanced or could lie. There is no sign, despite the great efforts of the spies to prove such motives, that the Luddites, or indeed any but a few unimportant, unrepresentative, irresponsible agitators, had any large or political designs.'

'Despite the most careful search no large dumps of arms, such as the spies talked about, were found. No connection could be traced between the disaffected in one district and those in others...' The secret committees in the Lancashire towns were a 'fungoid growth', controlled by spies or by men who made 'petty sedition their source of income'. And of the larger Luddite attacks, 'it does not appear that there was any more organization in these large mobs than there is in the crowd that carries through a spontaneous college 'rag'. There is nothing whatever other than the uncorroborated testimony of spies to prove that the Luddites ever took any secret or illegal oath at all'.

Caught up in the minutiae of day-to-day reports – phlegmatic officers here, panic-stricken magistrates there, incredibly tortuous stories of espionage in another place – it is possible to doubt the reality of Luddism altogether. But if we stand back from the minutiae for a moment, we shall see that the conclusions of these authorities are as unlikely as the most sensational conspiracy-theory of Luddism. Anyone who has conducted a raffle or organised a darts tournament knows that scores of men cannot be assembled at night, from several districts, at a given point, disguised and armed with muskets, hammers and hatchets; formed into line; mustered by number; marched several miles to a successful attack, to the accompaniment of signal lights and rockets – and all with the organization of a spontaneous college 'rag'. Anyone who knows the geography of the Midlands and North will find it difficult to believe that the Luddites of three adjoining counties had *no* contact with each other....

The chapter on 'Lancashire Luddism' is the least satisfactory chapter in *The Skilled Labourer*....The conclusions are little short of ridiculous. We are asked to believe that 71 companies of infantry, 27 troops of Horse Guards and Dragoons, as well as thousands of special constables (1500 in the Salford Hundred alone) were on active duty in Lancashire in 1812 because 'Old S', Young S' and 'B' [spies and informers] had made their employers' blood run cold with stories of insurrection and because some spontaneous food riots had taken place.

What is most noticeable in the Hammonds' handling of the sources is a marked disposition to commence their research with the assumption that any *bona fide* insurrectionary schemes on the part of working men were either highly improbable or, alternatively, wrong, and undeserving of sympathy, and therefore to be attributed to a lunatic, irresponsible fringe. It is difficult to see why, in 1812, this should be assumed. With a year's intermission, war had continued for almost twenty years. The people had few civil and no trade union liberties. They were not gifted with historical clairvoyance, so that they might be comforted by the knowledge that in twenty years (when many of them would be dead) the middle class would secure the vote. In 1812 the weavers had experienced a disastrous decline in their status and living standards. People were so hungry that they were willing to risk their lives upsetting a barrow of potatoes. In these conditions, it might appear more surprising if men had not plotted revolutionary uprisings than if they had; and it would seem highly unlikely that such conditions would nourish a crop of gradualist constitutional reformers, acting within a Constitution which did not admit their political existence....

Several of the historians who pioneered the study of this period (the Hammonds, the Webbs and Graham Wallas) were men and women of Fabian persuasion, who looked back upon the 'early history of the Labour Movement' in the light of the subsequent Reform Acts, and the growth of the TUC and Labour Party. Since Luddites or food rioters do not appear as satisfactory 'fore-runners' of 'the Labour Movement' they merited neither sympathy nor close attention. And this bias was supplemented, from another direction, by the more conservative bias of the orthodox academic tradition. Hence 'history' dealt fairly with the Tolpuddle Martyrs, and fulsomely with Francis Place; but the hundreds of men and women executed or transported for oath-taking, Jacobin conspiracy, Luddism, the Pentrich and Grange Moor risings, food and enclosure and turnpike riots, the Ely riots and the Labourers' Revolt of 1830, and a score of minor affrays, have been forgotten by all but a few specialists, or, if they are remembered, they are thought to be simpletons or men tainted with criminal folly....

From one aspect, Luddism may be seen as the nearest thing to a 'peasant's revolt' of industrial workers; instead of sacking the *châteaux*, the most immediate object which symbolized their oppression – the gig-mill or power-loom mill – was attacked....Even while attacking these symbols of exploitation and of the factory system they became aware of larger objectives, and pockets of 'Tom Painers' existed who could direct them towards ulterior [political] aims....

From another aspect we may see the Luddite movement as transitional. We must see through the machine-breaking to the motives of the men who wielded the great hammers. As 'a movement of the *people's own*', one is struck not so much by its backwardness as by its growing maturity. Far from being 'primitive' it exhibited, in Nottingham and Yorkshire, discipline, and self-restraint of a high order. One can see Luddism as a manifestation of a working-class culture of greater independence and complexity than any known to the eighteenth century. The twenty years of the illegal tradition before 1811 are years of a richness at which we can only guess; in particular in the trade union movement, new experiments, growing experience and literacy, greater political awareness, are evident on every side. Luddism grew out of this culture....It was a transitional phase when the waters of self-confident trade unionism, dammed up by the Combination Acts, strove to break through and become a manifest and open presence. It was also a transitional moment between Despard and 'Black Lamp' [i.e hare-brained revolutionary conspiracies fomented by an extremist minority] on the one hand, and Peterloo [reform movements attracting mass support] on the other....In the three counties [Yorkshire, Nottinghamshire and Derbyshire], the agitation for parliamentary reform commenced at exactly the point where Luddism was defeated....If we follow the logic through to its conclusion, we may credit the comment of a Derbyshire magistrate in 1817: 'the Luddites are now principally engaged in politics and poaching. They are the principal leaders of the Hampden Clubs which are now formed in almost every village in the angle between Leicester, Derby and Newark'....

When contrasted with the Radical years which preceded and the Chartist years which succeeded it, the decade of the 1820s seems strangely quiet....These quiet years were the years of Richard Carlile's contest for the liberty of the press; of growing trade union strength and the repeal of the Combination Acts; of the growth of free thought, cooperative experiment and Owenite theory....And at the end of the decade, when there came the climactic contest between Old Corruption and Reform [leading to the passing of the Reform Act], it is possible to speak in a new way of the working people's consciousness of their interests and of their predicament as a class....Working men formed a picture of the organization of society out of their own experience and with the help of their hard-won and erratic education, which was above all a political picture. They learned to see their own lives as part of a general history of conflict between the loosely defined 'industrious classes' on the one hand, and the unreformed House of Commons on the other. From 1830 onwards a more clearly defined class consciousness, in the customary Marxist sense, was maturing, in which working people were aware of continuing both old and new battles on their own....

The new class consciousness of working people may be viewed from two aspects. On the one hand, there was a consciousness of the identity of interests between working men of the most diverse occupations and levels of attainment, which was embodied in many institutional forms, and which was expressed on an unprecedented scale in the general unionism of 1830–34. This consciousness and these institutions were only to be found in fragmentary form in the England of 1780.

On the other hand, there was a consciousness of the identity of the interests of the working class...as against those of other classes; and within this there was maturing the claim for an alternative *system*. But the final definition of this class consciousness was, in large part, the consequence of the response to working-class strength of the middle class. The line was drawn, with extreme care, in the franchise qualifications of 1832. It had been the peculiar feature of English development that, where we would expect to find a growing middle-class reform movement, with a working-class tail, only later succeeded by an independent agitation of the working class, in fact this process was reversed. The example of the French Revolution had initiated three simultaneous processes: a panic-struck counter-revolutionary response on the part of the landed and commercial aristocracy; a withdrawal on the part of the industrial bourgeoisie and an accommodation (on favourable terms) with the *status quo*; and a rapid radicalization of the popular reform movement until the Jacobin cadres who were tough enough to survive through the Wars were in the main little masters, artisans, stockingers and croppers, and other working men. The 25 years after 1795 may be seen as the years of the long counter-revolution, and in consequence the Radical movement remained largely working-class in character, with an advanced democratic populism as its theory. But the triumph of such a movement was scarcely to be welcomed by the mill-owners, iron-masters and manufacturers. Hence the peculiarly repressive and anti-egalitarian ideology of the English middle classes....

The Reform Bill crisis of 1832...illustrates these theses at almost every point. The agitation arose from 'the people' and rapidly displayed the most astonishing consensus of opinion as to the imperative necessity for 'reform'. Viewed from one aspect England was without any doubt passing through a crisis in these twelve months in which revolution was possible....And viewed from another aspect, we can see why throughout these crisis months a revolution was in fact improbable. The reason is to be found in the very strength of the working-class Radical movement; the skill with which the middle-class leaders...both used this threat of working-class force, and negotiated a line of retreat acceptable to all but the most die-hard defenders of the *ancien regime*....Bronterre O'Brien [later a Chartist leader]...wrote of the Reform Bill 'We foresaw that its effect would be to detach from the working classes a large portion of the middle ranks, who were then more inclined to act with the people than with the aristocracy that excluded them'.

Source 142

The Birth of Class. From Harold Perkin, *The Origins of Modern English Society 1780–1880* (Routledge and Kegan Paul, 1969) pp.183–4, 188–9, 192–5, 208–13 and 215–6.

'The abdication on the part of the governors'

[An] anonymous contributor to *Blackwood's Edinburgh Magazine*...in 1820 lamented the change in 'the style and structure of society' since 'the time of our fathers':

> 'Everywhere, in every walk of life, it is too evident that the upper orders of Society have been tending, more and more, to a separation of themselves from those whom nature, providence, and law have placed beneath them....The rich and the high have been indolently and slothfully allowing the barriers that separate them from their inferiors to increase and accumulate....Men have come to deride and despise a thousand of those means of communication that in former days knit all orders of the people together.'...

'The abdication on the part of the governors', however, went far beyond snobbish aloofness and the withdrawal of sympathetic contacts. It consisted in the deliberate dismantling of the whole system of paternal protection of the lower orders which had been the pride of the old society and the justification of its inequalities. In the early years of the nineteenth century, practically the whole of the centuries-old legislation protecting the workers' standard of living and conditions of work was repealed, and a campaign waged, not less resented for being unsuccessful, to abolish the most symbolic of all paternal protections, the poor law....As late as 1795 [the ruling aristocracy] were still willing, in the form of Speenhamland [a system of outdoor relief for the poor], to pay the price of paternal protection in return for filial obedience. But from then onwards they began to exact the fruits of paternalism but refuse to pay the price....

The first symptom of this provocative change was the Combination Acts of 1799 and 1800 [Unit 3.1, Source 71 and 3.3 Source 147]....These were a mere generalization of old society attitudes towards industrial 'insubordination' and contained no new principle. What was new, however, was the context in which they were passed. Having within the same five years refused to regulate wages, Parliament now reiterated its traditional denial of the right of the workers to negotiate them for themselves. It was this outrageous demand to have their cake and eat it, to exact paternal discipline while denying paternal protection, which...was to exasperate the lower orders and awaken in them the spirit of class conflict.

How reluctant the lower orders were to be provoked can be seen in the immense efforts which they made to maintain the fabric of the paternal system. For a dozen years, from 1802 to 1814, workers in the traditional crafts petitioned and went to law for the enforcement of the legislation regulating wages and apprenticeship. In 1802 the Yorkshire and West of England weavers combined to employ an attorney and prosecute infringements of the special laws regulating the woollen industry. The response of parliament was to suspend the laws in 1803, and repeal them six years later....A number of London trades engaged a solicitor between 1810 and 1811 and at great cost obtained a few convictions for infringement of the apprenticeship clauses of the 1563 Act [Statute of Artificers], only to have the Lord Chancellor Ellenborough rule in 1811 that crafts established since 1663 were not covered by the Act....Finally, massive petitions to put the 1563 Statute in operation were met by the repeal of the wages clauses in 1813 and of the apprenticeship clauses in 1814, and the destruction of the machinery of industrial paternalism was complete.

This was not the end of the aristocratic onslaught on the paternal system, however. It achieved its zenith only with the attack on the poor laws in the years immediately following the Wars. The campaign to abolish the poor laws was the most flagrant breach of the principle of dependency on which the old society rested, and, though unsuccessful, did more to alienate the lower orders and provoke working-class antagonism than any other action of the aristocracy....

The demand of the landed rulers for power without responsibility offended not only the lower orders. The middle ranks, too,...were alienated by the unseemly haste with which at the first sign of peace the landowners brought in the Corn Laws to protect their rents at the expense of the rest of the community....From that moment the alienation of the middle ranks paralleled that of the lower orders. It was only a matter of time before they would unite to bury the old society which had destroyed itself from within.

We have seen, however, the reluctance of the lower orders, and to a less extent of the middle ranks, to abandon paternalism and be provoked into class antagonism. It is true that from the French Revolution onwards there were those who were not at all reluctant to apply the axe to the old society. Working men...joined the Corresponding

Societies in their hundreds,...only to be persecuted and brutally suppressed by the government. This gave rise to what may be called the conspiratorial theory of the birth of class. 'In the 1790s', writes the leading left-wing historian of the making of the working class [E.P. Thompson], 'something like an "English Revolution" took place, of profound importance in shaping the consciousness of the post-war working class. It is true that the revolutionary impulse was strangled in its infancy; and the first consequence was that of bitterness and despair.' But the tree of liberty had been planted, and the proletarian [working-class] seedling was nurtured through the long winter of repression by devoted cells of Painites [radicals influenced by Thomas Paine's *The Rights of Man*], whose propagandist labours at length united the hot breaths of the revolutionary working class into an artificial spring and made it burst into bloom....

The difficulty with the theory is twofold: it is doubtful to what extent Paine and the radicals of the 1790s were consciously proletarian, and it is still more doubtful whether the workers as a class supported them....The London Corresponding Society of 1792 [was] proletarian according to the theory but in fact composed of 'tradesmen, mechanics and shopkeepers' who in old society terms belonged to the middle ranks rather than the lower orders, or at least cut across both....Secondly, it is not the case that here was a mass-movement of the working class prematurely strangled by a tyrannical despotism. However numerous the working-men Reformers, the working-men supporters of the existing order were still more numerous. The government had no police and only a volunteer army, and it was not so much the mailed fist of the law which put the Jacobins [Painite radical reformers of the 1790s] to flight as the Church-and-King mobs, in which the heat and burden were borne by patriotic working men....If some of the Reformers were proletarian, how much more so were the mobs which burned and pillaged the houses of Thomas Walker and Joseph Priestley? [Walker and Priestley were leading reformers whose homes were destroyed during the Church-and-King riots in Birmingham and Manchester during 1791–2.] Indeed, it can be argued that the loyalist reaction played a far greater part in the development of class feeling than the movement which provoked it....

The Delayed Birth
As long as the great French Wars lasted, patriotism reinforced paternalism to hold overt class conflict in check....It was in the first five years of peace, between Waterloo and the Queen's Trial [an attempt to deprive George IV's estranged wife, Caroline of Brunswick, of her royal title for sexual misconduct] that the vertical antagonisms and horizontal solidarities of class came for the first time, clearly, unmistakably, and irrevocably, to supplant the vertical connections...of dependency....By this definition the working class almost sprang into existence with the Parliamentary Reform Movement of 1816–19....

It was not the leadership which gave the movement its working-class character: Cobbett was the nearest to a working man amongst them, while Orator Hunt...prided himself on being a gentleman....It was, first of all, the platform of the movement, household and then universal suffrage, and, secondly, the means, vast mass meetings with democratic resolutions carried by acclamation, both of which alienated practically everybody but the emancipated working class....

The significance of the working-class Reform movement in these five years was not the threat of revolution, which was confined to a few cranks and extremists. On the contrary, it was...the direct opposite: for the first time working-class protest, instead of exploding into riots and mob-violence – as indeed still happened in these years amongst the less sophisticated framework knitters and agricultural labourers – was organized on a national scale for a non-violent purpose....It was between 1815 and 1820 that the working class was born....

The union of the middle and working classes against the aristocracy was hastened and anticipated by two events which together marked the end of the period of birth, Peterloo and the Queen's Trial. The 'Manchester Massacre' hastened it by throwing into glaring contrast the provocative use of force by the ruling class and the manifest lack of revolutionary intent on the part of the working class....The Royal Divorce Bill although – or perhaps because – it diverted popular attention away from Reform, actually anticipated the successful alliance of the Great Reform Crisis....Loss of confidence and division of the aristocracy in the face of the united middle and working classes – this was to be the formula for the passing of the Reform Bill.

Source 143

From R.J. White, *Waterloo to Peterloo* (Heinemann, 1957) pp.112–3 and 128.

The favourite adjective [of members of the government], when referring to the labouring poor, was not 'revolutionary' but 'deluded'. They were intent less upon exaggerating the disturbed and dangerous state of the country (although they rightly realized that it was dangerously disturbed), than upon correcting the false impression that there was any necessary connection between political opinions and social distress.

In all this, the facts were for long enough on their side. There is scarcely any sign of political intention in the machine-breaking movement which raged in the Midlands and the north at the time when the Liverpool administration came into power. The disturbances of 1815 and 1816 were similarly the work of Luddites and bread-rioters. The Derbyshire Rising of 1817 was the action of deluded and desperate men whose declared intention was to 'turn out and fight for bread'....It was not until 1819 that popular agitation took on a coherent political character....Lord Liverpool...was still speaking in the last year of the Regency as he had spoken in the first year of that agitated epoch. In 1812 he accepted the report of the Secret Committee of the House of Lords on the nature of the Luddite disturbances: 'that the rioters were to a great extent tools in the hands of those whose turbulence and disloyalty derived no provocation from poverty...'. In 1819, in the debate on the conduct of the magistrates at Peterloo, he declared that the distress of the people arose 'from the state of an internal trade that was affected by foreign commerce....Whatever might be the circumstances of that distress, it was not connected with political causes.' His diagnosis was the same in both cases: a basis of distress occasioned by causes beyond the Government's control, and the provocative conduct of some few ill-disposed persons who wished to make political capital out of their fellow creatures' sufferings....

All the evidence goes to show that Luddism was an essentially local phenomenon, devoid of national and political ramifications; an affair of blackened faces, secret oaths, and threatening letters. General Ludd was something of an industrial Robin Hood. His headquarters were supposed to be in Sherwood Forest. His followers combined the morals of Robin Hood with the methods of gangsters. Their extraordinary loyalty to each other, their fearsome secret oaths by which they sought to wreak 'unceasing vengeance' upon traitors, invited the attention of spies and *agents provocateurs*, and the government depended upon the reports of these unscrupulous and often illiterate individuals for their perverted information as to what was going on. Thus, it was a certain 'B' (or 'Mr. Bent') who, in a number of semi-illiterate reports which still repose among the Home Office Papers for 1812, evoked in the imagination of his employers the fantasy of 'a general insurrection' which was due to occur on 1 May, or early in that month.

Source 144

From a review by W.H. Chaloner of R.J. White's *Waterloo to Peterloo*, in *History*, June 1958, Vol.43, no.148.

Mr. R.J. White's book...has a dual purpose, to ride a hobby horse by setting forth the alleged virtues of a mythical pre-industrial 'Old England' which has never existed outside the imagination, and secondly, to trace the impact of popular politics immediately after Waterloo on a government apparatus, both local and national, which was still largely that of the eighteenth century....Looking back, it is very doubtful whether there was ever any danger of a British revolution. Lord Liverpool, Sidmouth and Castlereagh, to whom Mr. White is fairer than most historians, seem to have fallen into the error of later writers and endowed the tumults and pitiful plottings of 1816–21 with an exaggerated importance.

Question

3. Read Hypotheses A and B and Sources 145–70.

Hypothesis A
In the period from 1790 to 1850, co-operation rather than conflict was the norm in relations between the newly-emerged working class and its political and economic masters.

Hypothesis B
Between 1790 and 1850, confrontational and sometimes violent action, or at least the threat of it, was the principal means by which the working class made its views known to, and wrested concessions from, its political and economic masters.

Which, if either, of these hypotheses accounts most successfully for the evidence contained in Sources 145–70?

Source 145

From a declaration by delegates from various radical societies following a meeting at Norwich in 1792.

We believe that instructing the people in political knowledge and in their natural and inherent rights as men is the only effectual way to obtain the grand object of reform, for men need only be made acquainted with the abuses of government and they will readily join in every lawful means to obtain redress.

Source 146

From a contemporary account of a 'Church and King' demonstration in Coventry on New Year's Day, 1793.

The effigy of Tom Paine, with the *Rights of Man* fastened upon his breast, was placed in a cart...and drawn through all the principal streets....He was taken to the Cross Cheaping, where a gibbet had been previously erected for his reception; where, after hanging the usual time, a fire was lighted under the gallows, which consumed him instantly to ashes, amidst the acclamations of a loyal multitude of surrounding spectators, who all joined heartily in the chorus of *God Save the King*.

Source 147

From the Combination Act, 1799.

All contracts and agreements made by any workmen for obtaining an advance of wages or for altering their usual hours of working, or for preventing any person from employing whomsoever he shall think proper to employ in his business, are hereby declared to be illegal.

Source 148

From a leaflet left in the market place at Chesterfield in 1812.

I am going to inform you that there are 6,000 men coming to you in April and then we will go and blow Parliament house up [because] us labouring people can't stand it no longer. Damn all such rogues as govern England, but never mind Ned Ludd, when General Nody and his army comes we will soon bring about the great revolution; then all these great men's heads will go off.

Source 149

From a letter written by Earl Fitzwilliam (Lord Lieutenant of the West Riding of Yorkshire, and a Whig) to the Home Secretary, Viscount Sidmouth, 25 July 1812.

Having yesterday had occasion to converse with different persons, I have the satisfaction of reporting that I am very confident the country is not in that alarming state it has been supposed to be. That there is combination for mischievous purposes, there can be no doubt…but it shows no symptom of preparation for resisting men in arms.…Moreover, the reports of nocturnal training and drilling, when one comes to close quarters on the subject, and to enquire for evidence of fact, dwindles down to nothing; they are the offspring of fear, quite imaginary, and mere invention.…Nevertheless combination indisputably exists, very formidable to property and persons: most probably entered into originally for the destruction of that species of property, machinery in manufacture, and afterwards directed against the persons of the proprietors of that species of property as one means of its destruction, through the medium of intimidation.

Source 150

From evidence presented by Thomas Broughton of Barnsley, weaver, before two JPs in the West Riding, 26 August 1812.

That last Monday morning at Barnsley, he heard a person, whose name he does not know, but whom he understood to come from Sheffield, declare to Joseph Isaacs, that there were 8,000 men nearly complete in arms, in and about Sheffield, and would be in a few days, and therefore they did not mind the soldiers.…That since he had been upon the secret committee, the informant has been told by his fellow committee men, that delegates had been at Barnsley, from Manchester, and Stockport, (but he was not present), whose business it was, to collect numbers and other information. That one Haigh now in York Castle for administering unlawful oaths, told the informant that there were 450 Luddites twisted in [sworn in by secret oaths], at Holmfirth; the greater part of the neighbourhood at Huddersfield, and a great number at Halifax, and that they met there as Dissenters under the cloak of religion, and also 7,000 or 8,000 in Leeds. The informant saith that a very great number of Luddites are local militia men. That the Luddites have in view ultimately to overturn the system of government, by revolutionising the country. That certain delegates at Ashton under Lyne, on the 4th of August told the informant that the first measure to be adopted in bringing about a revolution, would be to send parties to the different houses of the members of both Houses of Parliament, and destroy them, and then the people in London belonging to that Society would seize upon the Government.

Source 151

From Samuel Bamford, *Passages in the Life of a Radical*, 1859. Bamford was a handloom weaver and leading radical from Lancashire.

A series of disturbances commenced with the introduction of the Corn Bill in 1815, and continued, with short intervals, until the close of the year 1816. In London and Westminster riots ensued, and were continued for several days, whilst the bill was discussed; at Bridport, there were riots on account of the high price of bread; at Bideford, there were similar disturbances to prevent the exportation of grain; at Bury, by the unemployed, to destroy machinery; at Ely, not suppressed without bloodshed; at Newcastle-upon-Tyne, by colliers and others; at Glasgow, where blood was shed, on account of the soup kitchens; at Preston, by unemployed weavers; at Nottingham, by Luddites, who destroyed 30 frames; at Merthyr Tydfil, on a reduction of wages; at Birmingham, by the unemployed; at Walsall, by the distressed; and December 7th 1816 at Dundee, where owing to the high price of meal, upwards of 100 shops were plundered.…

The writings of William Cobbett [especially his *Weekly Register*, the first cheap edition of which appeared in November 1816] suddenly became of great authority; they were read on nearly every cottage hearth in the manufacturing districts of South Lancashire, in those of Leicester, Derby and Nottingham; also in many of the Scottish manufacturing towns. Their influence was speedily visible; he directed his readers to the true cause of their sufferings – misgovernment; and to its proper corrective – parliamentary reform. Riots soon became scarce, and from that time they have never obtained their ancient vogue with the labourers of this country.

Source 152

'A Peep into the Green Bag, or The Secret Committee of Magnifiers' (Marks, 1817), a cartoon satirizing the parliamentary committee appointed to examine papers presented to them in 'A Green Bag' by Lord Castlereagh, showing members of the committee busily magnifying the evidence of revolutionary designs

Source 153

From a report in *The Courier* of the demonstration at St Peter's Fields, Manchester on 16 August 1819. (See also Unit 1.6, Source 307 for a report of a similar meeting in Leeds a month later.)

Before 12 o'clock crowds began to assemble, each town or hamlet having a banner, and some a cap, with 'Liberty' upon it: each party, as they came through the streets, kept in military order, with sticks shouldered. A banner was painted 'Taxation and no Representation is tyrannical and unjust', and on the reverse 'No boroughmongering – Unite and be free – Equal representation or Death'. On another banner 'Die like men, and not be sold like slaves'. On a third, 'Major Cartwright's Bill and no Corn Laws'; on a fourth, 'Unity and Fraternity – Strength and Liberty'. It was 20 minutes after one o'clock before Hunt appeared. 'Gentlemen, I must entreat that you will be peaceable; a great deal depends upon that, and I trust all who hear me will remain quiet'.

Source 154

From a report in *The Times* of the 'Peterloo Massacre', 19 August 1819. The reporter, who was mistakenly arrested during the incident, claimed to hold the views of Hunt, who addressed the Manchester meeting, 'in as utter abhorrence as the most loyal subject of His Majesty'.

A posse of 300 or 400 constables marched into the field about 12 o'clock. Not the slightest insult was offered to them. The cavalry drew their swords and brandished them fiercely in the air: upon which they rode into the mob which gave way before them. Not a brickbat was thrown at them – not a pistol was fired during this period: all was quiet and orderly. They wheeled round the wagons till they came in front of them.

As soon as Hunt and Johnson had jumped from the wagons (to surrender) a cry was made by the cavalry, 'Have at their flags'. They immediately dashed not only at the flags which were in the wagon, but those which were posted among the crowd, cutting most indiscriminately to the right and the left in order to get at them. This set the people running in all directions, and it was not till this act had been committed that any brickbats were hurled at the military. From that moment the Manchester Yeomanry Cavalry lost all command of temper. A man within five yards of us had his nose completely taken off by a blow of a sabre.

Source 155

From the diary of John Campbell, moderate Whig MP for Stafford. The entries indicate how public opinion could influence the views of MPs, in this case over the passing of the Reform Bill.

2 March [1831]: We are quite appalled. There is not the remotest chance of such a Bill being passed by this or any other House of Commons.…This really is a revolution.…It is unquestionably a new constitution. The general sentiment is that the measure goes a good deal too far. It is applauded by the Radicals and by *some* Whigs, but it is very distasteful to a great part of the Whig party.

3 March: The general belief is that the Bill must be thrown out on the second reading. I expect that Ministers will then resign and anarchy begin.…I feel inclined as a choice of evils to support and even speak in favour of the Bill.

5 March: The measure takes very much with the country.

8 March: I still consider the Bill dangerously violent, but apprehend less danger from passing it than rejecting it.

Source 156

From an article by Bronterre O'Brien, a radical journalist and later a Chartist leader, in his newspaper, the *Poor Man's Guardian*, 1833. O'Brien was commenting on the growth of trade unionism in England.

A spirit of combination has grown up among the working classes of which there has been no example in former times.…The object is…to establish for the productive classes a complete domination over the fruits of their own industry.…They aspire to be at the top instead of at the bottom of society – or rather that there should be no bottom or top at all.

Source 157

From a letter to the Home Secretary, Lord Melbourne, from James Frampton, a Dorsetshire squire who, in 1834, prosecuted six agricultural labourers, the 'Tolpuddle Martyrs', for swearing illegal oaths during a trade union initiation ceremony. The men were sentenced to be transported to Australia for seven years.

The event of this trial has been looked forward to with the greatest anxiety by all classes in this county: the farmers feeling that on it depended whether they should in future have any control over their labourers; and the labourers only waiting to join the union as soon as they were satisfied they could do so with impunity. The conviction and the prompt execution of the sentence of transportation has given the greatest satisfaction to all the higher classes, and will, I have no doubt, have a very great effect among the labourers.

Source 158

From George Loveless, *The Victims of Whiggery*, 1837. Loveless was one of the 'Tolpuddle Martyrs' and wrote *The Victims of Whiggery* on his return to England after their sentence had been quashed following radical demonstrations and pleas in parliament on their behalf.

I believe that nothing will ever be done to relieve the distress of the working classes, unless they take it into their own hands. With these views I left England, and with these views I am returned.

Source 159

From D. P. Titley, *Machines, Money and Men* (Collins, 1969) p.90.

Robert Owen was born in 1771....He was apprenticed to a draper but by exceptional business ability he was soon managing his own spinning works. He married the daughter of David Dale, who owned large cotton mills at New Lanark in Scotland. By the time he was 29, Owen was already controlling these mills, and it was then that he tried to create a model factory and a model community. Owen firmly believed that employers had a duty towards their workers to treat them as human beings. He built pleasant houses for the workers and shops where they could buy good products at fair prices. Schools were provided for children and no child under ten was allowed to work in the mill. He paid higher wages than anyone else and when his mills were closed for four months because of lack of raw cotton he continued to pay his workers. His partners protested bitterly until they found that despite high pay and short hours the firm's profits increased. Owen had proved that it benefited both employers and employees if goodwill existed on both sides. He tried to force other mill owners to restrict hours when he promoted the Factory Act of 1819 [which prohibited children under nine from working in cotton mills and restricted those over nine to no more than twelve hours a day]. However, it proved unsuccessful in practice.

Source 160

From the 1833 Factory Act, which was more effective than the earlier Act promoted by Robert Owen in 1819.

No person under 18 years of age shall be allowed to work in the night...in any cotton, wool, [or other textile] mill...[or] shall be employed for more than 12 hours in any one day, nor more than 69 hours in any one week....It shall not be lawful to employ any child who shall not have completed his ninth year...[or] to employ for longer than 48 hours in any one week, nor for a longer time than 9 hours in any one day, any child who shall not have completed his eleventh year.

Source 161

From the Report of a Parliamentary Commission established in 1842 to enquire into the practice of employing children in mines.

The practice of employing children only six or seven years of age is all but universal. The children go down into the pit with the men usually at four o'clock in the morning and remain in the pit between eleven and twelve hours each day. The use of a child up to six years of age is to open and shut the doors of the galleries when the coal trucks pass and repass. For this object a child is trained to sit by itself in a dark gallery for the number of hours described.

Source 162

From the Coal Mines Regulation Act, 1842.

From and after Three Calendar Months from the passing of this Act it shall not be lawful for any Owner of any Mine or Colliery to employ any Female Person...under the Age of Eighteen Years within any Mine or Colliery...[or] to employ any Male Person under the Age of Ten Years.

Source 163

From the Report of a Parliamentary Commission established in 1845 to enquire into the state of public health in industrial towns.

This town [Merthyr Tydfil] is in a sad state of neglect. From the poorer inhabitants, who constitute the mass of the population, throwing all slops and refuse into the nearest open gutter before their houses...some parts of the town are complete networks of filth....There is no local Act for drainage and cleansing. In some localities, a privy was found common to 40 or 50 persons, and even up to 100 persons and more.

Source 164

From the Public Health Act, 1848.

Whereas further and more effectual provision ought to be made for improving the sanitary conditions of towns...be it therefore enacted...that 'The General Board of Health'...shall have and execute all the powers and duties vested in or imposed on each [local] board [of health established under the Act]....The General Board of Health may...direct a Superintending Inspector to visit such a city [with a high death rate or whose inhabitants request such a visit] and examine witnesses as to the sewerage, drainage, and supply of water, the state of the burial grounds, the number and sanitary condition of the inhabitants, and as to any local Acts of Parliament in force...for paving, lighting, cleansing, watching, regulating, supplying with water or improving the same.

Source 165

From the minutes of a meeting of the Working Men's Association, 15 May 1838.

Resolved, That the Members of the Working Men's Association fully concurring in the great principles of Universal Suffrage, Annual Parliaments, the Ballot, and all the other essentials to the free exercise of Man's political rights – and hearing that a meeting is to be held at Glasgow on the 21st of May in furtherance of those objects, do request our Honorary Members, Mr. Thos. Murphy and Revd. Dr. Wade to present to that meeting our pamphlet entitled the 'People's Charter', being the outline of an act to provide for the just representation of the people of Great Britain in the Commons House of Parliament – embracing the principles of Universal Suffrage, No Property Qualifications, Annual Parliaments, Equal Representation, Payment of Members, and Vote by Ballot prepared by a committee of twelve persons, six members of parliament and six members of the Working Men's Association.

Source 166

From an *Address to the People of England*, issued by the Working Men's Association in 1838.

What, we would ask, but legislation, has made the difference between democratic America, despotic Russia and pauperised and oppressed England? If the will of the American people, expressed through their legislature, has raised them from such a poor and heterogeneous origin, to become a nation better educated than any other under the sun – where two-thirds of the adults are proprietors and most of the others have the prospect of becoming so – what...is there in the character of Englishmen to prevent them from realising similar advantages, were the same political rights conferred on them as on their American brethren?

Granting that a number of our countrymen are in poverty, can [our opponents] show, by any valid reasoning, the absolute necessity of their being so....Can they trace the existence of that poverty to any other source than corrupt and exclusive legislation?...America had an adventurous and speculative race to begin with, intermingled with fanatics and convicts from Britain, and for the last half century the poor and the oppressed of all the countries of Europe have sought and found an asylum on her hospitable shores....But her salutary laws and institutions, *springing from Universal Suffrage,* have enabled her to reform, instruct and purify the mass, and...she is the most prosperous and free of all the nations of the earth.

Source 167

A contemporary illustration of the Chartist rising at Newport in 1839, where 24 men were killed or died from their wounds when fired on by soldiers defending the Westgate Hotel from an attack by Chartist rebels intent on seizing the town

Source 168

From William Lovett, *The Life and Struggles of William Lovett,* 1876. Lovett was a moderate Chartist leader and the principal author of the People's Charter. In this extract from his autobiography, he explains how the working and middle classes co-operated in founding the Complete Suffrage Union.

The Complete Suffrage Conference [held in April 1842], composed of 84 persons, both of the middle and working classes,...met at Birmingham....According to the arrangements previously agreed on, I brought forward the following motion:

'That this Conference having adopted such just principles of representation as are necessary for giving to all classes of society their equal share of political power, and as the People's Charter contains such details as have been deemed necessary for the working out of such principles,...in order to effect a cordial union of the middle and working classes, resolve in a future conference...to enter into a calm consideration of that document amongst plans of political reform, and, if approved of, to use every just and peaceable means for creating a public opinion in its favour'....

This having been adopted, the rules for the formation of a new society entitled 'The National Complete Suffrage Union' [were agreed]....This effort to effect a union between the two classes was to some extent successful; for a great many local Complete Suffrage Associations were formed in many towns. Great numbers of the working classes were, however, kept aloof from it by the abuse and misrepresentation of the *Northern Star* [a radical Chartist newspaper edited by Feargus O'Connor]....However, the members of the Union were not idle; tracts were printed, lectures given, meetings held and...two motions introduced into the House of Commons on the subject of the Suffrage by Mr. Sharman Crawford.

Source 169

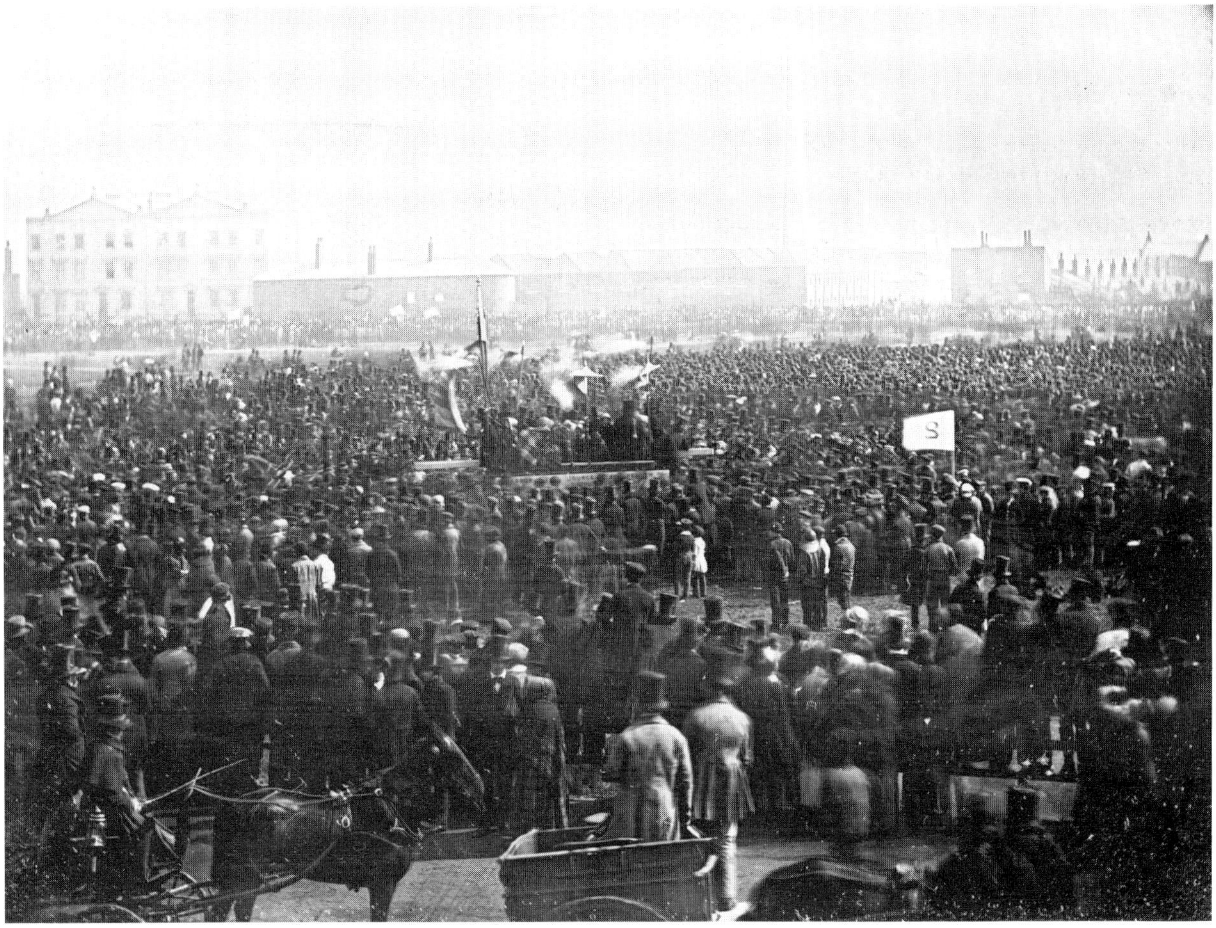

A daguerrotype [an early form of photograph] of the great Chartist meeting on Kennington Common, 1848

Source 170

From a report in the *Manchester Guardian*, 1861.

At this moment, there is not a manufacturing town in South Lancashire in which that trade pest, a strike, does not rage in some form, or that is not in daily fear of contagion. The adjacent counties are no less dangerously infected. Trade in Cheshire, Yorkshire and Lancashire languishes under the disease; and valleys are once more given up to silence and want, through the errors of the class most interested in the prosperity of the works which they reduce to inactivity.

Case Study: The Pentrich Rising

The Pentrich [or Pentridge] Rising took place in Derbyshire in June 1817 and has been a cause of dispute among historians since 1963, when Edward Thompson first published a controversial interpretation of it in his book, *The Making of the English Working Class*. Thompson claimed that 'we may see the Pentridge rising as one of the first attempts in history to mount a wholly proletarian insurrection, without any middle-class support.…It is a transitional moment between Luddism and the 'populist' Radicalism of 1818–20 and 1830–32'. His view challenged the orthodoxy that had been established earlier in the century by John and Barbara Hammond and by G.D.H. Cole and Raymond Postgate. It was the Hammonds who had first drawn historians' attention to the Pentrich Rising with the publication of *The Skilled Labourer* in 1919. Both they and Cole and Postgate had interpreted it as provoked and instigated by the spy and *agent provocateur*, 'Oliver' (whose real name was William Richards), who duped a few radical stocking-knitters in and around Pentrich to take up arms in the mistaken belief that they were merely a small part of a general insurrection. To these historians, it was a minor protest by distressed workers that was only invested with political significance because Oliver fed the Home Secretary, Sidmouth, with information that appeared to confirm the government's fears of an imminent general revolution. The rising was a pathetic farce and its sole importance lay in the evidence that it afforded of the disreputable methods employed by the Home Office. While some historians accepted Thompson's reinterpretation of the significance of the affair at Pentrich, at least in part, others have been more sceptical. R.J. White, for instance, sees it as one of the last of the old-style reactionary revolts triggered by economic distress rather than the first of a new breed of politically-motivated revolutions.

Before considering the different interpretations of the Pentrich Rising offered by these historians and the assumptions that underlay them (Sources 173–6), we must establish what happened on the rain-sodden moors between Pentrich and Nottingham on 8–9 June 1817. From March to May, the government informer, Oliver, undertook a tour of the northern industrial regions posing as a representative of the London Hampden Club. Acting on his information of a general insurrection planned for early June, delegates to a meeting at Thornhill Lees near Dewsbury were arrested by local magistrates on 6 June. This arrest provoked a march on Huddersfield two days later by several hundred weavers, but they dispersed without any loss of life after exchanging a few shots with a small detachment of troops sent to intercept them.

Meanwhile, Oliver had moved on to the Nottingham area, where he made contact with the veteran radical, Thomas Bacon, who appears to have suggested Pentrich as a suitable base for the planned rising because of its proximity to the Butterley ironworks, which could be commandeered to manufacture pikes and cannon. However, Bacon had no further involvement in what transpired, and it was a 27-year-old stocking weaver, Jeremiah Brandreth, who actually led the rising, whether at his own instigation or at Oliver's is not clear.

On 8 June, Brandreth, sometimes known as the 'Nottingham Captain', met members of the Hampden Clubs from Pentrich, Ripley, South Wingfield, Alfreton and Swanwick in the White Horse at Pentrich. There he explained his plan to collect arms and men from the surrounding villages and march to Nottingham to join with insurrectionary contingents from other areas. London was to be secured and a 'provisional' government established, which some at least of the rebels thought meant a government that would supply them with provisions. There was vague talk of ending taxation and the National Debt, of freeing some 'great men' from prison and of 'roast beef, rum and a hundred guineas a man'.

The following day Brandreth and his supporters began visiting houses and farms demanding weapons and men, accompanying their demands with threats where necessary. In one such incident Brandreth shot and killed a farm worker, Robert Walters. Having been turned away from the gates of Butterley ironworks, the rebels who numbered somewhere between 200 and 300, began marching towards Nottingham, with their resolve already weakened by lack of support and heavy rain. When they were confronted at Eastwood by a small body of troops, those who had not already slipped away fled into the night.

The government either genuinely believed Oliver's tales of a planned national insurrection or found it convenient to pretend belief. A determined effort was made to discover those involved in the rising and many arrests were made. Thirty-five men were tried for treason at Derby during October: 23 were sentenced to death, of whom three, Brandreth, Turner and Ludlam, were hanged and the remainder had their sentences commuted to transportation. No mention was made of Oliver throughout the hearings, although his part in the affair was widely known after a report in the *Leeds Mercury* in June which led to widespread revulsion against government methods.

Source 171

Jeremiah Brandreth in chains

Source 172

The execution of Brandreth, Turner and Ludlam, 7 November 1817

Questions

4. What assumptions and purposes can you detect underlying the accounts of the Pentrich Rising by the Hammonds, Cole and Postgate, E.P. Thompson and R.J. White in Sources 173–6? (To answer this question, you should interpret the evidence in Sources 173–6 in the light of the information about the historians and their views contained in Sources 138–40 and 144.)

5. How have the assumptions and purposes of these historians influenced their interpretations of the Pentrich Rising?

Source 173

From J.L. and B. Hammond, *The Skilled Labourer* (Longman, 1919) pp.360–2, and 371–4.

It is possible that in spite of his enthusiasm Brandreth would have obtained no following had not local indignation been stirred by the fact that some men from Mr. Jessop's foundry at Butterley had been discharged on the Saturday night 'in consequence of their Jacobinical principles, and calling themselves members of a Hampden Club'. As it was, a small number of workmen, at the most two hundred, probably fewer, from Pentridge, Wingfield, and Ripley were induced to join in a march towards Nottingham. Some thought that when they got to Nottingham there would be plenty of rum and a hundred guineas, others more vague 'wanted a bigger loaf and the times altering', and they all thought that something important was happening everywhere else....

With dwindling numbers and sinking spirits the rebels marched on in the early morning hours as far as Eastwood on their way to Nottingham. There at about 6 a.m. they met two magistrates who had come out with eighteen men of the 15th Light Dragoons and two officers to oppose them. What happened is best described by one of the magistrates, Mr. Mundy: '...the mob...no sooner saw the Troops than they fled in all directions dispersing over the fields and throwing away their arms....They did not fire a single shot and seemed only intent on escape.' Never was war levied against the King in more spiritless fashion.

Oliver's career is important in history because these methods of government were rapidly growing into a system. Probably no English Government has ever been quite so near, in spirit and licence, to the atmosphere that we used to associate with the Tsar's government of Russia as the Government that ruled England for the first few years of the peace. Oliver's adventures were the most daring examples of methods that had become habitual in the treatment of the poor by several magistrates, but the employment of spies, and of the kind of spies that pass readily into *agents provocateurs*, had become very common in the last few years, as part of the political system....

There is no reason to suppose that Sidmouth deliberately employed Oliver for the diabolical purpose of fomenting an abortive rebellion, although this view was undoubtedly held at the time. The guilt of the Government was grave enough but it was not this. They took Oliver into their employment without knowing anything of his character. Their own correspondents sent them information, early in his career, that would have put any Home Secretary who had the slightest sense of responsibility for the lives and liberties of his countrymen, on his guard. Then came the disclosures of the *Leeds Mercury*, which were brought to the notice of Parliament at the time by Burdett [a Radical MP]. When Brandreth and his fellow victims were on their trial the Government knew enough about Oliver to make them suspect that these foolish ranters had been drawn into their ludicrous escapade by the craft of the man who was receiving the money of the taxpayers and acting as their servant. The temptation to produce something that looked like a spontaneous disturbance was strong, for hitherto the life of the country had borne no resemblance to the picture drawn by the Government in the House of Commons.

Source 174

From G.D.H. Cole and Raymond Postgate, *The Common People 1746–1938* (Methuen, 1938) pp.222–3.

In March and again in June the magistrates pounced upon meetings of working-class delegates and arrested them all. These men were supposed to be engaged on making plans for a general insurrection; but apart from the evidence supplied by paid spies and informers, there is nothing to show that any such movement existed. Wild talk there doubtless was; but of any organized conspiracy there is no untainted evidence at all. No one can read today, without disgust, the facts set forth in Mr. and Mrs. Hammond's *Skilled Labourer*, on the unimpeachable authority of the Home Office official papers, and the evidence furnished by such contemporary writings as Samuel Bamford's *Passages in the Life of a Radical*, written by one who was himself arrested at this time and kept in prison without any offence being proved against him.

Throughout the spring of 1817 the spy, Oliver, was going to and fro in the industrial districts, posing as a delegate from the London 'Physical Force Party'. Wherever he went he assured the local Radicals that the rest of the country was ready for a general insurrection, and only that particular place was lagging behind. In most areas he had no success in provoking the radicals to take up arms; but in Derbyshire, where the framework-knitters were even nearer starvation than the rest of the textile workers, an unemployed knitter named Jeremiah Brandreth believed what Oliver said, and a small band of men from Pentridge and some neighbouring villages set out with such arms as they could gather to march upon Nottingham. They believed that they were but one contingent among many; but in fact they were alone. Only at one other place, Huddersfield, did a few of Oliver's dupes assemble in arms; and they dispersed at once when they found how few and weak they were.

The Derbyshire 'rebels' fared worse. They marched through the night, meeting no other contingents, till they came in sight of a small party of soldiers sent from Nottingham to intercept them. They fled at once; but most of them were captured. Thirty-five were tried for high treason; twenty-three were found guilty....Oliver, who was responsible for the whole wretched affair, had done his work well; but his name was not allowed to be mentioned at the trial. The prisoners, by taking up arms, had convicted themselves. There was no need to mention the spy who had induced them to commit this folly.

Source 175

From E.P. Thompson, *The Making of the English Working Class*, pp.712–7, 723–34.

A widely accepted account of the events of the spring and summer of 1817 is [that put forward by Cole and Postgate in Source 174]. This is the classic Whig interpretation of 1817, and it is also the defence used by the reformers of the time themselves. It is an interpretation which received scholarly backing in the Hammonds' *Skilled Labourer* [Source 173], which remains the most authoritative reconstruction of the career of the notorious Oliver.

The Whig case, however, is a serious over-simplification....There are overwhelming reasons for supposing that some kind of 'physical force' conspiracy was under preparation in 1817, which was inextricably intertwined with the counter-conspiracy of Government *provocateurs*. As early as December 1816 there was loose contact between the 'Jacobin' party in London and extreme reformers in the provinces...[and] plans of national communication and (perhaps) of secret organization were discussed. Thus when Habeas Corpus was suspended in the first week of March some sketchy system of national organization already existed. The authorities claimed that there were four centres of organization controlled by 'secret committees': 1. Nottingham, Derby and Leicester. 2. Birmingham and district. 3. Lancashire. 4. Yorkshire. There was undoubtedly a considerable passage of delegates and also of Radical correspondence....

In April, [Joseph Mitchell, a Lancashire radical] visited in London Charles Pendrill, the Jacobin shoemaker...who had recently helped a friend, known to him as William Oliver, out of debtor's gaol: soon after this Oliver '...expressed uncommon anxiety to know whether there were any political associations into which he might obtain admittance'. Oliver's professions were believed and by March he had been admitted to the inner circle of London reformers. In April he was introduced by Pendrill and other reformers to Mitchell...[who later recorded that] 'he told me that it was the desire of the London friends to form a connection with the country friends. I said...it was also much wished in the country'....Oliver prevailed upon Mitchell to be permitted to accompany him on his next tour in the provinces. The two men set off on 23 April on a tour which was to last (for Oliver) for 23 days and which was to secure for him introductions to leading reformers in the main centres of the Midlands and the north. It was a splendid coup of espionage, and Sidmouth was well served by Oliver's reports. On 5 May he reported attending a central delegate meeting at Wakefield, attended by men from Birmingham, Sheffield, Huddersfield, Barnsley, Leeds, and by Thomas Bacon for the North Midlands district – large promises were made as to the number of men who would rise in each district. The date of the rising was planned for 26 May, and Oliver promised that London 'would be ready'....

But – perhaps by a miscalculation – Mitchell had been arrested on 4 May, and Oliver proceeded, as 'the London delegate', on his own. Thereafter an extraordinary situation existed, in which insurrectionary preparations were going forward in several districts, but in which the only London contact-man who can be identified was a government agent....From this point the sources become heavily partisan. The reformers and Whig critics of government...were at pains to present every piece of evidence to show that Oliver was the main instigator and organizer of the events of 9 June. The authorities, on the other hand, alleged that Oliver's role was solely that of an informer....

The truth is probably more complex than either account. Oliver was not the only spy in the secret organization....But, at the same time, it is not true that the only instigators of revolution were spies. Bamford [see Source 151] was visited at Middleton in May, not by Oliver, but by delegates from Derby – Thomas Bacon and Turner – both of whom were to be involved in the Pentridge Rising....

The story of Pentridge is soon told. Brandreth, the 'Nottingham Captain', performed the part which he had undertaken....On the night of 9 June two or, at the most,

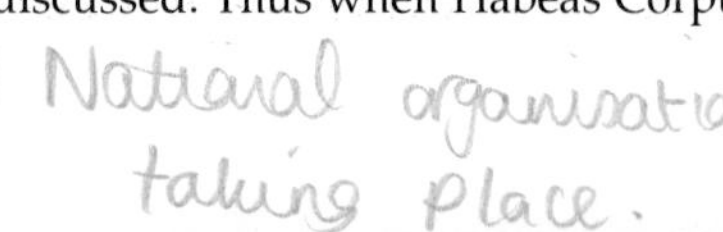

three hundred men were gathered from villages at the foot of the Derby Peak – Pentridge, South Wingfield, Ripley....They set off in the rain to march the fourteen miles to Nottingham, calling at farms and houses and demanding arms and support on the way. At one of these farms the only blood of the rising was shed; Brandreth, demanding imperiously entrance to a house where it was believed there was a gun, fired through the window and killed a farm servant. Brandreth led the increasingly despondent (and dwindling) party with grim determination. He...added more promises...: 'Nottingham would be given up before they got there', 'they should proceed from Nottingham to London and wipe off the National Debt'....To some reluctant recruits there was promised 'roast beef and ale', rum, and even a pleasure trip on the Trent. 'A provisional government' would be formed, and it would send relief into the country to the wives and children of those who had taken up arms....

As the column approached Nottingham the next day and found no support awaiting it, the men became more and more downcast and began to slip away, while Brandreth became more imperious, and threatened to shoot deserters. At length they saw approaching them a small force of Hussars. The insurrection ended in panic, as the men dropped their weapons and ran for cover, while the troops rode after them, or rounded them up in the next few days....

While Brandreth's case was a foregone conclusion (since he had killed a man), his followers might well have been accused only of riot. But the administration was determined to exact its full measure of blood. Thirty-five men were arraigned for high treason. Extraordinary care was taken in hand-picking the most compliant jury....[Following the revelations in the *Leeds Mercury*] the whole country was talking of Oliver, and it was confidently expected that the Defence would attempt to prove his instigation. But the spy's name was never mentioned....With Brandreth convicted, the Defence... pleaded that his associates had been under the spell of their charismatic leader....

We cannot accept the explanation that the Defence did not cite Oliver because Oliver in fact had no connection with Brandreth. In the first place, we know that he had. In the second place, Denman [one of the Defence counsel] knew this. Before the trial he wrote to a friend that he had reason to believe that Oliver was at the bottom of the 'whole business'. Defending his conduct in 1820 in the House of Commons he said that he had 'not the smallest doubt' that the rising was instigated by Oliver....He thought it unwise, however, to call spies as Defence witnesses because under the rules of legal procedure he could not cross-examine his own witnesses: 'they would, when cross-examination was impracticable, have thrown all the weight of their testimony against the prisoners'....Indeed, we now know that the brief for the prisoners' Defence is endorsed with a note to the effect that proof of instigation by Oliver 'is inadmissible, and if admissible, it does not lessen the Malignity of the Offence'....

But in this speculation it is easy to forget the prisoner. Who *was* Jeremiah Brandreth? The Hammonds, characteristically, describe him as 'a half-starved, illiterate, and unemployed framework-knitter', 'ready to... forward any proposal however wild'. This is pejorative writing. We know that Brandreth was not illiterate. If he was half-starved and unemployed, so were many hundreds of his fellow stockingers, notably in the 'Derbyshire Ribs' trade in which he was employed. We know that he had a house in Nottingham....In fact, these conspirators were not all unlettered yokels which some historians would have them to be. Because one of their followers thought that a 'provisional government' had something to do with 'provisions', we need not suppose that they all had straw in their hair....This suggests another way of viewing the insurgents. Persistent rumour suggested that Brandreth himself had been a Luddite – perhaps even a Luddite 'captain' [as had others]....There is reason, then, to suppose that some of those involved were not dupes but experienced revolutionaries....

We may see the Pentridge rising as one of the first attempts in history to mount a wholly proletarian insurrection, without any middle-class support. The objectives of this revolutionary movement cannot perhaps be better characterised than in the words of the Belper street song – 'The Levelution is begun...'. It is a transitional moment between Luddism and the 'popular' Radicalism of 1818–20 and 1830–32. Even without Oliver's patent provocations, some kind of insurrection would probably have been attempted, and perhaps with a greater measure of success. Indeed, in the Crown's view, not Oliver nor Mitchell, but Thomas Bacon, who himself had travelled between Nottingham, Derby, Yorkshire, Lancashire and Birmingham, was the main instigator of rebellion.

This offers...a shred of justification for the actions of Sidmouth and the Government. Believing that some outbreak was inevitable, they determined to handle it in such a way as to exact an example of terror and punishment which would silence, once for all, the monstrous sedition of the 'lower orders'. But this is not to suggest that in any circumstances in 1817 a working-class insurrection had any hope of success. Every detail of the story illustrates the weakness of the revolutionary organization, and the lack of an experienced leadership.

Source 176

From R.J. White, *Waterloo to Peterloo*, pp.170–6 and 181–5.

The Regency was to have its Revolution. History has forgotten it, partly because it took place in a remote countryside equidistant from the populous haunts of the cotton trade and the central stage of London, and partly because an affair of plots, pikes, night-marching and dragoons was something of an anachronism in a society which was undergoing an altogether more relevant revolution at the hands of manufacturers, journalists and Radical clubs. The revolution which bears the name of

Pentrich...has a singularly old-fashioned air. Its style and manner belong almost, although not quite, exclusively to the old England that was passing away. The Pentrich Revolution is revolution as Lords Liverpool and Sidmouth understood it, indeed, as they had for long anticipated it. It might have been arranged, if not by, at least for, the special benefit of the Home Secretary...an affair of pistols, pikes, bill-hooks and bludgeons, parading and marching with great force and violence in and through divers villages and highways....For its leader, also, possessed an old-fashioned and romantic mind. Jeremiah Brandreth was as little like the true revolutionary of the Regency – the politically-conscious, petition-making parliamentary reformer in fustian [a thick cotton cloth worn by many of the working class] – as John Ball or Jack Cade or Robert Kett. The adventure which he led through the wet summer night from the wet sunken lanes and cornfields of south-east Derbyshire to storm the battlements of Nottingham was about as relevant to the purposes which were served by Samuel Bamford and the working-class politicians of the Hampden Clubs as a blunderbuss is relevant to a ballot-box. Not once, throughout these colourful proceedings, did Jeremiah Brandreth utter the words 'franchise' or 'manhood suffrage' or 'annual parliaments'. His whole talk was of bread, rum, a hundred guineas for every man who reached Nottingham, a 'band of music', even a pleasure-trip up the Trent. When he was asked, by a practically-minded female, what kind of government was to supersede the borough-mongers, he replied 'a provisional government', and it is plain that he and his followers thought that a provisional government had something to do with provisions....

Jeremiah Brandreth was indeed the traditional rebel: the stalwart, desperate fellow who burns with desire to strike a blow for – something, although he may not know precisely what....He was old-fashioned almost to the point of reaction. He possessed one fixed idea: that the government must be overthrown and the poor men of England vindicated in the form of better victuals and brighter living....

The outcome of the Derby trials was a foregone conclusion. The Government took care of that. There was to be no risk of an acquittal this time, as after Spa Fields, because of public revelation of the activities of a spy. The case of Mr. Oliver had been a *cause célèbre*, both in the press and parliament, for many weeks after the exposure of his activities at Thornhill Lees by the *Leeds Mercury*: the exposure which had endangered his life and limbs on his southward retreat through Nottingham on the eve of the Pentrich rising. Every care was taken by the Crown Solicitors to arrange the proceedings at Derby in such a way that the Defence should have no chance to plead provocation. Those historians, however, who have chosen to see in this a diabolical machination on the part of the Government have neglected to observe one important fact which was perfectly obvious to the lawyers engaged in the case for the defence of the Pentrich men. It is expressed thus, in an endorsement on the reverse of the brief for the prisoners: 'In regard to the Proof that this Crime was committed by the Excitement of Oliver the Spy, it is to be apprehended that *such proof is inadmissible*, and if admissible, it does not lessen the Malignity of the Offence whether committed at the Instigation of a Government Spy, or at the Instance of any other Person'....Quite apart from the admissibility or otherwise of such proof, the Defence was well enough aware that it was also impossible. The Defence was unable to produce a single witness who could swear that he had heard Oliver inciting people to insurrection, or that any of the Pentrich prisoners had been present on any of the occasions when he had done this....Oliver was never mentioned by name....

A new kind of society was coming painfully to birth within the old, and both the minds of men and their political institutions were undergoing a difficult process of adaptation. In the unfolding of this larger story, the Pentrich rising was all but irrelevant. It contributed nothing to the growth of political self-consciousness on the part of the people.

Source 177

From M.I. Thomis and P. Holt, *Threats of Revolution in Britain 1799–1848* (Shoe String, 1977) pp.59–60.

Certain tentative conclusions might be offered about Oliver and his role. That groups of militants existed before Oliver appeared on the scene is quite clear; he did not create revolutionaries out of nothing, though he probably encouraged them both by what he said and what he did not say. Nor was he responsible for the notion of an armed insurrection, for that too had preceded Oliver, though he probably contributed more to the shaping and formulation of the insurrection that finally took place in June than he was ever prepared to admit. His connections with Brandreth are very tenuous and difficult to establish. A meeting between the two men has never been proved....Whatever Oliver's actual words to the companies among whom he moved, he conveyed an impression, whether by his speeches or his silences, that revolution was going ahead throughout the country and was himself understood to be the sign that there was a national leadership in London which expected revolution and was prepared to give it direction. Exactly how Oliver managed to convey this impression is more academic than important, but his villainous reputation within traditional Whig historiography remains largely undamaged.

The extent to which the Pentrich Rising *was* intended to be part of a national insurrection remains contentious, as does the role of Oliver in fomenting it (Source 177). However, the fact that historians differ about these issues does not negate the value of their interpretations. Each historian, by adopting a different perspective from others, will shed a different kind of light on the evidence and introduce a new dimension to our understanding of what happened at Pentrich in June 1817. Neither do the differences of interpretation mean that we must accept one viewpoint unequivocally, with all it entails, and reject others out of hand. If we are to retain our historical objectivity, we must follow in the footsteps of these historians and examine the contemporary evidence, extracts from which are provided below. Of course, much of the evidence is unreliable because it was gleaned from informers, from men implicated in the rising who had an interest in exculpating themselves or at least minimising their involvement, and from apologists for the government or for the radicals who had their own political axes to grind. Consequently, some sources of evidence will be of little value when judged on their own, but reflecting on the circumstances in which they were written (where they are known), cross-referencing between them and considering the weight of the evidence will enable conclusions to be drawn. Of course, these conclusions will be tentative and, in all probability, they will accept the validity of some aspects of each historian's interpretation, while rejecting others. If possible, they should attempt to reconcile the differences between competing viewpoints by offering a new synthesis that can be shown to be consistent with a reasoned interpretation of the available evidence.

Questions

6. How consistent are the accounts of the Pentrich Rising offered in Sources 173–7 with the evidence contained in Sources 178–82?
7. How would you explain the Pentrich Rising?

Source 178

From a report of the Select Committee of the House of Commons on the disturbed state of the country, 19 February, 1817.

It appears...that attempts have been made, in various parts of the country, as well as in the metropolis, to take advantage of the distress in which the labouring and manufacturing classes of the community are at present involved, to induce them to look for immediate relief, not only in a reform of Parliament on the plan of universal suffrage and annual election, but in a total overthrow of all existing establishments, and in a division of the landed, and extinction of the funded property of the country....

Your Committee cannot contemplate the activity and arts of the leaders in this conspiracy, and the numbers whom they have already seduced and may seduce; the oaths by which many of them are bound together; the means suggested and prepared for the forcible attainment of their objectives; the nature of the objects themselves, which are not only the overthrow of all the political institutions of the Kingdom, but also such a subversion of the rights and principles of property, as must necessarily lead to general confusion, plunder and bloodshed, without submitting to the most serious attention of the House the dangers which exist, and which the utmost vigilance of Government, under the existing laws, has been found inadequate to prevent.

Source 179

From a letter to the Home Secretary, Viscount Sidmouth, by Earl Fitzwilliam, Lord Lieutenant of the West Riding, 17 June 1817, in which Fitzwilliam reports on recent unrest in Yorkshire.

There certainly prevails very generally in the country a strong and decided opinion that most of the events that have recently occurred in the country are to be attributed to the presence and active agitation of Mr. Oliver. He is considered as the main spring from which every movement has taken its rise. All the mischievous in the country have considered themselves as subordinate members of a great leading body of revolutionists in London, as co-operating with that body for one general purpose, and in this view to be under its instructions and directions, communicated by some delegate appointed for the purpose. Had not then a person pretending to come from that body and for that purpose, made his appearance in the country, it is not assuming too much to say that probably no movement whatever would have occurred....

I consider that the spirit of resistance to legitimate government is not spread wide even in these districts, considered as the most disaffected of the Riding: on the contrary, that the number of revolutionists is very limited and confined, and that the mass of the people is still sound and well affected to the present [state] of things.

Source 180

From a deposition by William Stevens, a Nottingham needlemaker and Radical, reported in Cobbett's *Political Register*, 16 May 1818.

[After the suspension of the Habeas Corpus Act in January 1817] many hundreds...and, as he believes, many thousands, said that...it was time to resist....This was the way of thinking of a great part of the people in his town in the months of March, April and May 1817....Though the means of resistance were anxiously wished for..., no plan of resistance was formed until some time in the month of May....[When Thomas Bacon reported back to the North Midlands committee from the meeting he had attended at Wakefield on 5 May] Brandreth, Turner and Ludlam were present, as well as a great many more persons....About five or six days before the 26th of May, a letter from our friends at Sheffield came to Nottingham, informing us that the rising had been put off to the 9th of June in consequence of the advice of Oliver...because the nights would then be dark, and because the whole country would by that time be in a more perfect state for rising....In consequence of this, preparations continued to be made in Nottingham and the neighbourhood until the day of the rising....

On the 1st or 2nd day of June, Oliver came to Nottingham...to the house of this deponent. He said that all would be ready in London for the 9th of June....Oliver had a meeting with us now, at which meeting Brandreth and Turner and many others were present. At this meeting he laid before us a paper which he called a Plan of Campaign....

When Oliver had thus settled every thing with us, he prepared to set off to organize things in Yorkshire, that all might be ready to move in the Country at the moment that the rising took place in London, where he told us there were Fifty Thousand Men with arms prepared, and that they would take the Tower....

[After attending a meeting of northern delegates at Sheffield on 7 June, Stevens returned to his home in Nottingham.] At his own house he found Oliver, who now said that some treachery had taken place in Yorkshire; but that, as all was ready in London, all would go on well, if they did but remain firm to their promises at Nottingham and Derby. A meeting now took place at which Oliver was present...[after which he departed to] give the risers in London an assurance of the hearty cooperation of the Country.

Source 181

From evidence provided to the government by a local informer, probably H. Sampson of Bulwell.

I...went to Jerry Brandreth's between 6 and 7 this evening....We left his House...and met [Stevens] against the gaol....Stevens said I should have been here on Monday night....He stated that there was a London delegate, who reported that there were about 70,000 in London ready to act with us; and that they were very ripe in Birmingham....He was to be here again on Wednesday or Thursday, and to bring the determination of the time to be fixed upon for the Insurrection.

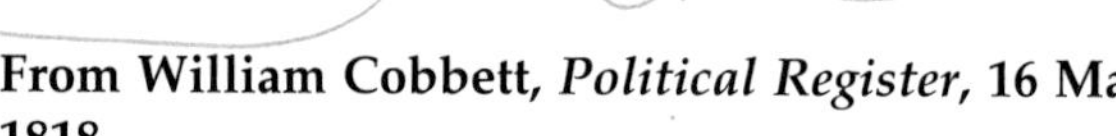

Source 182

From William Cobbett, *Political Register*, 16 May 1818.

Oliver drew towards London, leaving his victims successively in the traps that he had prepared for them....The employers of Oliver [the government] might, in an hour, have put a total stop to those preparations, and have blown them to air....[They] wished, not to prevent, but to produce those acts.

Cross-currents in historians' accounts and explanations

In this unit we have focused on the differences and conflicts between accounts of the making of the working class and explanations of the occurrence and significance of the Pentrich Rising produced by historians who had different purposes in writing and who made different assumptions about their subject matter. Although it is the contradictions and conflicts that we have stressed, there is a great deal of common ground between all the historians' accounts and explanations. This is hardly surprising since they are using the same sources of evidence and broadly the same techniques to interrogate those sources.

At the end of the previous unit, the complexity of historical development was stressed; it was likened to a river flowing in a general direction, but containing eddies, cross-currents and meanders. In terms of the present unit, this means that not all the elements that contribute to the making of the working class in the nineteenth century actually aided that process: some impeded progress, such as the attempts of employers to stamp out trade unionism; some both aided and hindered progress simultaneously, like the French Revolution which provided an impetus to working class radicalism but also led a fearful government to stamp on that radicalism more firmly than it might otherwise have done.

The same is true with explanations of why the Pentrich Rising occurred and its significance for the developing political consciousness of the working class. At one and the same time, Brandreth's pathetic little rising can be seen as showing the political weakness and gullibility of ordinary people in the early nineteenth century and perhaps their growing belief that they had a part to play in the political affairs of the nation. It illustrates both a continuation of the blind protest of the depressed and desperate that had been heard from time to time ever since the Peasants' Revolt, and most recently in the Luddite Riots, and, if E.P. Thompson is to be believed, the first faltering steps towards a more positive and coherent set of demands for reform and towards a national organization bent on achieving those demands.

When offering accounts and explanations of these things, we must be careful not to over-simplify and not to let our own assumptions and purposes, or those of the historians we read, lead us into over-tidy answers where everything points in the same direction. Our function as historians is to attempt to analyse the complex relationships between and significances of past events, not to sidestep the complexities by only using that evidence or accepting those interpretations that fit our assumptions. Our accounts and explanations must be clear, and preferably convincing, but they must also recognize that change takes place as a result of a complex interaction between different but related strands of development.

Question

8. How might aspects of the arguments put forward by E.P. Thompson and his opponents be interwoven to produce a complex account of the significance of the Pentrich Rising for the politicization of the working class during the eighteenth and nineteenth centuries?

Module 4: Reconciling competing lines of development

UNIT 4.1

TWO VIEWS OF RUSSIAN HISTORY

The first three modules of the Development Study traced and analysed developments in the exercise of power and in the reactions to the exercise of power in Britain. This module transfers the focus from British to Russian history so that you can apply in a totally different context the skills you have acquired in evaluating hypotheses, constructing alternative lines of development and assessing the significance of particular events within those lines of development. Unit 4.1 asks you to consider the relative merits of two different traditions regarding the development of Russian history, one of which ascribes the development of Russian political ideas and practices to western European influence while the other claims that Russian politics has developed in a uniquely Russian way that grew out of the experience of the Mongol conquest and rule from the thirteenth to the fifteenth century. Unit 4.2 requires you to reflect on the conflict between these two traditions in Russian history and to consider the ways in which and the extent to which the conflict between these traditions might be resolved. Finally, Unit 4.3 explores the relationship between the past and the present, arguing that, in both Russian and British history, the way we interpret the past is dependent on our experiences in the present and our aspirations for the future. In particular, you will be asked to consider the effect of the collapse of communism and the disintegration of the Soviet Union on our interpretation of Russian history. Does it, as Francis Fukayama has argued, signal the ultimate triumph of liberal democracy throughout the world and 'the end of history'?

Introduction

The history of Russia can be divided into seven periods of varying length.

1. The **tribal period** lasted until approximately the ninth century.
2. The **Varangian period** was ushered in by the arrival of Norse (or Varangian) traders and settlers who were led, according to legend, by Rurik. The Varangians established themselves first as rulers of Novgorod and then of Kiev. The principality of Kiev-Rus which they founded was the first recognizable Russian state and lasted from the tenth to the early thirteenth century. At its greatest extent during the eleventh century, it stretched from the Gulf of Finland in the north as far south as the Black Sea and from the Polish and Lithuanian borders in the west to those with the Volga Bulgars in the east.
3. A **Mongol period** of subjection to the rule of the warlike and autocratic Mongols (or Tatars, as they were known in Russia) began with the conquest of Russia by Batu Khan, grandson of Genghis Khan, in 1237. This period lasted until the late fifteenth century, when Ivan III, Grand Prince of Muscovy, threw off the Mongol yoke.
4. The principality of Muscovy, with its capital at Moscow, had been expanding at the expense of its neighbours since 1300, but between 1462 and 1580, under Ivan III, Vasili III and Ivan IV, it brought almost all of European Russia under its control and expanded its territory beyond the Ural mountains into Asiatic Russia. This **Muscovite period** was characterized by the growth of the Muscovite state, its transformation into a Russian Empire and the acquisition by its princes of the title 'Tsar of all the Russias'.
5. The **period of the Russian Empire**, from the end of the seventeenth century to 1917, saw increasing western European influence in Russian government. Peter the Great visited western Europe in 1697–8 to see for himself how government, the economy and society were organized and, on his return to Russia, built a new capital at St Petersburg. In the second half of the eighteenth century, Catherine the Great introduced the European principles of 'Enlightened Despotism' into the government of Russia.
6. The **communist period** began with two revolutions in 1917. The first deposed Tsar Nicholas II and established a provisional 'democratic' government under Alexander

Kerensky. The second ushered in a Bolshevik or communist regime, which changed the name of the state from Russia to the Soviet Union, restored Moscow as the capital and introduced fundamental changes into almost every aspect of government, economics and society.

7. The **post-communist** period has begun only recently with the dismantling of communism in 1990–91, the disintegration of the Soviet Union into a collection of smaller independent states and the first tentative, and often painful, steps towards the establishment of representative democracy and a market economy.

Key events within these seven periods are summarized in the table below.

Russian History from 800 AD to the Present Day

Date	
	Tribal period
6th–8th C.	Slav tribes migrated from the Danube into the Dnieper and Lovat valleys of Russia.
8th–9th C.	The Dnieper Slavs paid tribute to Khazars.
862	Rurik founded the Varangian dynasty in Novgorod.
	Varangian period
c.882	Novgorod and Kiev were united by the Varangian prince Oleg, who established the latter as the capital of Kiev-Rus.
911	Oleg secured a trade treaty with Byzantium following a successful military campaign.
966–71	Sviatoslav of Kiev defeated and destroyed the Khazar state and conquered Bulgaria.
988	Vladimir of Kiev made Eastern Orthodox Christianity the state religion.
1036	*Ruskaia Pravda* – first Russian law code issued by Iaroslav.
1051	First native Metropolitan of Kiev elected.
1126	First elected governor in Novgorod.
1147	First mention of Moscow in the chronicles.
1156	First elected bishop in Novgorod.
1223	First Mongol assault on Russia. A combined Russian-Polovtsian army was defeated at Kalka.
1237	Batu Khan began Mongol conquest of Russia.
	Mongol period
1240	Mongol-Tatar rule established in Kiev-Rus.
1243	Formation of the khanate of the Golden Horde with its capital at Sarai.
1257	Mongols conducted the first census of Russia.
1299	Metropolitan see transferred from Kiev to Vladimir.
1328	Metropolitan see transferred from Vladimir to Moscow. Rise of Muscovy began.
1380	Dmitri Donskoi defeated the Mongol army of Mamai Khan at Kulikovo.
1382	Moscow plundered and burnt by the Mongols.
1392	Muscovy annexed Nizhniy Novgorod and Suzdal.
c.1450	Mongol Empire (khanate of the Golden Horde) fragmented into lesser khanates.
1453	End of Byzantine Empire. Constantinople captured by Turks.
1477	Ivan III (the Great) conquered Novgorod.
	Muscovite period
1480	Ivan III ceased paying tribute to Mongols.
1480s	Massacres and deportations of leading citizens of Novgorod. Conditional land tenure (*pomeste* system) first introduced in Novgorod; later extended to other parts of Muscovy.
1514	Vasili III annexed Smolensk.
1547	Ivan IV (the Terrible) assumed title of 'Tsar of all the Russias'.
1549	First *Zemskii Sobor* (national assembly) met.
1552	Ivan IV conquered Kazan.
1555	Muscovy Company founded in London to trade with Russia.
1556	Astrakhan annexed.
1560	Moscow declared to be the 'Third Rome'.
1564–72	*Oprichnina*. Reign of terror.
1570	Novogorod destroyed and inhabitants massacred by *oprichniki*.
1577	Commercial links established with the Netherlands.
1582	Ivan IV conquered western Siberia.
1589	Patriarch of Moscow established as head of the Russian Orthodox Church.
1598–1613	The Time of Troubles.
1613	Mikhail I became the first Romanov tsar.
1649	The *Ulozhenie*, a new legal code was issued. Serfdom was legalized.
1670	Great peasant revolt led by Stenka Razin.
1697–8	Peter the Great conducted his 'Grand Embassy' to Europe.
	The Russian Empire
1711	Boyar council replaced by the senate.
1712	St Petersburg became the new seat of government.
1714	Salaries introduced for civil servants.
1718	Colleges (departments of state) introduced.
1722	Table of Ranks issued; henceforth nobility followed from rank in state service.

Date	
1762	Accession of Catherine the Great, who applied the principles of 'enlightened despotism' to the government of Russia. The gentry were freed from obligatory service.
1860	Vladivostok founded.
1861	Emancipation of the serfs.
1881	Assassination of Alexander II.
1891	Building of Trans-Siberian Railway began.
1905	New constitution permitted an elected Duma.
1917	February Revolution: Tsar Nicholas II overthrown.
	Communist period
1917	October Revolution brought Lenin's Bolsheviks to power.
1923	Formation of the Union of Soviet Socialist Republics.
1928	'Collectivization' of farms began.
1936–8	'The Great Terror': Stalin purged Bolshevik ranks.
1945–8	Imposition of communist rule in Eastern Europe.
1986	Mikhail Gorbachev elected leader of Communist Party.
1989	Collapse of communism in Eastern Europe.
	Post-communist period
1990	Communist Party renounced its monopoly of political power. Private ownership of businesses permitted. Restrictions on religious worship lifted. Lithuania declared independence.
1991	Communist Party banned. Soviet Union disintegrated, to be replaced by the Russian Federation, Belarus, Ukraine and 12 other newly independent states.

The geography of Russia

An understanding of Russian history is almost impossible without a basic knowledge of the geography and climatology of the region. Russia's most important physical characteristics are its size and its lack of a convenient coastline. Throughout history, the borders of Russia have expanded and contracted with the rise and fall of its political fortunes, but from ninth century Kiev-Rus to the twentieth century Soviet Union and its successor, the Russian Federation, the Russian state has always been large in comparison with western European countries. From Archangel on the White Sea to Sevastapol on the Black Sea is a distance north to south of over 1,400 miles; from the Polish border to the Ural Mountains is a similar distance east to west. Until the sixteenth century, Kiev-Rus and then Muscovy competed with rival principalities and with non-Russian peoples to establish dominance over the lands of this vast rolling plain. In the 1580s, the Russian empire expanded eastwards across the Urals into Siberia and by 1650 had established settlements at Okhotsk and Anadyr on Siberia's eastern coast. The distance from Anadyr to the Polish border is more than 5,000 miles.

Although modern Russia has an extensive coastline, it is inconvenient for the purposes of trade and seaborne contact with Europe and other parts of the world. Most of that coastline is north of the arctic circle and icebound for much of the year. There are three relatively small ice-free coastal areas, but all three are problematic from trading and strategic points of view. Russia's oldest ice-free coast lies at the eastern end of the Gulf of Finland, an arm of the Baltic Sea into which the River Neva empties. It was down this river that the Varangian traders and settlers entered the country from Scandinavia, and near its mouth that Peter the Great founded St Petersburg in 1712. While the Gulf of Finland gave access to the Baltic Sea and enabled trade to take place with states along its shoreline, contact with the rest of Europe has always been dependent on the good will of Denmark and Sweden, which between them control the narrow straits through which ships from the Baltic must pass before entering the North Sea. Russia's second ice-free coast lies on the Black Sea and was only acquired during the eighteenth century. The Black Sea flows into the Mediterranean through the narrow Bosporus channel controlled by Turkey. The Turks have often denied the Russians naval access to the Mediterranean and in times of warfare or diplomatic tension between the two states have also closed the Bosporus to Russian trading vessels as well. Since the disintegration of the Soviet Union in 1991, the Black Sea coastline is now divided between the Ukraine and the Russian Federation. The third warm water coast lies on the Sea of Japan around the port of Vladivostok, but is too far away from the main centres of population to the west of the Urals to provide a significant channel through which trade or cultural influences might enter European Russia.

Another major influence on the development of Russia has been its inhospitable climate. Average January temperatures in some areas reach −40 °C, and throughout most of northern Russia snow lies for more than 200 days a year and rivers freeze. In contrast, the average July temperatures in some southern areas exceed 30 °C. Rainfall tends to be heavy in the north west and sparse in the south and east. These climatic variations are reflected in the natural vegetation, which is characterized by endless coniferous forests in the north, giving way to deciduous forests and then the open plains of the steppes as one travels further south. The soils of the forest region are generally poor with the exception of the area around Moscow, but the black soils of the steppes are very fertile when irrigated to compensate for the shortage of rainfall.

Source 1

Russia

Some of the effects of these geographical and climatic features on the development of the Russian state and its inhabitants are summarized by Robin Milner-Gulland and Nikolai Dejevsky in Source 2.

Source 2

Robin Milner-Gulland and Nikolai Dejevsky, *Cultural Atlas of Russia and the Soviet Union* (Time-Life, 1989) p.16.

For the past thousand and more years several constraints can be seen in the relationship of the people and the land of Russia....

1 Russia is, and throughout history has been, large – very large on a European or even world scale....This huge extent has generally entailed poor communications and the threat of ungovernability.

2 Russia is thinly populated, and this was true even before it added the vast emptiness of Siberia to its territory.

3 Russia is agricultural. The often precarious harvests of field and forest have been the prime source of its wealth (and cause of its difficulties). Even in the industrialized twentieth century the rural population has been larger than the urban until the present generation.

4 Russia has lacked fixed frontiers. The unequivocal natural demarcations of seacoasts or high mountain ranges have been attained by Russians only very gradually, and through infiltration or conquest that has taken them far beyond their historic lands. Nor do the boundaries of the twentieth century Soviet Union or the Russian empire before it follow ethnic/linguistic demarcations at all closely.

5 Russia is astonishingly far north....Leningrad [which has now reverted to its pre-Revolution name of St Petersburg] is on the latitude of the Shetland Islands; nearly half the Soviet Union's territory is north of 60°, that is, on a level with Alaska, Baffin Island or Greenland.

6 Finally the Russian climate seems expressly designed to foil human habitation and activity. Winter lasts half the year or more, but the summer is actually often very arid, with rainfall slight and ill-distributed; vast tracts of desert are matched by even vaster tracts of waterlogged swamp.

Historians' views

Historians have been struck by Russia's geographical position on the edge of Europe – part of Europe and yet apart from it. All have been aware that there is a unique flavour to Russian history which stems from the geography and economy of the country and the culture, outlook and historical experiences of the Russian people. Nevertheless, Russia has not developed in a vacuum. It has been influenced by the states around it, and historians have argued whether the most important influences were European ones from the west or Asiatic ones from the east. Those arguing the greater importance of western influences can point to the Varangian settlers who helped to shape the early political development of the Russian state, the Orthodox Church centred on Byzantium (Constantinople) which became the state religion of Russia in the tenth century, traces of democratic traditions and institutions that may have originated in the west, the eighteenth century westernization by Peter the Great and Catherine the Great, and the influence of communism, which originated with the German socialist, Karl Marx. Those claiming that eastern influences were more significant tend to argue that Russian government and society derive mainly from the systems operated by the Mongol Empire that was at its height during the thirteenth and fourteenth centuries. The elements of Russian government most often claimed to have developed from Mongol origins are the autocratic government, the secret police and the use of terror as a political weapon.

Denis Shemilt summarized these two views as follows:

Hypothesis A
The development of Russian political ideas and institutions has been characterized by regular borrowing from the West. Each major turning point in Russian political life has been marked by the adoption of European ideas and institutions.

Hypothesis B
The development of Russian political ideas and institutions has been characterized by the continuity of autocratic traditions established during Mongol rule from the thirteenth to the fifteenth centuries. The ways in which this autocracy is maintained have changed, but the ways in which it works have not.

These two views of Russian history do not disagree about the facts, but they do conflict about which of those facts are more important in the development of Russian political history. Furthermore, the patterns and connections established between the facts will be somewhat different in a line of development constructed to support and illustrate Hypothesis A from those in a developmental account favouring Hypothesis B. Some of the conflicts between such accounts will be evident from the brief summaries below.

According to Hypothesis A, aristocratic and autocratic forms of government were brought to Russia by the Varangians, alongside which democratic traditions native to the Slav tribes persisted. Political theory was imported together with Orthodox Christianity from the Byzantine Empire based on Constantinople (also known as Byzantium) in the south-west. There was a strong Byzantine influence on law and administration. It was unclear which of three models of government would eventually triumph: democracy (strongest in Novgorod), aristocracy (associated with Kiev), or autocracy (associated with Muscovy).

The period of Mongol rule was an interlude that put Russian political ideas and practices into cold storage for 250 years or more. Native Russian political traditions persisted, but their further development was halted. When the Mongol yoke was cast off, the development of Russian political institutions resumed more or less from the point at which it had reached before the Mongol invasion. The main effect of the Mongol interlude was to aid the emergence of Muscovy as the strongest principality. Autocratic traditions of government were already well established in Muscovy before the Mongol conquest and were not altered significantly as a result of Mongol influence. However, Mongol patronage of the grand princes of Muscovy helped to ensure that it was Muscovite autocracy, rather than Kievan aristocracy or Novgorodian democracy, that came to dominate the future political development of Russia.

Source 3

The state seal of Ivan IV, showing the double-headed eagle inherited from Byzantium which was to remain the royal emblem until the monarchy fell in 1917

For the next 400 years, Russia lagged behind western and northern Europe, borrowing and copying from its more advanced neighbours in an attempt to catch up. Peter the Great, the first of the modernizing tsars, turned to western and northern Europe for models of political practice. The process of westernization continued through the 'enlightened despotism' of Catherine the Great, the emancipation of the serfs (1861–66) and the concessions made towards representative democracy in 1906. This phase ended in 1917 when the Bolshevik Revolution enabled Russia to leap-frog the whole of Russia and become, at least in theory, the most politically advanced country in the world. The Bolshevik Revolution created a political system inspired by the socialism of Karl Marx. In theory, all political power would devolve to the people, that is, to the workers, peasants and soldiers. The people would express their will through the organ of the Communist Party, a concept known as 'the dictatorship of the proletariat'. In practice, however, Marx's ideas proved difficult to put into practice, especially in a country with a long autocratic tradition. It is hardly surprising, therefore, that the ideals of the dictatorship of the proletariat were supported in theory, but that, in practice, what emerged was the dictatorship of the Communist Party leaders. The autocratic power of Josef Stalin, for instance, was every bit as strong as that of the tsars who had preceded him. It was not until the collapse of Russian communism in 1990 that Russian autocracy began to be seriously undermined by the importation of western democracy. However, at the time of writing, it is too soon to say whether this has finally brought to an end over a thousand years of Russian autocratic government.

Source 4

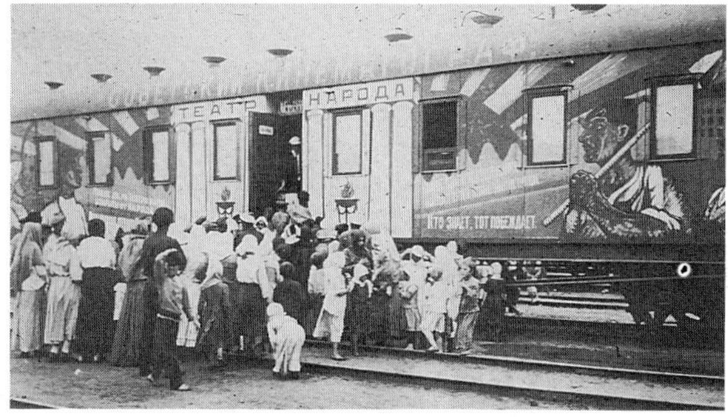

The agit train which travelled around Russia in the wake of the 1917 Bolshevik Revolution 'educating' the people about Marxism and the Revolution

Whereas in Hypothesis A, the period of Mongol rule was a discontinuity or interruption in the developmental flow of Russian political history, in Hypothesis B, it was a crucial turning point. It imposed upon the country traditions of autocracy, state service and political oppression that have lasted at least until the end of the communist period, and, some would argue, are still present in a modified form today. This view recognizes that aristocratic and autocratic forms of government were brought to Russia by the Varangians and that Byzantine culture and religion influenced the country's political development. It is argued that Russia retained an essentially Slavic political culture with a strong democratic element and that this Slavic culture was modified by contact with the Varangians and the Byzantine Empire. However, the crucial discontinuity in Russian history was the Mongol conquest which divided Russians into two categories: those who were agents and servants of the Mongol khan and those who paid taxes to him and were liable to conscription into his armed forces.

Source 5

Fourteenth-century Mongol warriors in cavalry pursuit

Source 6

Sixteenth century Russian cavalry used weapons and tactics that had been acquired from the Mongols

Once they had broken free of the Mongol yoke, the grand princes of Muscovy and their successors, the tsars of Russia continued the autocratic political traditions established under the Mongol khans, abandoning and crushing the native political traditions associated with pre-Mongol Novgorod and Kiev. The tsars regarded the Russian state as their personal property and claimed the disposal of all land, as the Mongol khans had; they strengthened the class of state servants (*pomeshchicki*) at the expense of the hereditary nobility (*boyars*); and terror was used as an instrument of state policy, most notably by Ivan III and Ivan IV. Meanwhile the Mongol conquest was reversed during the seventeenth and eighteenth centuries as European Russia carved out a huge empire in Asia, including much of the heartland of the former Mongol Empire.

The reforming tsars of the eighteenth and nineteenth centuries sought to modernize the administration of the Mongol-Muscovite state, while maintaining existing hierarchical power structures. Government remained essentially autocratic and state terror continued to be used as a means of quelling opposition. Russia built up the largest secret police force in Europe and was arguably the first 'police state'. Even the Bolshevik Revolution of 1917, which promised fundamental reform, ended with the exchange of one set of Russian autocrats for another. Communist Party officials replaced the royal family and developed further many of the powers and methods of government which the tsars had inherited from their Mongol predecessors. The people at the top changed; the ideology was new; the institutions were different; but the way the system worked remained essentially the same. The state still owned the land; the people still owed service to the state; a class of service nobility remained (the party officials); the police and labour camps were still there, and terror remained the ultimate political weapon – Stalin proving a worthy successor to Ivan the Terrible and Batu Khan.

Source 7

A German cartoon showing Stalin relaxing by a fire of human bones with the heads of communist officials executed in his purges hanging as trophies on his wall

Naturally historians do not always fit neatly into supporters of one view or the other. Nevertheless, a reading of the following extracts from the arguments put forward by various writers on Russian history should enable you to develop a clearer understanding of the nature of these hypotheses and of the arguments put forward in their defence.

Questions

Read Sources 8–17.

1. Which historians support Hypothesis A and what arguments do they put forward to justify their views?

2. Which historians support Hypothesis B and what arguments do they use to support their opinions?
3. What other interpretations of Russian history do Sources 8–17 suggest?

Source 8

From Daniel Kaiser and Gary Marker, *Reinterpreting Russian History* (Oxford, 1994) pp.4–5.

For a long time, the dominant view asserted that the first state to arise on this territory was indisputably Slavic, borrowing little from the other peoples known to have been resident across Eastern Europe. In its extreme form, this argument alleged that Kievan Rus was distinctly Russian, the historical predecessor to Muscovite Russia....

Historians impartially investigating the sources cannot, however, accept these generalizations. The available evidence...demonstrates unequivocally that the society which came together in the Middle Ages on the territory stretching from the Black Sea to the Baltic was distinctly multi-ethnic. Together with several Slavic tribes...Finnic and Baltic peoples also played important parts in taming the land....Furthermore, outsiders also had an impact on state and society. Particularly influential were the Vikings (normally called Varangians in Rus sources) who took their trading and plundering down the rivers of Eastern Europe just as they had done further west. That these Germanic peoples should have contributed anything positive to early Slavic civilization was an idea especially repugnant to Russian historians who had lived to see German armies cross Russian frontiers more than once and who...had heard Germans allege their native superiority to the less able Slavs.

So it was that many Russian historians blanched when they read in the *Primary Chronicle* a narrative which seemed to indicate that the medieval Slavs had invited the Vikings to establish a state in Rus so as to end the disorder over which they themselves were powerless. Long were the debates about the reliability of this evidence....[However,] the evidence demonstrates persuasively that the Vikings played an important part in the economy and society of Rus. What remains unclear is how far into the political life of Rus Viking influence extended.

Equally contentious has been the discussion about what kind of state it was that first arose in Rus. Historians have divided over this matter too, some discerning in Kievan Rus an ancient monarchic tradition, others alleging that only more recently did monarchs and autocrats abuse the more authentic, more antique democratic traditions of Rus. As might be expected, the evidence is open to more than one interpretation. Kievan Rus certainly had princes, and it is they who dominate the extant sources. We read in the chronicles about their making war and peace, about their decisions on war and religion, and much else....

There is, however, additional evidence which seems to point to another kind of political institution. In Kievan Rus, and later even more forcefully in Novgorod in the north, the city assembly (*veche*) seems to have taken a very active part in politics, sometimes even removing princes from their thrones. In Novgorod, the assembly left many traces of its authority, not least in the limitations which it came to impose upon its princes. Other evidence, too, seems to indicate that the princes of Rus played a small part in the lives of most people at that time. The oldest legal code, the *Pravda Ruskaia*, thought to have been compiled sometime in the eleventh century, makes no provision for the prince's court or any form of judiciary. Instead, the code recognizes blood revenge and a system of self-help which required little aid from the prince's state....From this perspective, then, the earliest state structures in Rus, if monarchic at all, gave plenty of expression to popular participation.

Source 9

From Tibor Szamuely, *The Russian Tradition* (Fontana, 1988) pp.16–19.

The first Russian state, established with its capital in Kiev towards the end of the ninth century, bore a close resemblance to the state formations then being set up in Western Europe. It ruled over a considerable territory, and possessed large and wealthy cities, important waterways, a flourishing foreign trade – and a culture derived not from Rome, but from Byzantium. By present day standards it seems to have been in certain respects a more civilized society than some that existed further to the west: for instance, it had neither capital nor corporal punishment (for freemen), nor the institution of judicial torture. Though its life-span coincided with the heyday of Western feudalism, Kiev Russia was not a feudal society;....fighting-men were free to enter and leave the prince's service at will; the bulk of the peasants were also free. Among the features that set Kiev apart from most contemporary European states, mention should be made of the fact that Kiev was a slave-holding society....

[As Kiev declined in the late twelfth and early thirteenth centuries], Rus disintegrated into a dozen or so separate territorial entities....There can be little doubt that, had this evolution continued unchecked, Russia would have irrevocably split up into several fully sovereign national states having little in common. In 1237, however, this process was brought to a sudden halt. In that fateful year the Mongol (or Tatar) army...descended upon the disunited, squabbling Russian principalities. The Tatar yoke, that was to press so heavily on the Russian people for the next 250 years and decisively to influence the further course of their history, had been firmly established....

Culturally the effect of the Mongol conquest...was to put Russia back several centuries – during precisely that crucial period when the European New Learning flowered into the Renaissance. But the Mongols, though ignorant of the finer things of life, were able to give Russia something of more lasting importance: a political and administrative system, a concept of society, quite unlike anything that was to be learned in the West....

The Mongol concept of society was based on the unqualified submission of all to the absolute, unlimited power of the Khan. Every member of society was allotted from above his specific position, to which he was bound for life....The Khan was not only vested with unquestioned authority over the lives of his subjects: he was also sole owner of all the land within his domains, and all other persons could hold land only on conditions of temporary tenure. Such then was the social and political system imposed upon a prostrate Russia by the merciless conqueror....

The first and most important effect of Mongol rule was the re-establishment of national unity, the foundation of a unified Russian national state....Ivan I of Muscovy, nicknamed Kalita, or 'Moneybags' (1325–41) founded his fortunes – and those of his successors and of the Russian national state as well – by a policy of total subservience to the Mongol overlords. The rewards were substantial....In return for services rendered, Kalita and his successors persuaded the Tatars to grant then the exclusive right of collecting taxes on the Mongol Horde's behalf, and also supreme judicial authority over all the Russian princes. These prerogatives, added to the prestige of having become the national religious centre following the removal of the Metropolitan (i.e. the leader) of the Russian Orthodox Church to Moscow, became powerful levers in the Moscow Grand Dukes' ceaseless campaign, aimed at unifying the Russian principalities under their rule.

Source 10

From George Vernadsky, *A History of Russia*, 1944, p.56.

The Mongolian state was built upon the principle of unquestioning submission of the individual to the group, first to the clan and through the clan to the whole state. This principle was in the course of time impressed thoroughly upon the Russian people. It led to the system of universal service to the state which all without exception were forced to give. Under the influence of Mongolian ideas, the Russian state developed on the basis of universal service. All classes of society were made a definite part of the state organization. Taken altogether, these ideas amount to a peculiar system of state socialism.

Source 11

From George Vernadsky, *The Mongols and Russia*, 1953.

A convenient method of gauging the extent of Mongol influence on Russia is to compare the Russian state and society of the pre-Mongol period with those of the post-Mongol era, and in particular to contrast the spirit and institutions of Muscovite Russia with those of Russia of the Kievan age....The picture changed completely after the Mongol period.

Source 12

From Sergei Platonov, *A History of Russia*, 1925.

How could the Mongol influence on Russian life be considerable, when the Mongols lived far off, did not mix with the Russians, and came to Russia only to gather tribute or as an army, brought in for the most part by Russian princes for the princes' own purposes?.... Therefore we can proceed to consider the internal life of Russian society in the thirteenth century without paying attention to the fact of the Mongol yoke.

Source 13

From Edward Acton, *Russia* (Longman, 1986) p.8–9.

The so-called 'Eurasian' school of historians, influential in the West since the 1920s, has depicted the Mongol invasion as the decisive event in Russian history. According to this view, the blow to the economy was matched by the Mongols' formative influence on the cultural and political life of the country. Russia was now cut off even from Byzantium and left to stagnate in an isolated backwater. Above all, she derived from the despotism of the Mongol Khan an arbitrary absolutism, extreme centralization, and disregard for individual property and liberty, which marked her off from the rest of Europe. This interpretation, however, has been subjected to effective criticism. The Mongol Empire and the smaller khanates which succeeded it were neither culturally dynamic nor politically stable. They had little in the way of models and ideas to offer the heirs of Kiev. They did not destroy the property rights of the boyars [landowners], and they positively fostered the wealth and influence of the Church, making no attempt to interfere with the faith of the Christian subjects. It was not until a century after the Mongol yoke had been broken that the Russian government began to acquire the kind of powers that were to distinguish it from Western states. The distinctive features of Muscovite and Imperial Russia can be explained with minimal reference to the primitive institutions of the semi-nomadic and heathen Mongol Horde.

Source 14

From Marc Raeff, 'Muscovy Looks West', in *History Today*, August 1986, pp.16–20.

Up to about the middle of the seventeenth century...Muscovy had existed in relative isolation from Central and Western Europe....It seemed to be a giant (the largest compact territorial state in Europe) condemned to passivity and stagnation....However, there was a silent stirring.... Foreshadowed first by Ivan IV (1533–84) and Boris Godunov (1598–1605) and pursued more consistently since the reign of Tsar Alexis (1645–76)...Moscow's policy had been turning away from its traditional fixation on the East (and South East), where it aimed at taking the place of the Mongol 'empire of the steppes'. Muscovy was now definitely seeing its main foreign policy tasks in the West (and South West). This was partly due to the internal weakening of Poland and Moscow's growing involvement in the diplomatic and military affairs of East Central Europe. But in some measure it was also the result of the economic aggressiveness of Dutch and English merchants. Indeed, by way of Archangel, these enterprising traders were bringing Western luxury and technical goods for the Kremlin's élite....

Russia's greater involvement in European wars required borrowing new techniques and tactics. The traditional mounted noble militia that had been the backbone of the Tsar's military establishment had to give way to the so-called 'newly-formed regiments' – units of professional soldiers, officered mainly by foreigners, and equipped with modern weapons. In short, a sizeable group of foreigners, settled for economic and military purposes, had become a fixed and significant element in Muscovy....Increasingly, members of the Tsar's court showed curiosity for things West European....However, they did so cautiously and selectively, without abandoning their traditional and religious outlook and customs....

West European intellectual achievements penetrated into Muscovy in a somewhat unexpected way....The Orthodox Church in the Ukraine [which had been absorbed into Catholic Lithuania during the fifteenth century and by the late sixteenth century was desperate to stem the tide of Catholic missionary work] needed to forge intellectual tools capable of countering Catholic arguments and educational efforts....One of the consequences of this effort was the ritual reforms of Patriarch Nikon and the resulting split with the Old Believers that destroyed the traditional religious-political consensus in the Russian state. [Adopting methods borrowed from their Western Catholic opponents, the Jesuits,] the first East Slavic institution of 'higher ecclesiastic learning' was founded by Peter Mohyla, Metropolitan of Kiev, in 1632. This academy became the centre for the intensive and modern training of the clerical élite and it also stimulated the development of a network of schools....Furthermore, the Academy arranged for more advanced study by its graduates at university centres in Western and Central Europe. In this way, intellectual movements prevailing in Europe were assimilated by the best of the Ukrainian clergy in the course of the seventeenth century....The incorporation of the Ukraine into the Muscovite state in the mid-seventeenth century only intensified these ecclesiastical and intellectual contacts. By the late seventeenth century, Kiev-trained clergy had established the Slavonic-Greek-Latin Academy in Moscow....

It is absolutely clear that Russia was forcibly dragged into Europe by Peter the Great; and it arrived there as an energetic and powerful giant, ready to undertake new tasks and play a big role in the affairs of Europe....The combination of his upbringing, personality and circumstances drove Peter to reorganize brusquely and ruthlessly the political and military machinery of Muscovy along lines suggested by the 'ideal type' of the well ordered police state (specifically borrowing from the practices of Swedish, Prussian, Dutch and other administrations)....It soon became obvious that there was no way back to Muscovy – not only did Peter I move the capital to St Petersburg..., but he had definitely focused the interests and curiosity of the Russian élites onto 'Europe'....

It should be emphasized that the overwhelming majority of the foreigners who contributed to the reorientation came from the northern Protestant parts of Europe....Protestantism's interpretation of Natural Law stressed the duties and responsibilities of the individual rather than his rights, and always viewed him as an inseparable part of a community to which he should owe his primary allegiance.

Source 15

From Fernand Braudel, *A History of Civilizations* (Allen Lane, 1994) p.540–5.

Russia turned more and more towards Europe. That was the crucial fact in its history in modern times, until 1917 and even beyond. By this policy, which it pursued with tenacity, Russia acquired modern technology....The Russian economy was improving too, if only because of contact with more and more active European trade in the Baltic outlets....Closer ties between Russia and the West multiplied and loomed larger with the bold, brutally hasty measures taken by Peter the Great (1689–1725) and the long, outwardly glorious reign of Catherine the Great (1762–96). As a result, the frontiers and external shape of modern Russia *vis-à-vis* Europe was greatly changed. In the eighteenth century, in fact, it continually sought to dominate and extend its own territory, if necessary at others' expense. The main link with the West was organized from St Petersburg, the new capital built from scratch on the Neva, starting in 1703. With more and more British and Dutch ships calling there, its trade continually grew. Russia was becoming more and more European....

Eighteenth century Russia called in countless Westerners to help it, even to build its industry – or what industry there was at the time. Crowds of engineers, architects, painters, artisans, musicians, singing teachers and governesses descended on a country eager to learn and ready to tolerate anything in order to do so....France played a privileged part in this cultural process. The autocratic Catherine was thought liberal in France because she had Mozart's *The Marriage of Figaro* staged in Russia before it was authorized by Louis XVI for performance in France. In reality, Catherine II's government was socially retrograde: it consolidated the power of the nobility and worsened the condition of the serfs.

Only aristocratic culture was readily influenced by Paris....In the background, revolution ran like a thread throughout the history of modern Russia, from the sixteenth century to the explosion of October 1917....In the Middle Ages Russia had remained backward. Feudalism took root in Russia just when it was waning in the West. From the fifteenth century to the twentieth, Russia became more and more European: but only a small part of the population was involved in the process....What was more, the growth of trade with the West, in Russia as in Central Europe, turned the aristocracy into wheat producers and merchants. A 'second wave of serfdom' was the obvious result. Peasants' liberties lost their meaning. Until then, serfs had had the right, unless they were in debt, to change masters every year on St George's Day. Now they lost it. Ivan the Terrible in 1581 forbade any further move. At the same time, rent and forced labour weighed ever more heavily on their shoulders....

The more time passed, the worse the plight of the Russian peasants became. For when the 'second wave of serfdom' began, there was also a 'second wave of aristocracy'. The boyars of the time of Ivan the Terrible were no longer the boyars of the Kiev Principality, similar to lords of the manor in the West, masters of their own land. Ivan had systematically crushed these independent noblemen: he had executed them by the thousand; he had confiscated their estates and given them to his own men, the *oprichniki* (noble officials who held their lands only for their lifetime). This being so, the very retrograde reform carried out by Peter the Great was the Entailment Law of 1714, which gave these officials and their heirs, in perpetuity, full possession of the lands they held. So the 'second aristocracy' was confirmed in its privileges, with its ranks fixed for good by the imperial court....This shows the double face of Russia in all its contradictions: modernity *vis-à-vis* Europe, medieval backwardness at home.

From that time onwards, a kind of pact united Tsarism with the aristocracy that surrounded and served it, always submissive and fearful in the face of the master's caprice. The peasants suffered in consequence: they were trapped in insoluble difficulties. Even mass emancipation, in 1858, 1861 and 1864, did little to help. Half the collective constraints imposed on the village, the *mir*, remained in place. Lands recovered from the lords could be bought back. What was more, the landlords still kept part of their domains. The question was not dealt with until 1917, when there was the greatest agrarian explosion in Russian history, a profound and practical reason for the Revolution. Even then, it found no permanent solution: for no sooner had the peasants thrown off their old fetters than collectivization began. Peasants in Russia had a very brief experience of owning their own land.

Source 16

From A.J. Toynbee, *The Impact of the Russian Revolution, 1917–67* (Oxford, 1967).

In Russian history...there is a governing factor that was operating before, as well as after, 1917. This governing factor is not one that has originated in Russia in the course of Russia's development. It is something that never would have disturbed Russia if it had not had the western world for its next-door neighbour. The constant disturbing factor in Russian history has been the accelerating progress of technology in the western world since the seventeenth century....When we survey Russian history during the ages before Russia's encounters with the West, we find nothing here that suggests that the Russians...would ever have dreamed of communism...if this ideology had not already been manufactured in the West and had not been waiting, ready-made for non-western peoples to import. Communism, like liberal democracy and enlightened autocracy, is a western invention which can be accounted for only in terms of the western civilization's previous history.

Source 17

From Richard Pipes, *Russia under the Old Regime* (Weidenfeld and Nicolson, 1974) pp.xvii–xviii.

One may say that the existence of private property as a realm over which public authority normally exercises no jurisdiction is the thing which distinguishes western political experience from all the rest. Under primitive conditions, authority over people and over objects is combined, and it required a complex evolution of law and institutions which began in ancient Rome for it to be split into authority exercised as sovereignty [over people] and authority exercised as ownership [of land and property]. It is my central thesis that in Russia this separation occurred very late and very imperfectly. Russia belongs to that category of states which...it has become customary to refer to as 'patrimonial'. In such states political authority is conceived and exercised as an extension of the rights of ownership, the ruler (or rulers) being both sovereigns of the realm and its proprietors. The difficulty of maintaining this type of regime in the face of steadily increasing contact and rivalry with a differently governed West has brought about in Russia a condition of permanent internal tension that has not been resolved to this day.

Questions

4. Use the evidence on pp.114–38 to construct an account in support of Hypothesis A (see p.108) that the key developments in Russian political history up to 1914 resulted from the adoption of European ideas and institutions.
5. Use the same evidence to construct an account in support of Hypothesis B that the main influence on the development of Russian political history up to 1914 was the autocratic tradition established during the period of Mongol rule.

The Tribal period to 862 AD

Much of the early history of Russia is complex and uncertain. However, we know that, among many population migrations into eastern Europe, a peaceful farming race, the Slavs, settled in the Danube basin and that from there different tribes of Slavs dispersed into central Europe, into the

Balkans and along the Dnieper River. The *Primary Chronicle* (Source 18) tells us that the eastern Slavs spread into lands to the north, east and west of the Dnieper, becoming separate tribes with a common language and that these tribes were subject to the successive domination of Cimmerian, Scythian, Sarmatian, Goth, Hun, Avar and Khazar conquerors. The *Primary Chronicle* also records that, while subject to Khazar rule, the Slav tribes established 'principalities'. Some historians argue that these were little more than tribal governments in which the tribal leader had assumed the title of 'prince'. Others, such as Edward Acton, claim that 'the relatively stable conditions established by the Khazars in the eighth century fostered the development of viable urban trading centres dominated by a native aristocracy on which a state could be built'. To what extent recognizable Russian principalities had come into existence before the arrival of the Varangians in the ninth century is, however, uncertain.

Source 18

An account of the origins of the various Slavonic tribes from whom the Russians evolved. From the introduction to the *Primary Chronicle*, compiled between 1037 and 1118 by monks of the Kievan Crypt Monastery.

These are the narratives of bygone years regarding the origin of the land of Rus, who first began to rule in Kiev, and from what source the land Rus had its beginning....

For many years the Slavs lived beside the Danube, where the Hungarian and Bulgarian lands now lie. From among these Slavs, parties scattered throughout the country....Certain Slavs settled on the Dnieper River and were called Polyanians. Still others were named Derevlians because they lived in the forests. Some also lived between the Pripet and the Dvina and were known as Dregovichians. Other tribes resided along the Dvina and were called Polotians....The Slavs also dwelt about Lake Ilmen...and they built a city which they called Novgorod. Still others had their homes along the Desna, the Sem and the Sula and were called Severians. Thus the Slavic race was divided and its language was known as Slavic....

The Polyanians...built a town and named it Kiev....The Derevlians possessed a principality of their own, as did also the Dregovichians, while the Slavs had their own authority in Novgorod, and another principality existed on the Polota where the Polotians dwell.

The Varangian period: 862–1240

As Edward Acton argues in Source 19, there is some dispute among historians about whether the early Russian city-states – Novgorod, Kiev, and others – were founded by the Varangian traders and settlers who came from Scandinavia in the ninth century, or whether the Varangians took over, strengthened and expanded small political entities which already existed. The *Primary Chronicle* suggests the latter. *King Harald's Saga* reinforces the view implied by the *Chronicle* that the Varangians supplied the military strength and political organization to enable the warring and disorganized Slavonic tribes to combine into what was to become the powerful and extensive state of Kiev-Rus.

Source 19

From Edward Acton, *Russia*, p.3–4.

It was in the ninth century that an independent Russian state emerged....Resistance to foreign overlordship was stiffened by merchant mercenaries from Scandinavia. Wave upon wave of Viking expeditions made their way down the waterways, attracted by the lucrative trade with Constantinople in the south, and willing to serve native chieftains. The precise relationship between these 'Varangians', as the Russian chronicles call them, and the Slav tribes is unclear. Russian national pride has taken offence at the notion that the first Russian state, centred on the city of Kiev, and the very name 'Rus' should have been of Scandinavian origin. Russian historians, moreover, have been at pains to demonstrate the organic evolution of East Slav society towards statehood. The chronicles, however, on which historians depend for much of their knowledge of the period, speak of the warring Slavs inviting the Varangians 'to come and rule over us'. This has given rise to the view that the state of Kiev was the creation of the adventurers from the north. The Varangians appear, in fact, to have acted as a catalyst, accelerating commercial and political development. They provided Kiev with the ruling house of Rurik, but his descendants and their retinue were rapidly assimilated by the native Slavs and made little cultural impact.

Source 20

A legendary account from the *Primary Chronicle* of the establishment of Kiev-Rus by the Varangians. The *Primary Chronicle* is organized on a yearly basis beginning in 852.

859 The Varangians from beyond the sea imposed tribute upon the Chuds, the Slavs, the Merians, the Ves and the Krivichians. But the Khazars [an Asiatic tribe] imposed it upon the Polyanians, the Severians and the Vyatichians....

860–862 The tributaries of the Varangians drove them back beyond the sea and, refusing them further tribute, set out to govern themselves. There was no law among them, but tribe rose against tribe. Discord thus ensued among them, and they began to war one against another. They said to themselves, 'Let us seek a prince who may rule over us and judge us according to the law'. They accordingly went overseas to the Varangian Russes....The Chuds, the Slavs and the Krivichians then said to the people of Rus, 'Our land is great and rich, but there is no order in it. Come to rule and reign over us'. They thus selected three brothers, with their kinsfolk, who took with them all the Russes and migrated. The oldest, Rurik, located himself in Novgorod; the second, Sineus, at Beloozero; and the third, Truvor, in Izborsk. On account of these Varangians, the district of Novgorod became known as the land of Rus. The present inhabitants of Novgorod are descended from the Varangian race, but aforetime they were Slavs. After two years, Sineus and his brother Truvor died, and Rurik assumed the sole authority....

870–879 On his deathbed, Rurik bequeathed his realm to Oleg, who belonged to his kin....

880–882 Oleg set forth, taking with him many warriors from among the Varangians, the Chuds, the Slavs, the Merians and the Krivichians. He thus arrived...before Smolensk, took the city and set up a garrison there. Thence he went on and captured Lyubech, where he also established a garrison. He then came to the hills of Kiev....Oleg set himself up as prince in Kiev, and declared that it should be the mother of Russian cities. Varangians and Slavs accompanied him and his retainers were called Russes. Oleg began to build stockaded towns, and imposed tribute on the Slavs, the Krivichians and the Merians.

Source 21

From *King Harald's Saga*, an Icelandic tale about the exploits of Harald Hardrada who spent a number of years in Kiev-Rus before becoming king of Norway and eventually meeting his death in England in 1066 at the battle of Stamford Bridge. The saga was handed down by word of mouth until written down in the thirteenth century by Snorri Sturluson.

Harald travelled east...into Sweden. There he met Earl Rognvald Brusason and many more of King Olaf's men....Next spring they got some ships, and that summer they sailed east to Russia to the court of King Iaroslav [ruler of Kiev Rus, 1019–54] and stayed with him over the winter....King Iaroslav gave Harald and Earl Rognvald and their men a good welcome. He made Harald and Earl Rognvald's son, Eilif, commanders of his defence force....Harald stayed in Russia for several years and travelled widely throughout the East....[He made his way to Constantinople, where he become the leader of the Varangian mercenary forces serving the Emperor in campaigns in Greece, Sicily, Asia Minor and Palestine.] When Harald arrived [back] in Novgorod, King Iaroslav gave him a most cordial welcome....That winter, King Iaroslav gave his daughter Elizabeth in marriage to Harald.

The political organization of medieval Scandinavia combined monarchy with a democratic tradition involving assemblies of leading citizens. The fact that both can be seen in medieval Russia – monarchy taking hold in Kiev, while the Veche Council held sway in Novgorod – may have been due to Varangian influence or perhaps, as Fernand Braudel suggests in Source 22, to indigenous Russian influences. Whatever the extent of Varangian influence, Scandinavia was not the only area of Europe to affect the political development of Russia. To the south west lay the Byzantine Empire with its Orthodox Christian religion, its imperial government and its advanced political ideas and civilization. Contact between Kiev and Byzantium was initially established through trade and military forays, but the event which ensured that Byzantium would have an important influence over the development of Kiev-Rus was the adoption by Vladimir I of Orthodox Christianity as the official religion in 988.

Source 22

From Fernand Braudel, *A History of Civilizations*, p.531–4.

Historians have noted that the cities of the Kiev Principality differed in some respects from their contemporaries in the West. The latter were surrounded by a sprinkling of small towns....The Russian cities were not. Nor were they sharply cut off from the surrounding countryside. Thus, the lords of the land round Great Novgorod sat in its assembly, the Veche, whose decisions were law in the city and in its vast hinterland. They were its masters, together with the Council of leading merchants....These, then, were 'open' towns like those of antiquity, such as Athens,...and not at all like the towns of the West in the Middle Ages, closed in upon themselves, jealously guarding the privileges of their citizens.

Through its conversion to Orthodox Christianity, the Kiev Principality determined Russia's future for centuries to come....The fact that the world and civilization of Russia were sucked into the orbit of Byzantium from the tenth century onwards helped to distinguish Eastern from Western Europe. In Slav countries the language in which religious services were conducted was Slavonic, into which Saints Cyril and Methodius (between 858 and 862) had translated the sacred texts. They had had to invent an alphabet for it, since the Slavonic into which they were turning the Scriptures was only a spoken language. Hence the importance of liturgical Slavonic in the cultural history of Russia.

Source 23

In Novgorod a bell summoned men to the meetings of the Veche, an assembly of free citizens which possessed considerable authority, including the power to expel a prince from the city

Source 24

From the *Primary Chronicle* describing Vladimir's adoption of Orthodox Christianity as the official religion of Kiev-Rus in 988. Christianity was known in Kiev-Rus before this date, its most important convert having been Princess Olga who ruled from 945 to 962.

988 Vladimir marched with an armed force against Kherson, a Greek city. Vladimir and his retinue entered the city, and he sent messages to the Emperors Basil and Constantine, saying, 'Behold, I have captured your glorious city. I have also heard that you have an unwedded sister. Unless you give her to me to wife, I shall deal with your own city as I have Kherson'. When the Emperors heard this message they were troubled, and replied 'It is not meet for Christians to give in marriage to pagans. If you are baptized, you shall have her to wife, inherit the kingdom of God, and be our companion in the faith. Unless you do so, however, we cannot give you our sister in marriage'. When Vladimir learned their response, he directed the envoys of the Emperors to report to the latter that he was willing to accept baptism, having already given some study to their religion, and that the Greek faith and ritual...had pleased him well. When the Emperors heard this report, they rejoiced, and persuaded their sister Anna to consent to the match....

Vladimir was baptized in the Church of St Basil, which stands at Kherson...After his baptism, Vladimir took the Princess in marriage....As a wedding present for the Princess, he gave Kherson over to the Greeks again and then departed for Kiev. When the Prince arrived at his capital, he directed that the idols should be overthrown....The Prince went forth to the Dnieper with the priests of the Princess and those from Kherson, and a countless multitude assembled....When the people were baptized, they returned each to his own abode. Vladimir, rejoicing that he and his subjects now knew God himself,...ordained that churches should be built and established where pagan idols had previously stood. He thus founded the Church of St Basil on the hill where the idol of Perun and the other images had been set, and where the Prince and the people had offered their sacrifices....He took the children of the best families and sent them to school for instruction in book-learning.

989 After these events, Vladimir lived in the Christian faith. With the intention of building a church dedicated to the Holy Virgin, he sent and imported artisans from Greece. After he had begun to build, and the structure was completed, he adorned it with images, and entrusted it to Anastasius of Kherson.

Source 25

Olga, the grandmother of Vladimir I, receiving religious instruction at Constantinople. Olga was one of the earliest Russian converts to the Orthodox religion

Source 26

From Basil Dmytryshyn, *Medieval Russia* (Holt, Rinehart & Winston, 1991) p.9.

Kiev's relations with Constantinople before the middle of the tenth century grew and became one of the basic foundations of Kievan economic prosperity and cultural greatness. In addition to war booty, the Kievans returned from Constantinople with an alphabet, calendar, Christian concepts – in short, culture.

Source 27

From Edward Acton, *Russia*, pp.4 and 7.

For Russian culture, the conversion was decisive. All levels of society, from prince to slave, gradually learned to articulate their values and aspirations through the medium of Byzantine Christianity....Neither the Renaissance nor the Reformation penetrated Russia, and it was not until the seventeenth century that Western influence made any significant impression on the Orthodox mould....It was as an institution that the Church played a very decisive role in shaping the Russian state. A network of monasteries, bishoprics and parishes spread rapidly across Kievan Rus and the Church became a major landowner. With the clergy having a near monopoly upon literacy until the seventeenth century, the Church was able to develop an unrivalled administrative structure. It penetrated the countryside in a way that the rudimentary power of the princes could not hope to do. Moreover, this formidable institution was under the unified jurisdiction of the Metropolitan of Kiev 'and all Rus', established soon after Vladimir's conversion. As such it constituted a formidable political force which the Metropolitan, supported and appointed (until the fall of Constantinople in 1453) by the Greek Patriarch, used to good effect. When Kiev broke up and the Russians came under the sway of stronger powers to east and west, the Church worked vigorously to maintain its own unity. In the process, it nourished the ethnic consciousness of the East Slavs and greatly assisted their eventual political reunification.

Despite the influence of Byzantium, the government of Kiev-Rus remained rather rudimentary. Vladimir Monomakh, for instance, who ruled the principality from 1113 to 1125, indicated in his *Testament* that he took personal responsibility for everything from major policy decisions to minute matters of administration. While the prince had great personal authority, there were occasions when assemblies of citizens deposed princes who failed to protect them or to govern wisely. For instance, when in 1068 Iziaslav, prince of Kiev, ignored their demands to arm them and lead them against the Polovtsians, who regularly raided Kiev, the citizens overthrew him and placed Vseslav on the throne. Later, the citizens had a change of heart and held an assembly at which they decided to restore Iziaslav. However, the incident illustrates that citizens meeting in assemblies sometimes played an important part in the government of the Kievan state.

The role of the citizens was also important in the administration of justice, which, as the extract from the *Ruskaia Pravda* indicates, relied more on self-help than on the activities of the prince, judges or law courts. Nevertheless, the *Statute of Grand Prince Iaroslav* provides evidence that the legal powers of the prince and his boyars and judges were greater than is implied by *Ruskaia Pravda*.

Source 28

From the Testament of Vladimir Monomakh, 1113–25.

In war and at the hunt, by night and by day, in heat and in cold, I did whatever my servants had to do, and gave myself no rest. Without relying on lieutenants or messengers, I did whatever was necessary; I looked to every disposition in my household. At the hunt, I posted the hunters, and I looked after the stables, the falcons and the hawks. I did not allow the mighty to distress the common peasant or the poverty-stricken widow, and interested myself in the church administration and service.

Source 29

From *Ruskaia Pravda*, an eleventh century Russian code of law. A *grivna* was a silver ring used as currency; *rezanas* and *kunas* were also units of currency.

1. If a man kills a man, the brother is to avenge his brother; the son his father; or the father his son; or nephews their uncles; and if there is no avenger [the murderer pays] 40 grivnas fine....
12. If someone steals another's horse, or weapon, or clothes, and the owner recognizes it within his township, he gets back his property and 3 grivnas for the offence....
14. If a trader is owed money by another and the latter refuses to pay, he must appear before a court of twelve men; and if he wrongfully did not pay his debt, then he is to pay the money and 3 grivnas for the offence....
19. And if a bailiff is killed in a highway attack and the people do not search for the killer, the fine will be paid by that locality where the killed official is found....
41. And whoever should apprehend a thief receives 10 rezanas; and a sheriff receives fifteen kunas from 3 grivnas [of fines collected]; 15 kunas go [to the Church] as tithe; and the prince receives 3 grivnas.

Source 30

From the *Statute of Grand Prince Iaroslav*, who reigned from 1019 to 1054. The *Statute* grants judicial powers to Church.

I, Grand Prince Iaroslav...have consulted with Ilarion, Metropolitan of Kiev and All Rus, and we have compared readings in the Greek nomocanon [code of laws]. Since a prince, or his boyars, or his judges ought not to have jurisdiction over these suits, I have given to the Metropolitan and his bishops [jurisdiction over the following]: divorce cases in all towns; the customs duty each tenth week is to go to the church and the

Metropolitan; and his people are not to pay the customs duty anywhere, nor the duty levied on goods entering a town.

The Varangians introduced into Kiev-Rus the practice of 'partible inheritance', whereby the lands of a prince were divided up between his sons when he died, rather than inherited by the eldest son. This often led to bitter fighting between brothers until one emerged victorious and reunited his father's lands under his own rule or until, weakened by years of conflict, they agreed to accept that each would rule a smaller territory than their father had held. Thus, partible inheritance weakened Kiev-Rus and contributed to its decline during the twelfth century. It is fair to say that Kiev-Rus was already very much a declining power when it was overrun by the Mongols in 1240.

Source 31

From the *Primary Chronicle*.

1054 Yaroslav, Great Prince of Rus, passed away. While he was yet alive, he admonished his sons [Iziaslav, Sviatoslav, Vsevolod, Vyacheslav, Vysheslav and Igor] with these words: 'My sons, I am about to quit this world. Love one another, since you are brothers.... The throne of Kiev I bequeath to my eldest son, your brother Iziaslav. Heed him as you have heeded me, that he may take my place among you. To Sviatoslav I give Chernigov, to Vsevolod Pereyaslavl, to Igor the city of Vladimir, and to Vyacheslav Smolensk'. Thus he divided the cities among them commanding them not to violate one another's boundaries....

1073 The devil stirred up strife among these brothers, the sons of Yaroslav. When disagreement thus ensued among them, Sviatoslav and Vsevolod united against Iziaslav....Sviatoslav was the instigator of his brother's expulsion, for he desired more power.

The Mongol period: 1240–1480

Early in the thirteenth century, far to the east of Russia, the Mongol chieftain, Ghengis Khan, built a powerful military empire based on the brilliant horsemanship of his tribesmen, the tactical skill of his generals and the ferocity of his rule. The empire he established was an autocratic one in which the ruler was the embodiment of the state and demanded total obedience and service from his subjects. Terror, cruelty and mass murder were used as deliberate aspects of state policy in an attempt to ensure loyalty through fear.

Although the Mongols (or Tatars, as the Russians called them) only broke into Russian territory briefly during the reign of Genghis Khan, they returned in 1237 under the leadership of his grandson, Batu Khan, and by 1240 had taken Kiev and all of Russia except the north western territories around Novgorod. The butchery and devastation was on a scale hitherto unknown in an age noted for its brutality.

Source 32

From *The Tale of the Ravage of Riazan by Batu*, written by an anonymous monk soon after the event, which took place in 1237.

The churches of God they devastated, and in the holy altars they shed much blood. And no one in the town remained alive....There was no one here to moan or cry – neither father and mother over children, neither brother over brother, nor relatives over relatives – but all lay dead together.

The autocratic nature of Mongol government is revealed clearly in the descriptions of the Mongol court provided in Sources 33 and 34. However, these Sources also reveal that the Mongol empire possessed an effective legal system and a well-developed bureaucracy staffed by paid officials who owed unswerving loyalty to the khan.

Source 33

From a description of the court of the Mongol Emperor, Kuiuk Khan, at Karakorum in 1246 by John of Pian de Carpine, an envoy sent by Pope Innocent IV.

It is a custom of the Emperor of the Tatars never to address in person a stranger, no matter how great he be; he only listens, and then answers through the medium of someone....Whenever they explain any business to Kadak [the procurator of the Mongol Empire], or listen to an answer of the Emperor, those who are under him (that is, his own subjects) remain on their knees until the end of the speech, no matter how great they may be. One may not, for it is not the custom, say anything more about any question after it is disposed of by the Emperor. This Emperor has a procurator, legal clerks and secretaries, and also all the other officers for public as well as private affairs, except advocates, for they carry out without a murmur all judgments according to the Emperor's decision. The other princes of the Tatars do in like manner as regards those things which pertain to their offices.

Source 34

From Robert Marshall, *Storm from the East* (BBC, 1993) pp.34–36 and 72.

Discipline was strict and subject to central authority, and the men were regularly trained to fight as a large unit and not as individuals. Those who broke ranks to loot or who engaged in private feuds were severely punished. Genghis's aim was to make the army the focus of each individual Mongol warrior's loyalty – and he himself the focus of the army's loyalty. Hard experience had taught him that the nation would have to be founded upon a personal following. Absolute autocracy was the key....

The *Yasa* issued by Genghis Khan in 1206 was a code of general laws....It enshrined Mongol attitudes towards religious tolerance, exempted priests and religious institutions from taxation, prescribed the death penalty for espionage, desertion, theft, adultery and, in the case of a merchant, being declared bankrupt for the third time....The *Yasa* became the institutional foundation of the Mongol empire....

The *darughachi* was a sort of all-purpose Mongol official who was stationed in conquered territory and became, in effect, a kind of provincial military governor. It was his responsibility to ensure that the local communities did not renege on the submissions they had made to the Mongols. These officials had a swift and reliable line of communication with the Great Khan, and any hint of revolt was dealt with immediately. However, the *darughachi*'s most vital responsibility was to ensure that the appropriate taxes were collected and forwarded to the central chancellery in Mongolia. *Darughachis* were recruited from the ranks of the *keshig*, the imperial guard, whose allegiance was to the life and well-being of the Great Khan. All lines of communication led to him.

The impact of Mongol rule on Russia was largely indirect. Russian princes were not deposed unless they proved disloyal. They were expected to swear allegiance to the Mongol khan, to pay taxes and to provide men when required for the Mongol army. Each new Russian prince was required to visit Batu's headquarters at Sarai, where he would swear allegiance and receive the *yarlyk* or investiture charter, giving him authority to rule. This was frequently sold to the highest bidder. The Mongol khan used the Russian princes to maintain order in their principalities, to collect taxes and to conscript soldiers. However, Mongol agents kept a close watch on their activities. If a prince disobeyed orders or was suspected of disloyalty, he would be summoned to Sarai for punishment, which might involve withdrawal of the *yarlyk*, public humiliation and possibly execution.

Source 35

From a thirteenth-century Russian chronicle which records how the Mongol Emperor, Batu Khan forced Prince Daniel of Galicia to do homage and pay tribute to him.

In 1250 the mighty Khan sent his envoy to Prince Daniel...[The envoy said] 'Surrender Galicia!'....Daniel conferred with his brother Vasilko and left for Batu's camp saying: 'I will not surrender half of my patrimony (inheritance). Instead, I will go to Batu in person'....He arrived in Pereiaslav where he was met by Tatar officials....From there he reached Batu's camp along the Volga in order to pay homage to him....

Oh Tatar honour is evil! Daniel Romanovich was Grand Prince, who, together with his brother ruled over such Rus principalities as Kiev, Vladimir in Volyn and Galicia, as well as other principalities. Now he sits on Batu Khan's knees and has identified himself as his servant. Moreover, the Mongols are asking tribute. There is very little hope for a better life. There are constant threats. Tatar honour is evil.

Mongol rule introduced into Russia:

- judicial torture;
- the annihilation of whole communities in order to terrorize others into submission;
- censuses and universal taxation;
- conscription for military service;
- the concept of service to the state overriding all other loyalties to family and community;
- the concept of the khan as the supreme autocrat who owned all land, embodied the state in his person and commanded absolute obedience.

Two of the most obvious effects of the Mongol yoke were the demise of the *veche*, the assembly of citizens, almost everywhere except in Novgorod, because such democratic institutions were regarded with deep suspicion by the autocratic khans, and the rise to prominence of Muscovy. At the time of the Mongol conquest, Muscovy was a small obscure principality in north west Russia, but, by loyalty and faithful service to the khan and aggression against their neighbours, its princes increased the size of their territory and gained the coveted title of 'Grand Prince', implying a pre-eminence over other principalities.

By 1380, Prince Dmitri Donskoi of Muscovy felt strong enough to rebel against the Mongols, defeating Mamai Khan at Kulikovo. The victory was short-lived because a Mongol army sacked and burnt Moscow two years later, but Kulikovo did no lasting damage to the special relationship between the Muscovite princes and their Mongol overlords, while enhancing the reputation of the former in the eyes of their fellow princes.

Source 36

Dmitri Donskoi defeats the Mongols at Kulikovo in 1380

Source 37

From Edward Acton, *Russia*, p.9–10.

What limited the impact of the Mongols on Russia's social and political development was the form that their rule took. In the north-west, the great principality of Novgorod escaped invasion when she accepted the advice of Prince Alexander Nevsky and consented to pay tribute. Cultural and commercial exchanges with the Baltic states were thereby preserved. In the south-west, Mongol rule was curtailed in the fourteenth century when the territory passed to the more tender mercies of Lithuania....It was the central and north-eastern principalities of the Great Russians which suffered most from the Mongols, only finally overthrowing them in 1480. But the Mongols' overriding concern was to collect tribute, and on occasion military recruits. After a brief period in which they imposed their own tribute collectors, they were content to leave even that to the Russian princes. Their rule was indirect and their interference in native custom and traditions relatively superficial.

Certain specific repercussions of Mongol rule do deserve emphasis. To apportion tribute, the Mongols carried out a crude census of the population, and in delegating responsibility to the Grand Prince of Vladimir [and later of Muscovy], they provided him with a powerful influence with which to assert his authority. The lesser princes were to hand over their contributions to the grand Prince, and he alone was to conduct relations with the Khan. Moreover, the urge to overthrow the Mongol yoke served to strengthen the desire for unity among the princes....But the basis for consolidation around the new focus of wealth and population in the north-east had been laid before the Mongols arrived, and the blow they dealt the economy outweighed any positive influence their intervention had on Russian political development.

Source 38

From Lionel Kochan, *The Making of Modern Russia* (Pelican, 1963) pp.34–6.

The ultimate defeat of the Mongols by no means put an end to Mongol influence. On the contrary, the departing Mongols left an indelible impression on Muscovite life and society. This may be seen in such matters as Muscovite military organization, Muscovy's method of collecting taxes, its criminal law and its diplomatic protocol....But more important than all this was the impetus that Mongol rule gave to the development of the Muscovite autocracy....The Mongol empire was not only erected on the principle of unquestioning, unqualified service to the State; the Khan also demanded the complete obedience of the individual to the State. The Khan alone embodied the State, and all those who shared in it (through, for example, the 'possession' of land or the holding of office) did so on sufferance and not as a matter of right....It was this specific Mongol colouring that distinguished Muscovite absolutism from that in the contemporary West....Ivan III, for example, was the first ruler of Muscovy to claim ownership of all the Russian lands; he vastly extended the internal authority of the grand prince; and he asserted the position of the autocrat as military leader.

The Muscovite period: 1480–1697

The end of Mongol rule came gradually, brought about by the rising power of Muscovy and a simultaneous decline in Mongol power as the Golden Horde fragmented into five separate warring factions. However, its symbolic end was the defeat of the Great Horde by Grand Prince Ivan III of Muscovy on the River Ugra in 1480 and the cessation thereafter of the payment of tribute by the Russian princes to the Mongols.

Ivan III (1462–1505) was known as Ivan the Great and accorded the title 'gatherer of the Russian lands' for his achievements in throwing off the Mongol yoke and absorbing most of the Russian principalities into the Muscovite state. During his reign, Yaroslavl, Rostov, Tver, Novgorod and Riazan were annexed by Muscovy, either peacefully or by force. In the case of Novgorod, its democratic traditions were effectively stamped out by the execution or deportation of many leading noble families, the abolition of Novgorod's institutions of government and the removal of the famous Veche bell to Moscow. The lands confiscated from the Novgorodian nobility were redistributed to a new class of service gentry, the *pomeshchiki*, who held their lands in return for military and governmental service to the state. Continued possession of these *pomeste* lands was dependent on loyal performance of the landholder's obligations to the state. This system of conditional land holding was extended to other areas, such that by the mid-sixteenth century there were 20,000 *pomeshchiki* in Muscovy, providing a reliable form of manpower and freeing the grand prince from military dependence on the boyar nobility.

Ivan III also began a war against Lithuania in which he forced its Grand Duke to recognize him as 'Sovereign of All Russia' and which, when brought to a successful conclusion by Ivan's successor, Vasili III, added Vyazma, Smolensk, Briansk and Chernigov to the rapidly expanding Muscovite state.

In 1453, Constantinople had fallen to the Turks. As the centre of Orthodox Christianity it had claimed to be 'the second Rome'. Following its fall, Moscow was left as the capital of the only significant Orthodox state and it soon exerted its claim to be 'the third Rome', the spiritual centre of the Orthodox faith, a claim that was strengthened by the fact that Ivan III had married the niece of the last emperor of Constantinople. This spiritual leadership of the Orthodox faith was exercised through the metropolitan of Moscow, who was elevated to the rank of patriarch in 1589, a rank which placed him on the same level as the patriarch of Constantinople. It was clear that Ivan saw Muscovy as the political as well as the spiritual successor to the Byzantine empire, a view he underlined by adopting the Byzantine double-headed eagle as the official emblem of the state.

Although the Muscovite princes had thrown off the Mongol yoke and had begun to carve out an empire of their own, they had risen to prominence under the tutelage of the Mongols and had learnt much of their statecraft from their former masters (Sources 39–40). However, they had also learnt a thing or two from their former spiritual guides in Byzantium, especially the idea that the church and state were inseparable (Source 41).

Source 39

From Sergei Platonov, 'The Transition from Appanages to a Unified Autocracy', in *Readings in Russian History* (Syracuse University Press, 1963) pp.65.

The Muscovite princes regarded their principality as a personal possession...and staked out claims to possess and control the whole vast state. This view was generally accepted; the people of Moscow always declared that they belonged to the great sovereign because they lived on his lands....The authority of the Moscow princes thus took on the character of the authority of a lord of the manor over its land and people, and was, therefore, complete and very autocratic.

Source 40

From Charles Halperin, 'The Ideology of Silence', in *Contemporary Studies in Society and History* 27 (1984) pp.459–66.

The Russians borrowed heavily from Mongol political, military, administrative and fiscal institutions; for example, the postal service which the Mongols had perfected to carry information and people across the Eurasian continent; the division of the army into the five divisions of advance guard, main regiment, left and right flanks, and rear guard; the Mongol customs tax, tax-collector and treasury; and Mongol diplomatic etiquette. The Russians showed good judgment in imitating the institutions in warfare and government which had permitted the Mongols to create and control an empire stretching from the Pacific to the Baltic and the Black Seas. [By the eighteenth century Russia was to possess an empire of similar dimensions.]...That the Mongols did not influence Russian culture was attributable to Russian religious practice....The Golden Horde enjoyed a respectable Muslim religious culture, which is precisely why the Russians could not borrow from it.

Source 41

From Sergei Averintsev, 'The Idea of Holy Russia', in *History Today*, November 1989, pp.41–2.

It is important who instructed the Russians in matters of faith. Their teachers were the Orthodox Byzantines who insisted, for the sake of asserting their own authority, the Church and empire were quite inseparable. In this respect the admonition administered to Vasili I, the Prince of Moscow [1389–1425], by Patriarch Anthony IV of Constantinople was typical. The former had dared to proclaim that the Russians shared a Church with the Byzantines but did not have an emperor, i.e. for them the Byzantine monarch, who was for the time being the only Orthodox emperor, was not their king. 'It is impossible for Christians to have a Church and not to have an Empire', noted the Patriarch. 'For Church and Empire form a great union and it is impossible for them to be separated'. Historically speaking, it is highly significant that these words were addressed by a spiritual leader to a secular lord, and by a Byzantine to a Prince of Moscow in the 1390s. The Byzantine empire would continue to exist for little more than half a century: soon after its fall the Prince's descendants would lay the foundations of the Russian empire....

It is further important that the rise of Moscow coincided chronologically with the fall of Constantinople to the Turks in 1453....In 1478 Moscow annexed the territory of Novgorod and in 1480 finally threw off the Mongol-Tatar yoke. The idea of a third Rome as an alternative to Constantinople is well known from the letter written by the *starets* [church elder], Filofei, in the sixteenth century: '...two Romes have fallen, the third stands, and a fourth there shall not be'.

Source 42

Ivan III, also known as Ivan the Great, (1462–1505), whose marriage to the niece of the last emperor of Byzantium (which claimed to be 'the second Rome') strengthened Ivan's claim that Moscow was 'the third Rome'

Ivan III also paved the way for the establishment of serfdom in Muscovy at a time when it was declining in the west. In a decree issued in 1463, he limited the time when Russian peasants could leave or change their masters to a few days in late November, after the harvest. However, even this very restricted freedom was of limited value since by then the Russian winter would have arrived and it would be a brave or foolhardy peasant who tried to find a new master or other form of employment at so unpromising a time of year.

Source 43

From an instruction issued by Ivan III in 1463 to Prince Ivan, who was responsible for local government in Iaroslavl.

The Abbot of Troitsk-Sergeev Monastery...has informed me that you accept people from his villages of Fedorovsk and Nerekhta as well as other villages during the entire year....[I am instructing you in future] not to accept any people from these villages during any other time than St George's Day [26 November]. And whoever shall leave monastery estates on other than St George's Day, I am ordering you to return him....Whoever wants to come from monastery estates to my estate in Iaroslavl, you may accept him only during two weeks of the year – one week before and one week after St George's Day.

It would be too easy to categorize autocratic Russian rulers from Ivan the Great to Peter the Great and beyond as simply following in the traditions of the Mongol khans. Edward Acton (Source 44) shows us that the true picture is more complex than that, with the boyars and the church being able to exercise considerable influence over the tsar.

Source 44

From Edward Acton, *Russia*, p.17–20.

Unification under Moscow had been accompanied by the creation of a powerful centralized monarchy. All appointments to military and administrative posts were in the gift of the Grand Prince. It was in his name that taxes were collected, the law enforced, war waged and treaties signed. His realm was bound together by an increasingly standardized legal code, gradually extended over newly incorporated areas, a rudimentary postal system, and uniform coinage, weights and measures. Executive, legislative and judicial authority flowed from him and there were no legal limitations on his power....

Yet the Grand Prince's position was in fact more complex than this picture suggests. Ivan III and Vasili III were not despots on the Asiatic model. The Grand Prince lacked a sizeable military apparatus directly responsive to his will. With the money economy spreading extremely slowly, he could only centralize very limited financial resources. The central bureaucracy was embryonic and his provincial officials were spread wafer-thin and proved very difficult to supervise. In these conditions, he was in no position to ride rough-shod over the interests of either the Church or the nobility....On the other hand, Muscovy's social élites did suffer from weaknesses which made them much less independent and their property much less secure than elsewhere in Europe....The Grand Prince faced neither parliaments nor Magna Carta; and individual landowners who fell foul of the monarch enjoyed no legal protection....

The most significant institution outside the state itself was the Church. The favour shown it by the Mongols had enabled it to consolidate its position across Russia long before the Muscovite state managed to do so. Culturally dominant and playing a pervasive role in the everyday life of élite and masses alike, it wielded enormous influence....In the early sixteenth century over 25 per cent of all cultivated land was in church hands. The combination of spiritual, cultural and economic influence at its disposal made the Russian Church in some ways better placed than its Western counterparts to resist the ambitions of the newly centralized state. When Ivan III manoeuvred to undermine the security of monastic property, he found himself unable to do so....[However, the Church leaders] feared to alienate the Grand Prince, who had a wide measure of control over appointments to the [Church] hierarchy....It was the Church hierarchy which orchestrated the remarkable development of monarchic ideology....The Metropolitan Makarii nurtured Ivan the Terrible's hugely inflated notion of his office, and prepared the dramatic ceremony which saw him crowned in 1547 not as mere Grand Prince but as unfettered 'Tsar'. Rather than checking the power of the state, the church thus increased it....

At the top of the social pyramid was the aristocracy, largely landowners whose families had long served Moscow (the boyars) and princes who had gradually been drawn to the metropolis....It was they who surrounded the monarch and provided most of his advisers. The boyars' *Duma* (Council) might lack closely defined rights, but by custom the Tsar legislated and acted in consultation with it....What limited their political weight, however, was the fragile nature of their landed wealth. In contrast to much of Western Europe, primogeniture [inheritance by the first born] was not practised in Russia: a father's property was divided among his heirs. Very quickly the greatest fortune tended to be dissipated among innumerable descendants. This process prevented even the most distinguished families from establishing the kind of firm territorial base which underpinned the political influence of western aristocracies.

The reigns of Ivan III and his successors, Vasili III and Ivan IV show a trend towards greater autocracy in government. Ivan III confiscated the lands of the nobility and, extinguishing political institutions such as the veche council in the lands he annexed, introduced the *pomeste* system. Vasili III extended his authority over the church, the nobility and the peasantry (Source 45). However, it was Ivan IV (the Terrible) who demonstrated how far a Russian ruler could go in using his already extensive powers, together with political savagery, to extend his own authority and cow his subjects into abject submission. Having acquired a deep distrust for the boyar nobility during his youth, when they used him as a pawn in their often bloody political intrigues, Ivan determined to bring them under control. Although he excluded the boyars from his councils, the early years of his reign were reformist rather than vengeful in character. In 1547, he had himself crowned 'Tsar of all the Russias'. *Tsar* means emperor and was a title adopted from the former Byzantine empire. In 1549, Ivan summoned the first *Zemskii Sobor* (Assembly of the Land) which contained representatives of the clergy, nobility and service gentry. This led to a series of reforms including the introduction of a new legal code, the reduction of corruption in government, and an increase in the numbers and importance of the *pomeshchiki*. During the same period, Ivan defeated and annexed the Mongol khanates of Kazan and Astrakhan.

However, in the mid 1560s, he introduced and participated in a blood-thirsty reign of terror in which he divided the country into a privileged and protected personal domain, the *oprichnina*, and the remainder of the country, the *zemshchina*, which was subjected to years of plunder, torture and murder (Sources 46–7). There are two possible explanations for this change in Ivan's policy and behaviour: one suggests that he became mentally unbalanced, a powerful psychopath; the other that he made cold-blooded and calculating use of torture and murder as instruments of state policy to destroy the power of the boyars. Whatever his reasons, by the time he ended the *oprichnina* most of the boyars were either dead or had had their lands confiscated and replaced by *pomeste* holdings in the new territories taken from the Mongols.

Source 45

From Sigismund von Herberstein, the ambassador to Moscow of the Holy Roman Empire [an empire centred on modern day Germany and Austria], 1517. Von Herberstein was describing the powers of Vasili III.

In the sway which he holds over his people, the Grand Prince surpasses all the monarchs of the whole world, and has carried out his father's plan of ejecting all princes and others from the garrisons and fortified places. He certainly grants no fortresses to his relations...but oppresses nearly all of them with close confinement; and whoever receives his orders to attend at court, or to go to war, or upon any embassy, is compelled to undertake whatever it may be at his own expense....

He uses his authority as much over ecclesiastics as laymen, and holds unlimited control over the lives and property of all his subjects: not one of his counsellors has sufficient authority to dare to oppose him, or even differ from him on any subject. They openly confess that the will of the prince is the will of God, and that whatever the prince does he does by the will of God....Metropolitans and bishops were formerly chosen at an assembly of all the archbishops, bishops, abbots and priors of monasteries....But they say that it is the custom of the present prince to summon certain ecclesiastics to him, and choose one of their number according to his own judgment.

All confess themselves to be *kholops*, that is, serfs of the prince. Almost all of the upper classes also have serfs, who either have been taken prisoners, or purchased; and those whom they keep in free service are not at liberty to quit at their own pleasure. If any one goes away without his master's consent, no one receives him.

Source 46

From Giles Fletcher, *The Russe Commonwealth*. Fletcher visited Russia in 1588 as an ambassador of Queen Elizabeth I.

The state and form of their government is plain tyrannical, as applying all to the benefit of the prince, and that after a most open and barbarous manner....To show his sovereignty over the lives of his subjects, the late emperor Ivan Vasilevich [the Terrible], in his walks or progresses, if he had disliked the face or person of any man whom he met by the way, or that looked upon him, would command his head to be struck off. Which was presently done, and the head cast before him....

Some there have been of late of the ancient nobility, that have held provinces by right of inheritance, with an absolute authority and jurisdiction over them, to order and determine all matters within their own precinct without...control of the emperor. But this was all abolished and wrung clean from them by Ivan Vasilevich....

Their highest court of public consultation for matters of state is called the *Zemskii Sobor*, that is, the public assembly. The states and degrees of persons that are present at this assembly are these, in order. (1) The Emperor himself. (2) Some of his nobility, about the number of twenty, being all of his council. (3) Certain of the clergymen, about the same number. As for citizens or others to represent the community, they have no place there: the people being of no better account with them than as servants or bond slaves that are to obey, not to make laws....

The late Emperor Ivan Vasilevich...meaning to reduce his government into a more strict form, began by degrees to clip off their [the nobility's] greatness, and to bring it down to lesser proportion: till in the end he made them not only his vassals, but his *kholops*, that is, his villeins or bond slaves. For so they term and write themselves in any public instrument or private petition which they make to the emperor. So that now they hold their authorities, lands, lives and all at the emperor's pleasure, as the rest do.

The means by which he brought this about against the nobility...were these.....He divided his subjects into two parts or factions....The one part he called the *oprichniki* or select men. These were such of the nobility and gentry as he took to his own part, to protect and maintain them as his faithful subjects. The others he called *zemskii*, or the commons. The *zemskii* contained the base and vulgar sort, with such noblemen and gentlemen as he meant to cut off, as suspected to mislike his government....The *zemskii* he put from under his protection: so that if any of them were robbed or killed by those of the *oprichniki* (which he accounted of his own part), there was no amends to be sought for by way of public justice, or by complaint to the emperor....And this liberty of the one part to rob and kill the other, without any help of magistrate or law (that continued seven years), enriched that side and the emperor's treasury, and brought about that which he intended by this practice; namely, to take out of the way such of the nobility as he himself disliked: whereof were slain within one week to the number of 300 within the city of Moscow....

Having thus pulled them down, and ceased all their inheritance, lands, privileges, etc.,...he gave them other lands of tenure of *pomeste*, that are held at the emperor's pleasure, lying far off in another country; and so removed them into other of his provinces, where they might have neither favour or authority, not being native nor well known there.

Source 47

From Heinrich von Staden, *The Land and Government of Muscovy*. Von Staden, a German, served in Ivan IV's *oprichniki* during the late 1560s.

The *oprichniki* did a number of indescribable things to the *zemskii* people to get all their money and property....The Grand Prince...murdered one of the chief men of the *zemshchina*, Ivan Petrovich Cheliadnin....The Grand Prince then went with his *oprichniki* and burned all the estates in the country belonging to this Ivan Petrovich. The villages were burned with their churches and everything that was in them....The *oprichniki* caused great misery in the country, and many people were secretly murdered....The Grand Prince continued to have one *zemskii* leader after another seized and killed as it came into his head....

The Grand Prince moved into Great Novgorod, into the bishop's palace, and took everything belonging to the bishop....He indulged his wantonness and had monks tortured, and many of them were killed. This distress and misery continued in the city for six weeks without interruption....Every day the Grand Prince could also be found in the torture chamber in person. Nothing might remain in the monasteries and the city. Everything that the soldiers could not carry off was thrown into the water or burned.

Source 48

Ivan the Terrible. The artist, Vasnetsov, has captured the awe and fear he inspired in his subjects as the first Grand Prince of Muscovy to be crowned 'Tsar of Russia'.

While most historians have interpreted the *oprichnina* as the actions of a blood-thirsty autocrat, some, including Mikhail Pokrovsky, have seen this drive to reduce the independent power of the boyars as the work of the 'townsmen and petty vassals' who had so often suffered at the hands of the boyars.

Source 49

From Mikhail Pokrovsky, *A Brief History of Russia*, 1933.

There is nothing more unjust than to deny that there was a principle at stake in Ivan IV's struggle with the boyars or to see in this struggle only political stagnation. Whether Ivan IV was himself the initiator or not – most probably he was not – yet this *oprichnina* was an attempt, 150 years before Peter's time, to found a personal autocracy like the monarchy of Peter the Great....Just as the 'reforms' had been the work of a coalition of the bourgeoisie and the boyars, the coup of 1564 was carried out by a coalition of the townsmen and the petty vassals.

The Rurikid royal house of Muscovy came to an end in 1598 with the death of Fyodor I, and this plunged Russia into 15 years of chaos, factionalism and virtual anarchy as different claimants fought for the crown. This 'Time of Troubles' came to an end with the accession of Michael Romanov in 1613, but the monarchy remained weak for some years thereafter. The *Zemskii Sobor* had elected Michael to the throne and for some years thereafter he and his successor, Alexei, relied on it for support. It sat in almost continuous session until 1622, helping to restore order and government to the war-torn country. However, as the new dynasty gained in strength this assembly met less frequently, vanishing from Russian life after its final meeting in 1653. Shortly before its demise, it ratified the new legal code, the *Ulozhenie* of 1649. This made land ownership and other privileges conditional upon service to the state – that is, to the tsar. All land owners were now servants to the tsar and held land *because* they were servants. It also completed the transformation of the rural peasantry from tenants into serfs, a process that had begun two centuries years earlier under Ivan III (Source 43). Henceforth, peasants simply became moveable property.

Source 50

From Martyn Rady, *The Tsars, Russia, Poland and the Ukraine* (Hodder & Stoughton, 1990) p.70.

The Romanov partnership with the service nobility is exemplified in the institution of the *Zemskii Sobor* or 'National Assembly'. Michael retained the assembly which had put him in power and throughout his reign he consulted frequently with this body in matters of domestic and foreign policy. Membership of the assembly was evidently determined by some form of election....It was the particular function of the assemblies to draw up petitions for the tsar's consideration and to advise on how 'to carry out such reform in all matters as may be best for the Muscovite state'....A number of historians have detected in the *Zemskii Sobor* an incipient parliament. This cannot be the case. Although a representative element was certainly involved in these gatherings, the assemblies lacked most of the distinguishing features of representative institutions elsewhere in Europe.

Source 51

From Basil Dmytryshyn, *Medieval Russia*, p.425.

One of the most important documents of seventeenth century Russia is the *Ulozhenie*, or Code of Law, of 1649. Prepared by the *Zemskii Sobor*, the *Ulozhenie* represents the first serious Russian attempt at legal codification. It consists of 968 articles....Among other things, [it] legalized the complete enserfment of the peasantry, granted the nobles broad privileges, furthered the consolidation of absolutism, and prohibited the further expansion of church and monastery estates. The *Ulozhenie* provided the direction for Russia's development, and many of its basic provisions remained in force until 1833.

While the power of the Muscovite monarchs expanded considerably during the sixteenth century, and recovered rapidly during the seventeenth century from the Time of Troubles, the power of the church also grew much greater, such that a German visitor, Adam Olearius, regarded the power of the patriarch as in many ways equal to that of the tsar.

Source 52

From Adam Olearius, *Voyages and Travels of the Ambassadors sent by Frederick Duke of Holstein to the Grand Duke of Muscovy*. Olearius visited Russia four times between 1634 and 1643.

The politic government of Muscovy is monarchial and despotical. The tsar is...so absolute that there is no prince or lord in all his dominions who does not think it an honour to act as his majesty's slave. No master has more power over his slaves than the tsar has over his subjects, whatever their condition or quality....Since there is no other difference between a legitimate government and tyranny than that in the one the welfare of the subjects is of greatest consideration, in the other the particular profit and advantages of the prince, we must allow that Muscovy inclines much towards tyranny....The tsar is not subject to the laws; he only makes them and all the Muscovites obey him with great submission....

The patriarch among them has the same authority as the Pope has in the Latin Church. The patriarch at Constantinople had heretofore the nomination of him. In time he came only to have the confirmation of him; but now of late he has lost both.... The patriarch's authority is so great that he divides the sovereignty with the tsar. He is the supreme judge of all the ecclesiastical cases, and absolutely disposes of whatever concerns religion, with such power that in things related to the political government, he reforms what he conceives prejudicial to Christian simplicity without giving the tsar any account of it, who, without any contestation, commands the orders made by the patriarch to be executed.

Olearius was by no means the only European visitor to Muscovy during this period. Trading and diplomatic links had been growing between Russia and western European nations, especially the Netherlands and England since trade relations were first established between Muscovy and England in the 1550s. European merchants, craftsmen and mercenary soldiers were to be found in Muscovy in such large numbers that a foreign quarter was established in Moscow.

Source 53

European ambassadors received by Tsar Alexis in the Kremlin, 1662

The St Petersburg period: 1697–1917

Many historians, including Martyn Rady (Source 56), regard the reign of Peter the Great (1682–1725) as an important watershed in Russian politics because of the wide-ranging westernizing reforms he introduced into Russian government and society following his 'Great Embassy' to the west in 1697–8. During this 'Great Embassy', he visited Germany, the Netherlands, England, France and Austria eager for knowledge of the government, economy, manufacturing industries, society, culture and military and naval systems of these countries. Following his return to Russia, much of the remaining 27 years of his reign was devoted to introducing western practices and influences into a great many aspects of Russian life.

- In 1703, he began constructing a new capital, St Petersburg, on the Gulf of Finland, a site chosen because it gave Russia 'a great window...looking into Europe', reflecting the closer ties that were being established between Russia and the west. The architect chosen to supervise this project was an Italian.
- The army was reorganized and trained in modern European methods of warfare. It was equipped with muskets imported from England until a native Russian arms industry could be established.
- A military academy was established to train more efficient officers, but its success was hampered by the lack of education of many of the boyars' sons who attended it. This led Peter to establish a system of elementary education for the sons of nobility in reading, writing, arithmetic and geometry. To encourage

Source 54

Nemetskaia sloboda (Moscow's foreign quarter) in the seventeenth century

reluctant boyars to send their sons to these new schools, Peter decreed that young noblemen would not be permitted to marry until they had obtained educational certificates.

- He reorganized local government into eight districts and restructured the local administration of the police and judiciary along Swedish lines. Similarly, central government was reorganized along more bureaucratic lines, employing the Swedish system of colleges, which were, in effect, departments of state. The ministers heading each college reported to the Senate, a central administrative council of nine, that held its administrative, financial and judicial authority direct from the Tsar.
- The church was also reformed in line with the new system of colleges. The office of patriarch was abolished and replaced by the Most Holy Synod, which, as a department of the state government, could be kept more firmly under the control of the tsar.
- Society was restructured during the 1720s with the introduction of the 'Table of Ranks' which derived from a similar system operating in Prussia. All officers in the government and the army were assigned to one of 14 noble ranks, depending on the services he performed and the responsibilities he held. The right to own land and serfs depended on membership of one of these ranks, which could only be attained by commitment to lifetime service to the tsar.
- He encouraged Dutch and German manufacturers to establish textile mills, ironworks and foundries in Russia.
- He altered the Russian calendar and clock to bring them into line with western practices. Until Peter's reign, the Russians had dated their calendar from the Creation of the World, and their New Year was on 1 September. Thus, what we would call 1 September 1699 was, in Russia, New Year's Day 7208. Peter introduced the European calendar by beginning the next New Year on 1 January 1700. He also changed the clocks 'so that the hours are shown in the European manner from one to twelve, that is from noon and from midnight and not (as now) from morning till evening with the figures running from one to seventeen'.
- In an attempt 'to sever the people from their former Asiatic customs', he taxed beards to induce the boyars to go clean-shaven, as was fashionable in western courts, and encouraged the aristocracy to adopt western manners and styles of dress.
- He ordered a reminting of the coinage using methods similar to those employed in London.

Source 55

Peter regarded the full beard traditionally worn by Russian boyars as uncivilized and placed a tax on beards to encourage them to shave. Those who refused wore a 'beard medal' to prove that they had paid the tax. In this contemporary cartoon, Peter is depicted as a barber removing the beard of a boyar.

Although the scale of European influence on Russia increased dramatically under Peter the Great, it is important not to forget that considerable European influence already existed prior to his reign.

Source 56

From Martyn Rady, *The Tsars, Russia, Poland and the Ukraine*, pp.84–86

For contemporaries and historians alike, the reign of Peter the Great amounted to a turning point in Russian history.... Under Peter's direction, Muscovy embraced the west and sought to transform itself into a modern European state. The reforms undertaken during Peter's reign affected every aspect of Muscovy's government and society and their legacy may be felt even to this day....[However,] thanks to the work of Peter's predecessors, Russia already had 'Europe and the West' firmly printed upon it. Peter's work of transformation rested on the achievements of others, and his reign demonstrated elements of continuity as well as of change.

At no time in its history was Russia ever 'severed' from the rest of Europe, for even during the grim years of the Mongol-Tatar yoke, Muscovy had managed to preserve some patchy contact with the west. These tenuous relations were established on a firmer and lasting basis during the fifteenth century when Ivan III opened up new diplomatic and commercial channels to the west....Despite these changes, Muscovite attitudes towards the rest of Europe were founded largely on suspicion and contempt....

The growing commerce with the rest of Europe revealed the technical inadequacies of Russian manufacture and war exposed Muscovy's military backwardness. Expansion into the Ukraine led in its turn to the discovery there of the fruits of Catholic learning and scholarship....During Alexei's reign [1645–76], a scholarly review of the ancient written Sources of the Orthodox faith led to a 'reformation' in religious practices and provoked a schism in the church between 'modernisers' and Old Believers. A particular complaint of the Old Believers was the replacement of old styles of icon painting by new techniques of representation borrowed from western Europe.

Source 57

From an explanation by Peter the Great of his motives in 1720 for abolishing the office of patriarch and replacing it with a council, the Most Holy Synod. Peter's view of the power of the patriarch is confirmed by Olearius in Source 52.

The fatherland need not fear from an administrative council the seditions and disorders that proceed from the personal rule of a single church ruler. For the common folk do not perceive how different is the ecclesiastical power from that of the Autocrat, but dazzled by the greater honour and glory of the Patriarch, they think him a kind of second sovereign, equal to or even greater than the Autocrat himself.

If Peter's reforms were prompted by European examples, his methods of enforcing compliance with his will owed more to autocratic Mongol traditions. He established a secret police bureau, known as the Secret Chancery, that soon became hated and feared for the brutality of its measures. Peter used terror as a means of forcing his subjects into obedience. When the *streltsi*, a corps of musketeers in the Russian army revolted during 1698 while Peter was engaged in his tour of western Europe, loyal forces crushed the mutiny, captured its leaders, executed some and imprisoned others. Nevertheless, when Peter heard about the revolt he hastened home from Vienna and instituted a further round of fierce and bloody reprisals in which 2,000 *streltsi* were executed.

Source 58

From Johan Korb, *The Diary of an Austrian Secretary at the Court of Peter the Great.*

Peter arrived in Moscow on 4 September [1698], a monarch to the well-disposed but an avenger for the wicked. His first anxiety after his arrival was about the rebellion....Who had dared to instigate such a crime? And as nobody could answer accurately upon all points...he began to have suspicions of everybody's loyalty, and began to consider a fresh investigation. The rebels that were kept in custody in various places were all brought in...to a fresh investigation and fresh tortures....No day, holy or profane, were the inquisitors idle; every day was deemed fit and lawful for torturing....The Grand Duke himself [Peter], in consequence of the distrust he had conceived of his subjects, performed the office of inquisitor....He examined the criminals, he urged those that were not confessing, he ordered such streltsi as were stubbornly silent to be subjected to more cruel tortures....The whole month of October was spent in butchering the backs of the culprits with the knout [a vicious whip] and with flames; no day were those that were left alive exempt from flogging or scorching, or else they were broken upon the wheel, or driven to the gibbet, or slain with the axe.

Source 59

The Mice Burying the Cat. A popular cartoon following the death of Peter the Great, showing a cat being drawn to its burial by the mice it had tormented. Traditionalists, Old Believers and other victims of his autocratic policies and harsh methods were among the 'mice' Peter had tormented.

While the Europeanization of Russia, which had advanced so dramatically under Peter the Great, could not be entirely undone, it had aroused strong resentment among traditionalists in the state and Old Believers in the church. This resentment, expressed somewhat crudely in Source 59, and the lack of reforming zeal among Peter's immediate successors, ushered in a period of sterility and reaction against European influence. Nevertheless, that influence remained. Anna's reign (1730–40) was known as a time of government by foreigners, due to the German origins of many of her ministers, and both Elizabeth (1741–62) and Catherine the Great (1762–96) were strongly influenced by French fashion, culture and political attitudes.

Catherine had been the consort of Peter III, whom she replaced on the throne following his deposition and murder. His short reign produced two liberalizing reforms: the closing down of the hated and feared Secret Chancery created by Peter I to act as a secret police force, and the issue of the Manifesto on the Freedom of the Nobility, which brought to an end compulsory state service for the nobility.

Source 60

From the *Manifesto on the Freedom of the Nobility* issued by Peter III in 1762.

We grant to the entire Russian hereditary nobility their freedom and liberty....All nobles who are presently in our service may continue as long as they wish or as long as their health may permit them. Those serving in the army should not ask for release or leave during a campaign or three months before a campaign; they should wait for release until the end of a war....Those nobles who will be freed from our service and wish to travel to other European countries should immediately receive the necessary passports...under one condition: namely, that should ever the need demand, those nobles should return home whenever they are notified....By virtue of this manifesto, no Russian nobleman will ever be forced to serve against his will...except in emergency cases and then only if we personally should summon them....No nobleman should keep his children uneducated under the penalty of our anger.

We hope that in return for this act Russian nobles...will continue to serve us loyally and zealously and will not withdraw from our service; on the contrary, that they will seek the service eagerly and will continue it as long as possible, and will educate their children attentively in useful knowledge. Those who will not perform any service...and will not educate their children...are not concerned with the general good, and we recommend that all our faithful subjects despise and avoid them. We will not allow such people any access to our court, nor will we tolerate their presence at public assemblies and festivals.

Some historians regard the Manifesto as a turning point in Russian history because it brought to an end the system whereby the gentry and nobility were regarded as the property of the tsar, to be ordered to serve in whatever capacity he chose, without any rights of their own. Instead, the Manifesto gave them a new sense of their own worth, encouraging them to serve the state out of moral obligation rather than through compulsion. By and large, they continued to serve the state and also responded to the inducement to educate their children. In consequence, the gentry and nobility contributed to an improvement in central and provincial administration and in agriculture, and contributed to the growth of intellectual and artistic society in Russia, which began to flourish under Catherine the Great.

Following the violent overthrow of Paul III shortly after the Manifesto was issued, it was left to Catherine to determine what to do with the service gentry and nobility, the *pomeshchiki*, now that their service was no longer compulsory. She developed a system of 'bureaucratic absolutism' in which she relied upon a modernized civil service, staffed mainly by the former *pomeshchiki*, to run the administration. She attempted to reform and codify the law in accordance with the principles of 'Enlightened Despotism' that were being expounded in western Europe and to ensure that the government operated within a legal framework. A Charter to the Nobility issued in 1785 defined the legal rights and privileges of the nobility, exempted them from the payment of taxes and from conscription, conferred absolute rights of ownership over lands and serfs, and enhanced their prestige and administrative role in the government of their districts.

Source 61

From the *Charter to the Nobility*, 1785.

The title of nobility is hereditary and stems from the quality and virtue of leading men of antiquity who distinguished themselves by their service....Neither a nobleman nor a noblewoman can be deprived of the title of their nobility unless they forfeit it themselves by an act contrary to the standards of noble dignity....A nobleman cannot be deprived of his title, his honour, his life or his property without due process of law....We confirm freedom and liberty to the Russian nobility on an hereditary basis for eternity....A nobleman is personally freed from the soul tax....We grant our faithful nobles permission to assemble in the *gubernias* [administrative districts] where they live, to organize in every district an Association of Nobles and to enjoy the rights, privileges, distinctions and preferences stated below. [These included the right to elect local officials, to advise the district governor and to petition the tsar or tsaritsa and his or her Senate council.]

The freedom and privileges granted to the nobility raised expectations that the serfs would also be freed. The argument ran as follows: since peasants had been enserfed so the nobility could perform their service to the state unhindered by cares about the management of their own estates, now that the nobility's compulsory service to the state was ended, there was no longer any need or justification for serfdom. The peasantry came to realize that Catherine was not about to emancipate them, when the tsaritsa issued a decree in 1767 prohibiting all complaints by serfs against their masters. This increased peasant restlessness and led to the outbreak of the first, and most serious, of a number of peasant revolts that were to break out over the next century. The rebellion was led by an obscure Cossack, Emelian Pugachev, who claimed to be the murdered tsar Peter III. During 1773–4 the rebellion blazed a trail of terror and destruction across the Volga Basin until Pugachev was captured and executed. Although the decree he issued reveals a number of complaints against Catherine's government, some of which can be traced back to the westernizing reforms of Peter the Great, emancipation of the serfs was the principal objective of the rebels.

Source 62

From the 'Emancipation Decree' issued by Pugachev, posing as Peter III, in July 1774.

We Peter III, by the Grace of God Emperor and Autocrat of All-Russia...grant freedom to everyone who formerly was in serfdom or in any other obligation to the nobility...; [to the Old Believers] we grant the right to use the ancient sign of the cross, and to pray and to wear beards; while to the Cossacks we restore for eternity their freedoms and liberties; we hereby terminate the recruiting system, cancel personal and other monetary taxes, abolish without compensation the ownership of land...and free everyone from all taxes and obligations which the thievish nobles and extortionist city judges have imposed on the peasantry and the rest of the population.

It was not to be until 1861, almost a century after the nobility gained their freedom, that the serfs would be emancipated. The position got worse before it got better, as the French artist, Gustave Doré (Source 63), illustrated in a famous cartoon showing how the peasantry were entirely at the mercy of the whims and caprices of their masters. It has been argued by many historians that the enserfment of the peasants to the nobility established a western-style feudal system in Russia at about the time that it was declining elsewhere. Adherents of this view point to similarities such as the existence of serfs in both systems and the obligations of service which the nobility must perform in return for their lands. However, other historians, including Tibor Szamuely (Source 64), claim that the similarities were no more than superficial and were outweighed by the differences, chief among which was the fact that in Russian 'feudalism' there was no reciprocal contract – the nobility had no rights in return for their service to the tsar and the peasants had no legal rights to protect them from injustice by their lord. Szamuely argues that the *pomeste* system of service to the state in return for land to which the peasants were tied by serfdom was evidence not of a western-style feudal system, but of an Oriental despotism.

Source 63

A French cartoon from 1854 depicting Russian landowners gambling with bundles of serfs

Source 64

From Tibor Szamuely, *The Russian Tradition*, pp.100–7, 110–1.

Of late it has become customary for western writers to place Russian society within the general framework of feudalism, and to call the system that existed in Russia until 1861 'feudal'....On the face of it, there would seem to be considerable resemblances between classical western feudalism and the Muscovite social system. One is immediately struck by the prevalence in both types of society of service land tenure, in combination with the military tenants' far-reaching authority over a subject and unfree peasantry....Upon closer examination, the resemblance is seen to be no more than a superficial and misleading one....In reality, nothing could be further apart than the pomeste system – land granted by the state...to enable its serving-man to fulfil his compulsory duty of unlimited and unconditional service – and the feudal fief, based on a strictly private agreement, and on a limited contractual relationship between the lord and his vassal....The system of vassalage...led inevitably to the growth of a powerful landed aristocracy...with private armies, private courts, private taxation....Yet far more important in the long run was the fact that a potent and privileged aristocracy constituted the strongest of checks upon the powers of the state, and that in this capacity it made a decisive contribution towards the evolution of democratic processes. De Tocqueville saw in the aristocracy, in its institutions and privileges, the chief rampart against the rise of despotism....

In Russia...the peasants were tax-paying chattel slaves, to be bought and sold, given away, lost at cards, or even deprived of life at their master's whim....As human beings they stood outside the law; they were not merely unfree, but un-people. The position of the peasant in feudal society was utterly different....He was unfree and personally dependent on his lord, but cannot by any stretch of the imagination be described as a chattel. He was subject solely to the jurisdiction of the lord, but this jurisdiction was exercised in accordance with local custom and the law of the land. Both his rights and his obligations were precisely defined....

The most detailed, lucid and influential exposition of Oriental despotism was made by Montesquieu in his celebrated *Esprit des Lois*....This was a system of government 'in which a single person directs everything by his own will and caprice', where mankind is 'all upon a level', and 'all are slaves'. The fundamental principle of despotic government is universal fear: 'In despotic states, the nature of government requires the most passive obedience;...man is a creature that blindly submits to the absolute will of the sovereign'....In despotic states no laws of property exist; 'the lands belong to the prince' – who is by the nature of things heir to all his subjects....Montesquieu often cited Russia as a typical example of the despotic state....

The Tatars, who, in the course of their centuries of rule, introduced into Russia the methods and concepts of Oriental despotism...were decisive both in destroying the non-Oriental Kievan society and in laying the foundations for the despotic state of Russia....From the Mongols Moscow inherited not only its claim to dominion over the Russian lands, and not only the methods of Oriental statecraft, of military organization, of finance, etc., but also the very ideas that lay at the heart of its system of government: the concept of universal compulsory service, of the unquestioning submission of the individual to the state; the idea of the prince as the supreme landowner; very probably too, the dream of a world empire.

Contact with the west increased during and after the Napoleonic Wars as Russia played an increasingly active role in European diplomacy. Prince Volkonsky (Source 65) was only one of many Russian intellectuals to become more aware of the limitations of the country's autocratic and repressive regime. During the reign of Alexander I (1801–25), a number of constitutional reforms were introduced which brought Russia more into line with the systems of government in operation in western Europe. For instance, Peter the Great's system of governing colleges was replaced in 1802 by government ministries, each headed by a minister of state, and in 1809 a draft constitution was produced which would have given the nobility a more important role in the government had it been implemented. Furthermore, Alexander introduced a state education system based on French practices, comprising six universities and a range of elementary and secondary schools. The status of education was improved by revising the Table of Ranks to incorporate university graduates. However, the reforms were piecemeal and were accompanied by increasingly repressive measures of censorship and police activity designed to suppress the rising tide of dissent. The value of the educational reforms was undermined by the strict control exercised over what could be taught.

Source 65

From the memoirs of Prince Volkonsky, a Russian liberal.

The campaigns of 1812–14 brought Europe nearer to us, made us familiar with its forms of state, its public institutions, the rights of its people. By contrast with our state life, the laughably limited rights which our people possessed, the despotism of our regime first became truly present in our heart and understanding.

Disillusionment that Alexander I's early reforms gave way to repression and censorship angered many among the educated élite, especially the army officers, who had come increasingly into contact with the constitutional ideas and institutions of western Europe. Following the death of Alexander in 1825, their frustrations boiled over into the Decembrist Revolt which sought to replace autocracy with representative government, to free the serfs and to reform the judicial system. Disorganized and weakened by divided leadership, the Decembrist Revolt was quickly crushed, but it was significant in being the first of a series of uprisings in which the gentry and nobility sought not personal gain but a better society. The new tsar, Nicholas I (1825–55) and his Minister of Public Education, Admiral Shishkov, blamed the revolt on lax censorship and the influence of the French Revolution.

Source 66

From a memorandum to Nicholas I from Admiral Shishkov, 1826.

No one doubts that the French Revolution...was caused by inadequate government supervision of book publishing. The prime reason for this was the presence [in France] of highly educated and...most impious individuals....Their sharp minds and their keen pens...implanted seeds which, when ripened, multiplied free thought and immorality and then destroyed faith and the throne....We are now seeing some signs of this plague [in Russia]. Loose talk, which never existed here about religion, freedom and government, has multiplied sects and dissidents among us, has stirred up common people, and has implanted in the inexperienced heads and hearts of young people the audacity to form a governmental system based on their dreams....We are witnessing now things that did not exist before; namely, frequent incitement of peasants against nobles and the resolute demand for freedom....We have witnessed with horror the development of last December. Its participants were not common people, but officials, princes, nobles and writers, who called themselves enlightened, who were endowed with keen minds and a worldly outlook....In France, as well as among us, all of them stemmed from the circulation and reading of mysterious immoral books and journals, which, because of the lack of proper review, passed the weak censorship system.

The Decembrist Revolt shook Nicholas I and the overthrow of the French king in 1830 and the revolutions in various parts of Europe in 1848 increased his sense of insecurity. Consequently, his reign was one of increasing repression and dictatorship. According to J.N. Westwood, 'Russia...resembled a modern police state, with strict censorship, numerous informers, arbitrary arrests, preventive punishments, and frequent denunciations of allegedly subversive citizens'. A new political police force, the Third Section, was established. Secret political police were nothing new in Russia, but the scale of operation of the Third Section dwarfed anything that had preceded it. The principal functions of the Third Section were to shadow, investigate, arrest, extract confessions from and punish those who were under suspicion of political or religious deviance, to supervise prison camps, to maintain surveillance on foreigners and to keep the tsar informed about the state of public opinion. It also carried out more conventional police duties, such as investigation of counterfeiting and the rooting out of corruption among provincial officials. Although the Third Section was later abolished by Nicholas's successor, Alexander II, its secret police functions continued under another guise.

The irony of the repression under Nicholas I was that it had the opposite effect from that which was intended. The harsh treatment meted out to the Decembrists made martyrs of them and inspired a generation of revolutionary thinkers; strict censorship gave rise to secret meetings of radical intellectuals and succeeded only in veiling, not in silencing, the social and political comment in the writings of such literary giants as Pushkin, Gogol, Dostoevsky, Turgenev and Tolstoy; while the tsar's refusal to contemplate emancipation of the serfs led to over 700 peasant uprisings during his reign. Revolutionary thinkers like Alexander Herzen fled abroad, where they could express more freely their opposition to the tsarist autocracy.

Source 67

From a letter written by Alexander Herzen while in Paris to his friends in Moscow, 1849.

In the worst days of European history we find some respect for the individual and a certain recognition of his independence....Not so in our country. The individual at home [i.e. in Russia], ever oppressed and neglected, has never made any attempt to get a hearing. Free expression of opinion at home was always regarded as an insolence; independence as sedition. The individual was absorbed in the state; was dissolved in the commune. The revolution effected by Peter I replaced the antiquated landlord rule of Russia by the European bureaucratic system. Everything that could be transferred from the Swedish and German codes was; everything that could be transplanted from Holland, a land of free municipalities, to an autocratic government of rural communes was borrowed. But the unwritten moral restraints on the government, the instinctive recognition of the rights of individuals, the right of thought, of truth, could not be transplanted and were not. Slavery in Russia increased with education; the state grew, improved, but the individual in no way profited by the process. Indeed, the stronger the state grew, the weaker did he become. The European forms of administration and of the judiciary, military and civil organization have developed into a monstrous, hopeless despotism....We saw the worst possible period of the imperial regime. We grew up under terror, under the black wings of the secret police, and were mutilated by hopeless oppression. We barely survived. But is that not too little? Has the time not come to loosen our hands and tongue for activity which would serve as an example? Has the time not come to awaken the slumbering consciousness of the people?...Open, frank acts are required.

Defeat in the Crimean War by Britain, France and Turkey exposed the backwardness and weakness of Russia and convinced the new tsar, Alexander II (1855–81), that reform could be postponed no longer. The 'Reform Period', as the early years of his reign have become known, began with a period of open discussion (*glasnost* in Russian) and led to four major pieces of legislation.

- Serfdom was abolished in 1861, but this did not grant the serfs the unlimited freedom for which they had hoped. Personal freedom was granted immediately, but it was meaningless without land. Peasants were entitled to a proportion of the land they had formerly worked as serfs, but they had to pay for it at prices that were determined by the owner of the estate. Having no capital of their own, they had to borrow the money and agree to excessive repayment conditions over the next 49 years. Furthermore, they could not buy the land individually, but had to do so as village communes, so that, while free in theory, in practice they exchanged serfdom to the nobility for economic dependence on the commune. The landlord--peasant relationship was modified from one of ownership to one of employment, and many landlords were bitter about the loss of their source of free labour.
- The first genuine system of local government was established in 1864 with the creation of *zemstvos*, which were local assemblies or councils comprising elected representatives from the landowners, the peasant communes and the citizens of the local towns. The *zemstvos* were given various responsibilities including education, welfare, public health, the promotion and regulation of local industry, commerce and agriculture and the maintenance of roads. However, their powers were severely limited because they were seriously underfunded and denied executive authority, which was retained by central government. As with the emancipation of the serfs, the creation of the *zemstvos* promised more than it delivered.
- A major reform of the legal system was enacted in 1864 and was more successful and wide-ranging than those that had preceded it. It was based on western European practice, with trial by jury, the right of representation for defendants, and the preliminary examination of defendants transferred from the police to examining magistrates.
- From 1863, a series of army reforms was introduced which increased its efficiency. The length of compulsory service for conscripts was reduced, discipline was made less brutal, basic education was provided for illiterate conscripts and automatic promotion for those of higher social rank was abolished. This made the army the most democratic institution in Russia.

In addition, the system of taxation was modified and expansion and improvements took place in secondary and higher education. These reforms not only affected the way the state was governed, introducing the first limited elements of representative government, but also altered the relationships between social groups.

Source 68

The emancipation of the serfs is announced on an estate near Moscow in 1861

Source 69

From the Statute on Local Government, 1864, which established *zemstvos*.

The matters that are subject to the jurisdiction of *zemstvo* institutions...are:

1. the management of the property, capital, and monetary levies of the *zemstvo*....
4. the management of *zemstvo* charitable institutions and other measures of care for the poor....
7. participation...in looking after public education, public health, and prisons....
13. The holding of elections for membership and for other positions in *zemstvo* institutions....

Zemstvo institutions function independently within the sphere of activity entrusted to them.

Source 70

From Larissa Zakharova, 'Autocracy, Bureaucracy and the Reforms of the 1860s in Russia', in *Soviet Studies in History*, Spring 1991, pp.6–33.

The abolition of serfdom in Russia in 1861 and the ensuing reforms are events of vital importance, a break and turning point in our country's history....The first powerful blow to Nicholas's system came from without. The defeat suffered in the Crimean War (1853–6) had shown the real state of Russia....Alexander II uttered his famous pronouncement before marshals of the nobility in Moscow on 30 March 1856, in which he spoke of the liberation of the serfs: 'It is far better that this come from above than from below'....A passionate, uncontrollable demand for society to express itself swept away the prohibition Nicholas I had imposed on the printed word, which had led from 1848 to 1855 to a 'terror of censorship'....This openness [*glasnost*] sprang spontaneously from below. The government lagged behind events; it renounced the worst forms of censorship but continued to eye openness with suspicion....

At first...innovation in domestic policy expressed itself in the removal of numerous prohibitions. This involved abolishing the restrictions that had been imposed on universities since 1848...reaching the decision freely to issue passports for travel abroad...easing censorship, offering opportunities 'to establish trading links with foreign countries and to import the latest European scientific achievements from them', and shrinking the army....Of special importance was a proclamation issued...freeing political prisoners....Nine thousand were released from administrative and police surveillance....

[In] 1859, Alexander II sanctioned the formation of a special commission [to draft the reforms]...modestly titled the Editing Commission....The new institution was primarily nontraditional in that most of its members were liberal activists....The liberal majority on the Editing Commission conceived of the peasant reform as a revolution embodied in a single legal act. The first stage would be to free landlord serfs from personal dependency; the final one to convert all of them into petty property owners while still preserving a substantial part of gentry land and large landlord estates. They planned to achieve their goal peacefully and avoid the revolutionary upheavals that had shaken countries in western and central Europe....

The change in the legal position of the peasantry was even more thoroughgoing and decisive. Abolishing personal dependency and depriving landlords of patrimonial power thrust many millions of peasants into the life of society....Peasants now could regulate themselves through regional and rural societies (based on the commune) with officials elected at meetings conducted by the peasantry.

Source 71

A meeting of the mir or village commune

While the impetus for social and constitutional reform came from the tsar, the inspiration for it came from the west. Whether reformers were radical intellectuals, many of whom had fled to western Europe during the reign of Nicholas I to escape the attentions of the Third Section, or government ministers, like Valuev (Source 72), the inspiration for their proposed reforms came from the ideas of western political theorists or from the representative institutions of European states. Nevertheless, most recognized that such ideas could not be imported unchanged into Russian government and society. Russia was different from the west, and western ideas would have to be modified if they were to find acceptance among a conservative and suspicious people and its nervous government.

Source 72

From a memo written by P.A. Valuev, Minister of the Interior, 13 April 1863.

One idea, apparently, has taken hold in all minds....Namely, that in all European countries various estates [i.e. classes] are given some degree of participation in the business of legislation or general administration of the state; and if this is so everywhere, then it should be the case with us. The establishment of the principles of such a participation is considered a sign of political maturity. Constantly stimulated in a tremendous number of Russian travellers by what they see abroad and in an even greater number of Russian readers both by the Russian press and by what is printed in all known languages, this notion cannot fail to have a strong, daily increasing influence.

Source 73

From a memo written by M.T. Loris-Melikov, Minister of the Interior, 28 January 1881.

I have to state to Your Majesty my profound conviction that for Russia it is impossible to organize popular representation in imitation of western patterns; not only are these alien to the Russian people, but they even could shake its basic political outlook and introduce troubles whose consequences are difficult to foresee.

As other rulers, in Russia and elsewhere, have found, the introduction of reform in a land long used to oppression leads not to contentment but to demands for further reform. The 1860s witnessed a marked growth in the activities of radicals and revolutionaries in Russia, which dampened Alexander II's earlier enthusiasm for reform. A failed attempt on the tsar's life in 1866 led to the arrest of suspected revolutionaries, stricter censorship and closer government supervision and control over students. However, indignation at police action overcame the fear of getting caught among many students, thus increasing the level of radical activity in the universities.

During the 1870s one group of revolutionaries, the *Narodniks* or Populists, advocated the development of a social revolution based on the peasantry. As a first stage, thousands of idealistic young intellectuals 'went to the people' by living and working alongside peasants in the hope that they would be able to enthuse them with revolutionary ideas. They failed, and many were turned over to the authorities by the peasants whom they had come to help. The trials of the arrested Populists and the long prison sentences meted out to many of them, won them sympathy and encouraged other revolutionaries to adopt more extreme and violent tactics. A militant wing of a group called Land and Liberty began murdering repressive officials, including the head of the Third Section and a senior official in the Kievan police.

The government responded with a brief but sharp programme of repression followed by a return to liberalization. The hated Third Section was abolished and its secret police functions were scaled down and transferred to the Ministry of the Interior. Alexander also began to consider further constitutional reform, but this was brought to a sudden and brutal end with the assassination of Alexander II by members of the People's Will, a revolutionary off-shoot of Land and Liberty.

Source 74

Alexander II, the tsar who liberated the serfs, but who, as this cartoon shows, was regarded by western Europeans as an autocrat, grinding his subjects under foot, and wielding a sword and a whip called a 'knout', which was used to administer punishment

The reigns of Alexander III (1881–94) and Nicholas II (1894–1917) represent a retreat from constitutional reform and a return to repression. The basic apparatus of a police state had been established by Nicholas I in the first half of the nineteenth century, but was extended much further under Alexander III and Nicholas II. Its main architect was K.P. Pobedonostsev, who served as chief minister in the Russian government from 1881 to 1905. He hated liberalism and democracy, claiming that representative government was 'the great lie of our time'. The origins of the police state under Nicholas I and its further development by Pobedonostsev during Alexander III's reign have been traced by Richard Pipes.

Source 75

From Richard Pipes, *Russia under the Old Regime* (Penguin, 1990) pp.293–302 and 311.

The new Criminal Code came out in 1845 and turned out to be a milestone in the historical evolution of the police state. Political crimes were dealt with in two chapters: No. 3 'Of felonies against the government', and No.4 'Of felonies and misdemeanours against the system of administration'. These two sections...constitute a veritable charter of an authoritarian regime. Other continental countries also had on the statute books provisions...for dealing with crimes against the state (a category of crime unknown in English and American law); but none attached to them such importance or defined them as broadly as Russia....Since 1845, with but one interlude between the revolution of 1905 and October 1917, it has been a crime in Russia to seek changes in the existing system of government or administration, or even to raise questions about such issues. Politics has been declared by law a monopoly of those in power....

This type of legislation [i.e. the Criminal Codes issued by Nicholas I in 1845 and by the Bolsheviks in 1927], and the police institutions created to enforce it, spread after the Revolution of 1917 by way of Fascist Italy and Nazi Germany to other authoritarian states in Europe and overseas. One is justified in saying, therefore, that Chapters 3 and 4 of the Russian Criminal Code of 1845 are to totalitarianism what the Magna Carta is to liberty....

Between 1878 and 1881 in Russia the legal and institutional bases were laid for a bureaucratic-police regime with totalitarian overtones that have not been dismantled since....In 1878, a terrorist striking in broad daylight on a St Petersburg street knifed to death the Chief of Gendarmes....A secret circular was issued [a few days later] detailing stiff preventive measures. These empowered members of the Corps of Gendarmes...to detain and even exile anyone *suspected* of political crimes....Until that time, a Russian citizen actually had to commit a subversive act (verbal or written expression being included in that category) before being liable to exile. From now on, to suffer this fate it was enough for him merely to arouse suspicion. This measure put in place a second pillar of the police state; the first, set in 1845, had made it a criminal offence for a private individual to concern himself with politics.; now he was treated as a criminal even if he only appeared likely to do so....

In August 1880...the Third Section was abolished and replaced by a central political police called...the Department of Police....It was organized into several sections, one of which dealt with 'secret' matters – that is, political counter-intelligence....The elaborate and rather flexible political police system established in Russia in the early 1880s was unique in at least two respects. Before the First World War no other country in the world had two kinds of police, one to protect the state and another to protect its citizens....Secondly, unlike other countries, where the police served as an arm of the law and was required to turn over all arrested persons to the judiciary, in imperial Russia and there alone police organs were exempt from this obligation....Its members had the right to search, imprison and exile citizens on their own authority, without consulting the Public Prosecutor....These two features make the police institutions of late imperial Russia the forerunner and...the prototype of all political police organs of the twentieth century....

To complete the picture of restrictive measures imposed by the government of Alexander III, mention must be made of policies subsumed under the term 'counter-reforms', whose avowed aim it was to emasculate the Great Reforms of Alexander II. Among them were limitations on the competence of *zemstvos*, abolition of the office of justices of the peace, and introduction of 'Land Commandants', local officials with much discretionary authority over the peasants.

Source 76

'Russian Civilization', a cartoon from Judy, *a London magazine, 3 March 1880, depicting political prisoners travelling under escort to exile in Siberia*

Pobedonostsev's reactionary and repressive measures did not stamp out revolutionary activity; they merely drove it underground and pushed many moderates into the arms of the radicals. Despite some economic reforms, discontent increased still further when Russia and its tsar were humiliated by defeat in the Russo-Japanese War of 1904–5. *Zemstvo* representatives began calling for a reform of political life and when these demands were rejected a crisis erupted. On a Sunday in January 1905 a priest, George Gapon, led a peaceful march of striking workers to present a petition to Nicholas II. The police fired on the protesters killing scores and wounding hundreds. This incident, known as 'Bloody Sunday', sparked off the 1905 Revolution.

Source 77

From Father Gapon's petition to Nicholas II, 1905.

Sovereign, there are thousands of us here; outwardly we resemble human beings, but in reality neither we nor the Russian people as a whole enjoy any human right, have any right to speak, to think, to assemble, to discuss our needs, or to take measures to improve our conditions. Our employers have enslaved us and they did it under the protection of your officials....They imprison and send into exile any one of us who has the courage to speak on behalf of the interests of the working class and of the people....

It is essential to have a popular representation; it is essential that the people help themselves and govern themselves. Only they know their real needs. Do not spurn their help; accept it; decree immediately to summon at once representatives of the Russian land from all classes....Let everyone be equal and free to elect or be elected, and toward that end decree that the elections to the Constituent Assembly be carried out on the basis of universal, secret and equal suffrage.

The massacre on 'Bloody Sunday' led to widespread unrest. There were riots, strikes and mutinies in the army and navy. Councils of workers, peasants, and soldiers, called *soviets*, were established in St Petersburg, Moscow and other cities. To restore order, Nicholas II granted some of the reforms that the revolutionaries were demanding. In August 1905, he promised to summon an elected national assembly, a *duma*, and two months later issued the October Manifesto, granting constitutional reforms which signalled the end of absolute monarchy in Russia. Freedom of speech and assembly and the announcement that in future laws would not come into operation without the approval of the *duma* set Russia, somewhat uncertainly, on the path towards constitutional monarchy. In addition, the hated redemption payments, which peasants had been paying since serfdom had been abolished in 1861, were ended.

Source 78

From the October Manifesto issued by Nicholas II in 1905.

We impose upon the government the duty to execute Our inflexible will:

1. To grant the population the sacred foundations of civic freedom based on the principles of genuine personal security, freedom of conscience, speech, assemblies, and associations.
2. Without postponing the scheduled elections to the State *Duma*, to admit in the participation in the *Duma*...all those classes of the population which presently are completely deprived of voting rights, and to leave further development of general elective law to the future legislative order.
3. To establish as an unbreakable rule that no law shall become effective without confirmation by the State *Duma*.

Source 79

The Duma in session, 1906

Nicholas had not become overnight a willing convert to constitutional monarchy. He still styled himself 'Autocrat' and dissolved his first *duma* after only a few weeks. A second *duma* met in 1907 but was dominated by radicals and lasted no longer than the first. Before a third *duma* was summoned later that year, the tsar amended the electoral laws to keep radicals out of parliament, strengthen the voice of the conservatives and weaken the voting power of the workers and of ethnic minorities. Nevertheless, the *duma* remained in existence; a third *duma* met from 1907 to 1912 and a fourth from 1912 to 1917. Had it not been snuffed out by the combined pressures of the First World War and the Bolshevik Revolution, it is possible that the constitutional monarchy that originated in 1905 would have established firmer roots.

The historical significance of the 1917 Revolutions

The February and October Revolutions

The First World War was disastrous for Russia and for tsarism in particular. The economy and the system of government were incapable of coping with the pressures of fighting a modern war. The vast Russian army was ill-fed and ill-equipped. In 1914, almost a third of the army lacked even a rifle with which to fight. Casualties were high – over four million Russian troops were killed or wounded in the first year of the war – and morale was low. By 1916, soldiers were deserting in increasing numbers.

Politically, the tsar's position became increasingly tenuous. Having taken on the direction of the war effort himself, Nicholas II hoped to boost his flagging popularity by taking personal credit for Russian successes. However, this also meant that he was in danger of being blamed for the defeats, which came with increasing frequency. His refusal to dismiss incompetent ministers and to work more closely with the *duma* and his failure to solve the deepening economic crisis alienated him further from his subjects. The reputation of the monarchy also suffered because of the influence of Rasputin, a disreputable monk notorious for his sexual promiscuity. He had worked his way into court circles and won the support of the tsarina Alexandra because of his apparent ability to relieve the suffering of her haemophiliac son. With Nicholas away at military headquarters for long periods, Alexandra and Rasputin virtually ran the government, promoting a series of incompetent ministers to high office.

Source 80

A cartoon showing Nicholas II and Alexandra as puppets manipulated by Rasputin

In 1916, Rasputin was murdered by a group of aristocratic conspirators intent on saving the monarchy. However, the damage had already been done. Nicholas had alienated almost all his potential supporters and Rasputin had damaged the reputation of the court and the government to such an extent that tsarism was beyond saving.

When, in February 1917, bread riots broke out in Petrograd (the new name given to St Petersburg in 1914), they spread rapidly; a general strike ensued and the army mutinied. This was not a planned revolution, but the tsar had so alienated his subjects that hardly anyone could be found to rally to his defence. In an attempt to save the crown, Nicholas II abdicated in favour of his brother, the Grand Duke Michael, but Michael refused to accept the crown on the grounds that it had not been offered to him by representatives of the Russian people. Thus, the Russian monarchy, once one of the most powerful autocracies in the world, came to an end, not as the result of a revolution engineered by its political opponents, but having collapsed due to its own incompetence.

Following this 'February Revolution', a Provisional Government was established under the leadership first of Prince Lvov and later of Alexander Kerensky. This was a liberal constitutional government based on the *duma*, but it made the fatal mistake of deciding to continue Russia's involvement in the First World War, when its people were close to starvation and wanted an end to the war so that the country could concentrate on feeding its people and repairing its shattered economy. It also ignored the demands for land being made by the peasants, some of whom had begun to take matters into their own hands by seizing and dividing up the estates of local landowners. Furthermore, there was something approaching a rival government in the form of the Petrograd soviet, a council of workers, soldiers and peasants dominated by socialist politicians that assumed effective authority over the capital. Other soviets sprang up in towns and cities throughout Russia.

These soviets soon came under the leadership of the Bolshevik Party, a group formed in 1903 whose principal leaders – Vladimir Lenin, Leon Trotsky, Joseph Stalin and others – had been in exile when the February Revolution had occurred, but had hurried back to Russia soon afterwards. In September 1917, Trotsky was elected chairman of the Petrograd soviet. The Bolsheviks told the Russian people what they wanted to hear, using simple, popular and readily-understood slogans such as 'Peace, bread and land' and 'All power to the soviets'. As a result, tens of thousands of workers and soldiers joined the Bolshevik Party, which began to lay plans to overthrow the Provisional Government by force. Although Lenin gave the order for the 'October Revolution' to begin, it was Trotsky who planned and directed it, using units of Bolshevik militia, known as Red Guards, to seize key installations. During the three days that it took the Bolsheviks to seize control (25–27 October), there was very little fighting and only five people were killed. This was largely because, throughout its brief life, the Provisional Government had never attracted much popular support due to its failure to end the war or satisfy any of the other demands of ordinary Russian people.

It must have seemed to many that the October Revolution was another step in the democratization of Russia that had begun with the 1905 Revolution. However, far from extending democratic rule, the Revolution quickly snuffed it out and replaced it with a one-party dictatorship.

Source 81

Soldiers take to the streets after the tsar's abdication in February 1917

Questions

6. What part do the 1917 Revolutions play in accounts which claim that 'each major turning point in Russian political life has been marked by the adoption of European ideas and institutions' (Hypothesis A)?
7. What part do the 1917 Revolutions play in accounts which claim that 'the development of Russian political ideas and institutions has been characterized by the continuity of autocratic traditions established during Mongol rule' (Hypothesis B)?

Marxism

The political philosophy of the Bolsheviks sprang from the teachings of Karl Marx (1818–83), the German founder of communism. Marx expounded the view that history was dominated by a series of class struggles between those who held political and economic power and those who did not. Mankind, he argued, had passed, and was still passing, through a series of ages, in each of which one class held power and used it to dominate and exploit the lower levels of society. This gradually built up resentment among the oppressed until they were strong enough to overthrow their oppressors in an armed uprising that brought a new class to power. Thus, feudalism, where power was in the hands of the landowners, was overthrown by means of armed conflict and replaced by capitalism, in which the bourgeoisie, the middle class, became the new ruling élite; society became industrialized and the proletariat, the industrial workers, became the new oppressed class.

Source 82

From Victor Kiernan, 'Marxism and Revolution', in *History Today*, July 1991, p.39.

Eighteenth century historians had arrived at a picture of the past as a succession of economic eras, each marked by one leading 'mode of subsistence'. Marx elaborated this into a series of 'modes of production', and identified a specific ruling class as the chief beneficiary of each in turn, until overthrown by a successor. He saw the dynamic of history in the combined forces of technological growth and human resentments and aspirations. The latest system to appear was capitalism, still in Marx's lifetime struggling to extend its sway over Europe, by dint of 'bourgeois revolutions'. It seemed to him...that the perfect model for these had been provided by the French Revolution of 1789. It replaced the dominance of one class and its mode of self-enrichment with another; a landowning nobility was supplanted by a rival capitalist class.

Source 83

From Karl Marx and Friedrich Engels, *The Communist Manifesto*, 1848.

The history of all hitherto existing society is the history of class struggles. Freeman and slave, patrician and plebeian, lords, vassals, guild-masters, journeymen, apprentices, serfs; oppressor and oppressed stood in constant opposition to one another, carried on an uninterrupted, now hidden, now open fight, a fight that each time ended either in a revolutionary reconstitution of society at large or in the common ruin of the contending class....The modern bourgeois society that has sprouted from the ruins of feudal society has not done away with class antagonisms...it has simplified them. Society as a whole is more and more splitting up into great hostile camps, into two great classes directly facing each other – bourgeoisie and proletariat....The advance of industry, whose... promoter is the bourgeoisie, replaces the isolation of the labourers...by their revolutionary combination, due to association....The fall of the bourgeoisie and the victory of the proletariat are equally inevitable.

As conditions of employment worsened under capitalism, the profits of industrialists grew and the gap between rich and poor widened, an armed struggle would eventually ensue between the bourgeois capitalists and the proletariat, which would end in the victory of the latter. The victory of the proletariat would be the culmination of this historical process, ushering in socialism or communism, in which the means of production would be in the hands of the workers and political power would be held by the proletariat. Class conflict would then cease and, as country after country experienced proletarian revolutions, the state would wither away as an outmoded means of suppressing the now victorious working class.

Marx believed that the proletarian or communist revolution would occur first in the industrialized countries of western Europe, and most probably in Germany or Britain. In his view, Russia was not yet ripe for a proletarian uprising because it had not yet had a capitalist revolution and did not have a large, industrialized urban workforce. He considered the uneducated and ill-informed rural peasants who made up the bulk of the Russian population to have little revolutionary potential.

Lenin and the Bolsheviks viewed the revolutionary potential of Russia in a more positive light, arguing that the industrialization that had begun during the 1890s had started to create an urban proletariat, which was capable of being led to revolutionary victory by Marxist intellectuals like himself. However, even as late as April 1917 he discounted the revolutionary potential of the rural peasants, declaring that 'it is not possible for a proletarian party to rest its hopes at this time on a community of interest with the peasantry'. However, the peasant land seizures which began to gather pace shortly afterwards changed his mind, and he fashioned a new brand of socialism, Marxist-Leninism, which envisioned industrial workers, peasants and soldiers working in harmony to overthrow the bourgeois government. Therefore, Lenin's initial aim on returning to Russia from exile in April 1917 was to achieve Bolshevik control of the soviets, since they represented the workers, peasants and soldiers. Having done so, he used the soviets to launch the October Revolution.

Source 84

From Fernand Braudel, *A History of Civilizations*, p.555.

By chance, the Socialist revolution occurred in the least industrialized country in Europe at the time. So it was impossible for it to take place in accordance with the Marxist scenario of a seizure of power by the proletariat. Power was seized by the Communist Party – i.e. by a tiny minority of the vast Russian population, perhaps some 100,000 people all told. This highly organized minority took advantage of the appalling stampede of 10 or 12 million peasants, escaping from the army and flooding back to their villages....When they arrived home, they began to commandeer the estates of aristocrats, the rich bourgeoisie, the Church, the convents, the Crown and the State.

The communist period: 1917–1990

The Bolsheviks won control of Petrograd, Moscow and other major cities with relative ease, but gaining control of the entire country was a much more difficult proposition. The Bolsheviks were a party of perhaps 340,000 in a country of 160 million, most of whom either knew little about Marxist-Leninism or else were opposed to it. The immediate tasks facing the new government were to establish control, to win widespread support, to make peace with Germany, to defeat the anti-Bolshevik forces ranged against them and to repair the war-ravaged economy. One of its first acts was to abolish ranks, titles and class privileges, but a new political élite rapidly emerged comprising members of the Bolshevik Party.

Source 85

From the Military Revolutionary Committee's announcement of victory for the Bolshevik Revolution in November 1917.

To the Citizens of Russia: The Provisional Government has been overthrown. The power of the state has passed into the hands of the organ of the Petrograd Soviet of Workers' and Soldiers' Deputies, the Military Revolutionary Committee, which stands at the head of the Petrograd proletariat and garrison. The cause for which the people have fought – the immediate proposal of a democratic peace, the abolition of landed proprietorship, workers' control of production and the creation of a Soviet Government – is assured. Long live the revolution of the workers, soldiers and peasants.

Source 86

From decrees abolishing classes and titles issued by Vladimir Lenin shortly after the Bolshevik Revolution.

1. All classes and class divisions, all class privileges...all class organizations and institutions, and all civil ranks are abolished.
2. All classes of society (nobles, merchants, petty bourgeoisie, etc.) and all titles (Prince, Count and others), and all denominations of civil rank (Privy State councillors and others), are abolished, and there is established the general denomination of Citizen of the Russian Republic.

The war against Germany was ended by the Treaty of Brest-Litovsk, but the cost was high. The new leaders of Russia ceded to Germany a million square miles of land inhabited by 45 million people in order to achieve peace. However, most of this was regained a few months later when Germany surrendered to its adversaries in the west. Faced with at least five separate anti-communist White armies inside Russia that were determined to crush the new government, Trotsky organized a Red Army which fought a bloody and costly Civil War against them, eventually defeating the last of its counter-revolutionary opponents in 1921. At the height of the Civil War, Tsar Nicholas II and his family, who had been under house arrest since his abdication, were murdered by members of the *Cheka*, a new political police force.

The response of Lenin's government to the challenges it faced was to establish a Bolshevik dictatorship. Lenin had no liking for what he called 'bourgeois democracy'. He believed that workers and peasants needed enlightened leadership to which they should give absolute obedience. This 'democratic centralism', as he called it, led him to vest power in a Council of People's Commissars under his own leadership and including Trotsky and Stalin among its members. This Council had the power to make laws by decree, without reference to any representative assembly. When a Constituent Assembly was elected in November 1917, the Bolsheviks won only a quarter of the seats and responded by forcibly dissolving it.

Shortly afterwards, they banned all political parties except their own, which they renamed the Communist Party, closed down all newspapers except their own and imposed strict censorship. The *Cheka* was a political police force established to silence critics and opponents, using methods that surpassed its tsarist predecessor in brutality and terror. The justification for the use of such methods was the need to subordinate everything else to the defeat of the White Armies in the Civil War. However, by the time the Civil War had ended, the *Cheka* and its repressive methods had become an established part of the Soviet government and remained so until communism was dismantled 70 years later. It went through various reorganizations and changes of name, from *Cheka* to OGPU, to NKVD, and finally to KGB, but political surveillance of the populace coupled with repression and terror remained the hallmarks of its activity.

Party dictatorship was also extended to the economy with the introduction in 1918 of 'War Communism'. Private enterprise was abolished as all industry and agriculture was taken into state ownership and organized to meet state needs and production targets, with forced requisition of grain and other foodstuffs introduced to alleviate the growing famine. Forcible requisitioning of grain provoked widespread violence and led peasants to produce less rather than more. Despite foreign aid, the famine worsened and an estimated ten million people died as a result of the combined effects of War Communism and the Civil War.

Source 87

From P.N. Stearns, *The European Experience Since 1815* (Harcourt Brace Jovanovich, 1972) p.236.

The Bolsheviks stayed in power by introducing a drastic programme called War Communism that included some nationalization of manufacturing, confiscation of land for distribution among the peasants, and a new legal system. The keynote was a single-party dictatorship and what Lenin called 'unsparing mass terror'. In December 1917, the government set up a secret police force called the Cheka to combat counter-revolutionaries....The Bolsheviks [launched]...a massive police effort that wiped out great numbers of their political opponents. All opposition newspapers were suppressed. Bolshevik control was now unchallenged, and in March 1918, they moved the central government to Moscow.

Source 88

From an order issued by the *Cheka* in 1918.

The All-Russian Extraordinary Commission to Fight Counter-Revolution, Sabotage and Speculation asks the [local] soviets to proceed at once to seek out, arrest and shoot immediately all members...connected in one form or another with counter-revolutionary organizations.

Source 89

From instructions issued by Felix Dzerzhinsky, the head of the *Cheka*, in 1918.

Do not demand incriminating evidence to prove that the prisoner has opposed the Soviet government by force or words. Your first duty is to ask him to which class he belongs, what are his origins, his education, his occupation. These questions should decide the fate of the prisoner.

Lenin was also unwilling to tolerate disagreement with his policies from within the party, and, as Alexandra Kollontai suggests, such disagreement could lead to one's arrest on trumped up criminal charges.

Source 90

From Alexandra Kollontai, a Bolshevik minister and ambassadress, 1922.

If you happen to read in the papers that Lenin has had me arrested for stealing the silver spoons in the Kremlin, that simply means that I am not entirely in agreement with him about some little problem of agricultural or industrial policy.

Opposition to War Communism began to grow among workers, soldiers and sailors in and around Petrograd, and found support among a few prominent Bolsheviks, including Alexandra Kollontai, who were also concerned that the party was serving its own interests rather than those of the people and was denying political rights to those on whose behalf it claimed to rule. In 1921, the opposition erupted into the Kronstadt Rising, in which a revolt by the previously loyal Kronstadt naval garrison was only put down after fierce fighting. Although the rising was suppressed, it focused Lenin's attention on the failure of War Communism, leading him to abandon it in 1921 and introduce the New Economic Policy (NEP). As P.N. Stearns explains, this represented a retreat from communist ideals with the reintroduction of a limited amount of private enterprise, but it had the effect of stabilizing the economy and creating much needed economic growth. Although War Communism was abandoned, the political repression against which the Kronstadt rebels had protested remained firmly in place.

Source 91

From P.N. Stearns, *The European Experience Since 1815*, p.284.

Victorious in the civil war but faced with massive economic problems, Lenin decided on a policy of relaxation in 1921. He replaced 'War Communism' with a 'New Economic Policy', which he called 'a step backward in order to go forward'. The NEP was a radical departure from War Communism and even represented a limited return to capitalism. The free market was stressed, particularly in agriculture. Peasants...could sell their surplus at free-market prices. Small businesses were returned to private hands, while foreigners were encouraged to invest in new industries. The state continued to own and operate all large-scale industries....Under this relatively loose guidance the Russian economy surged forward once more....In the countryside the NEP encouraged a minority of the peasants, the substantial *kulaks* [rich peasants], to acquire more land at the expense of the majority in order to produce more for the market. It thus furthered the growth of peasant capitalism that had begun...before World War I.

The effects of the 1917 Revolutions on Russian political life were undoubtedly dramatic: tsarism was abolished and, after the failure of a brief attempt at constitutional democracy, an entirely new system of government was erected based on the political theories expounded by a German socialist, Karl Marx. However, many historians have argued that this system was not as fundamentally different from the tsarist regime that preceded it as first appears. Party dictatorship replaced autocracy, but both were centralized authoritarian regimes based on coercion and employing a political police force to ensure obedience and suppress any form of dissent.

Source 92

From R. Bartlett, 'Images: Catherine II of Russia, Enlightened Absolutism and Mikhail Gorbachev', in *The Historian*, Spring 1991, p.8.

The political structure established by the new Soviet regime had much in common with the monarchy it replaced, insisting on a monopoly of political wisdom and power, and restricting to increasingly narrow prescribed limits the space for autonomous social opinion and action. The party élite, in its executive function and privileges, has been likened to the old nobility.

Source 93

From Fernand Braudel, *A History of Civilizations*, p.555.

Lenin is said to have asked: 'If Tsarism could last for centuries thanks to 130,000 aristocratic feudal landowners with police powers in their regions, why should I not be able to hold out for a few decades with a party of 130,000 devoted militants?'....'To hold out for a few decades' until Russia had reached a degree of development and industrialization that might have allowed a 'reasonable' revolution [one which would give power to the workers and peasants once they had acquired the education and political understanding to be able to use it effectively]: that, for years, seemed to be the crucial problem. It was also the motivation for an implacable dictatorship which was never the 'dictatorship of the proletariat' but that of the communist leaders – in the name of a proletariat that did not yet exist. Under Stalin, the dictatorship of the leaders even became that of one single man.

Source 94

From Michael Lynch, *Reaction and Revolutions: Russia 1881–1924* (Hodder & Stoughton, 1992) pp.145–6.

The collapse of tsardom left a power vacuum which the Provisional Government proved unable to fill. The reconstituted *duma* which succeeded the tsar in February held office, but it never held power....All the signs were that if Russia was to be modernized it could not be done by moderate means. The brief liberal experiment that followed the February Revolution was a temporary break in the authoritarian tradition. The Provisional Government had neither the time nor the ability to lay down democratic roots. It is arguable that the authoritarian tradition was so ingrained in Russia that modernization had to be imposed from the top. Although Lenin rejected the Russian past, he remained very much its heir. He had as little time for democracy as the tsars. Despite the upheavals of 1917, the rule of the Bolsheviks marked a continuation of absolutism in Russia. The Civil War...by intensifying the threat to the Bolshevik government, provided it with the pretext for demanding absolute conformity from the masses and the party members as the price of the Revolution's survival. Yet it is doubtful whether, even without that threat, Bolshevism could have developed other than as an oppressive system. Its dogmatic Marxist creed and its belief that it alone represented the force of history made it as intolerant of other political ideas as tsardom had been. The forcible dissolution of the Constituent Assembly in 1918 and the crushing of the Kronstadt Revolt in 1921 were the clear proof that democracy would never be allowed to restrict Bolshevik control. 1917 did not mark a complete break with the past. Rather it was the replacement of one form of state authoritarianism with another.

An insight into the similarity in governmental methods employed by the tsars and by the communist regime can be gained by comparing the following extracts from the Criminal Codes of 1845, 1927 and 1960.

Source 95

From the Criminal Code issued by Nicholas I in 1845.

Persons guilty of writing and spreading written or printed works or representations intended to arouse disrespect for Sovereign Authority, or for the personal qualities of the Sovereign, or for his government are on conviction sentenced...to the deprivation of all rights of property and exile for hard labour in fortified places from ten to twelve years.

Source 96

From the Soviet Criminal Code issued in 1927.

Actions defined as counter-revolutionary are those directed at the overthrow, undermining or weakening [of the government]....Propaganda or agitation, containing appeals to the overthrow, undermining or weakening of Soviet authority...and the spread or preparation of literature of such content carry the loss of freedom with strict isolation for no fewer than six months.

Source 97

From the Soviet Criminal Code issued in 1960.

Agitation or propaganda carried on for the purpose of subverting or weakening Soviet authority or of committing particular, especially dangerous crimes against the state, or circulating for the same purpose slanderous fabrications which defame the Soviet state....shall be punished by the deprivation of freedom for a term of six months to seven years.

Lenin died in 1922 and there followed a struggle for power from which Joseph Stalin emerged victorious. Trotsky, his main rival, fled into exile, eventually to be murdered in Mexico by Stalin's agents. Stalin ruled Russia until his death in 1953 and established what he called 'Socialism in One Country', which meant that he abandoned the notion of the imminence of worldwide communist revolution and concentrated on equipping the Soviet Union to survive in a world dominated by non-communist states. His first priority was to provide the foundations for a powerful modern state by improving the outdated methods of agricultural and industrial production and achieving vast increases in output (Source 98). A Five Year Plan was introduced in 1928, which set ambitious annual targets for the growth in output from the state-controlled heavy industries and from agriculture. This plan was completed ahead of schedule in 1932 and gave the Soviet Union an industrial base on which to build. Stalin boasted of this achievement (Source 99), but said nothing of the tremendous human suffering it cost (Sources 101 and 104–7). The first Five Year Plan was followed by a second from 1933 to 1937, with even more ambitious targets, and a third which began in 1938.

Source 98

Stalin on the first Five Year Plan, 1931.

We do not want to be beaten....[Russia] was ceaselessly beaten for her backwardness. She was beaten by the Mongol Khans. She was beaten by the Turkish beys. She was beaten by the Swedish feudal lords....She was beaten by the Anglo-French capitalists. She was beaten by the Japanese barons. She was beaten by all – for her backwardness. We are fifty or a hundred years behind the advanced countries. We must make good this lag in ten years. Either we do or they crush us.

Source 99

Stalin on the successes of the first Five Year Plan, January 1933.

The fundamental task was to convert the USSR from an agrarian and weak country, dependent upon the caprices of the capitalist countries, into an industrial and powerful country....The Party's confidence in the feasibility of the five-year plan and its faith in the working class was so strong that the party undertook the fulfilment of this task not in five years, but in four years.

What are the results of the five-year plan in four years?... We did not have an iron and steel industry, the basis for the industrialization of the country. Now we have one. We did not have a tractor industry. Now we have one. We did not have a machine tool industry. Now we have one. We did not have a big modern chemical industry. Now we have one. We did not have a real and big industry for the production of agricultural machinery. Now we have one. We did not have an aircraft industry. Now we have one. In output of electrical power we were last on the list. Now we rank among the first. In output of oil products and coal we were last on the list. Now we rank among the first.

Source 100

A Soviet propaganda poster showing a foreign capitalist mocking the Five Year Plan in 1928 as 'fantasy, ravings, Utopia'. After only four years he is silenced and dismayed by the achievements of the Plan.

Source 101

From P.N. Stearns, *The European Experience Since 1815*, pp.287–8.

The emphasis of the first Five-Year Plan, as well as the second, was on heavy industry, basic to industrial expansion and military equipment. Consumer goods were given little attention....Output in heavy industry soared, and by the end of the 1930s Russia was the world's third greatest industrial power.

Forced industrialization...was successful but only at great human costs. Workers were deprived of the freedom to choose their jobs and were without any outlet for protest....Russian workers...were given certain protections. The state inspected factories for safety and health conditions, provided old-age pensions...and afforded guarantees against unemployment....Without question, in Russia it was the State that guided and impelled workers to industrialize, rather than private capitalists as earlier in the West. It is not clear whether this factor made the process more painful or even less free for the workers involved.

Enforced collectivization of farming was introduced from 1928, whereby the land, livestock, crops and equipment of private landowners, mainly *kulaks*, were confiscated without compensation and reorganized into *kolkhozy*, or state-run collective farms, where whole villages laboured together to fulfil government production targets.

Stalin claimed at the start of the first Five Year Plan that collectivization would benefit the whole country (Source 102) and as the policy progressed his control over the media and the arts ensured that they portrayed a view that suggested the policy had been outstandingly successful (Source 103). However, output did not increase as fast as he claimed. Initially, collectivization had the reverse effect. Many *kulaks*, reluctant to give up their land and livestock without compensation, killed their livestock and destroyed their crops. Stalin responded by unleashing a reign of terror aimed at the 'liquidation of the *kulaks* as a class'. Millions were murdered or sent to harsh labour camps in Siberia (Source 104). The dislocation of agriculture caused by collectivization and the elimination of the *kulaks* caused a famine in which at least five million people died (Sources 106–7).

Source 102

Joseph Stalin on collectivisation, April 1928.

Agriculture is developing slowly, comrades. It should be developing with gigantic strides, grain should become cheaper and harvests bigger, fertilizers should be applied to the utmost and mechanical production of grain should be developed at high speed. But that is not the case, comrades, and will not come about quickly. Why?

Because our agriculture is a small-peasant economy, which does not lend itself readily to substantial improvement....We have about twenty-five million individual peasant farms....It is the most insecure, the most primitive, the most undeveloped form of economy....

Can we adopt the policy of encouraging privately owned, large capitalist farms in the countryside? Obviously we cannot. It follows that we must do our utmost to develop in the countryside large farms of the type of the collective farms and State farms and to convert them into grain factories for the country organized on a more scientific basis.

Source 103

'Collective Farm on Holiday', painted by S.V. Gerasimov, an official, idealized view of a policy which for a time brought famine and ruin to the countryside

Source 104

From V. Serge, *Memoirs of a Revolutionary 1901–41* (OUP, 1963) pp.246–8.

In 1928 the government began to force peasants to merge their land holdings into large collective farms. In this way, Stalin hoped to end the power of the *kulaks* [rich peasants] and create a rural social structure that would be more egalitarian and more efficient – and also easier for the government to control. When the *kulaks* resisted, they were attacked not only by government agents but by the poorer peasants as well. In their despair, the *kulaks* killed their own livestock and smashed farm machinery. As a result, famine returned to Russia and possibly as many as five million people died....

Trainloads of deported peasants left for the icy North, the forests, the steppes, the deserts. These were whole populations, denuded of everything; the old folks starved to death in mid-journey, new-born babes were buried on the banks of the roadside, and each wilderness had its crop of little crosses....Agricultural technicians and experts were brave in denouncing the blunders and excesses; they were arrested in thousands and made to appear in huge sabotage trials so that responsibility might be unloaded on somebody.

Source 105

A grain search in a graveyard during collectivization. Peasants who attempted to conceal grain stocks ran the risk of being exposed by 'shock brigades'. Those who were caught were usually executed or sent to labour camps in Siberia.

Source 106

From J.N. Westwood, 'The Authoritarian System', in Purnell's *History of the Twentieth Century*, 1969, p.1411.

In the year 1932–33 famine raged throughout the richest agricultural regions of the USSR....Five and a half million people died in a man-made disaster unacknowledged by the Soviet leaders. Its principal cause was Stalin's collectivization drive, which completely disrupted agriculture, and the government's requisition and export of foodstuffs to finance industrialization. Starvation was compounded with terror – ten million peasants were killed or deported for opposing the state. Some who were there at the time gave these accounts of what they saw.

'On a battlefield men die quickly, they fight back, they are sustained by fellowship and a sense of duty. Here I saw people dying in solitude by slow degrees, dying hideously, without the excuse of sacrifice for a cause. They had been trapped and left to starve, each in his home, by a political decision made in a far-off capital around conference and banquet tables'....

'The most terrifying sights were the little children with skeleton limbs dangling from balloon-like abdomens. Starvation had wiped every trace of youth from their faces, turning them into tortured gargoyles; only in their eyes still lingered the reminder of childhood. Everywhere we found men and women lying prone, their faces and bellies bloated.'

Source 107

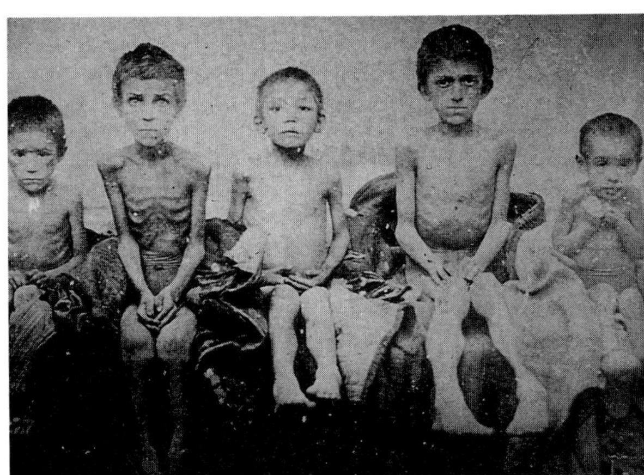

Starving, homeless Russian children, orphans created by the collectivization drive and the man-made famine

As the 1930s progressed, the violence and ruthlessness of Stalin's regime increased. Until 1934, his savagery was directed primarily against those who hindered or opposed his economic reforms, but in that year his protégé, Kirov, whom he had appointed chief of the party in Leningrad (formerly Petrograd), was murdered by a Communist Party member. This murder seemed to trigger a latent sense of insecurity and suspicion in Stalin who gathered more and more power into his own hands and became increasingly suspicious of party colleagues. Over the next four years, following Stalin's orders the secret police, recently reorganized as the NKVD, undertook a purge of the party which extended from its most senior leaders to ordinary members. It has been estimated that hundreds of thousands were executed and millions sent to labour camps. Show trials were organized in which former leaders, who had been tortured and brain-washed, confessed to crimes of which they were largely innocent, after which they were usually executed. Among the victims were Kamenev, Zinoviev, Bukharin and Rykov, all of whom played leading roles in the events of 1917 and had been senior members of the government during the 1920s.

Source 108

From P.N. Stearns, *The European Experience Since 1815*, pp.288.

In 1934 one of Stalin's deputies [Kirov] was assassinated. Stalin, shaken by this, insisted on questioning the murderer himself. He then resolved on a brutal house-cleaning. His old rivals...were tried for treason and executed and all branches of the government were purged. Only a handful of the pre-1914 Bolsheviks, those completely loyal to Stalin, remained alive. The purge reached far down into the ranks of the Communist Party and beyond – as many as eight million people were arrested, most of them subsequently deported to forced labour camps. Psychological pressure induced most of the prisoners to confess to treason they had not committed.

Source 109

Stalin with the men who were his colleagues in the 1920s and his victims in the 1930s. From the left, Stalin, Rykov, Kamenev and Zinoviev.

Source 110

Stalinist propaganda. Two photographs of the same meeting: in the first Trotsky is standing to the right of the platform from which Lenin was speaking in 1917, but he has been carefully removed from the second on orders from Stalin. After Trotsky's fall from power, Soviet historians rewrote the history of the Revolution and Civil War downgrading Trotsky's contribution.

Source 111

From Nadezhda Mandelstam, *Hope against Hope* (Collins, 1971) p.212. Nadezhda's husband, Osip, was a victim of Stalin's reign of terror during the 1930s.

The principles and aims of mass terror have nothing in common with ordinary police work or with security. The only purpose of terror is intimidation. To plunge the whole country into a state of chronic fear, the number of victims must be raised to astronomical levels, and on every floor of every building there must always be several apartments from which the tenants have suddenly been taken away. The remaining inhabitants will be model citizens for the rest of their lives....The only essential thing for those who rule by terror is not to overlook the new generations growing up without faith in their elders, and to keep on repeating the process in systematic fashion. Stalin ruled for a long time and saw to it that the waves of terror recurred from time to time, always on an even greater scale than before.

Alongside fear, Stalin used propaganda and misinformation to bolster his regime. This was used to vilify or simply eliminate from history his rivals and enemies, such as Trotsky, whose central role in the October Revolution and in the defeat of the White armies in the Civil War was ignored in everything from school textbooks to national newspapers. It was also used to build a 'cult of personality' around Stalin, creating the impression, as the tsars had done in earlier times, that he was essential to the continued well-being of the nation.

Source 112

The cult of personality. During celebrations in 1949 to mark Stalin's seventieth birthday, a photographic slide of Stalin was projected onto a cloud over Red Square in Moscow.

The Second World War brought a temporary halt to industrial and agricultural expansion and to the Stalinist terror as the country mobilized all its resources against Nazi Germany. Initially, Stalin had hoped to remain aloof from the war by signing a non-aggression pact with Hitler in August 1939. This Nazi-Soviet Pact partitioned Poland between Germany and Russia and enabled the latter to invade and annex the Baltic states of Latvia, Estonia and Lithuania. However, Hitler had no intention of honouring the Nazi-Soviet Pact and invaded Russia in 1941. In bitterly fought campaigns, German forces reached Stalingrad and came within 20 miles of Moscow before being pushed back. When the war ended Russian troops had driven the Germans out of Eastern Europe and had advanced beyond Berlin into the heart of Germany. Stalin had no intention of relinquishing this territory, which he proceeded to turn into satellites of the Soviet Union. In Poland, Czechoslovakia, Hungary, East Germany, Romania, Bulgaria, Yugoslavia and Albania communist governments were set up which, in all but Yugoslavia and Albania took their orders from Moscow. An 'Iron Curtain' was established between communist Eastern Europe and the non-communist West. Armed border guards prevented people from fleeing from the repression and poverty which beset most of Eastern Europe during the late 1940s, 1950s and 1960s to the greater political freedom and economic prosperity that could be found in the West.

Source 113

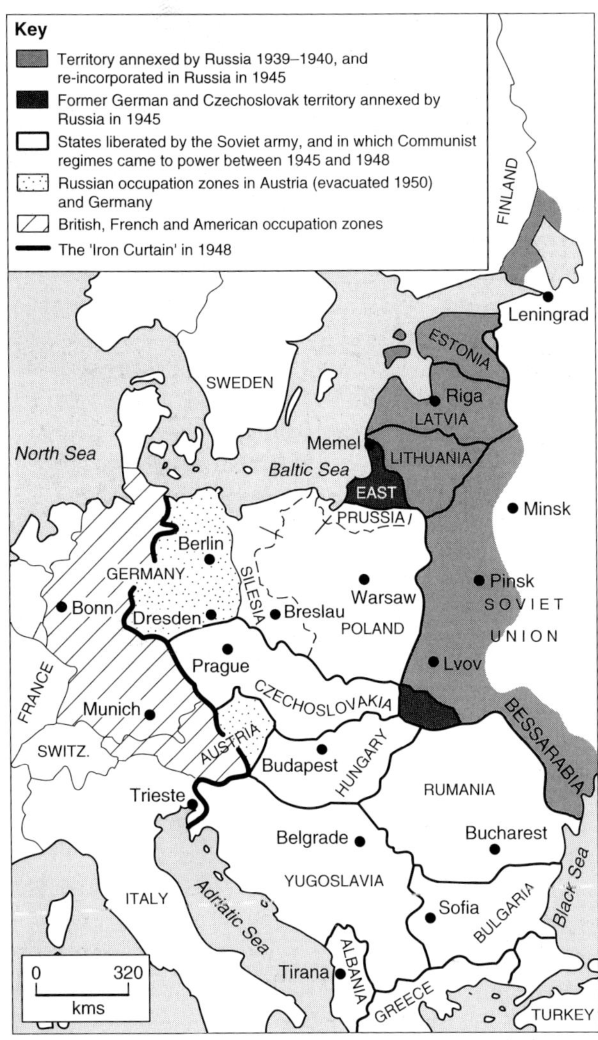

The Soviet Union in Eastern Europe 1945–48

The 'Iron Curtain' was one manifestation of the 'Cold War', a period of mutual hostility and rivalry between two armed camps, one led by the United States and extolling the virtues of democracy, the other led by the Soviet Union and comprising those states who believed in the virtues of communism. Stalin's modernization programmes had been achieved at enormous human cost, but they had established the Soviet Union as one of the world's two superpowers, second only in strength to the United States. However, superpower status and the Cold War imposed further burdens. In the post-war era, enormous amounts of money and resources were diverted into developing a nuclear arsenal, maintaining an army of over four million men, expanding the submarine fleet and participating in the exploration of space.

In 1953, Stalin died and a process of destalinization was initiated when Nikita Khrushchev came to power in 1955. The most obvious sign of changing times was the fate of Khrushchev's defeated rival, Georgi Malenkov, who remained a member of the Politburo, the most important decision-making committee in the Soviet Union, until 1957 and was then forced to retire. Under Stalin, defeated political opponents had not been allowed the luxury of retiring! Khrushchev denounced the excesses of Stalinism whilst being careful not to allow criticism of the Communist Party or of Marxist-Leninism. He introduced a cautious reform programme at home, the main element of which was the decentralization of economic planning, and in international relations contributed to a reduction in the level of hostility between the superpowers.

Khrushchev's reforms and decentralization, however, were only a matter of degree: criticism of Stalin was allowed and positively encouraged, the cult of personality associated with the leader was abandoned, as were the worst excesses of the secret police; but the Soviet Union remained an authoritarian state dominated by a single political party. The public had no political and little economic freedom, and few dared to deviate from the official party line on any matter for fear of attracting the attentions of the KGB, the new secret police organization which replaced the NKVD following the death of Stalin.

While Khrushchev's reformist policies were cautious, they went too far for many of the 'Old Guard' in the party, who accused him of damaging the economy by initiating ill-advised and poorly-planned reforms which devolved economic responsibility to local managers and reduced the importance of the party bureaucracy in Moscow. In 1964, Khrushchev's opponents in the Politburo banded together to force his resignation. His successors, Leonid Brezhnev and Alexei Kosygin, were more conservative, returning to a Stalinist emphasis on centralized planning and control over almost every aspect of Soviet life.

Source 114

From Robert Daniels, *The End of the Communist Revolution* (Routledge, 1993) p.58.

The Brezhnev-Kosygin regime was Stalinism without the mass terror of the Stalin era. People were not usually arrested unless they actually did oppose the government, and the death penalty was no longer meted out for the crime of falling from power. But the essentials of the system were maintained: rule by a privileged bureaucracy; the militarized command economy; a monopoly of the media to ensure...the manipulation of public opinion; police-state controls over everyone; a suspicious and confrontational attitude towards the outside world. The leadership...defined their system as 'developed socialism' or 'real, existing socialism'. Western observers were more inclined to call it totalitarianism.

The economy continued to grow under Brezhnev and standards of living improved, but politically it was an era of conservatism and stagnation. However, even in politics subtle changes were taking place. The absolute power of the party leader that had been enjoyed by Lenin and Stalin had been eroded by the success of the Politburo in ousting Khrushchev from office. Henceforth, the leader became the first among equals, wielding enormous power but no longer able to command absolute obedience, foster a 'cult of personality' around himself or ignore the opinions of other members of the Politburo.

Although in political terms the Brezhnev years were an 'era of stagnation', changes were taking place beneath the surface in the way of life of the population. Most important among these changes were the industrialization of society and the education of the masses. A population that had still been largely rural in 1945 had become more than half urban by 1979, according to official figures, and this had an effect on their attitudes, priorities and access to amenities such as education, culture, entertainment and consumer goods. Education expanded enormously during these years, such that by the late 1970s almost everyone received secondary education and those in university education had increased six-fold in 20 years.

The 1970s also witnessed the increasing influence of Western culture in terms of dress, music and, above all, attitudes. Unfavourable contrasts began to be drawn between Western and Soviet society by dissidents such as Alexander Solzhenitsyn and Andrei Sakharov. Although the Brezhnev regime attempted to silence the dissident intellectuals by arresting and torturing them, sending them to mental hospitals for 'treatment', imprisoning them in *gulags* (labour camps) or exiling them, the influence of the 'democratic movement' continued to grow through the distribution of *samizdat* material – hand-typed copies of dissident literature which were the only means of dissemination that could bypass official censorship. According to one political commentator, Martin Walker, 'the country went through a social revolution while Brezhnev slept'.

Meanwhile, the economy had become too complex for bureaucratic centralization, with its output targets, set prices and allocations of supplies, to maintain even a semblance of efficiency. Corruption was becoming such a problem that 'the country', according to Giulietto Chiesa, 'is just as if it were run by the Mafia'.

Brezhnev died in 1982 and was replaced by Yuri Andropov who, despite having been head of the KGB, began to initiate reforms. However, he died in 1984 before he could make a significant impression. His successor, the conservative Konstantin Chernenko, was dead within a year, bringing a younger man, the 53-year-old Mikhail Gorbachev, to power in 1985. He lost no time in introducing three new policies which, although he did not know it at the time, were to bring about the downfall of communism in Russia. These policies were *perestroika* or 'restructuring', *glasnost* or 'openness', and democratization. *Perestroika* was aimed primarily at dismantling the inefficient, bureaucratic, centralized planning and management of the economy, replacing it with a production model based on the pursuit of profit and on local management of factories and farms. In communist Russia, this was revolutionary stuff!

Source 115

From a speech by Mikhail Gorbachev at the time of his resignation in 1991.

When I found myself at the helm of this state it already was clear that something was wrong....We were living much worse than people in the industrialized countries were living and we were increasingly lagging behind them. This country was suffocating in the shackles of the bureaucratic command system. Doomed to cater to ideology, and suffer and carry out the onerous burden of the arms race, it found itself at the breaking point.

Source 116

From M. Frankland, *The Sixth Continent* (Hamish Hamilton, 1987) p.218.

Almost from the day he became leader Gorbachev started to make the point that the connection had been broken between how well people worked and how much money they earned. It might sound common sense abroad: inside the Sixth Continent [Russia] it was revolutionary....'Everyone, management, workers...all must...receive their pay according to their final product. If you do not get the final product, if profit is not created, then it means you cannot get paid.' When he said something similar at the twenty-seventh Party Congress he had to make a joke of the fact that no-one applauded him. It was radical talk because it suggested there could be no progress without a new approach to the problems of money and economic value, both of them uncomfortable subjects in the Soviet Union.

Naturally, there were many within the party who were not convinced of the need for *perestroika*, so Gorbachev sought allies among the intelligentsia and the media. For such people to be able to express their views in safety, there needed to be a new atmosphere of openness, in which people were free to criticize the government. He backed up his call for *glasnost* by reducing press censorship and by freeing the leading dissident, Andrei Sakharov, from exile in Gorky.

Source 117

From a private talk given by Mikhail Gorbachev to members of the Soviet Writers Union in 1986.

Restructuring is going very badly....The Central Committee needs support. You can't even imagine how much we need support from a group like the writers. We have no opposition. How then can we check up on ourselves? Only through criticism and self-criticism. The main thing is, through *glasnost*. A society cannot exist without *glasnost*.

Faced with increasing opposition to his policies of restructuring the economy and openness in the media and intellectual life, Gorbachev introduced the third strand of his reforms, democratization. At first, this was restricted to the party and was intended to use the support of ordinary party members to counteract the opposition of leading party bureaucrats. He began by calling for genuine elections to party committees and congresses in place of the old-style 'elections', which were nothing more than a rubber stamp for nominations made by senior party officials (Source 118). However, it was not long before he was calling for a more widespread kind of democracy involving all citizens (Source 119). By 1990, he was able to claim considerable success in having transformed the Soviet state into a democracy (Source 121).

Source 118

From M. Frankland, *The Sixth Continent*, pp.188–9 and 257.

In letters published in the party press [just before the 1986 Party Congress] Soviet Communists argued that the time had come for recognizably democratic elections at least [at local level]....The old rules had provided for secret elections to party committees at all levels, but the candidates, one for each post to be filled, were chosen by the party organization above....The usual practice was for a representative of the superior party organization to arrive at the election meeting and announce the nominee without informing anyone else....Several letter-writers stated the obvious truth that people could not be expected to be interested in elections that offered no choice. It was also argued that a competitively elected party secretary of a factory committee had a much better chance of doing a good job than one whose election had been uncontested.

Source 119

From a speech by Mikhail Gorbachev on the need to create a participatory democracy amongst Soviet citizens.

This is the way things should be today. Every working man...should be involved in everything. He has a right to have and should have real opportunities to make criticisms if they need to be made, about production as well as about consumer issues, educational issues and matters concerning discipline...and when it is not possible [to settle things quickly] then people must be told precisely and clearly why this is not possible. Don't be embarrassed, tell the truth, honestly.

Source 120

From Robert Daniels, *The End of the Communist Revolution*, p.23.

The Nineteenth [Party] Conference [in June 1988] was an epochal confrontation between two political cultures contending for the future of Soviet Russia. One was the old secretive, conspiratorial, xenophobic [anti-foreign] Muscovite political culture shared by the Stalinist bureaucracy and the peasantry from which it stemmed. The other was the political culture embodied in the Westernized intelligentsia since the eighteenth century, committed to a free, rational and cosmopolitan public life. It was to this culture that Gorbachev linked his fate.

Gorbachev was not able to get the party conference to shake up the membership of the Central Committee as he presumably had hoped to do, but he had virtually a free hand in winning endorsement of his economic reforms and his proposed constitutional changes. The latter were designed to shift power and responsibility, both central and local, from the party hierarchy to the system of elected soviets, all to be capped by a strong president (presumably himself). This plan would circumvent the party apparatus and give the civil government a status *vis-à-vis* the Party that it had not enjoyed since the Russian Civil War. It would open the door for genuine popular participation in politics, and would give Gorbachev and the reform movement a base entirely outside the party bureaucracy.

Source 121

From a speech by Mikhail Gorbachev to the Communist Party Congress in 1990.

The political system is being radically transformed; genuine democracy is being established, with free elections, a multi-party system, and human rights; and real people's power is being revived.... The atmosphere of ideological *diktat* [orders issued by the party] has been replaced by free thinking, *glasnost*, and the openness of society to information.

The post-communist period from 1990

In a sense, Gorbachev was too successful for his own good in achieving his three initial aims. *Perestroika* succeeded to a considerable extent in dismantling the bureaucratic centralization of the economy, but had little to put in its place. Consequently, the economy stagnated, then went into decline and finally into free-fall, causing economic chaos. *Glasnost* meant that the media and the general public were free to criticize not only the party bureaucracy but also Gorbachev himself as the economic crisis deepened. Democratization led, in 1990, to the loss by the Communist Party of its monopoly of power and in the following year brought about its dissolution.

Furthermore, *glasnost* and democratization released other unexpected forces, the most serious of which was nationalism. This led the Eastern European states to renounce communism and throw off the Soviet shackles in 1989. It also precipitated the break up of the Soviet Union into 15 separate independent states in 1990–91.

Gorbachev became Executive President of the Soviet Union with increased powers, but the break up of the Soviet Union shortly afterwards and increasing friction with Boris Yeltsin, the president of the new Russian Federation, made his position virtually impossible. A coup carried out by hardliners in August 1990 placed Gorbachev under house arrest at his holiday home in the Crimea. However, faced by determined opposition from Boris Yeltsin, the Russian parliament and its supporters on the streets of Moscow, the coup collapsed. Gorbachev returned to office, but effective power had shifted from him to Yeltsin. He was still President of the Soviet Union, but since the Soviet Union had effectively ceased to exist by the end of 1991, he resigned in December of that year.

Questions

8. How do the collapse of communism and the disintegration of the Soviet Union fit in with Hypotheses A and B on page 108 about the influence of Western European and Mongol autocratic traditions on the development of Russian political ideas and institutions?
9. What effect have the collapse of communism and the disintegration of the Soviet Union had on the historical significance of the 1917 Revolutions within these competing traditions in Russian history?

An epitaph for the Soviet Union was provided in 1990 by Viacheslav Shostakovsky, the rector of the Higher Party School in Moscow. He argued that communist Russia had come into existence in 1917 with a reform programme which it did not carry out. In 1990, the same issues of land for the peasants, worker control of the factories, political democracy and an end to hunger and deprivation were just as important as they had been in 1917.

Source 122

From a speech by Viacheslav Shostakovsky to the last Communist Party Congress in July 1990.

About the socialist choice. Yes, the people followed the Bolsheviks' slogans in 1917. But 73 years later we are repeating these slogans again and again: land to the peasants, factories to the workers, power to the soviets, peace to the people. We have not fulfilled these slogans. The land has ended up with the state; thus, it has ended up without a proprietor. The factories belong to the departments. Power belongs to the Party, and generally speaking there is no peace among the people. I would like to recall one more slogan from October [1917]: 'Bread to the hungry'. It is taking on a kind of new, tragic urgency.

Robert Daniels, in Source 123, claims that 1991 was 'one of the great turning points' in Russian history. The signs are that it will turn out to be so. At the time of writing (1994), Russia is lurching uncertainly towards the establishment of a constitutional democracy. It has an elected parliament and its first democratically elected president, but there are also signs that authoritarianism is not entirely dead. In the face of a deepening economic crisis and increasing friction between the president and parliament, Yeltsin has taken wide-ranging executive powers. He used these to chilling effect in 1993 when ordering tanks to bombard the White House, the Russian parliament building, into submission after parliament, led by Alexander Rutskoi and Ruslan Khasbulatov, began systematically to undermine Yeltsin's reform programme and then tried to overthrow his government. On the other hand, Yeltsin released Rutskoi and Khasbulatov from prison only a few months after their abortive coup. It is, perhaps, too soon to judge with any confidence whether Russia's future lies in a Western-style constitutional democracy or in a further manifestation of Oriental despotism under the leadership of some new dictator.

Source 123

From Robert Daniels, *The End of the Communist Revolution*, pp.1–2.

The year 1991 will go down in history as one of the great turning points, on a par with 1917. The attempted coup in Moscow in August by conservative Communists, the official demise of the Communist Party, the break-up of the Soviet Union into its constituent parts and the resignation of its president [Gorbachev] on 25 December, added up to a transformation that one might well consider as revolutionary and as world-shaking as the events that led from the fall of Tsar Nicholas II to the establishment of the Bolshevik dictatorship....Typically commentators both in Russia and in the West have hailed this great upheaval as the 'failure' of a wrong-headed 'experiment' that had been foisted upon the Russians and their associated minority nationalities by a bunch of utopian fanatics who only lost their grip and abandoned their global ambitions when their economic underpinnings rotted away....

The collapse of Communism was not a sudden plunge into revolutionary disorder like 1917; it came through step-by-step, cumulative change in the system, unwitting before 1985 and conscious after that date....In many ways we could argue that the most revolutionary moment in this process came not in 1991 but in 1989, and not just in the chain reaction of popular movements that put an end to Communist rule in the former Soviet satellite countries of Eastern Europe. The year 1989 was the turning point for the Soviet Union itself, in the dismantling of one-party totalitarian rule and the first steps to create a working constitutional structure. This year also saw the beginning of the precipitous economic collapse that more than any other circumstance tore away the forms of authority still linking the reformed Soviet realm with its past....

Something called 'Communism' prevailed as a political and economic regime in Eastern Europe for four decades and in the Soviet Union for many years before that. But this 'Communism' which the Soviet peoples and the Eastern Europeans finally put an end to was not a pre-cast machine nor a single-minded 'experiment'....If the Communists ever really pursued an experiment, it lasted for less than a year; the rest was a series of desperate expedients to keep power in the new world they had created, followed by the long darkness of Stalin's criminal and dishonest despotism, and the rearguard action by his successors to sustain their pretences and privileges and to keep real change to a minimum.

Source 124

From an editorial in the *Guardian*, 22 March 1993.

Call a spade a spade, so call this a presidential coup....The elected president of what is now supposed a friendly country, impatient with listening to too many opposition speeches, unilaterally seizes power to rule by decree. His action is taken, he alleges, to avert a Communist takeover. A hastily arranged referendum will be held to confirm his action. Opposition political activity can continue, but faces the prospect of restrictions....In any meaningful language, this is elective dictatorship.

But this is also Russia, the largest country in the world, a collapsed empire lacking effective state power or meaningful political institutions, wrestling with an economy on life support. The rules are different here, partly because they always have been – Russia has no history of democracy, no tradition of civil society....Mr. Yeltsin claims to embody democracy. But his democratic credentials, though genuine in certain ways, are certainly not beyond criticism. He fought stoutly against the August coup, and won the world's admiration for it, but the August coup was not simply a revolt against democracy so much as an attempted counter-revolution against the break-up of the Soviet Union. Mr. Yeltsin's immediate action after its failure was to ban the Communist Party and shut down its newspapers.

The causes of change in Russian history

When we seek to explain why change and development have come about in Russian history, we are concerned not so much with the causes of significant events, which will vary according to the nature of the event, as with the on-going factors which have influenced change and development in a recurring or continuous fashion. Hypotheses A and B on page 108 focus on two of these factors, the influence of European ideas and institutions and the effects of Mongol rule. Evidence for these factors can be found throughout the unit, but there is also ample evidence for the influence of other factors. The size and geographical position of Russia are of particular importance, as are Russian attitudes and beliefs, including religious beliefs, and the social and economic structure of the country.

Of course, these factors do not exist in isolation from one another, but interact to bring about, prevent, speed up or slow down change and development. Tibor Szamuely (Source 125) indicates how, in his view, some of these factors interacted to bring about and maintain the dominance of Oriental despotism in Russian history. Other factors, including religion, culture, education, trade and communications, and the desire to emulate a more developed civilization could be used to construct an explanation of why European ideas and institutions played such a prominent part in the development of Russia through the ages.

Source 125

From Tibor Szamuely, *The Russian Tradition*, pp.117–8.

What were the compelling factors that drove Russia...towards the development of a system which was in its main features indistinguishable from that of Oriental despotism? Two such factors existed. The first is the simple fact that throughout nearly the whole of written history...despotism was the only form of government capable of holding together and administering large territorial entities....Her sheer size, her giant, shapeless, frontierless bulk, irresistibly spilling over into the unsettled heartland of Asia, set Russia decisively apart from the nations of Europe....But the necessity that called forth the Muscovite variety of Oriental despotism was more pressing than the mere demand for effective administration....National survival depended upon the permanent mobilization and organization of all her meagre resources for defence, war and colonization, on a scale beyond the European comprehension.

Question

10. (a) What factors have shaped the development of Russian history on a continuous or recurring basis, and why?

    (b) Are some of these factors more important than others? If so, why?

If you peruse the work that you have already done on Russian history earlier in the unit, you will find that you have already identified a number of recurring causal factors which will contribute to an explanation of the development of Russian history. So all that is needed here is to draw those factors together into a coherent explanation, to explain their contribution and relative importance to the explanation and to evaluate your conclusions. Evaluation by means of a comparison can be done by comparing one era of Russian history with another to underline the continuing importance of a particular factor or by comparing developments in Russian history with those in a different country, say Britain, to show how different factors were at work and therefore brought about different types of development, or perhaps how similar factors brought about different outcomes because of the different circumstances in which they operated. Alternatively, a counterfactual evaluation might be put forward by suggesting why other possible development paths, such as those followed in Europe, were not followed in Russia and why the developments that did take place occurred instead.

UNIT 4.2

= RECONCILING CONFLICTS IN RUSSIAN HISTORY =

Introduction

It would be naive to think that the entire development of Russian history could be attributed exclusively either to European or to Asiatic influences, and none of the historians quoted in the previous unit make that claim. However, some of them argue that the most persistent and important influences that affected the political development of Russia can be found in the autocratic and repressive traditions of government that originated during the period of Mongol domination. Others, as we have seen, have argued that the most persistent and important influences originated in western Europe. Both cannot be right or, at least, both cannot be entirely right.

Equally, it would be difficult to argue that either is entirely wrong. Eminent historians can be found in both camps, each of whom is able to marshal persuasive arguments backed up by considerable documentary and other evidence in support of his or her interpretation. Therefore, if both contain some truth, it must be possible to reconcile, at least partially, the conflict between these two interpretations of Russian history and to produce an integrated account which recognizes that both interpretations played an important role and interacted with each other in shaping the political development of Russia through the ages.

Question

1. Use the ideas contained in this unit together with the accounts you produced whilst studying Unit 4.1 to construct an account of developments in Russian political history which reconciles the conflicts between Hypotheses A and B on page 108.

To produce an integrated account that synthesizes these two accounts and reconciles the conflicts between them requires more than a mere recognition that both were important in Russian history or that each played the predominant role during different periods of Russian history. The reconciliation of conflict also requires an integration of the accounts that demonstrates the relationship between them. In other words, to reconcile conflicts between the competing accounts of Russian history in the previous unit, we must show how the Mongol tradition and western influences *interacted* with each other. We must produce an account in which both strands are still visible, but in which they have been transformed by contact with each other into something that is distinctively Russian, rather than predominantly western or Asiatic. Alternatively, we could explain away the conflict between the accounts by showing that it is more apparent than real.

Integrating accounts

An integrated account might begin by showing how the earliest Slav settlers in what was to become Russia migrated from central Europe, but were subject to warlike nomadic tribes, such as the Goths, Huns and Khazars who emerged from central Asia and who exhibited traits, such as autocratic government and rule by terror, which were later to be characteristic of the Mongols. Western European influence made itself felt in Kiev-Rus through the Varangians, who contributed to the development of trade and of political and military organization. South-east European religion, culture and political ideas began to infiltrate Kiev-Rus as a result of Vladimir's conversion to the Orthodox faith in 988 and the close ties with Byzantium which resulted from this. Thus, even before the Mongol invasion, Russia was developing a distinctive political system which fused together elements from Slavonic, western European, Byzantine and Asiatic origins.

Following the initial Mongol invasion, which spread terror and destruction throughout most of the Russian principalities, Mongol rule was carried out largely by proxy. Russian princes continued to rule their principalities, but paid tribute to the Mongol khans who ruled over them indirectly from their capital at Sarai, near the mouth of the River Volga. The indirect nature of Mongol rule enabled Slavonic, Byzantine and even western European influences to remain a part of Russian political life. This was even more true of Novgorod, which had managed to escape Mongol conquest. Mongol influence undoubtedly affected the government of the Russian principalities, whose princes were impressed by the success of the methods employed by the Mongols and sought, where appropriate, to emulate them. This was particularly true of Muscovy, whose rulers rose to prominence through their loyalty and service to their Mongol overlords.

During this period, it would appear that Mongol ideas and institutions of government all but extinguished European influences on Russian life. However, the truth of this statement depends on one's interpretation of 'European influence'. Contact with western Europe certainly declined, and was not restored until Ivan IV established trading relations with England and the Netherlands in the 1550s and 1570s respectively. However, the influence of south-eastern Europe, in the form of the Byzantine Empire, remained strong right up to the fall of Constantinople to the Muslim Turks in 1453, and even beyond. Not only did the Orthodox faith continue to play an important part in Russian political life until 1917, but the idea of establishing a Russian empire, the title of 'tsar', the double-headed eagle insignia of the royal house and many institutions of government all entered Russia from Constantinople.

As Sergei Averintsev argues in Source 126, while Russia became isolated from the 'Catholic West', she retained close contact with the 'Orthodox West' as well as the Mongol East. She became a Eurasian power, facing both east and west, and with political ideas and institutions that were a peculiarly Russian mix of Byzantine and Mongol elements.

Source 126

From Sergei Averintsev, 'The Idea of Holy Russia', *History Today*, November 1989, p.43.

After the Tatar conquest, and especially after Ivan III had freed Russia again and Ivan IV (the Terrible) had triumphantly campaigned against the Tatars, Russia increasingly became a Eurasian entity; after the khanates of Kazan and Astrakhan had been conquered Moscow became no less of a Eurasian power than Byzantium, though in a different way. Each of these stages corresponds to an ever more conscious alienation of Russia from the Catholic West.

Russia's lack of contact with the Catholic West meant that she missed out on the cultural and political revitalization brought about by the Renaissance and the religious ferment of the Reformation. However, this isolation was never total and had already been eroded considerably by the time Peter the Great began his 'Embassy to the West' in 1697. It was not just the Catholic West, but also the Protestant states of northern and western Europe, from which he imported ideas, institutions and advisers into Russia. However, the brutal way in which he dealt with opposition to his westernizing reforms and asserted his autocratic power owed nothing to western influence and everything to a tsarist tradition that was founded on Mongol precedents and practices.

Throughout the eighteenth and nineteenth centuries, the government of Russia sought to wrestle with the problems, tensions and contradictions created by the importation of western ideas into a country whose tsars were determined to retain their autocratic powers, and whose Orthodox Church was equally determined to retain its privileged position and its hold over the minds of the masses. While European culture and certain political ideas, such as Enlightened Despotism, were welcomed by the rulers of Russia, other western ideas, such as representation, democracy, individual rights and liberty, and socialism, were distinctly unwelcome.

This illustrates another way in which we might seek to reconcile conflicts between the westernizing and autocratic traditions in Russian history: ideas from different traditions might have taken root in different sections of society. At certain times, especially during the nineteenth and twentieth centuries, western ideas such as those associated with democracy, liberty and social rights gained acceptance among the populace, while Asiatic-autocratic ideas continued to dominate the thinking of the political élite. As revolutionary and reform movements gathered pace during the nineteenth century, Russia evolved an ever more complex and repressive police state apparatus in an attempt to stamp out opposition. A secret police force employing informers to spy on the populace, and brutal methods of torture, imprisonment, exile and execution in an attempt to cow the populace into submission had come into existence largely to combat the influx of revolutionary ideas from Europe, but used methods which had their origins in the Mongol principle of government by terror.

Some tsars, such as Nicholas I and Alexander III, used repression to try to shore up the traditional social and political system; others, notably

Alexander II and, after 1905, Nicholas II, attempted a mixture of reform and repression. However, none were able to deal effectively with the problems created by the influx of progressive ideas from western Europe into a country with autocratic governmental practices rooted in Asiatic precedents and an inflexible and conservative religious hierarchy that had changed little since the demise of the Byzantine Empire. Thus, the conditions for a revolutionary upheaval existed long before the political and economic stresses created by the First World War triggered the revolutions of 1917, and these conditions owed much to the uneasy mixture of western European, Asiatic and Byzantine elements in the political ideas and institutions of tsarist Russia.

Source 127

An architectural drawing class for women students before the First World War. The women were training for a progressive, western-style career, but are seen at work here on designs for traditional Orthodox churches.

The tension between incompatible political traditions in Russia was not resolved by the communist regime. While the Orthodox Church was persecuted and marginalized, and the democratic potential of the soviets and the Constituent Assembly was swiftly stifled, the conflict between European democratic socialist ideas and Asiatic autocratic practices remained. The Marxist ideas and reforms to which Lenin and Stalin paid lip service were intended to place the means of production in the hands of the workers and to give 'Power to the People'. In practice, the means of production were placed in the hands of Communist Party bureaucrats, and Lenin and Stalin proceeded to erect an autocratic police state which was more brutal and repressive than the tsarist system had ever been.

It can be argued that the democracy that has been struggling to establish itself in the states of the Russian Federation since the demise of Soviet communism in 1990–91 is something that has been imported recently from the West, and so, to some extent, it is. However, as Bill Wallace argues in Source 128, it also has its roots in Russian history. Hidden beneath the autocracy of tsarist Russia and the Communist dictatorship of the Soviet Union lay a strand of democracy to which even such an uncompromising dictator as Stalin contributed unwittingly. It was this, argues Wallace, rather than recent democratic influences from the West, that brought about the disintegration of the Soviet Union. Furthermore, whilst implying that the soviets and the Constituent Assembly constituted a false dawn for the democracy which began in 1990 to establish itself in Russia, the extract from Wallace's account also illustrates how the Asian-autocratic and western-democratic traditions in Russian history coexisted and interacted with each other to bring about many of the important changes that have occurred in twentieth-century Russia.

Source 128

From Bill Wallace, 'The Democratic Development of the Former Soviet Union', *History Today*, July 1994, pp.46–52.

Democratic ideas were not new to pre-1917 Russia. Ever since Catherine the Great...and Alexander I, the notion that the subjects of the tsar should have some say in determining their own destiny had been seriously if fitfully discussed. Following defeat in the Crimean War, Alexander II was pressed to introduce a measure of representation and went so far as to yield limited participation in local government. Nobles were elected to provincial assemblies (*zemstvos*) and rich burghers to town councils (*dumas*) along with a few indirect representatives of the peasants and the urban poor. In the midst of the 1905 Revolution, Nicholas II went further, establishing an empire-wide *duma* that won the moderate revolutionaries to his side.

On the other hand, neither Alexander nor Nicholas yielded the autocratic principle. Alexander's institutions were confined to issues of social welfare. The franchise and powers that Nicholas allowed were strictly limited from the start and were reduced *duma* by *duma* until 1914....

The Western-style liberals who declared themselves a Provisional Government in February 1917 had some experience to build on...[but] they lacked leadership. Alexander Kerensky, who became prime minister in July,...lost his nerve at the critical point in October 1917 when faced by Bolshevik revolutionaries, thus surrendering the liberals' brief opportunity.

Another failure of the time was that of the *soviets* or councils. These were spontaneous regional assemblies that first appeared during the 1905 Revolution and spread rapidly in 1917, representing the grievances and aspirations of the small lower-middle class, the growing number of workers and the vast mass of peasants. They could easily have seized power in the summer of 1917 and have given Russia a remarkably representative government. But...when in the autumn the soviets did demand 'all power' for themselves, their actions proved to be to the detriment of democracy, since in the meantime they had been largely taken over by the Bolshevik Party....

Like many revolutionaries, Lenin claimed to be a democrat, arguing that government should represent the proletarian majority....In October he both seized power and began to rule by force on behalf of workers and peasants whom he claimed were still too weak to do things for themselves. Whatever his intentions, this led to the negation of democracy....He dissolved its properly elected, predominantly non-Bolshevik Constituent Assembly...and went on to purge the soviets of all who opposed his will....

Subsequent Soviet constitutions, seemingly democratic, were a complete sham. Lenin was lucky he did not live long enough to become as brutal in practice as Stalin. Khrushchev somewhat moderated the system by courting public opinion; and in his constitution, Brezhnev gave the Supreme Soviet a theoretical sovereignty. But neither tolerated opposition parties or dissident opinions. Yet in a perverse way all four autocrats contributed to the development of democracy....

Admittedly Stalin eliminated the better-off peasants,...but he also industrialized the Soviet Union by transferring half the population from scattered estates and farms to urban factories where they gradually acquired an education and eventually built up a store of aspirations and grievances....But in the 1960s and 70s, most ordinary people still gave little thought to politics. They voted as instructed since their living standards were getting better, if slowly, and their country was rising in international respect.

Then at the turn of the 1970s and 80s the economic situation deteriorated. Expenditure on the arms race with the West and on the war in Afghanistan proved too much for a centrally planned economy that had already produced inefficiency and obsolescence in industry and agriculture. The dictators had promised prosperity. When what materialized was hardship worsened by inequality it was time for Lenin's proletariat to turn to politics again. And they were no longer the simple peasants of 1917....

The emergence of Gorbachev as general secretary changed everything. It was not that he was economically a reformer or politically a democrat. But he was an improver who soon discovered that, to revitalize both industry and agriculture,...he had to dislodge the élite. One means of trying to achieve this was by exposing them....So the drive for economic restructuring (*perestroika*) led to open debate (*glasnost*). All the sins of the past came out, and a demand arose not just to improve the standard of living, but to democratize politics – to take up where the frustrated constitutional experiments of the early twentieth century had left off. The following year Gorbachev yielded so far as to authorize a Congress of Deputies on a less restricted franchise than the old Supreme Soviet. The Congress...did not constitute a properly representative and responsible parliament; but they were soon going through the motions of passing laws and making or unmaking ministers. Democracy had almost arrived.

What the public wanted, of course, was not so much a new form of government for its own sake as for what it would do for the economy....This would have been a difficult situation to handle even within a developed democracy. But the Soviet Union remained a one-party state in which the Communists were divided and embryo alternatives were already functioning....In spite of his authoritarian background, Gorbachev did remarkably well in parrying strands of discontent. But on one issue he did badly. In the wake of the collapse of Communism in Eastern Europe in 1989–90 he was not the only statesman to underrate the influence of nationalism on politics....So he failed to appreciate initially the seriousness of the Baltic independence movements and the implications of unrest in Ukraine and Georgia. When in the course of 1991 he came to realise the gravity of the situation, his conciliatory moves aroused the hostility of the diehards in the Party and the army.

It was they who in August attempted a *coup d'état*. That they failed was a victory for democracy....The same is true of the resignation of Gorbachev the following December. Certainly Yeltsin's determination to obtain revenge for previous insults by replacing Gorbachev played a crucial role. But even before the *coup*, Gorbachev had lost widespread support and he subsequently clung too long to the notion that the Communist Party should retain its virtual monopoly of power. However flawed the representative system, the majority of the population felt that Gorbachev's time was past; and again their will prevailed....

The events of 1989–91 demonstrated that seventy years after the Revolution, Soviet citizens were more sophisticated than their forebears and that, when given the chance, they could express their views and make them stick....

Following December 1991, Yeltsin did not immediately establish a new constitution for the Russian Federation....Nor did he organize a 'government' party to give himself parliamentary support....In addition, despite his previous advocacy of rapid economic reform, he proceeded hesitatingly. The result was growing resistance from former Communists in the Congress and Supreme Soviet without corresponding backing from moderate reformers; and as the state of industry and agriculture continued to deteriorate and prices began to soar, a further result was increasing public disillusionment with Yeltsin.

It was this that produced the crisis of October 1993 when, in total frustration, Yeltsin finally lost patience with his own economic impotence in the face of a rebellious parliament and sent in the tanks. In what, in other circumstances, would hardly have been described as democratic action he dealt with a small group of politicians pushing their own interests behind a supposedly constitutional screen. But amidst increasingly democratic pressures he could only do so on the promise of genuine political change and economic improvement.

With his advisers and supporters he had been preparing a new constitution, but in the end he had to rush it. Yet, when presented to the electorate in December, it was accepted. It is certainly more democratic than anything previous, not just in stipulating open voting...but in providing for a multi-party state....However, the rules of the constitution are weighted heavily in the president's favour; and this might well lead to friction between him and his parliament and could, in the wrong hands, open the way to a new dictatorship.

The results of the actual elections set alarm-bells ringing, not least because of the emergence of the extreme nationalist, Vladimir Zhirinovsky's inappropriately titled Liberal Democrats as the second largest party in the *duma*...and of the powerful showing of the revived Communists....

However, despite imperfections in the system and in its operation, democratic elections had been held and had returned the most representative body yet in Russian history....If Yeltsin can deliver a steady economic improvement without a heavy social cost, both he and the new political system will thrive. If not, they will be at electoral risk in accordance with the democratic norm; or the system will itself be destroyed by someone using their failure as an excuse to copy Lenin's 1917 Revolution against democratic progress....There is, however, an important safeguard against such an outcome. The population of the Russian Federation is now much more street-wise politically than it was.

At the time when Wallace was writing, many historians and political commentators were proclaiming the death of communism and the triumph of liberal democracy, but Wallace recognized that elements of the autocratic tradition that has played such an important role in Russian political history over the last eight centuries still exist. Such ingrained beliefs do not die easily, and we may yet see the development of a political system in Russia which combines elements of authoritarian centralism with liberal democracy and market capitalism.

Explaining away conflict

One might argue that some of the differences between the westernizing and Asiatic interpretations of Russian history are more apparent than real. For instance, some historians have interpreted the cultural and religious contribution of Byzantium to Russian history as evidence of western influence because Byzantium lies to the west of Russia, while others have regarded it as evidence of Asiatic influence because of the stronger cultural and trading links Byzantium had with Asia than with Europe. However, none would doubt that Byzantine religion and culture played an important part in the development of Russia.

As has been noted earlier, the heartland of Russia occupies territory on the border between Europe and Asia, between west and east; but it is not entirely clear where that border lies. As J.M. Roberts explains, to those living in Europe, Russia is to the east and displays characteristics that are alien to Europe and are therefore considered Asiatic. However, for those living in Asia, Russia lies to the west and, since many of the characteristics of its political system seem equally alien, they may be seen as European. Thus, whether Russian political ideas and institutions are regarded as European or Asiatic in origin may depend on one's geographical perspective.

Source 129

From J.M. Roberts, *The Triumph of the West* (BBC, 1985) p.170–4.

Whatever the disputes of Russian 'westernisers' and 'slavophiles' over their cultural destiny at home, and however alien Russia's ways might seem to western European and American liberals, she looked western to those who met her in Asia. 'In Europe', wrote Dostoevsky [a nineteenth-century Russian author], 'we were Asiatics, whereas in Asia we, too, are Europeans'

Russia's ambiguity can be traced back a long way. It shows in its central institutions, in the nature of Russian government itself. Muscovite political theorists who were keen on promoting their grand prince's authority began to use the title of 'Tsar' more and more in the fifteenth century....It went along with and helped to justify the transformation of a princely state into an empire of many peoples, heir to the Mongol Golden Horde and its successor states. Ivan the Great was the first Russian ruler to call himself 'Tsar'....So what was once the name of the Roman emperors, the Caesars, survived their empire...to pass into yet another empire's terminology. Ivan married a niece of the last eastern emperor, too; it may have been because of her that he adopted for the royal seal the Byzantine symbol of sovereignty, the double-headed eagle, which survived as part of the heraldic insignia of the Russian monarchy until 1917.

Time and time again, twists and turns in the road of Russian history have emphasized its difference from western Europe. The Tatars had devastated the Russian towns just as those of western Europe were showing their greatest vigour and independence. The continued consolidation of the state territory by centuries of acquisition from neighbours confirmed the military and autocratic bias of the regime. For good or ill, Russia carried forward into its age of expansion none of the western and 'feudal' stress on individual status and privilege, none of the tension between the religious and the secular, none of the 'liberties' of the western cities, none of the emphasis on group and corporate rights which led to the representation of 'estates' of the realm in parliament....Because she was Orthodox and had no Reformation, so Russia had no slowly emerging tradition of allowing more than one religion within the state. Her Scientific Revolution and Enlightenment had to be imported. When she first industrialized it was to be on the basis of a serf economy such as had virtually disappeared in other centres of industrialization, and serfdom was actually to increase its extent and its grip on Russian society at a time when it was in retreat in western European countries. Long to be preoccupied with Asia, which she penetrated by land, Russia played only a tiny part in the exploration and exploitation of the oceans. Drawn inevitably into the European diplomatic system, she was to remain ideologically aloof from it, even while using its language and forms, distanced mentally as well as geographically from the West and still debating right down to the present whether she is of it or not.

In the eighteenth century, Peter the Great moved the Russian capital to St Petersburg. There then began two centuries during which Russia's rulers often seemed to be trying to identify her firmly with the West. But in 1918...the capital was moved back to Moscow [where] the socialist international was created, the practical and official embodiment of the claim of Russia to lead international communism.

And we still do not know the answer to our queries. When Russia looks westward, she appears uneasy, threatened by lands from which a mortal danger has all too often come. Yet Russian expansion in Asia has long been justified as progressive, advanced, 'western', as it were....It is still hard to say where Europe 'ends' in the east.

UNIT 4.3

THE PAST AND THE PRESENT

The practical past and the historical past

For historians, there is an undeniable connection between the past and the present. E.H. Carr described history as 'an unending dialogue between the present and the past'; François Voltaire claimed, somewhat more irreverently, that 'history is a pack of tricks we play on the dead'. The point that both were making is that it is the purpose of the historian to make sense of the past to people living in the present or, as R.W.K. Hinton put it, to make 'sense of the present by placing it in the context of the past'.

However, the present is ever-changing and this influences our conception of what was important in the past. Historians writing in the first decade of the twentieth century lived in a world where Europe was divided into two armed camps but the horror of the First World War had yet to be experienced; where communism was no more than a theory expounded by a few radical intellectuals; where fascism was as yet unknown; and where monarchism, imperialism and liberal democracy were the contending political ideologies. Historians in Britain, Germany and other European imperial powers traced with pride the development of their countries' power and influence in the world and sought to explain the origins and workings of the 'balance of power' theories which had governed European politics for a century.

By the 1940s, '50s and '60s, the world looked very different. Historians living and writing then experienced the Second World War and the defeat of fascism; saw European nations lose their dominant role in the world to the emerging superpowers of the United States and the Soviet Union; witnessed the Cold War, in which two armed camps, one communist and one democratic, both armed with nuclear weapons, confronted each other in Central Europe across the 'Iron Curtain'; and saw imperialism begin to lose its grip as Asian and African countries struggled towards independence from their European masters. Historians of this age no longer celebrated imperialism, focusing more on its shortcomings and on the development of resistance to the imperial powers. Ideological issues had become more important as historians sought to explain the rise and fall of fascism, the growth and continuing expansion of communism, and what seemed like a world-wide struggle for supremacy between communism and democracy.

By the 1990s, the picture had changed again. International co-operation has become increasingly important: the role of the United Nations has expanded; states are co-operating to resist aggression and try to resolve conflicts in Bosnia, the Middle East and elsewhere; the European Community is expanding in both membership and powers; the Cold War has come to an end; and communism has collapsed in Russia and Eastern Europe. As in previous ages, historians are seeking to place these developments in their historical context, but some such as Michael Oakeshott, question whether this is what historians should be doing. He draws a distinction between the 'practical past', in which we 'read the past backwards from the present...[and] look in it for the origins of what we perceive around us', and the 'historical past', in which the past is studied for its own sake, assigning to events the significance they had at the time rather than that which they had for later generations.

Source 130

From Michael Oakeshott, 'On the Activity of Being a Historian', in *Rationalism and Politics* (Methuen, 1962) pp.147–8 and 153–5.

If we understand a past event merely in relation to ourselves and our own current activities, our attitude may be said to be a 'practical' attitude....The practical man reads the past backwards. He is interested in and recognizes only those past events which he can relate to present activities. He looks to the past in order to explain his present world....The past consists of happenings recognized to be contributory or non-contributory to a subsequent condition of things. Like the gardener, the practical man distinguishes, in past happenings, between weeds and permissible growths....If he is a politician, he approves whatever in the past appears to support his political views and denounces whatever is hostile to them....

But in the specifically 'historical' attitude...the past is *not* viewed in relation to the present, and is not treated as if it were the present. Everything that the evidence reveals or points to is recognized to have its place....The place of an event is not determined by its relation to subsequent events. What is being sought here is neither a justification, nor a criticism nor an explanation of a subsequent or present condition of things....This past is without the moral, the political or the social structure which the practical man transfers from *his* present to *his* past....In short, there is to be found an attitude towards the past which is discernibly different from the 'practical' attitude; and since this attitude is characteristic...of those whom we are accustomed to call 'historians'..., its counterpart may be called the specifically 'historical' past....

The attention of the practical man is directed to the past by a miscellany of present happenings which, on account of his current interests, ambitions and directions of activity, are important to him, or by the present happenings which chance puts in his way....But with the historian this is not so. His enquiry into the past is not determined by chance encounters with current happenings. He collects for himself a world of present experiences (documents etc.) which is determined by considerations of appropriateness and completeness. It is from *this* world of present experiences that the 'historical' past springs.

Oakeshott claims that historians are different from other mortals in that they divorce their minds from the concerns of the present and pursue an objective investigation of the past. While few would quibble with Oakeshott's claim that historians are – or at least should be – objective, it is clear from the comments of Carr, Voltaire and Hinton quoted in the first paragraph of this unit, and in extracts from numerous historians quoted throughout this volume, that historians *are* influenced by the age in which they live and *do* seek to explain the present as well as the past. In other words, while there is a difference between the objectivity of the 'historical past' and the contextualization of the present involved in the 'practical past', much, though by no means all, of the history that is written involves a fusion of the two. The questions historians seek to answer often emanate from the 'practical past', from a desire to make sense of or to contextualize forces that are shaping the present; but the methods employed to answer those questions, such as the objective assessment of evidence and the answering of questions raised by that evidence, derive from the 'historical past'.

The extent to which historians operate in the 'historical' or in the 'practical' past can be gauged by looking at some of the debates sparked off by the collapse of communism in Russia and Eastern Europe which, according to Francis Fukuyama, marked the ultimate triumph of liberal democracy and, with it, 'the end of history'.

The end of history?

In the summer of 1989, Dr Francis Fukuyama, a senior official in the American State Department, published an article in *National Interest* in which he claimed that communism as an ideology (that is, as a system of belief about how states should be governed) was dead. In support of this view, he cited the rejection of communism by the Eastern European states, the imminent collapse of the Soviet Union and of the Soviet Communist Party (neither of which had yet happened when the article was published), and the emergence of the pro-democracy movement in China which, although temporarily crushed following the June 1989 massacre of pro-democracy demonstrators in Tiananmen Square, Beijing, by the communist Chinese authorities, he predicted would rise again and overthrow communism in China. Fukuyama also argued that Western capitalism had triumphed over communism or socialism as an economic system, claiming that the introduction of capitalist market economies in Eastern Europe and the Soviet Union was being paralleled by similar, although slower, developments in China.

History, according to Fukuyama, was characterized by a struggle between contending ideologies and since, with the collapse of communism, liberal democracy supported by market capitalism had triumphed over all its ideological adversaries, history had now come to an end. By this, he meant that there were no longer any viable rivals to liberal democracy as the accepted system by which states should be governed.

Source 131

From Francis Fukuyama, 'The End of History', in the *Independent*, 20–21 September, 1989. This article represents a condensed version of the original published in *National Interest* a few weeks earlier.

Looking at the flow of events over the past decade or so, it is hard to avoid the feeling that something very fundamental has happened in world history. The past year has seen a flood of articles commemorating the end of the Cold War, and the fact that 'peace' seems to be breaking out in many regions of the world....

The twentieth century saw the world descend into a bout of ideological violence as liberalism contended first with the remnants of absolutism, then Bolshevism and Fascism, and finally an updated Marxism that threatened to lead to the ultimate apocalypse of nuclear war. But the century that began full of confidence in the ultimate triumph of Western liberal democracy seems at its close to be returning to where it started: not to an 'end of ideology' or a convergence between capitalism and socialism, as earlier predicted, but to an unabashed victory of economic and political liberalism.

The triumph of the West, of the Western idea, is evident first of all in the total exhaustion of viable systematic alternatives to Western liberalism. In the past decade there have been unmistakable changes in the intellectual climate of the world's two largest communist countries, and the beginnings of significant reform movements in both. But this phenomenon extends beyond high politics and can be seen also in the spread of consumerist Western culture....What we may be witnessing is not just the end of the Cold War, or the passing of a particular period of post-war history, but the end of history as such: that is, the end point of mankind's ideological evolution and the universalization of Western liberal democracy....

In the past century there have been two major challenges to liberalism, those of fascism and communism. The former...was destroyed as a living ideology by the Second World War....Communism's challenge was far more serious. Marx asserted that liberal society contained a fundamental and unresolvable contradiction – that between capital and labour – the chief accusation against liberalism ever since. But surely the class issue has actually been successfully resolved in the West. The egalitarianism [equal rights and opportunities for all] of modern America represents the essential achievement of the classless society envisioned by Marx....

But the power of the liberal idea would seem much less impressive if it had not infected the largest and oldest culture in Asia, China. In the past 15 years Marxism-Leninism has been almost totally discredited as an economic system....Economic reform was accompanied by enormous political and intellectual ferment that threw into question fundamental tenets of Chinese socialism. The tragic repression in Tiananmen Square this summer was in a way less remarkable than the massive pro-democracy movement that brought it on, and is likely to prove less enduring....Chinese Communism, rather than being the pattern for Asia's future, became an anachronism.

It is the developments in the Soviet Union under Mikhail Gorbachev which have driven the final nail into Marxism-Leninism's coffin, however. Although formal institutions are only now beginning to change, what has happened in the realm of ideas is a revolutionary assault on the most fundamental principles of Stalinism and their replacement by principles which do not amount to liberalism *per se*, but whose only connecting thread is liberalism. The Soviet Union could in no way be described as a liberal or democratic country now...but at the end of history it is not necessary that all societies become successful liberal democracies, merely that they end their ideological pretensions of representing different and higher forms of human society. And Gorbachev...has permitted people to say what they have privately understood for years: that the magic incantations of Marxist-Leninism were nonsense, that Soviet socialism was not superior to the West in any respect, but was in fact a monumental failure....

What are the implications of the end of history for international relations? Much of the Third World remains very much mired in history, and will continue to be a terrain of conflict. Nor are Russia or China likely to become liberal societies in the foreseeable future...[but] the passing of Marxism-Leninism...means the reduction of the likelihood of large-scale conflict between states. This does not by any means imply the end of international conflict *per se*, for the world at that point would be divided between a part that was historical [i.e. that had not yet achieved the ideal of liberal democracy] and a part that was post-historical [i.e. that had achieved liberal democracy]. Conflict between states still in history and those at the end of history would still be possible. There would still be a high and perhaps rising level of ethnic and nationalist violence since those are impulses incompletely played out, even in parts of the post-historical world.

The interest in Fukuyama's article can be gauged from the speed with which the issue of *National Interest* in which it appeared sold out. Interest, however, is not the same as agreement, and Fukuyama's article drew fierce criticism, and even ridicule, from historians around the world. This prompted him to clarify, expand and defend his views in a book published in 1992. Fukuyama pointed out that there was nothing new in the concept of 'the end of history', since it had been put forward by the German philosopher, Georg Hegel, at the beginning of the nineteenth century. Hegel claimed that history had 'ended' when the liberal goals of the French Revolution had been secured by Napoleon's victories. Fukuyama argued that Marx temporarily diverted the course of history by arguing that it would be the victory of the proletariat in the class struggle and the establishment of world-wide communism that would mark the end of history. Now, with the demise of Marxism, the victory of liberal democracy was assured. According to Fukuyama, Hegel had been right about history ending with the victory of liberal democracy, but he had been wrong about the date when this was achieved.

Source 132

From Francis Fukuyama, *The End of History and the Last Man* (Penguin, 1992) pp.xi–xxii.

The distant origins of the present volume lie in an article entitled 'The End of History?' which I wrote for the journal *National Interest* in the summer of 1989. In it, I argued that a remarkable consensus concerning the legitimacy of liberal democracy as a system of government had emerged throughout the world over the past few years, as it conquered rival ideologies like hereditary monarchy, fascism, and most recently communism. More than that, however, I argued that liberal democracy may constitute 'the end point of mankind's ideological evolution' and the 'final form of human government', and as such constituted the 'end of history'. That is, while earlier forms of government were characterized by grave defects and irrationalities that led to their eventual collapse, liberal democracy was arguably free from such fundamental internal contradictions....While some present-day countries might fail to achieve stable liberal democracy, and others might lapse back into other, more primitive forms of rule like theocracy or military dictatorship, the *ideal* of liberal democracy could not be improved on....

Both Hegel [a German philosopher] and Marx believed that the evolution of human societies was not open-ended, but would end when mankind had achieved a form of society that satisfied its deepest and most fundamental longings. Both thinkers thus posited an 'end of history': for Hegel this was the liberal state, while for Marx it was a communist society. This did not mean that the natural cycle of birth, life and death would end, that important events would no longer happen....It meant, rather, that there would be no further progress in the development of underlying principles and institutions, because all of the really big questions had been settled....

At the end of the twentieth century, does it make sense for us once again to speak of a coherent and directional History of mankind that will eventually lead the greater part of humanity to liberal democracy? The answer I arrived at is yes....

The most remarkable development of the last quarter of the twentieth century has been the revelation of enormous weaknesses at the core of the world's seemingly strong dictatorships, whether they be of the military-authoritarian Right, or the communist-totalitarian Left. From Latin America to Eastern Europe, from the Soviet Union to the Middle East and Asia, strong governments have been failing over the last two decades. And while they have not given way in all cases to stable liberal democracies, liberal democracy remains the only coherent political aspiration that spans different regions and cultures around the globe. In addition, liberal principles in economics – the 'free market' – have spread, and have succeeded in producing unprecedented levels of material prosperity, both in industrially developed countries and in countries that had been, at the close of World War II, part of the impoverished Third World.....

Moreover, the logic of modern natural science would seem to dictate a universal evolution in the direction of capitalism. The experiences of the Soviet Union, China, and other socialist countries indicate that while highly centralized economies are sufficient to reach the level of industrialization represented by Europe in the 1950s, they are woefully inadequate in creating what have been termed complex 'post-industrial' economies in which information and technological innovation play a much larger role....There is no question but that the world's most developed countries are also its most successful democracies.

Questions

1. Before reading any further, use your knowledge of developments in Russian and British history, and of current affairs in these and other countries, to consider whether Fukuyama is right in claiming that history has come to an end with the ultimate triumph of liberal democracy as a political ideal.
2. Read Sources 134–41, most of which were written in direct response to Fukuyama's thesis.
   (a) How acceptable is Fukuyama's thesis in the light of the arguments put forward in these sources?
   (b) In what ways do these sources suggest that the history of Russia and of Britain is being reassessed as a result of the collapse of communism?
3. To what extent do Sources 131–41 support or undermine Oakeshott's view that politicians are concerned with the 'practical past', while historians operate in the 'historical past'? (NB Fukuyama and the writers quoted by Whiteside in Source 136 are all politicians or political analysts; the remaining sources are all written by historians.)

We must guard against too hasty a judgment about the significance of the collapse of communism in Russia and Eastern Europe. On the one hand, it may, as Fukuyama claims, signal the death of Marxism as a viable ideology and the triumph of capitalism and liberal democracy. On the other hand, Marxism may recover its potency in a modified form, or it may be replaced in former communist states by nationalism and militarist dictatorship rather than liberal democracy. When Chou En-lai, a former leader of communist China, was asked what he considered to be the significance of the French Revolution, he replied, 'It is too soon to tell'. If it is too soon to be certain about the significance of a revolution that took place in 1789, any conclusions we draw about events that took place only a few years ago can be no more than tentative speculations.

Nevertheless, whether or not we accept Fukuyama's arguments, the collapse of communism must inevitably lead to some reassessment of Russian history since 1917 and may have wider implications for historical understanding in general. No longer can communism be portrayed as the ultimate achievement of the Soviet state; no longer can socialism be seen as the successor to capitalism and liberal democracy; and no longer can Marxists claim that communist revolutions will take place throughout the world. Although China and some Third World countries retain communist regimes, Marxism as a political ideology appears to be dead or dying. Instead of heralding the dawn of a great new age, the 1917 Russian Revolution now looks more like the entry into a cul-de-sac from which Russia is only now re-emerging.

Source 133

The end of Marxism in Albania. Crowds topple the statue of Albania's former Marxist dictator, Enver Hoxha, in the capital, Tirana, in 1991.

The following sources convey some recent reassessments of the history of Russia, and of certain aspects of British history, in the light of the collapse of the Soviet Union and of Marxist ideology. Those published by the magazine, *History Today*, are taken from a series of articles commissioned to respond to Fukuyama's 'End of History' thesis.

Source 134

From Edward Acton, 'From Tsarism to Communism', in *History Review*, December 1993, p.35.

Russia, they say, is the only country with an unpredictable past. Each dramatic change through which she passes brings with it a new version of her history. Villains become heroes and heroes become villains. Until the revolution, the tsars were celebrated as wise fathers of the people. After the triumph of the Bolsheviks, the tsars were vilified while an almost religious cult was built around Lenin. Now that Communism has collapsed, the signs are being changed again. There is growing sympathy for Nicholas II and the old regime in general whereas Lenin is being held responsible for all the calamities that have befallen modern Russia. But for him, Russian pupils are told, the Tsarist Empire would gradually have evolved along western capitalist and democratic lines, and avoided the horrors of the last 75 years.

John Roberts argues below that Marxism was never such a potent force in communist Russia as it appeared and that nationalism was behind the 'socialism in one country' practised by Stalin, and also lay at the heart of Chinese communism. The importance of nationalist aspirations in post-communist Eastern Europe and Russia cannot be ignored. The break-up of the Soviet Union began with independence movements in the Baltic states of Latvia, Lithuania and Estonia; Czechoslovakia divided along ethnic lines into two separate republics; first Croatia and then Bosnia of the former Yugoslav territories descended into bloody civil wars in pursuance of nationalist aspirations; and ethnic conflict has taken place in Georgia and Azerbaijan. Fukuyama admitted that 'nationalism and other forms of racial and ethnic consciousness have been behind much of the conflict of modern times', but argued that 'it is not clear that nationalism represents an irreconcilable contradiction in the heart of liberalism. Only such systematic nationalisms as Nazism qualify as formal ideologies on the level of liberalism or communism.' John Roberts disagrees, claiming that the *idea* of nationalism has provided a potent motivating ideology ever since the French

Revolution. Shaun Whiteside and the political commentators he quotes in his article agree, predicting that nationalism will be more important than liberal democracy in shaping the future of the states of the former communist bloc.

Source 135

From John Roberts, 'Goodbye to All That?', in *History Today*, August 1991, pp.40–2.

The French Revolution...launched on the world the idea that national identity should be the basis of statehood. The last two centuries have brought the triumph of that idea....The world is now almost totally organized in nation states....Of course, the story of nationalism's triumph is not one we have to admire....It has been one of massacre and counter-massacre, atrocity and counter-atrocity, blackmail, manipulations, myth-making, lies and cheating.. That there has been in the end successful resolution along national lines of some conflicts (often through exhaustion) hardly offsets the violence with which frustrated national sentiment infected the political settlements. That was much of the story of Central and Eastern Europe for a quarter of a century after the First World War.

True, other forces also shaped world history in the last two centuries. There were long trends – rising population, material wealth, the transformation of material culture and aspiration – visible the world round. One force though, once much feared, and from which much was once hoped, turned out to have no such vast importance. Marxism, which once promised so much, seems in retrospect hardly to matter in comparison: its importance now seems to have been only as a language...and a mythology to mask what was really happening. Russia would have been a world power anyway, and a great industrial state sooner, without the Bolsheviks....When Russia recovered as a great power once more [after the devastation caused by the First World War and the Revolution], it was under (and partly thanks to) Stalin. He talked Marxism, but is now reviled by many Marxists as a man who betrayed the faith. China, under Mao, built its independence on national reaction against the foreigner and on native tradition, puritanism and pragmatism, rather than Marxist doctrine, though continuing to use Marxist language.

Such movements and governments as proclaimed their commitment to Marxism in fact did very badly. In Europe, west of Russia before 1939 there were no Marxist regimes, except for brief moments. After 1945, there were many, though they were for the most part imposed by the military force...of the Red Army, not by revolution springing out of class-struggle....In the 1980s Marxist Eastern Europe collapsed....By then, Marxism had almost universally blighted the Eastern European economies. The effect of Cold War in the East had been to impoverish, and in the West to enrich, the working class.

Meanwhile, Marxism as doctrine first petrified and then dissolved....The doctrine dissolved more and more rapidly after Stalin. There had always been doctrinal adjustments, even in Moscow (was it not during the war that it was suddenly asserted that the withering-away of the state need not take place after all?). But the intellectuals began to qualify more and more....Today, we no longer know what 'Marxism' means. Like 'Christian', the word requires specific supplementation to be comprehensible....It was never a very good idea to talk about 'the end of history',...but to speak of the end of Marxism...is now clearly justifiable.

Source 136

From Shaun Whiteside, *Fin de Siècle* [the End of an Era], a pamphlet published in 1992 to accompany a Channel 4 television series of the same name.

The immediate reaction of the small states formerly under the sway of the Soviet Bloc has been a resurgence of nationalism, first in the Baltic states, then, most dramatically, in what was formerly Yugoslavia, with the war between the Serbs and Croats. The narrative has changed....For Misha Glenny, author of *The Rebirth of History*, a different, unfinished narrative is reawakening: 'The peoples of Eastern Europe have fought for their existence and for their democracies. Now, with the odds – as always – stacked against them, they must fight for their dignity and stability. History is by no means dead. In Eastern Europe it has emerged dramatically from its hibernation after forty years, and it has much to catch up on.'

For the last 50 years or so, the nations of Eastern Europe have had to hide their great historical diversity behind the Communist monolith. Some of these areas are highly industrialized – East Germany, Bohemia – others, such as Albania and Romania, put up with Third World conditions. Some parts have democratic traditions, others have only seen dictatorship and violence. Small wonder, perhaps, that nationalism is one of the first responses to liberation. At the same time, and despite the impending unification of the European Community, Western Europe faces nationalist problems of its own....

Stuart Hall sees the phenomenon of nationalism in Eastern Europe as quite understandable. The peoples that have been forgotten by history now want to catch up on lost time: 'The little nations, former parts of the Soviet Union, think that the nation is the way in which they can...make the drive for entering the West, entering modernity, becoming part of the European Community, etc.'

Salman Rushdie explains the more damaging aspects of East European nationalism as follows: 'The Soviet state held down for its period of existence a very large number of previously existing enmities and goblins...whether they be anti-Semitism, whether they be different kinds of racial and ethnic rivalries.' But this, says Rushdie, is the spirit of the age.

While accepting that Marxism is dead, or at least in severe decline, as a political ideology, we should think carefully before rejecting completely Marxist analyses of the past. A philosophy that could have such a marked influence on the world for most of the twentieth century must have some insights to offer that should be preserved from the wreckage. Edward Acton identifies two particular concepts – those of class-struggle and of the essential interrelationship between the state and the ruling class – which, in his view, will continue to play an important role in historians' explanations of developments in Russia and elsewhere during the nineteenth and twentieth centuries.

Source 137

From Edward Acton, 'Imperial Russia – Marxism à la Carte', in *History Today*, August 1991, pp.43–6.

For so long [Soviet historians] have celebrated modern Russian history as a 'law-governed' epic depicting the triumph of reason and justice over the chaos and inhumanity of capitalism. Now they are told from all sides that it is nothing more than a cautionary tale. Soviet socialism...it suddenly seems, is doomed to recede into the past as a bizarre detour from the highway of private enterprise and the free market....If Soviet socialism is a cul-de-sac, does it not show that far from being 'law-governed', the Bolshevik Revolution was a ghastly accident? Does it not demonstrate that it was only because Russia became engaged in the First World War at a singularly delicate moment in her modernization that she was vulnerable to Bolshevik conspiracy and was forced off the evolutionary path of capitalism and parliamentary government? In short, the political and ideological retreat of Communism looks set to give a second wind to what might be termed the 'primitive liberal' view of nineteenth century Russian history....

Before it is allowed to do so, it is worth pausing to consider whether anything may be salvaged from the Marxist approach....Take the notion that class struggle is fundamental to the course of history. It is difficult to deny its importance where imperial Russia is concerned. The conflict between peasant and landlord provided the theme of domestic developments. It was a crucial factor in undermining the tsarist regime's commitment to serfdom. It conditioned the counter-reforms of the 1880s. And it was central to the great peasant risings of 1905–7 and the social upheaval of 1917–18....Equally, nowhere has a working class acted with such sustained militancy or with so powerful a sense of common interest as in late imperial Russia....The workers' collective sense of hostility to management, employers and privileged society in general, and the crucial role they played in destroying both tsarism and the Provisional Government of 1917, is undeniable....The radical intelligentsia, conscious that their only hope lay in mass revolt, were under the most powerful compulsion to adapt their ideas and tailor their programmes to ensure that they had mass appeal....The Bolshevik party owed its triumph in 1917 less to its much exaggerated internal discipline and organizational prowess than to its success in articulating the aspirations of workers, soldiers and peasants....Its strength derived from the fact that it was identified with the very policies on which the masses were determined.

Perhaps the Marxist insight that remains of greatest value for understanding pre-revolutionary history concerns the role of the State. Marx offers the basic proposition that the State acts as the 'executive committee' of the ruling class, to which he adds the rider that in certain conditions the State enjoys a measure of autonomy from the ruling class because of the balance of social forces. This provides a framework tailor-made to analyse the relationship between Alexander II and the landed nobility. The relative autonomy which the tsarist State enjoyed in the mid-nineteenth century enabled it to take the initiative in the commitment to Emancipation, despite the opposition of the great majority of the noblemen. But the nobility acquiesced precisely because it was borne in upon them that their own government...had concluded that serfdom was too dangerous to perpetuate....

It is not necessary to treat Lenin as holy writ...in order to acknowledge strengths in the Marxist analysis of imperial Russia....The irony was that it was precisely at the moment of the Bolshevik triumph and the consolidation of Europe's first Marxist government that the Marxist view of the relationship between State and society began to lose its explanatory power. Under Stalin the State enjoyed a degree of autonomy that went far beyond anything Marx had envisaged. The superstructure proved able to pulverise and remould the social base in a manner that defied the...dogma of Marxism-Leninism.

The death of Marxism has had an effect not just on the former communist states and not just in the sphere of politics. It has also led historians to begin to reassess the history of the last two centuries, to ask different questions and to explore different issues from those which have dominated so much of the history written since the end of the Second World War. Tony Judt provides a brief survey of some of the new directions which historical research is beginning to take, while Gareth Stedman Jones and Peter Clarke offer reassessments of Victorian Britain and of the rise of the Labour Party in twentieth-century Britain.

Source 138

From Tony Judt, 'Chronicles of a Death Foretold', in *History Today*, October 1991, pp.48–50.

In order to appreciate the impact of the 'death of Marxism' upon the historical study of the twentieth century, it is important to note...the distinction between Marxism as a methodological tool and Communism as a political practice....The impact of the Russian Revolution and Communism upon modern historical writing was profound. Not only did the heritage of 1917 provide the subject matter of much historical research, but it coloured the approach to everything else. The history of Italian strikes, French politics, German democracy or British 'peculiarity' was very often written with half an eye to a question not even asked: why were Communists strong (or weak) in a particular political tradition or working-class culture? What was it about a particular national political or economic experience which rendered it penetrable, or otherwise, by the sorts of revolutionary currents born of Lenin's revolution?....Moreover, the impact of the Soviet state upon European geography – the fact that it had, by 1949, effectively re-forged in its own image much of Central and Eastern Europe – encouraged historians to write the history of twentieth century Europe in two distinct compartments, East and West. With this outcome in mind, much of the earlier history of Eastern Europe, for example, was written as though its major task was to explain the circumstances (backwardness, the absence of a middle class) which rendered that region vulnerable first to authoritarian dictatorships, then to Soviet totalitarianism.

With the declining appeal of the Soviet Union, and the European revolutions of 1989, all that has changed....The emphasis in recent years has not only moved away from previously fashionable themes of labour protest, social transformation and political radicalism, but has returned, refreshed, to older pastures. Economic history especially is thriving....While the image of Soviet Revolution still retained its power, and the history of the poor, the angry and the insurrectionary seemed to matter so much more than the tastes and thoughts of their oppressors, cultural history suffered; it is not altogether by chance that it has had to borrow from neighbouring disciplines (anthropology, psychology, literary theory) in order to...restore its claim to importance....

One of the issues which most appeals to historians from the Soviet Union, and their counterparts in newly democratic Poland and Czechoslovakia is that of liberalism and democracy itself. This curiosity about the weakness of liberalism in their own political culture thus echoes a new-found enthusiasm among Western historians for the history of political ideas. Hitherto the history of recent political thought in Europe was distorted towards a focus on the history of Marxism....But with the demise of Marxism as a political theory has come a return of interest in other traditions. Where once students of twentieth-century thought...felt it incumbent upon themselves to write about the impact of Marxism...recent work...has paid much closer attention to liberal and conservative traditions.

Source 139

From Gareth Stedman Jones, 'The Changing Face of 19th Century Britain', in *History Today*, May 1991, pp.36–9.

It is evident that the fall of Communism and the conclusion of the Cold War have not brought history to an end. But what has been undermined, perhaps now irretrievably, is a way of organizing the narrative of modern history, which, until recently, dominated the imagination of historians....In this scenario, history since the end of the eighteenth century was to be understood primarily as the unravelling of a single process, the process of modernization, rationalization and secularization. This process was carried forward irresistibly by the advance of industrialization....

Viewed from this angle, political history from the French Revolution onwards became little more than a sequence of successful or unsuccessful adjustments to these inexorable forces of social change. The crucial agents of change in this transition were not organizations, institutions or specific forms of practice or belief, but broad social classes and functionally defined groups – workers and peasants, large and small capitalists, traditional and modernizing élites. The key term was revolution. Modernization was a revolutionary process....

Nowhere was this more evident than in the study of nineteenth-century Britain. British society had generated the first industrial revolution...which created a new economy that in turn transformed the world....Victorian Britain was not only the pioneer of liberal capitalism, but of working-class socialism as well. In the various movements which culminated in Chartism in the first half of the nineteenth century, Edward Thompson discerned in *The Making of the English Working Class* (1963), an outline of the political and cultural components of class identity, which, if true, vindicated much that had been claimed in a socialist and Marxist tradition....The formation of an industrial proletariat was a global product of modern capitalism. But the experience of the English working class was nevertheless formative both because it was the first and because it provided a basis for Marx's own reflections....The *Communist Manifesto's* portrayal of the advent of industrial capitalism with its accompanying class struggle between bourgeois and proletarian was a global generalization drawn from the account given by Frederick Engels in his *Condition of the English Working Class in 1844*. Chartism together with the French Revolution provided the foundations upon which the Marxist conception of class struggle was built....

The high tide of this sense of expectation about the nineteenth century was probably reached in the mid-1970s. Thereafter, changes in the political climate increasingly undermined the assumptions upon which it had been built. The growth of the women's movement disrupted conventional narratives of progress and challenged the use of simple equations between class and ideology in historical explanation. The revolution in Iran contradicted widely held beliefs about the secular and modernizing character of revolts in the Third World....

These changes made an impact upon the interpretation of nineteenth-century Britain some years before the ending of the Cold War. In economic history, detailed research failed to reveal a sudden jump in the proportion of national income devoted to investment in the 1750–1850 period, or indeed any dramatic acceleration in the growth rate of the economy, justifying the term 'revolution'. The spread of factory production before 1870 was shown to have been far more gradual and localized than had once been thought....There was no substantial shift in the distribution of wealth from London and the home counties to the new industrial regions of the north....

It was not simply that the supposed chronology of the formation of a working-class movement no longer coincided with the revised dating of industrialization. More fundamentally, there was a questioning of the whole tradition of interpretation which saw the one as a response to the other....The target of Chartism was not a class of employers, but an unrepresentative state largely controlled by a landed aristocracy. For these reasons, Chartism did not herald the class struggle between bourgeois and proletarian depicted in the *Communist Manifesto*. It rather formed part of a cluster of radical and democratic movements which had gathered pace from the last third of the eighteenth century and declined in the years around 1848....

In short, what has gradually been dismantled has been the assumption that the working classes in nineteenth-century England can usefully be studied as if they were, or were about to become, a homogeneous political or cultural force....Thus, for historians actively engaged with the nineteenth century, a revision of interpretation was well under way before the dramatic global changes at the end of the 1980s. Marxism had ceased to inspire new research.

Source 140

From Peter Clarke, 'Love's Labours Lost', in *History Today*, September 1991, pp.36–8.

Until relatively recently, our notions of the main trends and the most significant developments [in twentieth-century British history] have been saturated with...Marxist assumptions. Thus it is assumed that the social structure can best be analysed in terms of class, with special alertness for the emergence of the working class....It is also assumed that the shape of politics followed this supposed sociological infrastructure, conjuring up an image of the Labour Party stretching itself and flexing its muscles preparatory to its ultimate triumph. It is further assumed that government policy was a reflection...of these pressures, with the appointed destiny in the form of the welfare state, the mixed economy, trade-union incorporation, full-employment policies, mass council housing and comprehensive schools....This was winners' history, with the giant's share of the historiographical winnings going to the Labour Party....

We should spot...a lurking fallacy in this cumulative conceptual collapse [of Marxist assumptions]. The fallacy surely lies in talking about 'the death of Marxism' as though it implies 'the end of history'. What a curious back-handed tribute this equation is – to the intellectual dominance of Marxism, no less! For the assumption here is that if the history of existing society is not, as hitherto contended by the faithful, the history of class struggles, then there is no history left worth the name. In this sense 1991 already brings its riposte to 1989. The dramatic configurations of a world no longer riven by class struggle but instead ravaged by national, ethnic and religious rivalry and oppression already stare us in the face....

Historians of twentieth-century Britain are already exploiting the opportunity to address the real issues....In *The Progressive Dilemma: from Lloyd George to Kinnock* (Heinemann 1991), David Marquand offers a devastating critique of Labourism. He starts with a political paradox: 'Conservative or predominantly Conservative governments have been in office for fifty of the seventy-odd years since the Labour Party first became the official opposition in the House of Commons, and Labour governments for only twenty'. It is not enough to explain away the recent failures of the Labour Party in the era of Thatcherite ascendancy and three-party politics....It makes better history to acknowledge that Labour's failure has been persistent precisely in so far as it has clung to a myth of its role as a class-conscious party guided by a socialist ideology.

Once Labour's history is liberated from this sub-Marxian perspective, it is apparent that its one great period of success – in the 1940s – was a result of particular historical causes. In particular, the experience of the Second World War endowed Labour with a broad appeal, cutting across the narrow class and trade-union loyalties of its hard core of support....Labour's success as a determinedly working-class party rooted in the trade unions now looks like a failure to put together a broad-based reform coalition such as the Liberals did at the beginning of the twentieth century....

Anti-Marxist triumphalism, however, is out of place....Surely we have not discarded a Marxist obsession with class as the sole structural explanation of history only to mould our ideas on it as a sort of template which faithfully turns this proposition inside-out. If historians resolutely ignore the role that class plays in historical change they will surely be blind to significant sources of structural inequality which can lead – albeit in unpredictable ways – to social conflict. Reports of the death of Marxism may, in this respect, turn out to be much exaggerated. The questions which lie at the heart of the Marxist tradition remain worth asking. The point is that they are no longer – if they ever were – the only questions; and that no one now regards the Marxist answers as automatically valid.

As we have seen, historians have criticized from a range of different standpoints Fukuyama's claim that the collapse of Marxist ideology in Russia, Eastern Europe and elsewhere marks 'the end of history'. Some have even questioned whether it marks the end of Marxism as a political concept or as a tool for historical analysis. Fukuyama replied to his critics by reasserting that 'the end of history' meant there was no longer, and presumably never would be again, a political ideology that could challenge the dominant position of liberal democracy or an economic ideology that could challenge market capitalism. However, this did not mean that all the states in the world had yet achieved liberal democracy and market capitalism or that they would do so in the near future.

According to Fukuyama, other forces such as communism, nationalism and Islamic fundamentalism would continue to exert an influence for some time to come, but would not and could not threaten the triumphant position of the dominant ideology.

Source 141

From Francis Fukuyama, 'The End of Hysteria?', in the *Guardian*, 15 December 1989.

To refute my hypothesis, it is not sufficient to suggest that the future holds in store large and momentous events. One would have to show that these events were driven by a systematic idea of political and social justice that claimed to supersede liberalism....[Critics] have posited several sources of ideological competition to modern liberalism: communism itself, Islamic fundamentalism, and nationalism. Let me consider these in order.

The most common criticism has been that I have been very premature in writing off communism. In support of this charge, various writers have pointed to the incompleteness and fragility of the reform processes in the Soviet Union, China and Eastern Europe, and the continuing vigour of hard-line Communists....I would be the first to admit that the reform processes under way in the Communist world are incomplete and fragile. The tragic repression that occurred in Beijing in June set back the cause of liberalization in that country many years, and one would be foolish to assert that such a reversal could not occur in any one of the countries currently undergoing reform....Nonetheless, I question whether such a reversal could bring back the Soviet Union we knew and feared....

Islamic fundamentalism is not only a competitor to liberalism in the Islamic world, but has won a clear-cut victory over liberalism in many countries. And yet, for all of Islam's pretensions of being a universal religion, fundamentalism has had virtually no appeal in communities that were not Muslim to begin with....

One is inclined to take the threat of nationalism much more seriously....While this suggests that the post-historical era will not be free of significant conflict, we still have to put that conflict in perspective. Conflicts between Hungary and Romania,, or Bulgaria and Turkey, or Armenia and Azerbaijan, tragic as they may become, simply do not begin to reach the scale of the big, continent-wide nuclear wars that we have been fearing and planning against these past 40 years. Alan Bloom has suggested that virulent nationalism could still arise, even in the heart of Europe, as an outgrowth of one of the existing right-wing, anti-immigrant parties in France or Germany...though I don't see any of these extremist parties upsetting their political systems in the near future. The country where fascism may have the greatest potential may be the Soviet Union itself....If post-Tito Yugoslavia in some sense represents the Soviet Union's future, one should worry whether there is not some Russian Milosevic [the Serbian nationalist leader] waiting in the wings – a party bureaucrat who one day blossoms into a fascist demagogue, rousing the dominant nationality to reassert its 'rights' against all the others.

While they disagree on many things, almost all the historians and political commentators from whom extracts have been quoted above are agreed on one thing: that the abandonment of communism in Eastern Europe and the disintegration of the Soviet Union have opened up opportunities for, and almost necessitate, fundamental reassessments of many aspects of the history of the last two centuries. This seems to undermine Oakeshott's argument in Source 130 that historians should be concerned with an objective assessment of the 'historical past', in which the 'practical past', viewed 'in relation to ourselves and our current activities', has no place. Oakeshott claimed that historians are not 'directed to the past by a miscellany of current happenings', but study the past for its own sake. However, there is ample evidence in this unit that historians *are* influenced by current happenings.

This does not undermine or invalidate the history that is being written and constantly re-written by successive generations. Current political, social and cultural influences help to focus the attention of historians on particular aspects of the past and to frame the questions that they ask, but historical methodology requires that their use of evidence to answer their questions and to interpret the past should be impartial and objective. In other words, the 'practical past' may help to frame the questions historians ask, but it should play no part in the answers to those questions.

Index

Page numbers in italics refer to an illustration of the subject